The Benefits of Psychotherapy

MARY LEE SMITH is director of Evaluation Research Services in Boulder, Colorado, and an assistant professor at the Laboratory of Educational Research, University of Colorado, Boulder.

GENE V. GLASS is co-director of the Laboratory of Educational Research, University of Colorado, Boulder. He is also professor of education at the university.

THOMAS I. MILLER is director of research and evaluation, Department of Human Resources, City of Boulder.

The Benefits of Psychotherapy

Mary Lee Smith
Gene V. Glass
Thomas I. Miller

THE JOHNS HOPKINS UNIVERSITY PRESS
Baltimore and London

The Johns Hopkins University Press, Baltimore, Maryland 21218
The Johns Hopkins Press Ltd., London

Library of Congress Cataloging in Publication Data

Smith, Mary Lee.
  The benefits of psychotherapy.

  Bibliography: pp. 223-61
  Includes index.
  1. Psychotherapy—Evaluation.   I. Glass, Gene V.,
1940-   joint author.   II. Miller, Thomas I.,
joint author.   III. Title.   [DNLM: 1. Psychotherapy—
Methods.   2. Outcome and process assessment (health
care)   3. Mental disorders—Drug therapy.   4. Evaluation studies.   5. Drug therapy—Methods.   WM420
S6554d]
RC480.5.S57   616.89'14   80-11610
ISBN 0-8018-2352-8

To our parents

Science is built up with facts, as a house is with stones. But a collection of facts is no more a science than a heap of stones is a house.

Poincaré, *La Science et l'Hypothèse*

Contents

Figures

....

Tables

....

Preface

The writing of any book is a cultural phenomenon—not *Hoch Kultur*, but culture in the sense of persons or groups working cooperatively. This book has its own small history and sociology; the former must be recorded for the sake of accuracy, the latter for the sake of courtesy.

Our work on integrating the psychotherapy-outcome research literature began in January 1975, when we first asked a seminar of clinicians and counselors to think about the problem with us. This small beginning encouraged us to persevere. That we were able to continue owes much to the Spencer Foundation, Dr. H. Thomas James, president, which granted us the first of two sums of money that made our work possible over the succeeding three years. In April 1976, some preliminary findings were reported in the second author's presidential address to the American Educational Research Association. Eighteen months later, an extended, but still cryptic report of our work was published in the *American Psychologist* (Smith and Glass 1977). This book represents a significant expansion of the work previously published and its extension to the research on drug treatment.

We could fill pages with the names of persons to whom we feel an obligation to thank. No one would understand if we reached back to our student days and recalled the names of professors and colleagues who set us on the path and showed us how to walk. And they would be embarrassed by our having broken a convention to pay overdue debts. It is conventional to thank those persons, many of them new acquaintances, who contributed directly to the work published; it is a convention we gladly honor, no less mindful of older and indirect contributions.

The financial support of the Spencer Foundation deserves to be acknowledged again. Several established scholars in the field of psychotherapy were generous with their encouragement and advice: Hans H. Strupp, Vanderbilt University; Victor Raimy, University of Colorado; Lester Luborsky, University of Pennsylvania; R. Bruce Sloane, University of Southern California; Herbert J. Schlesinger, University of Colorado–Medical Center. Our concerns about certain statistical problems were quieted by John W. Tukey, Princeton University. We were gratified and reassured by the exchange of correspondence on methodology with Robert Rosenthal, Harvard University. Our work brought us many new acquaintances, but three were particularly agreeable: Dirk Revenstorf, Max-Planck Institute for Psychiatry–Munich, Diana Shapiro and David Shapiro, University of Sheffield.

Two brief leaves from our duties at the University of Colorado expedited our work. We wish to acknowledge the support during those visits to the

Max-Planck Institute for Psychiatry–Munich and the Center for the Study of Evaluation, University of California–Los Angeles. As always, our work owes much to the interest and support of our colleagues and students in the Laboratory of Educational Research, University of Colorado. Two persons labored with us over the manuscript. Evi Bassoff struggled to make the prose simple and direct, but there is only so much one person can do. Our secretary for the past five years, Victoria Bergquist, announced when we handed her the first chapter that she was pregnant; the final typing took only six months, but then it is not so complicated a work as that which she was about.

The Benefits of Psychotherapy

Chapter 1

Psychotherapy-Outcome Research: Science in the Service of Controversy

"No responsible writer has ever reviewed the evidence of outcome studies and concluded that counseling and psychotherapy . . . have an average benefit beyond that seen in comparable control groups"; so wrote Truax and Carkhuff in 1967 (p. 13). Their categorical statement is not isolated, but represents a widespread view that research has proven psychotherapy to be ineffective as a treatment for psychological disorders. Who were these responsible reviewers and what were the bases for their conclusions? In 1952, Hans Eysenck began a controversy that has still not subsided by reviewing two studies of the spontaneous improvement of psychologically distressed individuals and comparing their improvement rates with those of clients of psychotherapy. He concluded on the basis of this comparison that the effectiveness of psychotherapy was unproven. In 1961 and 1966, Eysenck added eight research studies to his review and concluded that the results were uniformly negative. He saw no alternative but for therapists to concede that "current psychotherapeutic procedures have not lived up to the hopes which greeted their emergence fifty years ago" (1961, p. 720).

Later reviewers echoed this gloomy message. Bergin (1970) reviewed Eysenck's methods and results, disputing them successfully on many points. He reviewed some fifty studies of psychotherapy outcomes. Although his view was more favorable than Eysenck's, he could not "point to more than a moderately positive average effect" (p. 229). Bergin even argued that many clients were worse off after therapy than they had been before. When a few positive cases were sorted in with the negative ones, the overall average rates of improvement were not much greater than those of the untreated persons in the study.

Rachman (1971) reviewed the psychotherapy-outcome literature and concluded that, "we do not have satisfactory evidence to support the claim that psychotherapy is effective. It would seem therefore that those psychologists and psychiatrists who advocate and/or practice psychotherapy carry the burden of having to demonstrate the value of their views and practices" (p. 162).

Attacks against psychotherapy based on outcome research have not been confined to the academic community. The most recent and vitriolic of such attacks written for the general public is *The Psychological Society* by Martin Gross (1978). Basing his opinions on the reviews of Eysenck and others, Gross called psychotherapy the *"key ritual in our twentieth-century religion"* (p. 34). "The breakthrough in evaluating psychotherapy has come from the use of a simple scientific method, the *controlled study*. Therapy has built its inflated reputation on *clinical claims*, the anecdotal recounting of 'cured' cases, which, like stories of chiropractic 'miracles', hypnotized an anxious society. Backed by a strident propaganda campaign, psychotherapy protested that it did not need studies to verify its beneficence" (p. 24).

The experiences of hundreds of thousands of individuals contrast sharply with the negative views of Gross and the academic critics. In a relatively free market, psychotherapy continues to prosper. More than seven million persons engage in psychotherapy each year, paying over two billion dollars, according to Gross. He would interpret this fact, however, as indicative of the successful conspiracy of propaganda by psychotherapists and not as testimony by clients of a successful experience.

What Gross failed to recognize is that he had wandered onto the battlefield of an internecine war. Although there are many combatants—Freudians versus cognitivists versus humanists—the principals in the war are behaviorists and nonbehaviorists. These groups have called each other names and traded high-sounding insults. But the issue was not over psychotherapy versus no psychotherapy, but over brand A psychotherapy versus brand B psychotherapy. Even Eysenck—believed to be the archenemy of psychotherapy by most American scholars—espouses a therapeutic philosophy that hundreds or thousands of American clinicians call psychotherapy. If Gross had reported on the debate over a gold or a silver standard at the end of the nineteenth century, he would have transmogrified it into a battle over a money economy versus a barter economy, and he would have made the objections of each protagonist against the other monetary standard look like arguments against money itself.

Each of the reviewers of research used some part of the research literature to set up "traditional" (a euphemism for whatever forms of psychotherapy have gone before) psychotherapy as a straw man to be knocked down by a new conception of psychotherapy or treatment. For Eysenck and Rachman, the preferred alternative to traditional psychotherapy was behavior therapy. "Fortunately," according to Eysenck, "we now have an alternative method of treatment rationally based on scientific concepts developed in psychological laboratories, and deriving its methods from modern learning theory. Behavior therapy has already been shown to be a shorter, and for many neurotic disorders a much more effective method of treatment than psychotherapy ... we are in the position of having two contenders in the ring between whom a rational choice should not be impossible" (1964, p. 99).

Eysenck thus provided a pugilistic metaphor that may be aptly applied to the history of psychotherapy research. Different forms of therapy were viewed as adversaries, competitors, or contestants, and the arena of conflict was the controlled experiment. The referee judged the performance and results and declared one therapy the winner and the other the loser. To the winner went the spoils—acclaim, superiority, grant money, journal space. Unfortunately for the winner, however, a rematch always reversed the outcome. Who, then, is the real winner?

Although this picture is overdrawn for the sake of emphasis, it better represents the state of psychotherapy-outcome studies and reviews thereof than does the common view of science as the accumulation and refinement of evidence, gathered by neutral, objective observers, gradually converging on the single, true conclusion.

The contest between verbal psychotherapy and behavior therapy was over in many peoples' minds by 1970. Academic psychologists and therapists of all stripes were prone to concede that behavior therapy had won. Yet the victory rested on little more than brash claims and ex cathedra statements that one way of doing therapy was "scientific" and the other way was not. There were few comparative studies—studies in which verbal and behavioral therapies were compared directly—prior to 1970; but those that did exist were seldom cited as the basis for the contention that behavioral therapies had won and would soon sweep the consulting rooms of the world.

Critics of psychotherapy in its various forms, supposedly basing their claims on the accumulated research, are not neutral third parties but proponents of alternative forms of psychotherapy. Polemics and rhetoric—saying it loud, often, and categorically—more frequently characterize the literature than does the careful, dispassionate, and fair evaluation of evidence. Perhaps this is a natural stage of development for a science. As Thomas Kuhn wrote in *The Structure of Scientific Revolutions* (1962), "the pre-paradigm period [in the development of a science] is regularly marked by frequent and deep debates over legitimate methods, problems, and standards of solution, though these serve rather to define schools than to produce agreement" (pp. 47–48).

Later reviews of the outcome literature resulted in quite different conclusions and were subjected to criticisms of liberal bias. Meltzoff and Kornreich (1970) reviewed 100 studies and found the bulk of evidence supportive of the effectiveness of psychotherapy. Luborsky, Singer, and Luborsky (1975) reviewed 30 studies and found that "a high percentage of patients who go through any of these psychotherapies gain from them" (p. 1003). They found no differences in the effectiveness of behavioral and nonbehavioral psychotherapy.

These conclusions are at variance with those reached by Eysenck, Rachman, and Bergin. Which are to be believed? The observer—bewildered by the conflict and unable to read all the primary sources for himself—is left with unanswered questions: Is psychotherapy really effective for dealing with psychological distress? Is one form of therapy any more beneficial than another? Are people with one sort of distress helped more than those with other sorts?

Those who have sought to address these questions, using the research literature, have reached different, even contradictory conclusions. This occurred despite their use of similar methods—research reviews—and despite the fact that they often read and reviewed the same collection of studies. But traditional research-reviewing techniques are inadequate. They lack essential features of scientific investigation—replicability and objectivity. Traditional reviewing techniques involve the narrative description of each study, a critical evaluation leading to a decision to accept or reject the study as evidence on the question at hand, and then an implicit summing up of the findings, with qualifications made to account for discrepant results. Hundreds of studies bear on the question of therapeutic effectiveness, however, rendering impossible the narrative summary of all their findings. The problem we confront in this book is how to turn these thousands of pieces of evidence into an integrated representation of the benefits of psychotherapy, and how to do so according to a set of rules that can be specified and repeated so that prejudice and idiosyncracy can fade into the background and the evidence can take its rightful place as the center of concerned attention.

The method used is called meta-analysis. It is the statistical summary of the numerical outcomes of each study. We attempted to find and include all the controlled studies of psychotherapy outcome; that is, all the research in which one group of persons was treated for psychological conditions and compared with another, roughly equivalent untreated group. Studies were not excluded from consideration on arbitrary grounds; for example, because they used relatively inexperienced therapists or clients who had volunteered for the experiment, or had crude outcome measures. We suspected that contradictory conclusions of previous reviewers were largely the result of the arbitrary imposition of criteria for deciding which studies constituted valid evidence. These criteria had often been applied so as to favor a favorite hypothesis or vested ideological interest. The statistical results of each study were quantified to yield an estimate of the magnitude of therapeutic effect. These measures were summarized and then related to other features of the research, such as the kind of client, treatment, and outcome. This allowed us to examine the amount of bias injected by those who excluded studies based on the validity of their design, length of treatment, experience of therapists, or whatever.

We hope that what emerges at the end of this meta-analysis will strike the reader as being fair, nonideological and clear. The results should seem connected closely to the original data (i.e., the findings of hundreds of outcome studies themselves) so that the reader suffers few worries about being several steps removed from the primary evidence. Although he is inevitably some distance from the tens of thousands of pages of the original studies, he should be able to trace precisely the steps that were taken to reach the promontory from which the landscape of the psychotherapy-outcome literature can be seen. If he does not trust the view we show him, at least now he knows why. The remainder of the book is organized into eight chapters described below.

Chapter 2 contains a more detailed account of the debate over psychotherapy effectiveness introduced in Chapter 1. The reviews of Eysenck, Bergin and Rachman are presented and the assumptions and methods of each are analyzed. Several of the numerous published responses to these reviews are included. The more recent reviews of the evidence are also detailed. A table is presented in which the results of the major reviews are summarized. A case is made for considering the validity of review conclusions on standardized, published criteria.

The issues involved in the evaluation of psychotherapy are presented in Chapter 3. Research is contrasted with evaluation, the latter being more descriptive of studies of psychotherapy effectiveness. The controlled study should be the basic building block of therapeutic effectiveness, yet there are many objections to the use of this method. These objections—that control groups are unethical or that therapies or clients are too variable to be compared, for example—are analyzed. The rationale for meta-analysis as an advance over other techniques for research integration is presented, as are methodological considerations of meta-analysis.

Chapters 4 and 5 deal with the methods and results of the psychotherapy meta-analysis. The definition of the population of outcome studies, sampling from that population, classification of variables from the studies, quantification of outcomes, and analysis of data are the topics of Chapter 4.

The results of these processes are reported in Chapter 5. Results are presented as a whole to answer the overall question: How effective is psychotherapy? More specific analyses yielded estimates of the effectiveness of different forms of psychotherapy and estimates of the effects of therapy for different kinds of clients and outcomes. The question about the relationship between the quality of the study's design relative to the size of effect produced is answered.

Chapters 6, 7, and 8 refer to a separate investigation—the meta-analysis of studies of the effects of drug therapies on psychological disorders. The two meta-analyses were separated because of obvious differences in the two populations of studies. Studies that involved drugs or drugs in conjunction or competition with psychotherapy also involved clients who were older, more seriously disturbed, and more likely to be hospitalized, as compared with clients in the psychotherapy studies. We suspected substantial differences in motivation and expectation for medical as opposed to psychological treatment between the two sets of subjects. Chapter 6 contains the methods and results of earlier reviews of the efficacy of drug therapy. There is less acrimonious debate in the history of these reviews, in comparison with the psychotherapy reviews (Chapter 2). Still, there is some disagreement about the comparative value of drugs and psychotherapy for the treatment of psychological disturbance. There is even less consensus on what research proves about the interaction of drugs and psychotherapy. Do psychoactive drugs inhibit or facilitate the effects of psychotherapy? Do drugs make psychotherapy obsolete for seriously disturbed patients?

The details of the methods used in the drug therapy meta-analysis are presented in Chapter 7: the population of studies, the sample, the classification of study variables, quantification of outcomes, and summary data analysis. The results of the analysis are presented in Chapter 8. The questions about the overall effectiveness of drug treatment are answered and effectiveness is compared to psychotherapy. The interaction of drug and psychotherapy effects is estimated.

Chapter 9 contains the conclusions reached in the two meta-analysis investigations. The effects of psychotherapy and drug therapy are described in very general terms; the conclusions are only those few so thoroughly supported by the evidence derived in our analyses that one may hope for a consensus. Some implications of these findings are suggested for research, policy, and practice.

The meta-analyses to be presented here permit conclusions about the effectiveness of psychotherapy as a whole and in its several forms. Yet we do not expect that a rapprochement among the warring factions will follow the publication of our findings. Responses to our previous work have led us to expect that those who are pleased with the results of the analyses will praise the study and that those whose favorite "contender in the ring" is not favored in the results will criticize not only the findings but our methods and our motives as well—such is the adversarial atmosphere of psychotherapy research.

Chapter 2

Reviews and Controversies in Psychotherapy-Outcome Research

Tendentious and adversarial, the debate about the effectiveness of psychotherapy has proceeded through a series of research reviews and commentaries on these reviews. Variable, often contradictory, conclusions have been reached by reviewers not only because of opposing philosophical and theoretical positions but also because of a lack of methodological sophistication in research reviews. In this chapter, we develop an analogy between the methods of research reviews and the methods of primary research design and use this analogy as a point of departure for analyzing the major reviews, beginning with Eysenck's (1952), and the controversies generated in response to them. Standards for judging the adequacy and fairness of reviews also are presented.

Reviews as Primary Research Design

Rarely is the objective of a reviewer of research to list the separate pieces of research on a topic. More often his objective is to analyze and present the separate studies in such a way that an overall conclusion can be reached about the nature of the process studied. As soon as the researcher reaches for that conclusion, he is engaging in a process of inference or generalization from separate data. Data in the form of findings from research studies are aggregated or accumulated almost in the same way as measurements on individuals are accumulated in primary research to form conclusions about the variables studied.

In research reviews, findings are aggregated and colligated to form conclusions. When the findings of the individual studies do not agree, or the characteristics or contexts of the studies are different, as is usually the case in social science research, the reviewer is faced with the problem of how to qualify his general conclusion, or how to weight differentially the separate studies to arrive at the general conclusion. It is common to see reviewers impeach a study based on its research design (e.g., "although study X showed conflicting results, flaws in design preclude its further consideration"). Similarly, a reviewer may throw out the results of one study in which the population was defined in a somewhat different way than the populations of the remainder. This process of discarding conflicting findings is almost always judgmental and done post hoc. Although clothed in elaborate rationalizations, the process is dangerously vulnerable to the injection of prejudice and bias. We are never sure whether the results of the rejected study were known prior to the reviewer's decision to reject.

Developed over decades of methodological thought and research, the rules for reaching a generalization within an individual empirical study are fairly well accepted in most quarters. These rules are not so obvious and well articulated in the case of research reviews. However, the processes involved in the two kinds of research and the rules for arriving at generalizations and judging whether these generalizations are valid can be seen as analogous.

The steps in an empirical study are familiar. The researcher states a hypothesis about the expected direction of results. He defines a population for study and samples from it. He measures variables and analyzes data. From these data, conclusions are drawn. The reader can follow the steps taken and judge the validity of the conclusions. The steps in a research review are similar and are described below.

Hypotheses. Like the primary investigator, the research reviewer usually has a hunch about probable conclusions to be reached from an analysis of the accumulated research. This hunch comes from familiarity with one or two studies done by the reviewer or his colleagues, from theory or from prejudice or proclivity. The hypotheses may be implicit and unstated, but they are present at least in the mind of the reviewer and guide the activities that follow.

Population and Sample. The independent variables (characteristics of the studies) and dependent variables (e.g., rate of improvement or magnitude of effect) are defined. The population of studies is identified (e.g., "all experimental studies of need achievement," "all survey studies of dogmatism published after 1970"). The research reviewer may include all studies that fit his definition of the population or he may sample according to some decision rules. Just as in empirical studies, the fairest rule would be the random sampling of experimental units (studies from the population of studies). On the other hand, the reviewer may ignore some studies or fail to locate others. To the extent that the sample is not representative of the population, the conclusions reached on the basis of the sample may be biased.

Measurement. Features of the study are abstracted and categorized; these may include the quality of the research design, the nature of the population studied, and the statistical procedures used to analyze data. The findings of the study are often related to these characteristics; that is, the effects produced by a study are correlated with different features of the study. The findings of the individual studies are abstracted from statistical tables and narrative discussions into a common metric for subsequent use in analysis of data. For example, a table of results from an individual's multifactor test battery is collapsed into a single judgment of "improved" or "unimproved." Or, the study is listed as having produced "significant" or "nonsignificant" effects. Or the statement is made that this study produced an improvement rate of 70 percent. Judgments, listings, or statements such as these become the dependent variables or outcome measurements from the studies.

Analysis. Just as measurements from subjects in an experiment must be somehow aggregated, there must be some means for accumulating the findings from the separate studies into a review summary. This may be as simple as adding up the measures and dividing by the number of measures, defining a median improvement rate, or comparing the means for various portions of the data (e.g., comparing the average improvement rates for subjects treated by drugs vs. rates for those treated by electro-shock therapy). Another common method is the cross-tabulation of study effects with characteristics of the study, its subjects, or treatment. More complicated descriptive and inferential statistics may also be used to draw general conclusions. The data analysis process is sometimes implicit and must be inferred. Also accessible by examination is the weighting scheme the reviewer uses. For example, all studies might be given the same weight in arriving at the conclusion. In other cases, the reviewer might decide that the findings of poorly designed studies should not be given any consideration (weight = 0) in adding the findings to reach a conclusion, or should be given less credence (weight = 0.5) than findings of well-designed studies. The reviewer might decide to count dropouts from the treatment group as treatment failures, or instead to decrease total sample size by the number of dropouts. These decisions have a great effect on the final statistics, and they are infrequently obvious. Many reviewers are apt to disqualify studies and exclude them from the research review. The grounds for such exclusion are frequently personalistic, post hoc, and not independent of the findings of the study.

Conclusions. Based on the descriptive statistics, the comparisons or the narrative treatment of review findings, conclusions are drawn. These conclusions may be qualified by the reviewer according to the specificity of limitations both within the individual studies and with respect to the procedures of the research review.

Conclusions based on comparisons of findings within studies and among studies can be subjected to the standards for evaluating validity set up by Campbell and Stanley (1966). Suppose that a research reviewer analyzes twenty studies in which subjects receiving insulin therapy were compared experimentally with untreated control groups and twenty other studies in which subjects receiving electro-shock therapy were compared against control groups. By fair and reliable procedures, the improvement rates were shown to be 50 percent for insulin treatment and 40 percent for electro-shock treatment. But the difference in relative improvement rates must be qualified, since the comparison is not experimental (subjects were not randomly assigned to the two experiments). In addition to the effects of the treatments, there may be other possible causes for the observed difference, such as any initial differences in severity of illness between subjects in the two experiments. This is true in spite of the high internal validity of each of the two sets of studies. This example illustrates the "selection threat" to the internal validity of the *research review*. Although this is the most common, other threats to internal validity (e.g., history, instrumentation, mortality—see Campbell and Stanley 1966) must also be considered in the evaluation of the validity of the research-review conclusions. There may be a set of studies in which two or more treatments are directly compared. Suppose in the previous example of a research review some studies directly compared the effects of electro-shock and insulin, with patients randomly assigned to one treatment or the other or to the control group. Aggregating across this group of studies to arrive at a comparison of treatment effects avoids the threats to internal validity of selection, instrumentation, and history, thus increasing our confidence in the results.

Psychotherapy-Outcome Research Reviews

Failure to distinguish between the validity of the primary studies on which research reviews are based and the validity of the research reviews themselves has contributed to confusion and controversy in the psychotherapy-outcome literature.

Eysenck's 1952 Review

Eysenck (1952) began the debate with a review of research in which he compared the results of two studies of untreated neurotics with the results of 24 studies of the cure or improvement rates of neurotics treated with psychodynamic or eclectic psychotherapy. The two original studies of "spontaneous remission" among untreated neurotics were done by Landis (1938) and Denker (1946). The Landis study used the improvement rate (proportion rated by the physician as "cured," "improved," etc.) of hospitalized neurotics as a standard by which psychotherapy outcomes must be judged. Even with no therapy and only custodial care, two-thirds of the hospitalized neurotics were discharged as recovered or considerably improved within one year. Denker found a similar figure of spontaneous recovery after two years for neurotic patients who made disability claims to an insurance company. These two studies provided a baseline of recovery without benefit of psychotherapy, and Eysenck contrasted it with the improvement rates reported in 24 uncontrolled studies of psychotherapy outcomes. The improvement rates in each of these studies were placed by Eysenck into categories: "cured or much improved" was grouped with "improved;" "slightly improved" was grouped with "not improved, died, left treatment."* Since the primary studies reported different categories of improvement, some judgment had to be exercised to derive a common set of categories. Eysenck stated that this judgmental process produced no distortions in the pooled results. The numbers of patients in each improvement category were added up and transformed into percentages of total subjects who were classified as "cured, much improved, improved." Eysenck recorded the following findings: "Patients treated by means of psychoanalysis improve to the extent of 44 percent; patients treated eclectically improve to the extent of 64 percent; patients treated only custodially or by general practitioners improve to the extent of 72 percent. There thus appears to be an inverse correlation between recovery and psychotherapy; the more psychotherapy, the smaller the recovery rate. This conclusion requires certain qualifications" (1952, p. 322).

The qualifications involved the definition of a treatment terminator as a treatment failure, the differences between the populations studied by Landis and Denker and those of the therapy-outcome studies, and the differences in outcome assessment in the research reviewed.

The conclusions reached by Eysenck were condemning and uncompromising:

[The data] fail to prove that psychotherapy, Freudian or otherwise, facilitates the recovery of neurotic patients. They show that roughly two-thirds of a group of neurotic patients will recover or improve to a marked extent within about two years of the onset of their illness, whether they are treated by means of psychotherapy or not. . . .

The figures quoted do not necessarily disprove the possibility of therapeutic effectiveness. . . . Definite proof would require a special investigation, carefully planned and methodologically more adequate than these *ad hoc* comparisons. But even the much more modest conclusions that the figures fail to show any favorable effects of psychotherapy should give pause to those who would wish to give an important part in the training of clinical psychologists to a skill unsupported by any scientifically acceptable evidence (1952, pp. 322–23).

Responses to Eysenck's 1952 Review

Widely quoted in the popular and professional literature, Eysenck's findings and conclusions had a far-reaching impact. Many clinicians and clinical

---

*"... a patient who fails to finish treatment is surely a treatment failure" (Eysenck 1952, p. 322).

researchers responded critically to Eysenck. Two of these responses are examined here.

Rosenzweig (1954) criticized the Eysenck review and the primary studies on which it was based. He noted that Landis (1938) had urged caution, precision, and a minimum of generalization of his findings, due to the fallibility of diagnostic, treatment, and outcome definitions. Eysenck was not as cautious in his own generalizations, according to Rosenzweig, making only a "polite bow of recognition to the sources of difficulty outlined by Landis which are then lightly dismissed" (p. 298).

Rosenzweig demonstrated that by using alternative assumptions and methods of allocating subjects to the improvement categories one could find nonnegligible differences in the final outcome rates. He questioned whether the severity of the illness in the treated and untreated groups was comparable. After analyzing the reports of the primary studies, he concluded that Denker's baseline group was probably less severely ill (the need for treatment being compounded by the secondary gains of receiving disability payments) than the treated groups. The Landis group was probably more seriously ill, enough so to be hospitalized. Eysenck's failure to establish commonality in patient populations in the two sets of studies led to an invidious comparison in his review.

Challenging the assertion that the subjects studied by Denker and Landis were actually untreated, Rosenzweig suggested that these groups actually received a variety of psychotherapeutic procedures, such as attention, reassurance, and suggestion. This being the case, "the necessary contrast between the baseline and the experimental groups becomes markedly attenuated" (p. 303).

The question of common criteria for improvement was also raised. Rosenzweig stated that improvement (symptom disappearance) sufficient for dismissal from the hospital does not approximate the more rigid standards of psychoanalysis for a cure.

[Eysenck's improvement rates—44 percent for those treated with psychoanalysis, 64 percent for those treated with electic psychotherapy, and 72 percent for those treated custodially—do not] prove the improbability that the more intensive the psychotherapy, the less benefit to the patient; rather it reflects the probability that the more intensive the therapy, the higher the standard of recovery (p. 302).

Eysenck's data and arguments fail to support his thesis that psychotherapy cannot be shown to facilitate recovery. . . .
The only safe deduction is that . . . broad generalizations as to the effectiveness of treatment are to be avoided (p. 303).

Eysenck (1955) responded by suggesting that he and Rosenzweig were "in complete agreement as to the main conclusion"—that available evidence fails to prove the effectiveness of psychotherapy. "All through his article, Rosenzweig seems to criticize me for having attempted to prove that psychotherapy is ineffective. This, however, I have never attempted to do. I was not trying to prove the null hypothesis, which would be foolish as well as inadmissable; I was simply examining available data to see whether these data *succeeded in disproving* the null hypothesis'' (p. 147). To Rosenzweig's criticism that Landis had urged more caution in dealing with these data than Eysenck had used, Eysenck replied that including such cautions would have made the paper too long, repetitious of the original data with which everyone should be familiar, and ripe for an editor's deletion. Eysenck also neglected to discuss Rosenzweig's demonstration that the former's method for allocating subjects to improvement categories biased the results. Eysenck did not reply to the points raised about invidious comparisons due to variations in the severity of patient illness, treatment definitions, and standards of outcome. Instead, he repeated the complaint about the lack of knowledge of the nature of the process under investigation and this lack of controlled studies (in the absence of which his conclusions held).

Luborsky (1954) replied to Eysenck with many of the same criticisms as did Rosenzweig and other respondents—differential criteria in the two sets of studies reviewed, differences in initial severity of illness in the two populations, the high probability that the ''untreated'' groups received nonspecific therapeutic treatment, and the differences introduced by variance in allocation of subjects to improvement categories (particularly in counting those who had died during treatment). Luborsky also raised the issue of whether the effectiveness of treatment might not vary over the course of history, i.e., whether it is fair to compare one group treated in the 1920s with another group treated in the 1940s.

In addition, Luborsky made the crucial point about the invalidity of Eysenck's comparisons.

I do not believe Eysenck has an adequate control group nor that comparisons of groups can be made within the experimental group. . . .

To conclude as he does, Eysenck must assume patients do something they do not do: randomly self-select themselves to psychiatrists, general practitioners, and state hospitals. His ''treatment'' versus ''non-treatment'' groups are composed along very selective lines. Many of the ''insurance'' group would probably never have visited the doctor if it were not required. As a whole the group is probably of higher social and economic level than other groups. Very likely the choice of a general practitioner rather than a psychiatrist to treat their psychoneurosis reflects a not-to-be ignored difference in attitude to their illness. And, for all we know, different brands of psychiatrists may get self-selective by different samples of patients. Eysenck says we need better control groups, but fails to take his own statement seriously (p. 129).

Eysenck (1954) published a rejoinder to Luborsky in which the same arguments made in response to Rosenzweig's critique were repeated, viz., that Eysenck had not stated that psychotherapy was ineffective, but merely that no evidence existed to prove its effectiveness. Eysenck did not respond to the methodological criticisms raised except to reiterate that the failings of the studies he reviewed precluded more specific conclusions.

His critics had the best of the substantive and methodological argument, but the rhetorical victory was Eysenck's. However, careful reading of the original studies, the responses, and the ripostes leads one to the conclusion that he deftly sidestepped certain methodological criticisms to hold to his conclusion. The criticisms dealt with Eysenck's own invidious comparisons, yet he deflected these criticisms by saying that the studies (and not he himself as reviewer) employed inappropriate comparisons. Although a comparison between a treated group and a nonequivalent control group does not rate high on anyone's index of internal validity, a nonequivalent comparison group was precisely the "design" used by Eysenck in his review. Viewed this way, conclusions emerging from his review are deficient with respect to selection, history, and instrumentation (threats to internal validity discussed by Campbell and Stanley 1966), and therefore no conclusions are warranted at all. This would be true *even if the primary studies he reviewed had been internally perfect*.

Eysenck's protestations that he did not conclude that psychotherapy was ineffective (merely that its effectiveness was not proven) also defused criticism while maintaining the original finding. Some would think such a maneuver disingenuous, since many readers in the therapeutic community, as well as the general public, do not understand the distinction between failure to disprove the null hypothesis and the failure of the treatment itself. This ambiguity was virtually eliminated in Eysenck's later publications.

Eysenck's 1961 Review

In a subsequent research review, Eysenck (1961) included four sets of research studies: studies using control groups, studies establishing a base-rate of spontaneous remission, a research review by Levitt (1957) involving effects of psychotherapy on children, and studies comparing treatments based on behavioral theories that provide alternatives to psychotherapy.

Eysenck delineated requirements for an adequate experiment and presented alternative definitions of psychotherapy—showing the differences among them—and settled on one that involved prolonged interpersonal relationship, a trained and experienced therapist, the patient's felt dissatisfaction as the motive for entering treatment, psychological treatment methods based on some theory, and amelioration of dissatisfactions as the aim of treatment.

He summarized four controlled studies of the effect of psychotherapy: by Teuber and Powers (1953), Brill and Beebe (1955), Barron and Leary (1955), and Rogers and Dymond (1954). The first three produced no differences between treated and control groups. The fourth showed findings generally supportive of psychotherapy, but was excluded from the conclusions because of flaws in its design. A nonequivalent control group had been used in the Rogers and Dymond study, and the time interval between testings was not the same for the treated group and a second, more comparable, control group.

Because of these flaws in the fourth study, Eysenck drew his conclusion on the basis of three studies that showed no effects.

For the second set of data, Eysenck used the two uncontrolled studies of spontaneous remission (reviewed in Eysenck 1952), adding a study by Shepard and Gruenberg (1957). In the latter, analysis of the incidence and prevalence rates of neurosis covered by insurance claims suggested that a neurotic disorder will run its natural course and remit without formal treatment within two years. Combining these three data sources, Eysenck constructed a curve that related percent improvement to the passage of time. This curve was used as a baseline with which to compare the rates of improvement due to psychotherapy produced by the 24 uncontrolled treatment evaluations previously reviewed (Eysenck 1952).

The review of the effects of psychotherapy with children (Levitt 1957) was also used. Levitt had followed the lead of Eysenck (1952) in comparing improvement rates of studies of psychotherapy with children with base rates of untreated populations from other studies. In this case, the untreated were those who had applied for, been accepted, but failed to engage in therapy at child guidance centers.*

The fourth set of studies consisted of comparisons of verbal psychotherapy with alternative modes of therapy—reciprocal inhibition (Wolpe 1958), "assertion-structured therapy" (Phillips 1957), and "rational psychotherapy" (Ellis 1957). Although no untreated control groups were used to test the spontaneous remission rates (as Eysenck pointed out), the "learning-theory based" alternatives proved to be more effective than the psychoanalytically oriented psychotherapies in assessments of rates of improvement.

Having added up these four sets of studies, Eysenck arrived at eight conclusions. The following are the most inclusive:

When untreated neurotic control groups are compared with experimental groups of neurotic patients treated by means of psychotherapy, both groups recover to approximately the same extent (p. 719).

Neurotic patients treated by means of psychotherapeutic procedures based on learning theory† improve significantly more quickly than do patients treated by means of psychoanalytic or eclectic psychotherapy, or not treated by psychotherapy at all (p. 720).

Eysenck reviewed his 1952 conclusion that research fails to disprove the "null hypothesis" of therapeutic ineffectiveness. "The additional studies which have come to hand since, particularly those using a control group, have been so uniformly negative in their outcome that a somewhat stronger conclusion appears warranted. . . . It rather seems that psychologists and psychia-

---

*Interestingly, Eysenck criticized Levitt for the noncomparability of the latter's control group.

†"Ellis does not attempt to derive his rational psychotherapy from learning theory, but this would not be impossible" (p. 719).

trists will have to acknowledge the fact that current psychotherapeutic procedures have not lived up to the hopes which greeted their emergence fifty years ago" (p. 720).

Eysenck updated his review in 1966, finding eight studies, seven of which were considered as negative evidence. The one study showing positive results was disallowed because of design flaws. Otherwise, his conclusions were identical to those reviewed above.

Bergin (1970) presented a review of controlled studies of therapeutic effectiveness and a critique of the methodology employed by Eysenck (1952, 1961, 1966). In particular, Bergin examined the original studies of remission rates for neurotics. Using different assumptions and procedures for establishing common improvement rates from the different improvement categories used in the primary studies, he arrived at a remission rate of 30 percent. He achieved his principal objective in this analysis: to show "how investigators with differing biases can arrive at different rates of improvement" (p. 218). Nevertheless, he carried the 30 percent figure as a baseline for spontaneous remission against which rates of improvement from uncontrolled studies of therapeutic effects could be compared.* He added data from several other uncontrolled studies to corroborate his baseline figure. The uncontrolled studies of therapy outcome reviewed by Eysenck (1952) were reexamined. Improvement rates for eclectic psychotherapy were confirmed, but rates for psychoanalytic treatment were higher than those estimated by Eysenck.

Bergin chose 52 studies of psychotherapy outcome. He called these a "cross-section of the literature," probably culled from the bibliography of approximately 500 empirical studies of "therapy in practice" (Strupp and Bergin 1969). The sampling procedure was not specified. Half of the studies reviewed had control groups. None dealt with behavioral therapy. The studies were categorized on the basis of therapist experience, presence of a control group, adequacy of the research design, duration of therapy, type of therapy (analytic, eclectic, or client-centered), and whether there was one therapist or more than one in the study. Studies were tabulated on the above variables and cross-tabulated on the results of therapy—positive, negative, or in doubt.

The criteria for categorizing the studies and judging the success of the outcomes were not fully documented. The criteria for inclusion or exclusion of studies were not clear, and eight controlled studies were not included in the cross-tabulation but did appear in a later but unrelated section of the paper.

Of the 52 studies, Bergin judged 22 to be positive as to the effectiveness of psychotherapy, 15 were negative, and 15 were in doubt. There was a slightly positive relationship between design quality and outcome. Duration and type of therapy were unrelated to outcome. His conclusion was clearly at odds with any that Eysenck had ever drawn: "psychotherapy, on the average, has modestly positive results."

---

*By so doing, Bergin recommitted the essential error in research reviews—concluding from a comparison with nonequivalent groups.

The paper then changed in focus from an evaluation of the effects of psychotherapy into an argument for the existence of a deterioration effect of psychotherapy and an argument for the unspontaneous nature of "spontaneous" remission. Although these sections of Bergin's paper laid the groundwork for a series of articles about the deterioration effect, the argument will not be presented here. Searching for the true spontaneous remission rate is unnecessary. Such estimates will never substitute for control groups; there is now a sufficient number of controlled studies. Both lines of argument made Bergin's article vulnerable to criticism and obscured his primary conclusions about the effectiveness of psychotherapy.

Rachman's Review

Rachman (1971), a frequent collaborator with Eysenck, reviewed the psychotherapy literature in response to Bergin. His conclusion followed that of Eysenck—that there is no evidence to prove the effectiveness of psychotherapy, and the burden of proof remains with those who advocate it.

He repeated Eysenck's argument and the methods used in supporting it, and he listed and attempted to refute the major criticisms of that work. Coming under particular attack was Bergin's treatment of the spontaneous remission problem. After reviewing the (uncontrolled) studies Bergin used to arrive at a remission rate of 30 percent, Rachman concluded that Bergin's rate was ill-founded and misleading and that Eysenck's figure of 65 percent was still more credible. Rachman's technique was to rereview some of the studies presented by Bergin and impeach each one that was inadequate in some respect. Thus, a study was disallowed because the subjects studied were delinquents or psychosomatic disordered rather than neurotic. Or a study might be disallowed for reasons of research design or measurement of outcome.

The impeachment process was heavily used in Rachman's review of controlled studies. No attempt was made to describe how the studies reviewed were chosen from the population of such studies. There was no attempt to categorize features of the studies and no explicit procedure for aggregating their results.* The author merely described several studies in some detail, noted whether the outcome was favorable or unfavorable to psychotherapy, and then made some concluding statement that impeached the study, based on flaws in its design, population, or outcome assessment. If not impeached, the study was included in the summary.

An analysis of this review reveals that of the 23 studies, Rachman declared only one as showing tentative evidence for the effects of verbal psycho-

---

*In developing a table that summarizes the results of several reviews, we have included the studies in Rachman's chapters 4 (psychoanalysis), 5 (psychotherapy), and 7 (Rogerian psychotherapy). To gain some commonality in the table, we have excluded his reviews of psychotherapy with children and psychotics. Behavioral treatment studies were also excluded.

therapy. Five studies produced negative effects (i.e., treated groups failed to exceed control groups or baseline remission rates on outcome criteria). Seventeen studies were impeached for a variety of reasons. Only two of these showed negative effects; these were disallowed because of nonrandom assignment of subjects to groups and because two therapies were compared directly without reference to a control group. Reasons for impeaching the fifteen studies showing positive results were the following: use of the Thematic Apperception Test or self-concept Q-sorts as criterion variables, exclusion of premature therapy terminators from sample size (thus unfairly inflating improvement rates), failure of all outcome measures to show improvement or advantage to the treated group (e.g., where three measures showed positive results and one showed negative results), nonequivalent comparison groups, failure of observed benefit at termination to be maintained at the time of follow-up, use of hospital admissions as an outcome criterion, use of improvement ratings by raters who were not blind as to group composition, use of inexperienced therapists, use of patients who were not neurotic, use of an unpublished test as a criterion measure, inadequate data presentation ("... all their results are presented as averages and these are shown in the form of a graph," p. 76; parentheses and italics original).*

Both Davis (1972) and Shapiro and Shapiro (1977) reviewed Rachman (1971) and found evidence that the latter used inconsistent standards for evaluating evidence of the superiority of behavioral therapy over psychotherapy. Shapiro and Shapiro claimed that Rachman explained away the negative results of *behavior therapy* experiments and willingly accepted positive studies with methodological weaknesses. These same weaknesses in studies of psychotherapy effects would have resulted in their automatic impeachment.

The most stinging indictment one could make against Rachman's work is that he ignored the spontaneous remission argument in his analysis of behavior therapy experiments. In his criticism of psychotherapy studies, he demonstrated the failure of psychotherapy to show effects greater than for untreated controls who spontaneously remit after two years—such being the natural history of psycho-neurotic disorders. Yet, in none of the studies of behavior therapy reviewed by Rachman (or published since then) was this standard met.†

Rachman can also be faulted for his research review strategies. First is the matter of representative sampling of studies. Many more studies were readily available to Rachman (to Bergin and Eysenck as well) than he included. He

---

*Later in the book Rachman presented a table of forty experiments on the effects of systematic desensitization, a "behavioral therapy." Of these, thirty-three were accepted as positive evidence for the effect of this treatment; one was negative; six were in doubt.

†This statement is meant not to criticize behavior therapy, but rather to illustrate the use of a double standard for evaluating evidence.

did not even review all those discussed by Bergin. His selection procedures were unexplained and cannot even be inferred from the text.

Second, and more important, is that the strategy of ex post facto impeachment of some studies based on design quality and outcome measurement is unsupportable. This strategy presumes an objectivity and distance from the problem that is rare among acknowledged advocates and adversaries. No study is above criticism. All studies vary on a number of dimensions of quality and rigor. Where any reviewer draws the line—assigning a study the status of acceptable or unacceptable—is purely an exercise in professional judgment. Any judgmental strategy permits the introduction of bias in the conclusions.

Even prespecified decisions to include or exclude the results of studies may inject bias, unless there is independent evidence or rationale for doing so. That is, if it is known that good and poor designs produce different outcomes, one strategy might be to exclude studies with poor designs. If many years of research have shown that a certain test battery never reflects therapeutic change, then studies using only that battery may be excluded. If different diagnostic categories produce qualitatively different effects, then one might exclude studies involving all but one diagnostic type. However, these relationships have not been substantiated. They are empirical questions that do not support a particular exclusion strategy in reviews of research.

Subsequent Reviews

Meltzoff and Kornreich (1970) started their work with the major premise that a great deal of evidence exists about the effectiveness of psychotherapy—much more than was acknowledged by Eysenck and others. They adopted a method of arriving at overall conclusions about therapeutic effectiveness by tabulating the results of the separate studies. This method was defended by their statement of purpose: "... to find out if there are demonstrable effects of any systematic attempts to modify pathological behavior, regardless of kind or type. . . . Whether or not anyone has been able to demonstrate satisfactorily that individuals with emotional disturbances (of any type) can be more benefitted by psychotherapy (of any variety) than by lack of it over the same time span. What does the current balance of the evidence reveal?" (p. 75).

The authors defined and illustrated several categories for classifying studies. Research designs to be included were either "adequate" (free of major design flaws, use of an adequate control group, use of adequate outcome measures) or "questionable" (less adequate design or less comparable control group, less defensible measurement and analysis of outcome criteria, or use of an analogue procedure). Outcomes were categorized as "positive" (statistically significant differences in favor of the treated group), "negative" (statistically significant differences in favor of the untreated group, or "null" (no statistically significant difference). The outcome was further categorized as demonstrating major or minor benefits. The authors provided a narrative description of each study and entered its results in a cross-classification table based on the above-described characteristics. Although the search and selection of studies were not described, apparently the authors included all the studies that they could find that fit their definition of psychotherapy. One hundred and one controlled studies were found. There was no ex post facto impeachment of studies.

Based on the tabulation of study results, Meltzoff and Kornreich found that 80 percent of the studies yielded positive results. The rest had null or negative results. There was a positive relationship between quality of the research design and the production of positive results. Of the 57 studies categorized as "adequate," 48 (84 percent) yielded positive results about the effectiveness of psychotherapy. Among the 44 studies categorized as "questionable," one-third yielded positive results.

The authors concluded that there was much evidence to demonstrate the effectiveness of psychotherapy, and the bulk of this evidence was positive. Furthermore, Eysenck's results were biased because of his small and unrepresentative selection of studies. The statement by Truax and Carkhuff (1967) that no responsible writer has ever reviewed the evidence and found that psychotherapy has an average benefit beyond control groups is invalid.

Malan (1973) pointed out that Meltzoff and Kornreich treated the methods and results of the research they reviewed "ruthlessly" but "dispassionately" and "fairly." However, they were rather uncritical with respect to outcome measurement and follow-up. Although their conclusion about the effects of psychotherapy in general was valid, it did not necessarily pertain to dynamic psychotherapy with neurotic clients, according to Malan.

For their review of psychotherapy-outcome studies, Luborsky, Singer, and Luborsky (1975) used inclusion criteria that were more stringent than those of Meltzoff and Kornreich and more carefully and fairly delineated than those of other previous reviewers. Luborsky et al. included all reasonably controlled studies on "real" clients; that is, those who recognized problems and sought psychological treatment. Thus, studies of behavioral treatments on volunteer populations were excluded. The types of therapy in the studies reviewed included the traditional verbal therapies based on psycho-dynamic and client-centered theories plus behavioral treatments on "real" or "bona fide" clients.

The premise of this review is as follows: "Comparative studies of psychotherapies is not an area where one or two decisive experiments can be telling—one must rely on the verdict of a series of at least passably controlled studies. Ideally, one would want to have an impeccable definitive study that would settle the question of comparative worth once and for all, but it is not possible, since *every* study has some uniqueness of sample characteristics, measuring instruments, and other less easily defined aspects. A consensus of many studies is what we must hope for'' (p. 995).

Each study to be reviewed was categorized on several dimensions. Research quality was determined on the basis of twelve criteria, among them, the methods for assigning subjects to comparison groups, procedures for dealing with therapy dropouts, use of real clients, use of experienced therapists, the equal valuing by the experimenter of each of the treatments compared, the tailoring of outcome measures with therapeutic goals, independent and objective measurement of outcomes, and adequate sample size. The scores on these criteria were summarized into grades for research quality—A through E. A grade of E excluded that study from the summary of results. The results of each study were categorized according to whether there were significant differences in favor of the treated group (+), the comparison group (−), or no significant differences between the groups (0). These results were summarized in a table of "box scores," i.e., the number of statistically significant studies broken down by psychotherapy vs. behavior therapy, high quality design vs. low quality design.

The results of 33 studies in which psychotherapy treatment groups were compared with untreated groups showed 20 studies with treated groups statistically significantly better off than were the controls and 13 studies with no significant differences between treated and untreated groups. In no study was the control group superior to the psychotherapy group. For those 19 studies with nonpsychotic populations, 11 yielded results in favor of the psychotherapy groups, 8 "ties," and no studies in favor of the control groups. The reviewers found no relationship between the quality of the design of the study and its outcome.

The review extended to comparisons between individual and group psychotherapy (no differences), time-limited and time-unlimited therapy (no differences), behavior therapy and psychotherapy (no differences), psychotherapy and medical treatment for psychosomatic symptoms (psychotherapy plus medical treatment was superior to medical treatment alone), and psychotherapy and psycho-pharmacotherapy (see Chapter 6).

The conclusion based on this review was as follows: *"The controlled comparative studies indicate that a high percentage of patients who go through any of these psychotherapies gain from them"* (p. 1003).

Except for a somewhat derisive and nonsubstantive criticism by Rachman (1977) about Luborsky's use of baseball-like boxscores, no published criticism of the latter's 1975 work could be located. Two general concerns should be stated. Using statistical significance as a means of determining whether a study yielded positive or negative effects shows impartiality and a single standard for evaluating evidence. However, studies with large samples are given greater weight than those with small samples, since statistical significance is related to sample size. Second, the exclusion of "analogue" studies may cause the effectiveness of behavioral treatments to be underestimated. It is difficult to draw the line between "real," bona fide clients and "volunteer" populations, between therapists with "sufficient" and "insufficient" training. Minimally trained therapists may still effect change. Volunteer clients usually have identified symptoms that therapy can ameliorate.

The work of Luborsky and others was built upon by Smith and Glass (1977), who statistically integrated the results of 375 studies of psychotherapy effectiveness. They used the definition of psychotherapy of Meltzoff and Kornreich and attempted to find all the controlled studies in which psychotherapy was tested. They did not exclude analogue studies, but categorized the studies on a variety of dimensions. Some of these dimensions had been used by earlier reviewers to define and exclude analogue studies. The magnitude of effect produced by a study was then studied in relation to variation on the characteristics of that study. The internal validity of the study bore no relation to the size of therapeutic effect produced. However, the type of instrument used to measure outcome did show a relationship to magnitude of effect. Behavioral and nonbehavioral therapies produced about the same average effect once preexisting differences among the studies had been statistically and experimentally controlled. The overall effect of psychotherapy was about 0.67 standard deviation units, a size that supported the conclusion that psychotherapy is effective.

Summary of Reviews of Psychotherapy-Outcome Studies

One's belief in the conclusions of any particular review should be influenced by the representativeness of the sample of studies reviewed relative to the population of all possible studies on the topic, the clarity of assumptions and method, the absence of ex post facto exclusion of studies based only on the judgment of the reviewer,* the absence of bias in translating the results of each study into a common metric for the summary, the extent to which the conclusions of the review follow from the findings, and the unprejudiced attitude of the reviewer through each step in the procedure. Finally, the conclusions of the review that are based on comparisons within and among the studies reviewed should themselves meet the tests of internal validity usually applied to studies as separate entities.

The reviews presented in this chapter vary greatly in the extent to which they honor these standards. The reader may make his own judgment about the credibility of these reviews and ours to follow. Irrespective of credibility differences, the results of the major reviews are summarized in Table 2-1. For the sake of comparability within the table, the results of studies on children and psychotics are excluded, as are studies of the effectiveness of behavior therapy. The table contains the number of studies listed by the reviewers as

---

*Or at least the independence of judgments of the inclusion of a study with the results the study produced.

positive (by the reviewer's criteria), the number of "null" studies, the number of studies with miscellaneous categorizations, the number impeached by the reviewer, and the total for that row of the table. Because of varying criteria used by the different reviewers, the same study may appear in different columns (e.g., impeached by one, treated as positive by another). Therefore, no overall conclusions are possible, except to illustrate the different results that arise from different methods for studying the same topic by means of a research review.

Table 2.1. Summary of major reviews, tabulating the numbers of controlled studies of psychotherapy outcome, showing positive, negative, and other results

Reviewer	Date	Number of studies (% of total)				
		Positive	Null[a]	"Mixed" or "In doubt"	Impeached	Total
Eysenck	1961	0 (0%)	3 (75%)	0 (0%)	1[b] (25%)	4
Eysenck	1966	0 (0%)	7 (87%)	0 (0%)	1[b] (13%)	8
Bergin	1970	22 (37%)	15 (25%)	23[c] (38%)	0 (0%)	60
Rachman	1971	1 (4%)	5[d] (22%)	0 (0%)	17[e] (74%)	23
Meltzoff & Kornreich	1970	81 (80%)	20 (20%)	0 (0%)	0 (0%)	101
Luborsky et al.	1975	7 (78%)	2 (22%)	0	0[f]	9[g]

[a] Includes studies in which treated groups did not significantly differ from controls, in which controls were superior, in which treated groups did not exceed baseline

[b] Disallowed due to methodology (positive results)

[c] Fifteen studies were "in doubt," and eight not included in table for unknown reason (mixed results)

[d] Treatments for children, psychotics, and behavioral treatments are excluded from summary table

[e] Seventeen studies were impeached (fifteen positive and two null results)

[f] Number impeached is unknown due to method of reporting and excluding studies based on low design quality

[g] Behavioral treatments and treatments on psychotics are excluded from summary table

Chapter 3

A Defense of Psychotherapy-Outcome Research and Its Integration

The work presented here is basically a complicated piecing together of the findings of literally hundreds of psychotherapy outcome studies. What is eventually presented as evidence of the benefits of psychotherapy depends in part on the logical integrity of the constituent elements, the individual evaluations themselves. Many questions have been raised in the past about the logic and methodology of psychotherapy-outcome research: Is it possible? Is it sensible? Is it fair? Is it humane? Challenges to the meaningfulness of individual studies are challenges by implication to the sense of their integration. First challenges should be met first.

Psychotherapy-outcome research is the treatment of persons and the assessment of the effects. In our opinion, it must be comparative; that is, roughly equivalent groups of persons, one of which receives treatment and the other of which does not, must be compared on the outcome measures. We do not deny the existence of other, nonexperimental ways of knowing, but we maintain that only the controlled experimental method has the power to persuade a wide audience of contemporary scholars and educated laymen. Psychotherapy-outcome research encompasses an enormous variety of treatments and measures. But this is common to all of its forms: persons are treated for psychological conditions in two or more different ways and their progress is subsequently measured with a common instrument.

A fundamental distinction underlies many misconceptions about psychotherapy-outcome research. It is embodied in the name itself, which, considering the use to which the findings are put, ought to be "psychotherapy outcome evaluation." Evaluation is different, in important ways, from scientific research. Evaluation is not simply the application of psychology, even when the claims being evaluated emanate from the discipline of psychology. Evaluation and research differ in their techniques and their goals. The distinction has been made frequently before: in connection with psychotherapy, Edwards and Cronbach (1952) distinguished "administrative" and "critical" outcome research; addressing a broader domain, Tukey (1960) distinguished "decision-oriented" and "conclusion-oriented" inquiry; Scriven (1959) elaborated in detail on how an evaluative experiment on psychoanalysis would differ from a theoretical one; Glass (1972) added little to these distinctions when he offered "evaluative" and "elucidatory" inquiry.*

Elucidatory inquiry is the process of obtaining generalizable knowledge by contriving and testing claims about relationships among variables or generalizable phenomena. (There is an obvious empirical social-science bias in the definition and the thinking to follow.) This knowledge results in functional or statistical relationships, models, and ultimately theories. When the results of elucidatory inquiry are combined with knowledge of particular circumstance, one obtains *explanations*.

Evaluative inquiry is the determination of the worth of a thing. It involves obtaining information to judge the worth of a program, product, or procedure. According to Scriven (1967, p. 40): "The activity consists simply in gathering and combining of performance data with a weighted set of goal scales to yield either comparative or numerical ratings; and in the justification of (a) the data-gathering instruments, (b) the weightings, and (c) the selection of goals."

1. *Motivation of the Inquirer.* Elucidatory and evaluative inquiry appear generally to be undertaken for different reasons. The former is pursued largely to satisfy curiosity; the latter is done to contribute to the solution of a practical problem. The theory builder is intrigued; the evaluator (or at least his client) is concerned.

2. *The Objective of the Search.* Elucidatory and evaluative inquiry seek different ends. The former seeks conclusions; evaluation leads to decisions.

3. *Laws versus Description.* Closely related to the distinction between conclusion-oriented and decision-oriented are the familiar concepts of nomothetic (law-giving) and idiographic (descriptive of the particular). Elucidatory inquiry is the search for laws, i.e., statements of relationships among two or more variables or phenomena. Evaluation merely seeks to describe a particular thing with respect to one or more scales of value.

4. *The Role of Explanation.* Explanations are not the goal of evaluation. A fully proper and useful evaluation can be conducted without producing an explanation of *why* the product or program being evaluated is good or bad or *how* it operates to produce its effects. Elucidatory inquiry is characterized by a succession of studies in which greater control ("control" in the sense of the ability to manipulate specific components of independent variables) is exercised at each stage so that relationships among variables can be determined at more fundamental levels.

5. *Properties of the Phenomena Which Are Assessed.* Evaluation is an attempt to assess scientific truth. Except that truth is highly valued and

*The contrast between elucidation and evaluation is well-established in aesthetics. Elucidatory aesthetics attempts to explain what constitutes art, or, more generally, beauty. Evaluative aesthetics concerns the discrimination between good and bad art (what is beautiful and what is less beautiful) without explaining why an art work is good or bad.

worthwhile, this distinction serves fairly well to discriminate elucidatory and evaluative inquiry. The distinction can be given added meaning if "worth" is taken as synonymous with "social utility" (which is presumed to increase with improved health, happiness, life expectancy, increases in certain kinds of knowledge, and decrease with increases in privation, sickness, and ignorance,) and if "scientific truth" is identified with two of its possible forms: (1) empirical verifiability of statements about general phenomena with accepted methods of inquiry; (2) logical consistency of such statements. Elucidatory inquiries may yield evidence of social utility, but only indirectly, because empirical verfiability of general phenomena and logical consistency may eventually be socially useful.

6. *Universality of the Phenomena Studied.* Perhaps the highest correlate of the elucidatory-evaluative distinction is the universality of the phenomena studied. Elucidatory inquirers work with constructs having a currency and scope of application that make the objects one evaluates seem parochial by comparison. A psychologist experiments with "reinforcement" or "need achievement," which he regards as neither specific to geography nor to one point in time. The effect of positive reinforcement following upon the responses he observes is assumed to be a phenomenon shared by most men in most times; moreover the number of specific instances of human behavior that are examples of the working of positive reinforcement is great. But the evaluation of a specific type of therapy (e.g., Synanon or acupuncture) may address the question of the value of a particular arrangement of techniques and even personalities that in themselves are of no general scientific interest.

Dewey, an optimist on the question of the practical value of the scientific method, wrote that nothing is as practical as a good theory. This statement can be true without it being true that every good theory is of practical value, e.g., cosmological theories—excellent in scientific terms, but hardly touching the lives of this generation of humans or their children. Likewise, something can be of practical significance and be neither explained by a theory nor of any theoretical import, e.g., aspirin, Teflon, and jogging.

We have concentrated so much attention here on the distinction between research and evaluation because the failure to appreciate the difference has spawned so much derogatory commentary on the psychotherapy-outcome literature. Persons whose efforts are directed solely toward one aim (whether it be the evaluative or the scientific) fail to understand the motives and purposes of persons working toward the other goal. They declare each other's efforts meaningless and worthless. For example, in commenting on what we regard as the single best outcome evaluation of psychotherapy ever accomplished, Bandura (1978, p. 87) wrote:

A widely publicized study by Sloane, Staples, Cristol, Yorkston, and Whipple (1975) comparing the relative efficacy of behavioral therapy and psychotherapy, similarly contains the usual share of confounded variables, unmatched mixtures of dysfunctions, and inadequately measured outcomes relying on amorphous clinical ratings rather than on direct assessment of behavioral functioning. As is now predictable for studies of this type, the different forms of treatment appear comparable and better than nothing on some of the global ratings but not on others. With such quasi-outcome measures even the controls, who receive no therapeutic ministrations, achieve impressive improvement. Based on this level of research, weak modes of treatment are given a new lease on life for those who continue to stand steadfastly by them.

Leach the arrogance and self-interest out of this assessment and a large measure of simple misapprehension remains. That the importance of the Sloane et al. study could be so utterly misjudged speaks to the inability of persons immersed in one form of inquiry to appreciate the efforts of others whose work serves purposes different from their own.

Not all issues about the evaluation of psychotherapy are as grand and sweeping as what has been dealt with thus far. Many are simpler and easier to analyze. A natural form for stating these issues is to present a traditional objection to the psychotherapy-outcome evaluation and attempt to answer the objection.

Objection 1. *Control groups are unethical because some persons are deprived of treatment.* If the efficacy of the therapy is truly undetermined, then placing persons in control groups could hardly be depriving them of a known good. Moreover, "wait-list" control groups (persons from whom therapy is withheld until the experimental group has been treated and measured) are common devices for overcoming this objection; unfortunately, their use obviates long-term follow-up comparisons of treatment and control groups.

If before a study there is a widely shared expectation that a treatment will be beneficial, then the ethical issue of using untreated control groups is reached more seriously. It is generally wise evaluation practice to compare a new therapy against a relevant competitor; for example, one that has a reasonably favorable past record. Then no one is deprived of treatment; the needs of persons are satisfied as well as the need to know. Suppose further that a new therapy, A, of unknown efficacy is to be compared in an experiment with an old therapy, B, regarded currently as the method of choice for the problem shown by the clients. An untreated control group might even be required by an ethical examination of these circumstances. Imagine that 150 persons are available for the experiment. Assigning 75 persons each to therapies A and B is statistically hardly preferable at all to having 50 under each therapy. But if only 100 persons are involved in the A vs. B comparison, the remaining 50 should be held out (as an untreated control group) and given either therapy A or B at the end of the experiment, depending on which proves superior. Thus, the interests of the persons are best served by placing them in an untreated control group. The only contingency that nullifies this argument is the hypothesis that there are critical periods during which persons who are suffering must receive psychotherapy if it is to be effective; persons in wait-list control groups may be denied therapy during such a critical period. We know of no evidence that such critical periods exist.

Objection 2. *It is impossible to ensure that persons in control groups will not seek help from other professionals, friends, parents, self-help books, and the like.* In short-term studies that last only a few weeks, the possibility that control subjects will seek "outside" therapy is not a serious problem. In long-term studies in which therapy may extend over several months, the objection may apply with more force, but it is hardly a fatal flaw. (Notice how it was dealt with in the Sloane et al. [1975] experiment.) The outcome data can be analyzed separately for those control group members who seek outside help and those who do not.

However, if one assumes a particularly apt evaluation perspective, this objection is quite irrelevant. Consider the evaluation question phrased as follows: "Is the thing called 'psychotherapy' more valuable than the general activities people in distress engage in, whether those be seeing a clergyman, buying hot tubs, taking ocean voyages, or whatever?" To place control groups in suspended animation for what were regarded as necessary experimental purposes would only produce unrepresentative comparisons, not like life and irrelevant to the question of what value psychotherapy adds to life as people typically live it.

Even if psychotherapy were shown to be no better than help that distressed persons obtain from friends and colleagues, the finding might not be devastating to psychotherapy. Theoretical and professional psychotherapy may be responsible in large part for the existence of many skilled helpers in the general population. Unraveling such possibilities is a problem in historical analysis of major proportions.

Objection 3. *Psychotherapy is complex and not standardized; no two clients are treated in the same way by even the same psychotherapist; so psychotherapy cannot be labeled method A or method B and studied experimentally.* The eminently sensible premise of this objection does not lead to its pessimistic conclusion. Like all arguments that lean too heavily on the word "same," this one has no logical defense. No two empirical instances of anything are "the same;" the very statement of the contrary position is self-contradictory. The question one faces in any attempt to establish empirical knowledge is whether two instances may meaningfully share a common label. The meaning in a group of instances will depend in part on the purposes of the inquiry. Most ways in which two instances of psychotherapy differ will be irrelevant from anyone's perspective; for example, whether the therapist is dressed in natural instead of synthetic fibers, or whether the client sits at 27° instead of 18° to the line of vision of the therapist. How many elements must be shared by instances of psychotherapy before they can reasonably be grouped under the rubric "psychotherapy" or "behavioral modification therapy" is a decision that will be made differently, depending on why an evaluation is undertaken and how its findings will be used. For one purpose, it will be sufficient to label as "psychoanalysis" all therapy practiced by therapists who report on a questionnaire that they find Freud a more congenial model than Skinner. For another purpose, it may be necessary to verify by direct evidence that the psychoanalysis being evaluated is conducted by a graduate of an approved analytic training institute, is reported by more than three-fourths of all patients to adhere strictly to the rule of free association, whether the analyst keeps a couch in the office, and so forth.

Uses dictate definitions and labels. The meaning and integrity of labels depend on the larger purposes of the inquiry in which they are used. Understanding this point would obviate of itself a remarkably large proportion of academic quibbling about psychotherapy research.

A related point about the role of definitions in evaluative inquiry can be made usefully at this point. There is no particular level of specificity at which a phenomenon must be defined so that it can be evaluated. Evaluating "labels" may be quite adequate in many circumstances. More than twenty-five years ago, the American Psychoanalytic Association undertook to evaluate the outcomes of psychoanalysis. The committee vested with the responsibility decided that logic demanded that a thing must be defined before it is evaluated. There followed years of fruitless debate in search of the proper definition of psychoanalysis; the evaluation was never completed, indeed it was never actually begun. The world would have happily settled for an evaluation based on a simple, stipulative definition of psychoanalysis in terms of a few obvious characteristics.

Objection 4. *Psychotherapy is more art than science; thus it is outside the realm of experimental scientific study.* One can feel a good deal of sympathy for this view, if not for the defensive way in which it is frequently advanced to justify uncomplimentary findings. The position reflected in this objection deserves some respect when it is articulated by scholars who have attempted to study human behavior in traditional scientific ways and have learned the essential manner in which it is unique and complex.

However, for the purposes of the inquiry reported here, the answer to this objection hinges on the distinction between research and evaluation. Art, which is appropriated to the critic's purpose in this objection, gave rise to the distinction between elucidatory and evaluative criticism. In this distinction lies a resolution of the objection. Although art is poorly understood by science—even, as we suspect, science presents currently a most incomplete and unsatisfactory understanding of psychotherapy—art is not beyond the reach of evaluation, as witness art auctions, art awards, art appraisals, and the awarding of advanced degrees in fine arts. Art and psychotherapy differ in many respects, but in one way they are alike: people value both and are continually drawn to assess their worth. If psychotherapy is an art, then like art it can be observed, reviewed, criticized, appreciated, disliked, sold, and bought.

Objection 5. *Anything as complex, elusive, and human as psychotherapy and its effects cannot be quantified and measured.* In most significant respects, research on psychotherapy fails to approach the sophistication of measurement in the physical sciences. A few ancillary phenomena (e.g., response latency, GSR) may be described in the gram-meter-second language of physics; but most concepts unique to psychotherapy are not so measurable. Freud acknowledged that his essentially quantitative concepts of id, ego, and superego were only qualitatively recognizable; thus, many predictions of behavior (the resultant of forces of different magnitudes) were impossible within psychoanalytic theory.

These shortcomings of psychotherapy measurement are beside the point of most outcome evaluation. Psychotherapy evaluation is based fundamentally on the recognition and counting of events and the perception of gross order relationships among them. "The subject was drunk six times within a month after therapy"; "The subject continues to complain much more about his wife's cruelty than his daughter's indifference." To deny that this kind of measurement is possible undercuts not just the empirical evaluation of psychotherapy, but its practice as well; for if key acts (symptoms, utterances, etc.) cannot be recognized and recorded, then therapy itself can hardly be managed. How is the therapist to know when therapy should be begun or terminated, when a therapeutic effort in a particular direction should be redoubled or abandoned—how any of a hundred decisions is to be made if clients' progress cannot be seen and evaluated?

Objection 6. *Since all individuals are different, it is illogical to measure the progress of unique individuals against a standard or uniform scale.* The uniqueness of humans is a truism, but so is their communality. If two organisms were unique in every respect, they would not be recognizable as members of the class organism. Of the countless ways two persons are different, most are quite irrelevant to the concerns of psychotherapy-outcome evaluation. Furthermore, that two persons present themselves for psychotherapy is evidence of their having a great deal more in common than either has with a person who would seek relief from a witch doctor, a faith healer, or an acupuncturist. At some useful level of abstraction—even if as general as "satisfaction with life"—there are communalities among psychotherapy clients that can be measured and compared. Aspirin is intended as an analgesic; and whether the source of the pain is tension, fatigue, menses or whatever, it makes sense to measure pain reduction from aspirin and compare it with other means, such as meditation, warm baths, and laxatives.

Objection 7. *Certain outcome measures are biased in favor of certain types of psychotherapy; comparisons based on them are unfair.* This objection to some psychotherapy outcome evaluations is more cogent than most. It is indeed true that the outcomes sought by some types of psychotherapy are more thoroughly understood and quantifiable than those aimed at by others. "Smoking behavior" is more readily seen than "ego capturing territory from the id." We do not mean to suggest that the former is ipso facto better, more scientific, or more rational; it may even reduce complex human emotions to trivial details. The principal point is that psychotherapies that work toward more easily measured outcomes will tend to look better on existing outcome measures. When this obvious warning is forgotten, researchers begin to sacrifice the art of treatment to the tyranny of measurement. Different psychotherapies will frequently work toward different goals even with comparable clients. The evaluator will often be well-advised to measure both goals and not press obstinately to resolve the difference and find the true or proper goal. But where the goals of one therapy are well measured with the available technology and the goals of the other are not, the risk of an unfair evaluation is great. Perhaps the benefit of the doubt should be granted to theories that lack technologies readily applicable to outcome evaluation, without at the same time condoning the evasiveness of some theoreticians who seek escape in the immeasurable niches of psychology from the embarrassment of facts.

Objection 8. *Asking whether psychotherapy works is a virtually meaningless question; it is like asking whether medicine is good or schools worth keeping open.* To rebut this argument by citing the views of romantic social critics (Rozak, Ilyich), who do indeed question the value of such respectable social institutions as schools and medicine, is to miss the gravamen of the complaint. Those who raise this criticism of psychotherapy-outcome research are making a less sweeping indictment; essentially, they are advancing a point about method. The basic point can begin to be seen in a quotation from Truax and Carkhuff (1967, p. 18): "Thus, to ask whether psychotherapy is indeed therapeutic, and to attempt to answer that question by comparing . . . change in counseled or 'control' groups, is very much like a pharmacologist asking, 'Is chemotherapy therapeutic?' and then conducting his research by randomly giving unknown kinds and quantities of drugs to one group of patients with various complaints and no drugs to a similar 'control' group.''

The chemotherapy researcher that Truax and Carkhuff satirize needs a voice raised in his defense. Outcome research somewhat like what is described in the caricature was, in fact, very important in the history of chemotherapy. Unknown drugs—in the sense that they were known only to be psychoactive—were given to experimental groups and the quantities administered were not always carefully controlled. Yet it produced crude but important findings.

The methodological point that Truax and Carkhuff appear to reach for but fail to grasp was made more explicit by Kiesler (1966) in a frequently cited paper. Kiesler accused psychotherapy-outcome researchers of believing in myths that rendered their findings useless. He named these the "uniformity myths."

The Patient Uniformity Myth: *Patients at the start of treatment are more alike than they are different.* Kiesler (1966, p. 111) remarked about this myth that: "Far from being relatively homogeneous, patients coming to psychotherapy are almost surely quite heterogeneous—are actually much more different than they are alike. . . . Because of these initial patient differences, no matter what the effect of psychotherapy in a particular study (be it phenomenally successful or a dismal faulure), one can conclude very little if anything.''

On strict quantitative grounds, Kiesler's statement of this myth is meaningless; hence, no one could be accused of believing it. To describe persons as more alike than different ignores any specification of the respect in which they are to be regarded and fails to define how similarity is to be measured. The vacuousness of the statement is clear when a specific form of it is stated: Bob and Joe are more alike in height than they are different in height.

Kiesler's statement of the myth is better regarded rhetorically. From the sense of the surrounding discussion, it should be taken to mean that psychotherapy researchers frequently fail to distinguish types of clients who might be affected differently by therapy.

The Therapist Uniformity Myth: *Therapists are more alike than different and whatever they do with their patients is properly called "psychotherapy."* Kiesler judged this myth to be devastating to psychotherapy research. He alleged that outcome researchers make the mistake of believing that psychotherapy is a uniform, homogeneous treatment. More effort must be invested in defining psychotherapy and in identifying and measuring the therapist variables so relevant to eventual outcome. "To continue the practice of assigning some patients to psychotherapy and others to a 'control' group seems futile" (p. 113). "Until our designs can incorporate relevant patient variables and crucial therapist dimensions—so that one can assess which therapists behaviors are more effective with which type of patients—we will continue to perpetuate confusion" (p. 113).

It is dangerous to speculate on what personal motives Kiesler may have satisfied in articulating this position; but it is difficult to imagine that they were irrelevant. He had just emerged from the arduous and largely unsuccessful attempt of the Rogers group to treat schizophrenics with client-centered psychotherapy. The research showed virtually no differences, on the average, between treatment and control groups. It was the habit of that group of researchers to separate treatment patients after therapy into those who received high and low levels of the Rogerian therapeutic conditions. Large outcome differences were then typically observed. So it came to be believed that the label "therapy" was too crude and the true benefits of therapy could only be seen by specifying what therapy genuinely involved. Of course, one can see now that this ex post facto separating of the data rested on an assumption that the therapist's behavior caused changes in the patient: the Unidirectionality Myth, one might name it. If in fact patients' changes and progress (arising from nontreatment influences) could cause the therapists to bring about higher levels of the therapeutic conditions, then the obtained data would likewise have been observed: no average differences between therapy and control groups, but average differences between therapy patients who "receive" high and low levels of the therapeutic conditions. The presumption in assuming that the therapist's influence on the client is what is tested in these post hoc analyses is clearly revealed when the correlation is described in the opposite direction: these researchers showed that patients who are getting better versus those getting worse bring about more therapeutic-appearing behavior in their therapists (cf. Lambert 1976).

Paul (1967, p. 111) posed what he regarded as the only meaningful question for psychotherapy-outcome research: *"What* treatment, by *whom*, is most effective with *this* individual with *that* specific problem under *which* set of circumstances?"* Even if the reference to *"this* individual" were changed to *"this* type of individual"—an essential change if the statement is to avoid advocating a belief in paralyzing idiosyncrasy—it is impossible to defend the assertion that this is the only meaningful question for outcome research. Paul avers that the question of whether psychotherapy works is meaningless, because there are so many kinds of psychotherapy. He denies, then, the possibility or the utility of a generalization.

Those who fight protracted battles in the academic wars understandably come to view much of the world as it is reflected in their own corner. A scholar may be shocked that an administrator or politician would lump together instances that the scholar is fond of distinguishing, such as behavioral and verbal psychotherapy.

One can endorse the general good sense in Kiesler's and Paul's recommendation—after all, it merely expresses the scientist's sentiment: refine, specify, control—without agreeing that it puts forth the sine qua non of psychotherapy-outcome research. Indeed, as a statement of methodology, it is misleading and untutored. Kiesler fails to distinguish the purposes of scientific research from those of evaluation; and with the theory of evaluation, he neglects crucial distinctions between unconditional and conditional value claims (or "main effects" and "interactions" in the argot of statisticians).

The concern for specificity is an old one. It appears as a central concern in one of the earliest methodological papers on psychotherapy-outcome research (Edwards and Cronbach 1952), and it is repeated more and more often today. Perhaps it is emerging as a more salient concern in contemporary research because the general question, "Does psychotherapy work?" has been answered to the satisfaction of all but the most obdurate skeptics. But to advance the concern zealously for specificity in design gives bad advice on many old and new research questions. The general question of benefit needs to be answered for many new, exotic flora in the therapy garden (Rolfing, Primal Screaming, EST, and the like).

The scientific temperament seeks more refined conclusions. Generalizations are anathema to it. Analysis of a phenomenon at one level leads inevitably to the attempt at analysis at a more fundamental level, and the answer to each "why" leads inevitably to further interrogation. Evaluation serves different purposes. Establishing value claims is different from analytic research. Fortunately, determining "how good" does not depend on determining "why." A road test can determine which car is the best buy, even though one lacks even a minimally adequate theory of the automobile. Whatever might be appealing in Kiesler's and Paul's argument, because it suggests a more scientific character is needed for psychotherapy-outcome research, is appealing to an uncritical respect for science. Many purposes of psychotherapy-outcome research are fundamentally not scientific, and it is likely that the advice to become more scientific (in widely accepted terms) is bad advice (Meehl 1978).

But the nub of Kiesler's and Paul's misconception is that they seem to regard unconditional value claims as invalid, or at least confusing and futile. An unconditional value claim is an assertion about the worth or value of a class of things: "Datsuns get good gas mileage" or "psychotherapy is better for you than a Tarot reading." Conditional value claims specify subclasses within the class: "The Datsun 240 Z gets good gas mileage on the highway, but the Datsun 510 is a better buy for city driving." Unconditional value claims are general; conditional value claims are specific. Finally, a conditional value claim is only conditional in relation to a more general, unconditional claim, i.e., the concept is essentially relational; there are no (interesting) inherently conditional value claims.

The important point is that no number of conditional value claims, or even the possibility of their existence, renders an unconditional claim invalid, or futile or confusing. Whether conditional value claims should be the objective of an assessment of worth is not a philosophical question; it is a pragmatic matter governed by the needs and interests of decisionmakers, the tolerance of audiences for specification when they seek general guidelines, the hope of finding meaningful subdivisions of the class across which value differs, and many other concerns.

It is presumptuous, and a bit egocentric, to tell persons that they must be interested in a particular type of value question. Policymakers—and we use the term fully conscious of how these anonymous persons are often invoked to justify one's own fancy—may act rationally when they view psychotherapists as a species of identical stripe; and they may ask sincerely and logically whether the latter are accomplishing anything worthwhile. Picking out one form of psychotherapy from the many may well be a connoisseur's distinction; and they may rightly feel it is not their place to design the profession of psychotherapy, rather they face the decision whether the enterprise in toto as it now stands is worthy of support. The researcher who fails to appreciate the mentality or circumstances that force a policymaker to reach general evaluations might reflect on whether he ever voted the Republican ticket, say, because he felt it was time the Democrats were turned out lock, stock, and barrel, even though there are good ones among them and even though the bad ones aren't all bad.

Even where audiences can tolerate a large number of conditional value claims—as academics can, for example—advice such as Kiesler's and Paul's may well force an unnecessary burden on outcome researchers. If psychotherapy-outcome research should only be undertaken where clients and therapists are measured, observed, distinguished, and categorized, the costs of such research will multiply; and surveying the research of the last ten years, there is little reason to hope that more elaborate designs will produce better findings. On the contrary, academics routinely impose hundreds of quite useless distinctions on clients' behavior and the process of therapy. Even a few that once excited great hopes pale upon closer scrutiny, e.g., the A vs. B therapist distinction. In a field where interactions are much larger than main effects and there is imminent possibility of finding many of the former and putting them to good use, Kiesler's and Paul's point might be worth heeding; but there is little to suggest that psychotherapy-outcome research has reached such a propitious point.

Issues in Integrating Psychotherapy-Outcome Studies

The important questions about the benefits of psychotherapy have grown too complex and numerous to be addressed by a single study, or even a series of studies. The myth of the critical experiment that resolves broad issues of inquiry was born in the physical sciences and refuses to die in the minds of many who know the social sciences casually but not intimately. The number of important questions about the efficacy of psychotherapy is so huge that even dozens of experiments leave many of them unanswered: what are the effects of time-limited therapy, experience of therapists, group vs. individual treatment; how does the type of psychotherapy interact with the diagnosis of the clients, their age, social and cultural background, mental ability, the particular presenting problem; how large are the effects of therapy in terms of specific behavioral change, personality change, social adjustment; how great are the benefits of psychotherapy immediately after treatment compared to six, twelve, eighteen, etc. months later? To describe the benefits of psychotherapy requires not just an examination of one Herculean study or even a score of smaller studies, but the systematic compilation and analysis of literally hundreds of controlled experiments.

One must add to this variegated landscape of psychotherapy-outcome research the fact of diversity of findings even where uniformity is sought and expected. The "same" study yields contradictory, or at least conflicting, evidence in different laboratories at different times in the hands of different experimenters. Such multiplicity and diversity vex theoreticians who understandably seek to reduce them. The least productive approach is to attempt to explain away inconsistent findings with prejudicial and a priori arguments about technical details of the studies. In Chapter 2, we saw the rhetorical depths to which this approach can reach. The multiplicity and diversity that confound researchers who hope in vain for great precision in psychotherapy give vigor to pragmatic inquiry and to evaluation. They permit the assessment of the robustness of conclusions, the examination of the sensitivity of effects across the rough grain of actual practice, and the probing of the limits of generalization. The literature on psychotherapy stretches from the antiseptic atmosphere of rigorously controlled laboratories to the septic environs of clinics and mental institutions. The waxing and waning of the effects of therapy from one site to the next are not simply a pragmatic concern, but a matter of genuine importance for the theoretical enterprise itself.

Multiplicity and diversity are vital elements of an empirical literature; they are complications as well. Finding the meaning in many studies, separating what is clear and consistent from what is idiosyncratic and ephemeral, reaching the needed general conclusions and qualifying them where necessary and useful—in short, making sense of a large, diverse body of evidence is an intellectual problem and a problem in research more complex than most that psychologists now confront. In what follows in this chapter, we shall illustrate and analyze a new approach to this problem.

Past Methods of Research and Integration

Traditional methods of research integration were fashioned to accommodate much smaller bodies of literature than are encountered today. They seldom distinguished theoretical and evaluative purposes. They lacked safeguards against prejudiced application and subjective bias. Indeed, the standards of objectivity, verifiability, replicability, and clarity against which primary empirical research was judged were ignored or forgotten when scholars turned to the problem of integrating the primary evidence. Two common methods for integrating the findings of many studies can be distinguished: the narrative integration and the "box-score" integration.

Narrative Integration

Narrative integrations are attempts to portray multiple findings in a connected, verbal report; they are written like stories, sometimes with themes, dramatis personae and even a denouement. They can be entertaining, but they seldom portray a body of literature as it really is. To readers who know the same literature well, narrative integrations often seem like exercises in forcing an intransigent literature into the Procrustean bed of a foregone conclusion.

The narrative method was insensitive to the need to adopt consistent definitions and standards of evidence. The findings of one's allies and those of one's enemies were often measured against a double standard, as Shapiro and Shapiro (1977) have shown for reviews in psychotherapy.

This method of research integration may have emanated from an epistemology of uniformity, an expectation of consistent findings from homogeneous materials such as a physicist might expect to see. The method was ill-equipped to cope with the variability of the social sciences. As time passed and literature grew to enormous dimensions, the problems of narrative integration became more acute. The impossibility of reading several hundred experiments, reflecting on their findings, and then writing a narrative description was clearly apparent. After all, who would suggest to an experimenter that he merely gaze at the 200 scores his laboratory animals produced, reflect on them, then write a story about his experiment?

To retain the narrative approach, reviewers had to find ways of reducing a field of dozens or hundreds of studies to only a few. Various strategies of exclusion have been followed. One of the most common is simply to ignore huge areas of the literature where much work lies readily available; the doctoral dissertation literature is a prominent example. It is rich with important findings on any question in psychology, yet it is unaccountably seldom referenced in research reviews. The justification for ignoring it that holds it to be of "poor quality" is a patently false overgeneralization and a bit of defensive stereotyping, and it takes far too seriously the imperfect journal reviewing process that some theses survive but many do not.

The principal means that narrative reviewers have used to cut a large literature down to manageable size is to exclude the majority of studies through a series of arbitrary stipulative definitions of concepts and a priori judgments of quality. A central concept that has been used in psychotherapy research to trim down the literature is the "analogue study." Reviewers often excluded "analogue" psychotherapy experiments and concentrated on "real" psychotherapy. Different reviewers defined "analogue study" differently, and it was often unclear which definition was being used. Meltzoff and Kornreich (1970) cast a wide net and excluded little; they used the term "analogue study" only twice: once in reference to a study that used volunteer clients and psychotherapy lasted only twenty minutes (p. 133); and later in reference to a study that used completely inexperienced "therapists" and dealt with letter writing and interviewing (p. 305). Luborsky et al. (1975) excluded many analogue studies. They included only "research in which *bona fide patients* were in *bona fide treatment*" (p. 1000). Psychotherapy-outcome studies are routinely excluded from consideration by reviewers when the therapy cannot be clearly distinguished from normal practice, or it may be a prototype of some future form of psychotherapy. Bandura (1978, pp. 84–85) argued against the arbitrary labeling of studies as "analogue," as did Kazdin (1978).

A second device for cutting the literature to fit the scope of the narrative method is to impose a priori standards of quality on the techniques of the outcome studies. If experimental designs are not of a certain type, if measurement is "unreliable," if statistical analysis is handled ineptly, the findings of the study are thrown away. These methodological rules, learned as dicta in graduate school and regarded as the touchstone of publishable articles in prestigious journals, were applied arbitrarily; for example, note again Rachman's high-handed dismissal on methodological grounds of study after study of psychotherapy outcomes. Textbook standards of research technique were applied by rote. The wisdom and experience that reveal this flaw in design to be fatal and that flaw in measurement to be benign were utterly lacking. It was methodology by recipe, and it was indigestible methodology. But the true purpose was well served: most of the literature was eliminated, and what few studies survived were consistent, probably because they had been conducted by the reviewer himself, his students or his friends.

The "Box-Score" Integration

Narrative integrations were improved on when reviewers adopted standard definitions and began to keep tallies of how the studies came out: "aye" or "nay" on the hypothesis. With one or two refinements, this more inclusive, systematic and quantitative approach became known as the "box-score" or "voting" method of research integration. Light and Smith (1971, p. 433) described it thus:

All studies which have data on a dependent variable and a specific independent variable of interest are examined. Three possible outcomes are defined. The relationship between the independent variable and the dependent variable is either significantly positive, significantly negative, or there is no significant relationship in either direction. The number of studies falling into each of these three categories is simply tallied. If a plurality of studies falls into any one of these three categories, with fewer falling into the other two, the modal category is declared the winner. This modal categorization is then assumed to give the best estimate of the direction of the true relationship between the independent and dependent variable.

This method is standard practice in reviews of research on psychotherapy. The most serious shortcoming of the box-score method is that it ignores considerations of sample size in the studies integrated. Large samples produce more statistically significant findings than small samples, *ceteris paribus*. Imagine that nine small-sample studies yield not quite statistically significant results, and the tenth large-sample study is significant. The box-score is 1 for the hypothesis and 9 against, a conclusion quite at odds with one's best instincts—so much the worse for the voting method.

A second deficiency of the voting method of research integration is that it discards good descriptive information. To know that aversive conditioning beats directed imagery in 25 of 30 studies—if, in fact, it does—is not to know whether it wins by a nose or in a walkaway. One ought to integrate measures of the strength of experimental effects or relationships among variables (according to whether the problem is basically experimental or correlational).

Researchers commonly believe that significance levels are more informative than they are. Tallies of statistical significance or insignificance tell little about the strength or importance of a relationship.

The Meta-Analysis of Research Studies

In the past several years, we have developed and applied a method of research integration designed to overcome deficiencies in past techniques (Glass 1976; Glass 1977; Glass and Smith 1979; Smith and Glass 1977; Miller 1977). Our colleagues and students have applied these methods to problems in education (Hartley 1977; Hearold 1979; White 1976). Rosenthal (1976) developed a similar approach and applied it to problems in social psychology, as did his student Hall (1978). The method was designed to satisfy three basic requirements: (1) studies should not be excluded from consideration on arbitrary and a priori grounds; boundaries must be drawn around fields, but it is better to draw them wide than narrow; (2) study findings should be transformed to commensurable expressions of magnitude of experimental effect or correlational relationship; (3) features of studies that might mediate their findings should be defined, measured, and their covariation with findings should be studied. It is assumed that the only data consistently available to the reviewer are those that appear in written reports of a study, which rarely contain raw data. Hence, the methods developed must begin with the results of data analyses (means, variances, *t*-tests, and the like) that are typically reported by researchers. An integrative analysis is then carried out on the results of the primary data analyses. This analysis of analyses, or *meta-analysis*, then becomes the means by which studies are integrated and understood. An illustration or a small problem will provide concrete examples of these general observations.

An Example of Meta-Analysis: Psychotherapy and Asthma

A small published literature exists on the benefits of psychological treatment of asthma. Eleven controlled outcome studies were located in which one group of asthmatics received psychotherapy and a control group received no treatment or standard medical treatment for asthma. Each study was read and several of its features were noted: (a) the type of psychotherapy given to the patients, (b) the average age of the patients, (c) the number of hours of therapy given, (d) the type of treatment given the control group, (e) the number of weeks elapsing between the end of therapy and the measurement of the outcome (follow-up time), (f) the type of outcome measured, and (g) a measure of the magnitude of the benefit of the treatment in comparison to the control (the experimental effect size). Many other features of the studies could be noted and recorded but were not, so that the illustration would not grow

Table 3-1. Findings of eleven studies of psychological treatment of asthma

Study (a)	Therapy type (b)	Age (c)	Hrs. of therapy (d)	Control group (e)	Follow-up time (wks.)	Dependent var. (g)	ES (h)
1. Ago et al. (1976)	Eclectic (4-somatic, 4-therp.)	34	20	Medical treatment	120	Remission of asthma symptoms	1.51
2. Alexander et al. (1956)	Jacobson relaxation training	12	3	No treatment	0	Pulmonary functioning (peak expiratory flow)	0.82
3. Barendregt (1957)	Eclectic (4 dynamic)	42	100	Medical treatment	0	Increased hostility, decreased oppression & damage; Rorschach	0.57
4. Citron, K. M. (1968)	Hypnotherapy	30	12	Relax training	0	Symptoms, wheezing	0.52
5. Groen & Pelser (1960)	Psychodynamic (group)	45	50	Medical treatment	24	Rated improvement	1.36
6. Kahn (1977)	Counter-conditioning	12	15	No treatment	32 32 32 32	Use of drugs & medication Emergency Room visits Hospitalization Asthma attacks	0.29 0.49 0.19 0.24
7. Kahn et al. (1973)	Counter-conditioning	11	15	Medical treatment	40 40 40	No. of ER visits Amt. of drugs & medication No. of asthma attacks (one hospitalization in control group, none in therp.)	0.76 1.11 0.66
8. Maher-Loughman et al. (1962)	Hypnotherapy	25	20	No treatment	0	Symptoms, wheezing	0.64
9. Moore (1965)	Reciprocal inhibition	21 ½ adults ½ children	4	Relax training	0	Lung functioning No. of asthma attacks	1.41 0.88
10. Sclare et al. (1957)	Psychodynamic	30 (19–42)	28	Medical treatment	0	Remission of symptoms	0.66
11. Yorkston et al. (1974)	Verbal desensitization	42	3	Relax training	0 96 96	Lung functioning Psychiatrist's rating of improv. Use of drugs	1.00 1.00 1.52

unwieldy. The data for the nineteen separate measurements taken in the eleven studies are recorded in Table 3-1.

The meaning of most of the information is obvious. For example, in the ninth study (Moore 1965), a group of asthmatics, half adults and half children averaging twenty-one years of age, received four hours of reciprocal inhibition psychotherapy; immediately after treatment they were compared with a control group that received only relaxation training, on measures of lung capacity and incidence of asthma attack. The final column of Table 3-1 contains the measures of experimental effect known as "effect size,"*ES*. Perhaps this is the only variable in the table whose meaning is not obvious.

The comparison of treatment and control groups was made by subtracting the average score on the outcome variable for the control group from the average score for the experimental group; then the algebraic sign of the difference was arranged so that a positive difference corresponded to greater benefits for the treatment group. Negative differences are possible, of course. Although this simple difference reflects on the size of the benefits of the treatment, it is meaningful only to one who knows the scale properties of the outcome variable. For example, a psychotherapy versus control group difference of 5.61, say, could be on a scale of lung capacity measured in inches or centimeters, or it could be large or small; and only an expert might know for certain. However, by standardizing the difference in a particular way, arbitrary choices among scales (e.g., inches vs. centimeters, hours vs. days) can be made irrelevant and the magnitude of the difference can be transformed to a common scale. The standardizing quantity is called the *standard deviation*, the familiar statistic descriptive of the variability of a set of scores. The complete definition of the effect size, *ES*, then is:

$$ES = \frac{\bar{X}_{\text{Therapy}} - \bar{X}_{\text{Control}}}{s_x}$$

where: $\bar{X}_{\text{Therapy}}$ is the average score for the psychotherapy group on the outcome measure,

$\bar{X}_{\text{Control}}$ is the same, but for the control group, and

s_x is the standard deviation of the control group.

The value of *ES* so calculated describes the experimental effect in standard deviation units; and, after a harmless assumption is made, it reveals the degree of overlap in the distributions of scores for the therapy and control groups. Notice, for example, that on the lung functioning outcome measure in the Moore study, the therapy group was, on the average, 1.41 standard deviations superior to the control group (relaxation training). If one assumes normal distributions (the ubiquitous bell-shaped curve) of lung functioning scores, then it is calculable that the average or 50th percentile person in the therapy group scores above 92 percent of the persons in the control group. Furthermore, the relative distributions of the lung function scores would appear as in Figure 3-1.

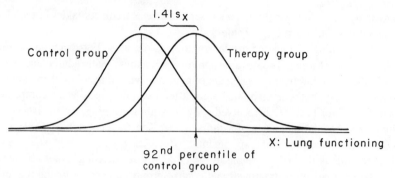

Figure 3-1. Illustrations of the results of the Moore study for the lung functioning outcome variable, assuming normal distribution of scores

The *ES* measure of experimental effect can be directly compared from one outcome variable to the next. For example, the effect of therapy on lung functioning in the Moore study (1.41) is very much larger than the effect of therapy on "wheezing symptoms" in the Citron study (0.52). We will return to this matter, since it is a point of concern, if not contention, with some persons.

From the perspective that meta-analysis affords on the data in Table 3-1, they are viewed as raw data for statistical analysis. The gain in meaning that this perspective lends is greater when there are many more studies than eleven, for then it is apparent that nothing short of an extensive analysis of the data will reveal the relationships and general character of the findings. With as few studies as there are recorded in Table 3-1, the application of meta-analysis is more *pro forma*; however, the only point of this small example is to illustrate the form of the method.

It is immediately apparent that none of the effect sizes is negative. The odds are overwhelming against the possibility, then, that these eleven studies are a sample of a much greater number of studies in which positive findings are outweighed by negative findings. (The odds are overwhelmingly against these eleven studies being a sample of anything, since they were all the studies that could be located by an extensive search; but such is the stylized reasoning of much of inferential statistical theory.) The effect sizes, *ES*, average 0.82. Thus, psychotherapy treatment of asthma results in average benefits of about eight-tenths standard deviation above control conditions. Two normal curves separated by 0.82 standard deviations at their means depict this relationship in Figure 3-2. There one sees that the average patient treated by psychotherapy ends up being better off than 79 percent of the control patients. The standard deviation of the nineteen *ES*'s is 0.42; this measure gives an idea of the consistency of the effect measures across different studies. It can also be used to set a confidence interval around the population average $\overline{ES}$. For example, a 95 percent confidence interval around $\overline{ES}$ is calculated from $\overline{ES} \pm$

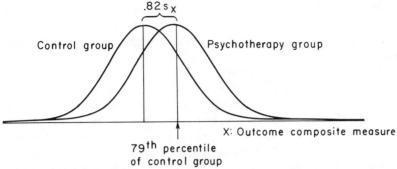

79th percentile
of control group

Figure 3-2. Illustration of the composite overlap of curves for the 11 asthma studies in Table 3-1

$_{.975}t_{18}s_{ES}/\sqrt{n}$, where $\overline{ES}$ is the sample average, s_{ES} is the sample standard deviation, n is the number of effects in the sample, and t is the appropriate percentile in the t-distribution, and in this instance, equals (0.62, 1.02). The sense in which this interval gives estimates of a parameter and the assumptions under which it does so are quite standard, though problematic. If the nineteen ES's in Table 3-1 are considered a random sample of independent observations from a population of effect measures, then the interval (0.62, 1.02) was generated by a process that has 0.95 probability of capturing the population mean value. That the population in question is hypothetical instead of real is a complication with which social scientists are learning to cope. The more serious complication is that the nineteen observations cannot sensibly be regarded as independent. One study yields four ES measures; two yield three ES's each. It is clear that the different effect sizes in the same study are more alike than ES's from separate studies; the average within-study standard deviation of the twelve ES's for the Kahn, Moore, and Yorkston studies is 0.26, compared with the overall standard deviation of 0.42. This clustering of effect measures within studies implies that the confidence interval is at least truly no shorter than the (0.62, 1.02) interval calculated under the assumption of independence. If lack of independence among the nineteen ES's became an overriding concern, the multiple ES's within a study could be averaged, and all analyses could be performed on the eleven average ES's for each study. For example, the two ES's for the Moore study would be replaced by their average, 1.15. Choosing to work with eleven independent observations of this type now gives an average ES across the studies of 0.87, hardly different to any important degree from the average of the nineteen individual ES's, 0.82. Furthermore, the standard deviation of the eleven study-level ES's is 0.38, which yields a 95 percent confidence interval around the mean of (0.62, 1.12)—amazingly close to the interval of (0.62, 1.02) calculated on all nineteen effects. In this instance, the choice of a level or unit of analysis ("study" or "individual ES") proves not to be very important, although one cannot assume this will always be so. One would prefer to analyze the data of Table 3-1 with all nineteen *ES*'s represented, since the eleven study averages obscure distinctions among types of outcome measure and follow-up intervals, for example.

The varied pattern of circumstances described in Table 3-1 invites more refined analyses. Two investigators (Moore and Yorkston) used a treatment for a control comparison, relaxation training, that a third investigator (Alexander) used as his experimental treatment. Three of the studies involve control groups that received no treatment, and five studies compared psychotherapy with medical treatment of asthma. These observations suggest partitioning the studies in various ways to isolate these instances. The average effect size measures for some partitionings are reported in Table 3-2.

The new groupings of the studies in Table 3-2 cast little light on the findings. The worst showing ($\overline{ES} = 0.45$) is made by studies that used untreated control groups. In fact, the five studies in which psychotherapy was compared to medical treatment showed more than twice the effect of the three studies in which psychotherapy was compared to untreated controls. Before concluding that asthma symptoms are iatrogenic (i.e., caused by medical treatment itself), it is well to note that there are several dissimilarities among the two groups of studies. In particular, the studies using untreated controls had patients nearly half as old (14 years vs. 26 years) as the studies comparing psychotherapy and medical treatment, and they applied therapy for only about one-third as many hours (14 hours vs. 35 hours). These inequalities may explain the unexpected difference in results. An equating of studies of the two types with respect to patient age and duration of therapy would clarify matters, but many more studies would be needed than are now available.

Some things about psychotherapy and its effects on asthma might be learned by correlating various features of the studies with the magnitude of effect that is shown. For example, the effects produced by different kinds of psychotherapies can be compared. Of the nineteen values of *ES*, four were produced by a psychodynamic therapy, twelve by a behavioral or other learning-theory based therapy, and two by hypnotherapy. The average effects for these three general types of psychotherapy are shown in Table 3-3. This

Table 3-2. Average effect sizes for different groupings of the eleven studies in Table 3-1

Grouping	$\overline{ES}$.	Number of studies	Number of *ES*'s
1. Psychotherapy compared with "no treatment" control groups	0.45	3	6
2. Psychotherapy compared with medical treatment	0.95	5	7
3. Psychotherapy compared with "no treatment" or medical treatment (relaxation training eliminated as a control condition)	0.72	8	13
4. Psychotherapy compared with relaxation training as a control condition	1.06	3	6

Table 3-3.   Comparison of effect sizes for three types of psychotherapy

	Behavioral or learning-theory based therapy	Psychodynamic psychotherapy	Hypnotherapy
$\overline{ES}$.:	0.80	1.03	0.58
N:	12	4	2

comparison may well be more courageous than enlightening; the small number of effects of psychodynamic and hypnotherapy render the estimates untrustworthy.

When the nineteen values of ES were correlated with the average age of the patients in the study, a coefficient of 0.43 was obtained. This correlation indicates that the older the patients, the larger the effect. Psychotherapy has greater benefits for older asthmatics than younger ones. A coefficient of this magnitude calculated on a sample of nineteen independent cases would be statistically significantly different from zero at the 10 percent level, but not quite significant at the 5 percent level (Glass and Stanley 1970, p. 536). If the degrees of freedom are actually fewer than the assumption of nineteen independent observations would imply, then the correlation is even less statistically significant than indicated by these tests. So the correlation of 0.43 falls in limbo, where its friends call it suggestive and its enemies call it illusory. The correlation between ES and the duration of the psychotherapy in hours for the data in Table 3-1 is $-.12$. (This correlation has no friends.) The duration of psychotherapy (at least in the range 3 to 100 hours) appears not to be related to the benefits it produces in the treatment of asthma.

The correlation of ES with the number of weeks after therapy at which ES was measured is $+.42$. Since this coefficient is the same size as the correlation of age and ES, its statistical significance is of the same order. However, it is considerably harder to understand; one has every reason to expect a negative correlation: the longer after therapy the measures are taken, the smaller the measured effect. Conceivably, this correlation in the opposite direction arose from variation in a third variable that is correlated simultaneously with ES and follow-up time. For example, if older patients derive greater benefits from psychotherapy (i.e., have larger ES's) and also happened to be involved in studies that measured effects at later follow-up times, then the correlation of age with follow-up interval might account for the surprising positive correlation of follow-up time and ES that was observed. The means of answering this question is to partial age out of the correlation between follow-up time and ES (Glass and Stanley 1970, pp. 182–86). The resulting partial correlation estimates what the correlation would be between follow-up time and ES if all the patients were of the same age. The value of the correlation of age and follow-up time across the nineteen effects is only $+.20$, which gives a partial correlation of follow-up time and ES of $+.37$—smaller than $+.42$, but not by much. Differing ages of patients do not fully explain the unexpected correlation.

It may help to take a closer look at the data in Table 3-1. One datum probably has a major influence on the correlation of follow-up time and *ES*. The Ago et al. study measured effects nearly two years after treatment and showed an *ES* of 1.51, only 0.01 less than the largest *ES* in all the data. Some details of the Ago study are pertinent. The psychotherapy group comprised 46 patients who were willing to learn about mind-body relationship and were enthusiastic about receiving therapy. The control group comprised 42 patients who were unwilling to learn about the mind-body relationship and rejected the offer of psychotherapy. This is an uncommonly bad experimental design (far worse than any other in Table 3-1) and was coded as such in all of our more detailed analyses. The weakness in design constitutes independent reasons for removing the Ago study and recalculating the correlation between *ES* and follow-up time. When this was done, the correlation dropped from + .42 to below + .25, and the greater part of the mystery of the unexpected correlation was solved.

In view of the problems surrounding the Ago study, it would be wise to recalculate the average effect sizes with the Ago *ES* of 1.51 removed. The overall *ES* drops to 0.78 from 0.82—a trivial change. However, when the Ago study is removed, the average of the four *ES*'s for psychodynamic therapies in Table 3-3 drops to 0.87, essentially equal to the average of 0.80 for behavioral and learning-theory based therapies.

The issues in the analysis of the asthma example have grown progressively more complex and esoteric to illustrate a point: summary data from many studies can be analyzed in the same variety of ways as can be used to analyze primary data in a single study. The asthma example is limited and small. Many issues that would emerge in the analysis of a large collection of data cannot be illustrated in a didactic example. Furthermore, the power of the method to resolve specific issues cannot be demonstrated where only one or two studies address a narrow question.

An Assessment of Meta-Analysis

The approach to research integration illustrated here is nothing more than the attitude of data analysis applied to quantitative summaries of individual experiments. By recording the properties of studies and their findings in quantitative terms, the meta-analysis of research invites one who would integrate numerous and diverse findings to apply the full power of statistical methods to the task. Thus, it is not a technique; rather it is a perspective that uses many techniques of measurement and statistical analysis.

A tenet of evaluation theory is that self-assessment is always more suspect than assessment by a neutral party. There is a tone of false promise in professing to criticize an endeavor in which one has invested himself heavily.

Although we cannot promise to deal with the strengths and weaknesses of the meta-analysis approach with an even hand, we can assure the reader that most of the objections raised against the procedure by critics of earlier applications are recorded and discussed below.

Some critics are radical skeptics. They suspect that all outcome research on psychotherapy is biased and flawed at the core. For them, no integration of studies would serve any useful purpose: the sum of a thousand zeroes must remain zero. They variously attribute the problems of the literature to invalid experimental designs or bias (consciously or unconsciously introduced) in the original data. This position is patently extreme and incredible. Suppose it were true. Then to explode the myth, some young researcher (presumably exquisitely trained in experimental design, measurement, and statistics) would only have to perform a few experiments and win fame as the debunker of the fiction. But no one has done so. Could it be that such studies have been done but that the psychotherapy establishment controls publications and rejects the reports submitted? Hardly. Editors don't report receiving careful experimental work on the effects of psychotherapy that shows negative results. And there is such a ready audience for publications that speak ill of psychotherapy that potential debunkers can be published when they have no data at all to substantiate their claims. Furthermore, many empirical studies have been undertaken by critics of psychotherapy who were hostile toward it, and their findings are little different—and hardly less positive—than the findings of the studies by psychotherapy's friends. Many experiments are designed to include two quite different types of therapy and an untreated control group; the experimenter clearly wants to prove *his* type of therapy superior, and he would be delighted to see the other type of therapy proven ineffective, i.e., equal to the control group. But these studies are no less supportive of the benefits of both types of therapy than are all the other studies in the literature. The claim that all psychotherapy-outcome research is a cover for a sham is ridiculous. One might as well believe that an afternoon's telephoning could prove that President Kennedy was assassinated by an international conspiracy, and no one will bother to make the calls. The point-counterpoint organization of objections to psychotherapy outcome research and rejoinders used earlier in this chapter may serve here as well.

Objection 1. *The meta-analysis approach to research integration mixes apples and oranges. It makes no sense to integrate the findings of different studies.* Indeed the approach does mix apples and oranges, as one necessarily would do in studying fruit. If two studies were the same in every respect, there would be no point to integrating them since their results would be the same as well. Only studies that are different need to be integrated. The amount of difference among studies that an observer will tolerate before he raises the tired old bromide about "apples and oranges" is entirely a matter of personal preference or necessity of scope of generalization. When, in an early application of meta-analysis to psychotherapy research, the question of the relative

efficacy of behavior therapy and psychotherapy was addressed, some behavioral psychologists regarded it as "too global to be meaningfully answered." There is no correct level at which to pose scientific questions, much
less questions of value and utility. To fail to see the sense in a comparison of
behavior therapy and psychotherapy tells more about the intellectual prefer-
ences of the critic than about inquiry, its pursuit, and its uses.

Objection 2. *The meta-analysis approach "advocates low standards of
judgment" of the quality of studies.* Although Eysenck (1978) saw us as
advocating low standards of research quality, other critics have viewed us
merely as being incapable of telling the difference between good and bad
studies. We have been accused of relying on an undiscriminating volume of
data rather than on quality of design and evidence. In the academic wars
waged over the questions of the benefits of psychotherapy, the judgment of
quality of design and evidence has usually been the ad hoc impeaching on the
methodology of the studies of one's enemies.

Somewhere in the history of the social sciences, research criticism took an
unhealthy turn. It became confused with research design. The critic often
reads a published study and second guesses the aspects of measurement and
analysis that should have been anticipated by the researcher. If a study "fails"
on a sufficient number of these criteria—or if it fails to meet conditions of
which the critic is particularly fond—the study is discounted or eliminated
completely from consideration. Research design has a logic of its own, but it
is not a logic appropriate to research integration. The researcher does not want
to perform a study deficient in some aspect of measurement or analysis, but it
hardly follows that after a less-than-perfect study has been done, its findings
should not be considered. A logic of research integration could lead to a
description of design and analysis features and study of their covariance with
research findings. If, for example, the covariance is quite small between the
size of an experimental effect and whether or not subjects were volunteers,
then the force of the criticism that some experiments used volunteers is clearly
diminished.

Our early work on the effects of psychotherapy (Smith and Glass 1977)
never strayed far from a sensitivity to design and methods in the studies
integrated. However, across the field of psychotherapy-outcome evaluation,
there was basically no correlation between the "quality" (in the sense of
Campbell and Stanley 1966, and others) of the design and the size of
psychotherapy effect (Smith and Glass 1977, p. 758, Table 4). Thus, any
distinctions between "good" and "bad" studies would leave the overall
picture unchanged—a fact that should be clear to anyone who understands
what the absence of correlation implies. No purpose would have been served
by reporting results separately for "good" and "bad" studies, since they
would have been essentially the same. In a meta-analysis of educational
research on the effect of class-size on achievement, Glass and Smith (1979)
found that quality of research design (essentially the degree of control exer-

cised over the assignment of pupils to classes) was the highest correlate of effects. The sensible course was elected, and results were presented only for the studies in which careful experimental control was exercised.

An early attempt at meta-analysis was characterized somewhat cynically by a critic as follows: "Although no single study was well enough done to prove that psychotherapy is effective, when you put all these bad studies together, they show beyond doubt that therapy works." This skeptical characterization, with its paradoxical ring, is a central thesis of research integration. In fact, many weak studies can add up to a strong conclusion. Suppose that in a group of 100 studies, studies 1–10 are weak in representative sampling but strong in other respects; studies 11–20 are weak in measurement but otherwise strong; studies 21–30 are weak in internal validity only; studies 31–40 are weak only in data analysis; and so on. But imagine also that all 100 studies are somewhat similar in that they show a superiority of the experimental over the control groups. The critic who maintains that the total collection of studies does not support strongly the conclusion of treatment efficacy is forced to invoke an explanation of multiple causality (i.e., the observed difference can be caused either by this particular measurement flaw *or* this particular design flaw, *or* this particular analysis flaw, *or* ...). The number of multiple causes that must be invoked to counter the explanation of treatment efficacy can be embarrassingly large for even a few dozen studies. Indeed, the multiple-defects explanation will soon grow into a conspiracy theory or else collapse under its own weight. Respect for parsimony and good sense demands an acceptance of the notion that imperfect studies can converge on a true conclusion.

Objection 3. *The meta-analysis approach lumps studies into gross categories and fails to separate treatments that ought not to be grouped.* The search for meaningful generalizations necessitates grouping different things together. If one opposes all groupings of unlike instances, then knowledge itself becomes impossible. It has been remarked by philosophers that knowledge is gained by the orderly discarding of information.

Psychologists seem to take offense at groupings for territorial and political reasons, not for epistemological reasons. The objections to grouping are frequently expressed after the fact and with full knowledge of their impact. For example, if psychotherapy A, which produced effects of size 1.0, is grouped with its neighbor psychotherapy B, which produced effects of size 0.5, then proponents of A will be heard to remark on the meaninglessness of ever speaking of therapies A and B in the same breath. Therapy B followers will hold a discrete silence.

Psychology seems to suffer from a common bad habit of thought, which is especially prevalent in the theoretical literature on psychotherapy. Before the fact of the existence of empirical data, theorists press for a huge number of distinctions most of which mark no real or important underlying differences. Then when complimentary data arise and can be claimed, theoretical thinking becomes labile, distinctions are dropped, and boundaries are redrawn. Thus are humanists wont to emphasize their behavioral connections and behaviorists to remind us that they are human beings as well.

Objection 4. *The meta-analysis approach suffers from conceptual difficulties in its definition of effects and it works with data and evidence that are flawed by several serious shortcomings of the published literature:* (a) *selective reporting;* (b) *incorrect primary data analyses;* (c) *insufficient reporting of primary analyses;* (d) *inadequate description of original studies* (Jackson 1978). These points deserve serious consideration, but they do not preclude the necessity of working with research reports as primary data to draw conclusions. If researchers were to carry out many studies, but publish only those few with favorable findings, the deception would be tragic. One can take some comfort in knowing that the odds against this being true for psychology are astronomical (Rosenthal 1979). The more serious problem is that original studies are frequently reported badly: much that was done is not recorded, statistics are reported that obviously have been miscalculated, and too often data are reported in a form that makes it impossible to calculate fundamental descriptive information, such as means and standard deviations. Basic statistics like the mean and the variance are needed to calculate the effect size *ES*, the standard measure of experimental effect.

Although *ES* is simple, it can present many difficulties in both conception and execution. Where there are more than two experimental conditions and means are not reported, there is little hope of ever recovering an *ES* from the report. There are several circumstances of incomplete data reporting in which a harmless assumption and some simple algebra will make it possible to reconstruct *ES* measures: (1) one knows the value of t and whether $\bar{X}_E$ or $\bar{X}_C$ is larger; (2) one knows the significance level of a mean difference and the two sample sizes; (3) one knows $\bar{X}_{E1}, \bar{X}_{E2}, \ldots$, and the value of F; (4) one knows $\bar{X}_E, \bar{X}_C$ and the value of some multiple comparisons statistics, such as Tukey's q or Dunn's or Dunnett's statistics.

One example worked out in detail should suffice to illustrate how to proceed in these general circumstances. The report of an experiment contains J means $\bar{X}_1, \bar{X}_2, \ldots , \bar{X}_J$, the sizes of each group $(n_1, \ldots , n_J)$, and an F statistic. Suppose that $\bar{X}_1$ is the mean of the experimental condition of interest and that a second condition is a control yielding $\bar{X}_C$. The value of the F statistic was calculated by the original investigator from the following formula:

$$F = \frac{\Sigma n_j (\bar{X}_j - \bar{X})^2/(J - 1)}{\Sigma (n_j - 1)s^2_j/(N - J)} = \frac{MS_B}{MS_W} ,$$

where the only symbol that might not be obvious is N, which equals $n_1 + n_2 + \ldots + n_J$. Under the assumption that the variance, s^2_j, in each group is the same, the above expression can be readily solved to obtain s_x^2, the assumed homogeneous variance:

$$s_x^2 = \frac{MS_B}{F}$$

The effect size follows directly:

$$ES = \frac{\bar{X}_E - \bar{X}_C}{s_x}$$

Reports sometimes give only the sample sizes and an indication of whether a mean difference was statistically significant at a customary level. A conservative approximation to the *ES* can be derived by setting a t-ratio equal to the critical value corresponding to the reported significance level and solving for $(\bar{X}_E - \bar{X}_C)/s_x$, under the assumption of equal within-group variances.

Nonparametric statistical techniques hide essential information about the magnitude of effects, since they are not built on basic concepts of means and variances, but instead are constructed primarily for inferential purposes. Since they do yield significance levels for distribution differences, one could equate the α-level to that of a parametric t test and employ the techniques set forth in the above paragraph. This method would be doubly conservative, for the reason already indicated for the t test and also because the nonparametric test is likely to be less powerful.

Experimental outcomes are frequently measured in crude dichotomies where refined metric scales do not exist: remained sober vs. resumed drinking, convicted vs. not convicted of a crime. It seems inappropriate with such data to calculate means and standard deviations and take a conventional ratio.

Effect-size measures on hypothetical metric variables can be obtained simply by differencing the standard normal deviates corresponding to the percentages observed in the experimental and control groups. The reasoning followed is essentially the same as that which underlies *probit analysis* in biometrics (Finney 1971; Glass 1977).

The definition of *ES* appears uncomplicated, but heterogeneous group variances cause substantial difficulties. Suppose that therapy and control groups have means and standard deviations as follows:

	Experimental	*Control*
Means	$\bar{X}_E = 52$	$\bar{X}_C = 50$
Standard deviations	$s_E = 2$	$s_C = 10$

The measure of experimental effect could be calculated either by use of (a) s_E or (b) s_C or some combination of the two, such as (c) an average or the square root of the average of their squares or whatever. The differences in effect sizes ensuing from such choices are huge: (a) 1.00, (b) 0.20, and (c) 0. 33, respectively.

The third basis of standardization—the average standard deviation—probably should be eliminated as pointless. (Regrettably, there is no alternative to averaging when a standard deviation must be reconstructed from many test statistics like F and t.) It must be acknowledged that both the remaining 1.00 and 0.20 are *correct*. It is true, in fact, that the experimental group mean is one standard deviation above the control group mean in terms of the experimental group standard deviation; and, assuming normality, the average subject in the control group is superior to only 16 percent of the members of the experimental group. However, the control group mean is only one-fifth standard deviation below the mean of the experimental group when measured in control group standard deviations; thus, the average experimental group subject exceeds 58 percent of the subjects in the control group. These facts are neither contradictory nor inconsistent; rather they are two distinct features of a finding that cannot be captured by one number.

In the meta-analysis of psychotherapy reported here, the problem of heterogeneous standard deviations was resolved from a quite different direction. Suppose that therapies A, B, and Control are compared in a single experiment, with the following results:

	Therapy A	Therapy B	Control
Means	50	50	48
Standard deviations	10	1	4

If effect sizes are calculated using the standard deviations of the therapy, then ES_A equals 0.20 and ES_B equals 2.00—a misleading difference, considering the equality of the therapy means on the dependent variable. Standardization of mean differences by the control group standard deviation at least has the advantage of allotting equal effect sizes to equal means. This seems reason enough to resolve the choice in favor of the control group standard deviation.

None of these deliberations helps resolve an even more perplexing situation that is likely to arise. One might want to summarize a collection of experiments in which methods A and B are compared to an untreated control condition, in order to determine which is more effective. Experiments are certain to turn up in which A and B are compared without a control. Such experiments may be quite informative but do not permit calculation of effect sizes of methods vis-à-vis the missing control condition. A certain percentage of "control-referenced effects" constructed along the following lines seems tolerable. Suppose an experiment comparing only A and B yields a difference in favor of A of 0.50 standard deviations, the standard deviation being taken as the common s_x in each group; and assume that all other available comparisons of A and B with the control condition yield average effect sizes of 2.00 and 1.00, respectively. Then assigning effect-size measures of 1.75 to A and 1.25 to B has the advantage of being closest to the respective average effects, while corresponding to the difference obtained in the experiment in question.

A final example will illustrate the complexity of describing experimental findings. The size of "within-group" standard deviations, and hence the size of *ES*, is affected by both the homogeneity of the experimental subjects and the number and type of classification factors in the design. Suppose that client-centered psychotherapy is approximately 10 points superior to the untreated control condition on the Hopkins Symptom Checklist. If Jones performs an experiment with a typical group of mental health center out-patients whose standard deviation on the outcome measure is 20 points, he will obtain an *ES* for client-centered therapy vs. control of +0.50. However, if Brown conducts a similar study with a more homogeneous group of in-patients (e.g., with a standard deviation of 5), an effect of +2.00 will be obtained. Clearly, the discrepancy arises for good reason; one *ES* is not right and the other wrong. A similar circumstance may be encountered in a single study. An investigator compares client-centered therapy against untreated controls for both in-patients and out-patients and reports the results in a two-factor analysis of variance, Treatment *X* In- vs. out-patient. Is the proper standard deviation for calculating *ES* the standard deviation within the four cells of the factorial design, or the standard deviation within treatments, ignoring the in-patient vs. out-patient stratification? The difference between the effect-size measures calculated by the two methods might be substantial. If some attempt is not made to deal with this problem, a source of inexplicable and annoying variance will be left in a group of effect-size measures. At least two techniques can help reduce the problem. If the scale of measurement of the outcome variables is familiar, it may be possible to calculate all effect-size measures using the known population standard deviation. For example, if the outcomes of therapy are measured with the MMPI, the experimental vs. control mean difference can be divided by $s_x = 10$. An alternative approach based on less bold assumptions and requiring less a priori knowledge is to regard the homogeneity of the subjects as a characteristic of the studies. Effect-size measures could then be tagged as having arisen from studies with low, average, or highly homogeneous subjects, for example. One can then examine the covariance of *ES* with the homogeneity of the subjects used in the experiment.

These and countless other problems crop up in reading hundreds of studies, quantifying their characteristics, and measuring their outcomes. We have documented our attempts to resolve them in the chapters that follow and in the Appendixes where several of the more technical solutions are recorded.

Final Defense

General arguments to the effect that psychotherapy outcomes can be studied and that different studies can be woven into general conclusions may be convincing in part; but the final defense against objections to the meaningfulness of both psychotherapy-outcome research and its integration is the concrete demonstration of its existence, to which we move in the remaining chapters.

Chapter 4

....

Methods of the Psychotherapy Meta-analysis

The purpose of the meta-analysis was to determine the state of knowledge about the effects of psychotherapy. The principal methods consisted of gathering, studying, and integrating the results of research designed separately to test those effects. Guiding this project was the motive to reach unbiased conclusions based on adequate representation of the body of evidence and statistical methods for integrating separate studies. This chapter is divided into the following sections—population definitions, sampling and search procedures, classification of studies, and analysis of data. Chapter 5 contains the findings and conclusions of the psychotherapy meta-analysis.

Population Definition

All controlled studies of the effectiveness of any form of psychotherapy formed the population of interest for this project. Further elaboration is necessary for two parts of this statement—the concept of controlled study and the concept of psychotherapy.

Controlled studies refer to those research investigations in which the experimenter treated one group of clients with a form of psychotherapy, while another more or less comparable group remained untreated, were put on a waiting list for a period of time equal to the time of treatment, received a placebo treatment, or received a second form of psychotherapy. The assumption was made that control groups yield the only reasonable baseline against which the effects of psychotherapy can be measured. Present knowledge about psychopathology—its origins, natural history, and remission—is insufficient to permit the use of naturalistic baselines as standards of comparison for treatments. However, complete knowledge about an illness is not necessary to evaluate the effect of treatment purporting to cure it. Within an experiment, two client groups, one to be treated and the other untreated, can be initially equivalent on all characteristics—age, sex, severity of illness, for example—which might affect the outcome of therapy. All the characteristics associated with the treatment (duration of therapy, qualification of therapists, time and type of outcome measurement) may be held constant, varying only the treatment between the experimental and control groups. At the end of the experiment, differences between the groups are due to treatment effects, therefore, and not to initially different characteristics. Judging the validity of the experiment is not a matter of personal judgment, but the acknowledged canons of experimental science.

The definitional boundaries of psychotherapy used in this project are liberal, but defensible. More stringent definitions would rule out arbitrarily large bodies of pertinent evidence. For example, some earlier reviews excluded studies of rational-emotive psychotherapy; others excluded analogue studies. Although such a procedure appears to preserve theoretical distinctions among theories of psychotherapy, the commonalities among therapies, both in terms of processes and outcomes, may be greater and more important than the distinctions. We chose empirical methods to identify which distinctions produce observable differences in effectiveness.

Definitions are inherently unsatisfying. Nothing appears to be wrong or excessively liberal about Meltzoff and Kornreich's (1970) definition of psychotherapy: "Psychotherapy is taken to mean the informed and planful application of techniques derived from established psychological principles, by persons qualified through training and experience to understand these principles and to apply these techniques with the intention of assisting individuals to modify such personal characteristics as feelings, values, attitudes, and behaviors which are judged by the therapist to be maladaptive or maladjustive" (p. 6). Yet several critics (e.g., Howard and Orlinsky 1972; and Malan 1973) took exception to the studies Meltzoff and Kornreich used, many of which did not fit the critics' personal conceptions of psychotherapy. Limiting a review to only those studies that fit some personal conception of psychotherapy may introduce bias into the conclusions of the review. For example, exclusion of studies that use volunteer subjects solicited by experimenters probably introduces a bias against behavior therapies in a comparative review. Our aim throughout the meta-analysis was to eliminate the possibilities of bias even at the expense of blurring distinctions that have theoretical importance, but only minor importance in evaluation research.* No form of psychotherapy was excluded if the therapy (1) involved clients identified by themselves or others as having some emotional or behavioral problem; (2) if the clients sought or were referred for treatment to ameliorate this problem; (3) if the treatment or intervention was psychological or behavioral; and (4) if the person delivering the treatment was identified as a psychotherapist by virtue of training or professional affiliation. Within this definition are studies of the effects of psychodynamic psychotherapy, behavior therapies, cognitive therapies, client-centered therapy, hypnotherapy (when used for psychological and psychosomatic problems), transactional

---

*The studies are classified so that the reader with a different definition of psychotherapy is able to reconstruct effects for that definition.

analysis, and eclectic forms of psychotherapy. Studies of vocational and personal counseling were included when their characteristics conformed to the above definition. Many distinctions have been drawn between psychotherapy and counseling. The two processes have been described as varying on a number of dimensions, such as the severity of illness of the clients treated, the amount of training of the professionals delivering the treatment, the goals of the treatment, and the psychological depth of the treatment. However, in the middle ranges of these dimensions, it is impossible to make reliable distinctions between psychotherapy and counseling. Drawing a line between the two involves an arbitrary judgment, with the possible admission of bias. Furthermore, the effect of therapy relative to the diagnosis of the client, the training of the therapist, and the type of treatment should be studied directly, not by arbitrary exclusion of portions of the evidence.

What some reviewers (Luborsky et al. 1975) have called analogue studies and excluded from consideration are included in this meta-analysis. The label of "analogue" is usually used to designate studies of short-term behavioral therapies practiced on volunteer clients (sometimes identified by extreme scores on inventories of specific phobias) by relatively inexperienced therapists. Usually, the rationale for exclusion of analogue studies is that "real" therapy is not tested, nor "real" clients, nor therapists. The important question is whether the effects of therapy vary with the severity of client illness, experience of therapist, and length of treatment. We believe that this question is best addressed empirically by studying the relationship between severity of illness, length of treatment, and experience of therapist on the one hand, and the effect of therapy on the other.

The following treatments were excluded from the population definition: psychopharmacological treatments (these were analyzed separately and included in Chapter 7), bibliotherapy, sensitivity training, consciousness-raising groups, encounter groups (except when led by a psychotherapist and identified with client-centered or gestalt therapies), hospital milieu therapy (except when a specific program of psychotherapy was included), education and training programs, peer counseling, meditation therapies, electro-shock treatment, occupational or recreation therapy, and the like.

Sampling Procedures

Our original intention was to include all studies with the characteristics defined in the preceeding section. To locate and assemble all these studies, standard search procedures were used. The studies named by previous reviewers were obtained. *Psychological Abstracts* was searched as was *Education Resources Information Clearinghouse* (ERIC), and studies named in relevant abstracts were gathered. The major outlets for outcome studies (e.g., *Journal of Counseling Psychology, Journal of Consulting and Clinical Psy-*

chology, Behavior Research and Therapy, Journal of Abnormal Psychology)
were searched from their initial volumes to 1977. The bibliographies of
studies obtained by the above methods were searched for related research.
Colleagues familiar with early phases of the project provided further leads or
sent unpublished works. Papers delivered at meetings of such associations as
the Society for Psychotherapy Research were obtained. *Dissertation
Abstracts* in psychology and education were searched from 1900 to 1977.
Those that fit the population definition were purchased.

We failed to exhaust the defined population for various reasons. Some
studies simply slipped through the net of our search procedures. Studies
published in foreign language journals were probably largely missed. Approximately fifty studies were unused because the statistics used in them escaped
even our tenacious attempts to convert them into common metrics. Sampling
procedures were used in two areas where studies were numerous. We sampled
dissertation studies of ordinary school counseling at a rate of 25 percent. No
bias was introduced by this sampling procedure, because this body of work is
remarkably uniform in the amount of effects produced by the counseling, as
well as in type of outcome, duration of counseling, type of treatment, experience of counselor, and so forth. Studies of systematic desensitization of snake
phobias were also so numerous and uniform that little error was introduced by
omitting, not selectively, 10 percent of them. Finally, approximately thirty
studies were omitted because they were not fully analyzed by the deadline for
proceeding with subsequent steps in the meta-analysis. Decisions to omit
studies were not related to any characteristic of the study or to its results. Four
hundred seventy-five studies were fully analyzed and account for the conclusions reached in these analyses. These include 25 percent of the school-
counseling studies and probably 75 percent of the population as defined. The
error in generalizing from this sample to the population is probably relatively
small.

One sometimes hears from critics of research that there is a bias among
journal editors to publish only statistically significant findings, that reviews of
published research, therefore, have a positive bias. The case has even been
made—facetiously, perhaps, or for effect—that the published research consists only of Type I errors; that no studies of psychotherapy are truly positive,
that those that are published are the 5 percent of false positives and that the 95
percent that show nonsignificant effects remain inaccessible. This "file
drawer problem" has been addressed by Rosenthal (1979), who showed that
many thousands of unpublished manuscripts would have to exist unpublished,
lying in file drawers, for a finding based on a few hundred studies to be
averaged out to zero. We consider this to be unlikely in the case of the
psychotherapy-outcome literature. To study this problem within the meta-
analysis, we compared the results of published with unpublished research. If
the published literature had contained only Type I errors, there would be a
large difference between the average effects produced by published studies

compared to those of dissertations and other unpublished works. The observed difference was small enough to discount this problem.

There remains a pressing question to which we can offer no compelling answer. How alike are the therapists, patients, and practices represented in the data base, and therapists, patients, and practices in the day-to-day world of psychotherapy? We know much less about the latter than the former, which is variously tabulated and described in the results that follow. We trust that the two are not incomparably different.

Classification of Studies

One objective of the meta-analysis was to investigate the relationship between the effect produced by the therapy in a study and other features of the study, such as the characteristics of the clients, the therapy, the outcomes, as well as the technical features of the study itself. To do this, it was necessary to develop a coding sheet on which the important characteristics could be described and quantified. The characteristics included on the coding sheet were based on two criteria: (1) the characteristic was claimed to have a functional relationship with therapy outcomes (see, for example, Luborsky 1975), and (2) it was likely to be reported by the experimenter. There tend to be more of the former than the latter. The coding sheet was revised after a pilot test with fifty studies and was further refined over a two-year period of use. The final version was used to classify all studies in the meta-analysis.

An example of the form appears in Appendix 1. It contains the following variables on which each study was classified: date of publication; form of publication; professional affiliation of the experimenter; the degree of blinding used in the study; whether more than one treatment was simultaneously compared against the control group; client diagnosis; previous hospitalization; intelligence; age; sex; similarity of client to the therapist; the means by which the clients were obtained for the study; means of assigning clients and therapists to comparison groups; mortality (loss of subjects) from samples; internal validity of the study; the type, duration, modality, and location of the treatment; sample size; therapist experience; type and reactivity of outcome measure and the time after therapy when it was measured; whether factorial effects were tested; and the statistical procedures for determining the size of effect produced by the therapy. Each variable is further described below.

Each study was read and a coding form was completed for each outcome and each comparison in the study. This task presented a range of difficulty depending on the clarity of the research report and the conformity of the experimenter to standard research practices. A list of coding conventions was developed during the pilot phase of the project and was used to guide the classification of studies whose characteristics were ambiguous. These conventions are explained in the following paragraphs.

To judge the reliability of the coding procedures, twenty studies were coded by the authors and members of a graduate-level seminar in clinical and counseling psychology. Each person was given a copy of the study, coding conventions, and an abbreviated coding form consisting of twenty variables. Reliability was construed as the consistency of ratings. Over all twenty studies, there was a 92 percent agreement in ratings assigned to the classification variables.

Classification Variables

This section contains the description of each coding variable and the conventions that were developed to assist in its coding. Naturally, these variables do not exhaust the possible influences on therapeutic effect. However, they do reflect what information experimenters provide in their reports. It would have been desirable to know the age, sex, verbal ability, style, and place of training of each therapist, the source of funding for the study, the distribution of outcome test scores, and many other characteristics that may have influenced the effectiveness of therapy. But unfortunately authors do not report this information, even when no restrictions are placed on the length of the manuscript.

Date of Publication. This was recorded as stated on the manuscript. Some studies were published more than once, and in this case the earliest date was recorded.

Form of Publication. The study was classified according to the form in which it appeared: journal article, book, dissertation, or unpublished manuscript. If more than one form was used, such as a dissertation later published in a journal, the study was designated in its most accessible form.

Professional Affiliation of Experimenter. The study was classified, according to the affiliation of the experimenter, as either psychology, education, psychiatry, social work, or "other." This classification was determined by the institutional and departmental identification on the manuscript, or by membership in the American Psychological Association.

Blinding of Experimenter. This variable represents the degree of blinding that prevails in the assessment of outcomes or in the administration of these in the study. If the experimenter or the outcome evaluator was kept uninformed about whether each subject was in the control group or the treated group, the study was classified as "single blind." If no information was provided that showed that the experimenter or evaluator was kept uninformed about group composition, the study was categorized as either "experimenter did the therapy'' or ''experimenter knew the composition of groups but didn't personally treat the client.''

Client Diagnosis. It has often been said that clients with different problems and diagnoses profit to different degrees from psychotherapy. The challenge has been put to researchers by Kiesler (1966), and others, that they must no longer try to find out how therapy works in general, but instead design studies to find out what kind of therapy works with what kind of client by what kind of therapist. The counterargument is that there are common factors in therapy that work for all types of client. In the meta-analysis, the diagnostic label that the experimenter used was recorded and classified into a twelve-category diagnostic system. The categories were (1) neurotic or true (complex) phobic, (2) simple (monosymptomatic) phobic, (3) psychotic, (4) normal, (5) character disordered, (6) delinquent or felon, (7) habituee (e.g., alcohol, tobacco, drug addiction), (8) emotional-somatic disordered, (9) handicapped (physically or mentally), (10) depressive, (11) mixed diagnoses, and (12) unknown. Table 4–1 contains the diagnostic labels that were grouped under two diagnostic types: ''handicapped'' and ''emotional-somatic disordered.'' Other diagnostic labels grouped under diagnostic types are presented in Appendix 2. The neurotic category posed knotty problems, in the end becoming a catchment not only for clients the researchers called neurotic, but for a variety of nonpsychotic and nonspecific clients as well. They ranged from persons in stressful training programs to distressed low academic achievers to persons seeking personal growth through therapeutic groups. The problem with the neurotic category is not specific to this project, however, but is wrestled with throughout the professional and scientific communities.

Hospitalization. The number of years of previous hospitalization, as stated or implied by the author, was another indication of the severity of client distress and was recorded.

Table 4–1. Diagnostic labels for two diagnostic types

Diagnostic type	
Handicapped	Emotional-somatic disordered
Mentally retarded	Insomniacs
Vocational rehabilitation client	Sexual dysfunction
Handicapped children with behavior problems	Eneuresis
Speech defects	Obesity
Brain-damaged	Migraine headaches
Learning disabled	Dysmenorrhea
	Asthmatic
	Heart attack patients
	Dialysis patients

Intelligence. Intelligence of the client is frequently cited as mediating the effects of psychotherapy. The intelligence of the group was rated as "below average" for IQ scores less than 95, "average" for IQ scores between 95 and 105, and "above average" for IQ scores above 105. The source of information about client intelligence was also recorded. In 4 percent of the studies, IQ was reported by the experimenter. In 61 percent of the studies, IQ could be inferred (at least with the accuracy necessary to make the three gross distinctions) from the clients' placement in some institution, such as a college or a treatment facility for the mentally retarded. In 35 percent of the cases, client intelligence could not be assessed from the report and therefore was estimated as average.

Client-Therapist Similarity. The socioeconomic and ethnic similarity between client and therapist is also thought to influence the outcome of therapy. The cultures of the therapist and the client are similar in the sense that they share common languages, value systems, and educational backgrounds. The more healthy the client, the more he resembles the therapist. The studies were rated for similarity between the client and the typical white, middle-class, well-educated therapist. The highest value (4) was used for studies of white, middle-class, well-educated, and mildly or moderately distressed clients. The lowest value (1) was used when the typical therapist treated lower-class minority or severely disturbed clients.

Solicitation of Clients. The use of volunteers in therapy studies has been sufficient cause for some previous reviewers to disallow these studies as tests of therapeutic effect. Yet in the case of most analogue studies, the volunteers reported symptoms, requested and were given psychological treatments to remedy them. It is possible that they differ only in degree from "real" clients who independently seek treatment. The studies were classified according to whether (1) the subjects were solicited for therapy by the experimenter (usually by offering treatment to psychology students who obtained extreme scores on anxiety measures); (2) the subjects came to the treatment program in response to an advertisement; (3) the subjects recognized the existence of a problem and sought treatment; (4) the subjects were referred for treatment; or (5) the subjects were committed to the treatment, with no choice.

Assignment to Groups. A characteristic often afforded most importance in judging the validity of a comparative study is how the experimenter allocated subjects to treated and control groups. Random assignment insures, within probability limits, that the two groups are initially comparable and that differences between them on the post-test are attributable either to chance (with probability equal to the significance level) or to the treatment and to no other source of influence.* Matching pairs of subjects is the next best method, although using it presumes that all sources of influence on therapy are known and can be used as matching variables. Moreover, it renders significance levels meaningless when calculated in the usual ways. Ex post facto matching, covariance adjustments, and equating on pretest scores are less satisfactory allocation methods, but still better than no matching at all. Studies were classified according to the assignment of both clients and therapists to groups.

Experimental Mortality. Dropouts from treatment and control groups represent a critical problem in psychotherapy research. Eysenck and Rachman (see Chapter 2) declared that a dropout must be considered a treatment failure. Yet early termination can be explained by a variety of reasons other than treatment failure. These include economic problems, family or work problems unconnected with the psychological difficulties, amelioration of symptoms, scheduling changes, physical illness unrelated to treatment, and even death. Unless these alternative explanations are accounted for, the premature terminators cannot be classified as either successes or failures. Yet the decision to include or exclude terminators from final statistics may have a substantial effect on the findings of a study. Because the decision is made on professional judgment rather than independent empirical justification, the decision invites bias.

Premature termination is best regarded as a problem of the internal validity of the study and not confounded with outcome measurement. In this study, the percent mortality was coded separately for treated and untreated groups. These figures were occasionally difficult to ascertain and involved comparing degrees of freedom in post-test analyses with the numbers of subjects originally allocated to groups. A study might also have different rates of mortality at the times of the post-test and the follow-up. These different mortality percents were noted separately.

Internal Validity. The internal validity of a study was judged on the basis of the assignment of subjects to treatment and the extent of experimental mortality in the study. To be judged high on the internal validity scale, a study must have used random assignment of subjects to groups and have a rate of mortality less than 15 percent and equivalent between the two groups. If mortality was higher or nonequivalent, internal validity was still rated high if the experimenter included the scores of the terminators in the post-test statistics or established the initial equivalence of terminators and nonterminators. Medium internal validity ratings were given to (1) studies with randomization

---

*Matching the two groups on several variables, then randomizing the matched pairs into experimental and control groups is often thought to be the preferred allocation method. However, this procedure does not make the groups any more comparable then does simple randomization.

but high or differential mortality; (2) studies with "failed" randomization procedures (e.g., where the experimenter began by randomizing, but then resorted to other allocation methods, such as taking the last ten clients and putting them into the control group) with low mortality; and (3) extremely well-designed matching studies. Low validity studies were those whose matching procedures were quite weak or nonexistent (e.g., where intact convenience samples were used) or where mortality was severely disproportionate. Occasionally, statistical or measurement irregularities decreased the value assigned to internal validity, such as when an otherwise well-designed study employed different testing times for treated and untreated groups. This measure of internal validity was not contaminated by sample size, reactivity of measures, or the degree of blinding employed in the study. All four constructs were assessed separately.

Much has been written concerning the use of imperfect research studies as evidence to arrive at general conclusions about a topic. Yet it is clear that no study is unassailable, and research criticism can become no more than a textbook exercise, frequently not independent of the findings of the study critiqued. The important question in surveying a body of literature is to determine whether the best-designed studies yield evidence different from more poorly designed studies. If the answer is yes, then one is compelled to believe the best ones. If not, then the studies may be weighed equally and considered together. In this study, the effects would have been differentially weighted if high internal validity studies had produced results different from low validity studies. Since the correlation of size of effect with internal validity was $r = 0.03$, no differential weighting was necessary (see Chapter 5).

Allegiance of the Experimenter. Faith in the therapy on the part of the therapist has been mentioned as a putative cause of positive therapeutic effects. From the tone and substance of the research report, it was usually possible to determine whether the experimenter was partial to the treatment evaluated. For example, when the report contained enthusiastic endorsements of the therapy, this variable was coded as positive. Where a second therapy was clearly a foil for the favored therapy, this variable was coded as negative. Placebo treatments were always coded as negative. Where the experimenter was the therapist, this variable was coded positive.

Therapy Modality. Each study was coded for the modality in which the therapy was delivered—individual, group, family, mixed modalities, automated, or "other."

Treatment Location. Each study was coded according to the location in which the therapy was delivered—school, hospital, mental health center, other clinic, private practice, college facility, prison, residential facility, or "other."

Therapy Duration. The duration of therapy, both in number of hours and weeks, was recorded. The rate (hours per week) of therapy was computed from these two variables.

Therapist Experience. The number of therapists used in the study and their experience in years was recorded. Because reports were frequently lacking this information, the following conventions were developed for translating relevant bits of information into years of therapist experience when no more specific information was given:

Undergraduates or other untrained assistants	= 0 years
MA candidates	= 1 year
MA-level counselor or therapist	= 2 years
Ph.D. candidate or psychiatric resident	= 3 years
Ph.D.-level therapist	= 5 years
Well-known, Ph.D.-level therapist	= 7+ years

Outcome Measurements. Previous reviewers have struggled with the philosophical and technical problems connected with the selection and measurement of outcomes. A reviewer might count a study as supportive or not supportive of the effectiveness of psychotherapy based on the statistical significance of the outcome measure. Yet most studies employed more than one outcome measure, using different instruments or the same instrument given at different times after therapy. When different measures produced different results, several strategies were employed to cope with this problem. A study could be counted twice, for example, with one vote for and one against the therapy. Or, if a study showed positive effects at therapy termination, but no effects at the follow-up, that study could be listed as a negative indicator of therapeutic effectiveness. This strategy exemplifies a confusion between the use of empirical research for theory building and research done for evaluative purposes, i.e., to determine the effects and practical value of a treatment. Other reviewers have listed a study as a failure if significant effects were not found on *each* of the outcome measures used. Still other reviewers quibbled about the experimenter's choice of instruments, accepting findings from instruments on grounds that were psychologically and psychometrically problematic.

Different procedures were used in the meta-analysis. Statistical significance was not used to determine whether the study produced supportive or nonsupportive evidence. Instead, each outcome was converted into a standardized effect (see "Effect Size Calculation" below). No outcome measure was impeached on theoretic or psychometric grounds. Instead, the outcome measure was listed, classified into outcome types, rated for its "reactivity" and for the number of weeks after therapy the measure was administered. In this way, it could be determined whether the size of the therapeutic effect covaried with the type of outcome measure, reactivity of the measure, or the time it was taken. The direction of desirable therapeutic effect was obvious in nine out of ten cases by examining the research hypotheses stated by the experimenter or the narrative description of results. In the remainder of cases, the *Mental Measurements Yearbooks* were consulted, or other studies that had employed the same measure. Each outcome measurement listed by the experimenter was used in the meta-analysis. Each measure was weighed equally; however, redundant measures were eliminated. If, for example, a second measure matched the first in outcome type, degree of reactivity, follow-up time, and approximate size of effect, the second measure was deemed redundant and ordinarily not included in the meta-analysis. When subtest scores of multifactorial test batteries (e.g., MMPI) were reported, and the subtests yielded results that were only randomly different from one another, an average of the subtests was used. Total test battery results were used in favor of separate subtest scores.

The specific outcome was recorded and grouped into one of twelve outcome types: (1) fear or anxiety measures; (2) measures of self-esteem; (3) tests and ratings of global adjustment; (4) life indicators of adjustment; (5) personality traits; (6) measures of emotional-somatic disorders; (7) measures of addiction; (8) sociopathic behaviors; (9) social behaviors; (10) measures of work or school achievement; (11) measures of vocational or personal development; and (12) physiological measures of stress. Table 4–2 contains the outcome measures that were grouped within two outcome types: life indicators of adjustment and social behaviors. Other groupings of outcome measures within outcome types are located in Appendix 2.

Reactivity of Outcome Measure. Highly *reactive* instruments are those that reveal or closely parallel the obvious goals or valued outcomes of the

Table 4–2. Outcome labels grouped into two outcome types

Outcome type	
Life indicators of adjustment	Social behaviors
Number of times hospitalized	Interpersonal maturity
Length of hospitalizations	Interpersonal interaction
Time out of hospital	Social relations
Employment	Assertiveness
Discharge from hospital	IPAT sociability scale
Completion of tour of duty	Acceptance of others
Recidivism	FIRO-B
	Dating behavior measures
	Problem behavior in school social setting
	Social effectiveness
	Social distress
	Sociometric status
	Social distance scale
	Social adjustment

Table 4-3.   Conventions for assigning values of reactivity to tests and ratings

Reactivity value	Tests and ratings of therapy outcome
1 (lowest)	Physiological measures (PSI, Pulse, GSR), grade point average
2	Blinded ratings and decisions—blind projective test ratings, blind ratings of symptoms, blind discharge from hospital
3	Standardized measures of traits having minimal connection with treatment or therapist (MMPI, Rotter I-E)
4	Experimenter-constructed inventories (nonblind), rating of symptoms (nonblind), any client self-report to experimenter, blind administration of Behavioral Approach Tests
5 (highest)	Therapist rating of improvement or symptoms, projective tests (nonblind), behavior in the presence of therapist or nonblind evaluator (e.g., Behavioral Approach Test), instruments that have a direct and obvious relationship with treatment (e.g., where desensitization hierarchy items were taken directly from measuring instrument)

therapist or experimenter; which are under control of the therapist, who has an acknowledged interest in achieving predetermined goals; or which are subject to the client's need and ability to alter his scores to show more or less change than what actually took place. Relatively nonreactive measures are not so easily influenced in any direction by any of the parties involved. Using this definition of reactivity, it was possible to define a five-point scale with the low end anchored at unreactive measures, such as physiological measures of stress (e.g., Palmar Sweat Index) and anchored at the high end with therapist judgments of client improvement. Points on the scale are further illustrated in Table 4-3.

The reactivity scale is not meant to be evaluative in the sense of defining good and bad instruments. Nor is it a measure of the centrality or importance of the measure to objectives of therapy. The scale is related to the concept of blindedness. Even projective measures may have low reactivity if the evaluator scoring the responses is kept uninformed about which clients are treated and which are untreated. The subjectivity of an instrument is not important for our purposes if the variable is defined and measured without prejudice in each experimental group. Objective, mechanical measurement is not the *sine qua non* of reliability and validity.

Reactivity is also not necessarily related to whether the scale involved the observation of a current act or recall or self-report of behaviors. Measures of observable, countable behaviors are not necessarily less reactive than psychometric measures. On the Behavioral Approach Test, often used after systematic desensitization of snake phobias, the closer the client can come to the snake, including even picking it up and holding it, the higher the score. In most cases, the experimenter, evaluator, or even the therapist is in the room, knows the desired outcome (close for the therapy group, farther away for the control group), and may provide subtle cues for the client's behavior. The client knows the desired outcome, may want to please the evaluator, reward the therapist, or reduce his own dissonance. He will probably never need to touch another snake and can willfully walk closer to the snake than he would under any other circumstances.

This is the worst possible scenario for conducting the Behavioral Approach Test. However, it illustrates the possibilities, in a measurement situation, of influencing the direction and degree of effect. These possibilities have been confirmed in several experiments that showed the extent to which tests of this sort can be influenced by the presence of an experimenter and the "demand characteristics" in the test situation (Bernstein 1973; Bernstein and Paul 1971; Bernstein and Nietzel 1973).

Behavior therapies are not the only ones vulnerable to a judgment of highly reactive outcome measurements. Therapists' judgments about the rate of improvement of their clients are highly reactive. Obviously, the therapist has a vested interest in the outcome and may see or report progress more favorable than real. When self-defeating behavior is the focus of a cognitive therapy, and the outcome criterion is a measure of self-report of self-defeating behavior, that assessment would also be judged highly reactive. The client could readily perceive the connection between treatment goals and outcome measurement and alter his responses accordingly.

The concept of reactivity used here does not indicate that the results were in fact influenced by the experimenter, therapist, or client in known and socially desired directions. The score instead indicates the potential for influence. As will be shown in Chapter 5, the reactivity of a measure bears a strong relationship to the size of effect produced on that measure.

Effect Size. Nearly all previous reviewers of psychotherapy-outcome research have relied on the statistical significance found on the outcome measure to indicate whether that study supported or failed to support therapy effectiveness. However, using statistical significance confounds the magnitude of the effect produced by a treatment with the size of the sample and other technical features of the experiment, independent of the treatment effect (see Chapter 3). Therefore, a statistic was chosen to represent only the magnitude of therapeutic effect. The definition of the magnitude of effect—or "effect size" (ES)—was the mean difference between the treated and control subjects divided by the standard deviation of the control group, that is, $ES = (\bar{X}_T - \bar{X}_C)/s_C$. An effect size of + 1 indicates that a person at the mean of the control group would be expected to rise to the 84th percentile of the control group if he was given treatment.

Because the effect-size statistic is a standardized mean difference, using it allows comparisons among outcomes assessed by different instruments and rating devices. Selection of outcome measures is always the prerogative of the experimenter, a matter of professional judgment, and therefore never likely to be identical among many different experimenters. If the measures are not identical, how much difference among them should be tolerated before generalizations across studies can be made? In the strictest sense, it is not even justifiable to combine data from two forms of the same achievement test or from individual intelligence tests administered by different psychologists. Yet these are distinctions that some observers have attempted to press. Maintaining distinctions such as these precludes any possibility for generalizing across different studies. Yet such generalizations are both defensible and common. Making statements about "what the research says" involves an implicit generalization across studies (all with slightly different outcomes), and such a statement is merely a less systematic variation of the meta-analysis procedure.

Each independent experimenter makes a choice among outcome measures, based on a number of considerations—the characteristics of the clients to be studied, what outcomes the treatment is likely to produce in that population (based on theory, previous experimentation, *ES* values, and professional judgment) and the psychometric characteristics of the assessment devices. Each experimenter chooses an instrument and establishes in hypotheses the desired direction of change (in spite of the diversity of measures resulting from these decisions, all the measures relate in some way to a construct of "general well-being"). This relationship is endorsed by colleagues and editors. A definition of positive outcome of a systematic desensitization treatment as *an increase in fear* of the phobic object would never be tolerated. For groups of neurotic clients receiving client-centered therapy, a mean decrease in self-acceptance would never be accepted as a positive outcome. Therefore, in spite of a diversity in measurement instruments, there are implicit norms for general well-being and all measurement instruments must relate to them. To the extent that all instruments estimate that construct of well-being, they are comparable at a general level. The primary job is to standardize them statistically so that they appear on a common scale, record as many characteristics of them as possible, and then compare the magnitude of effect with the characteristics of the instrument. In this way, it is possible to determine whether therapy in general or specific therapies produce larger effects on measures of fear and anxiety than on measures of self-esteem, for example.

Calculating effect sizes was straightforward for those studies with means and standard deviations reported. If means and standard deviations were not reported, effect sizes were obtained by solving equations from t or F ratios or from other inferential statistics. Statistical procedures for solving these equations are located in Appendix 7. Probit transformations were used to convert percentages (e.g., improvement rates) to effect sizes (Glass 1977). Original data were requested from several authors when effect sizes could not be derived from any reported information.

Effect sizes were calculated on each (nonredundant) outcome measure (see above). The procedure used to calculate the effect size (e.g., means and standard deviations, probit transformation, solution of formulas from t or F statistics, nonparametric transformations) was recorded in each case, as were the final sample sizes on which the statistics were based, and whether any factorial or covariance effects were tested.

Treatment. To determine whether the therapeutic effect produced in a study was related to the type of treatment used, a system for categorizing treatments was developed. Four levels were used. At the first level, the treatment as labeled by the experimenter was recorded. At the second level of aggregation, the specific therapies were grouped into nineteen therapy types based on the description of the therapies in the study and correspondence of these descriptions with key concepts and proponents within theories and schools of thought in therapy. At the third level of generality, therapy types were grouped into subclasses by psychophysical scaling techniques; and at the fourth and highest level, subclasses were organized into classes of therapy. Each of these levels is explained in detail below.

There were two major reasons for organizing therapies into groups of differing levels of specificity. Different audiences have varying appetites for specificity and generalization. A therapist who works exclusively with systematic desensitization is probably most interested in how that therapy compares with others. .Someone whose role is establishing policy in public health is probably interested in broader questions (e.g., Are therapies based on learning theories really superior to other types?).

A category system with different levels of specificity was also necessary for achieving statistical precision. For example, in the complete body of data collected, there are only two effects each for therapies labeled "ego therapy" and "micro-group psychotherapy." Comparing the means for these two therapies results in a statistically unstable comparison. However, grouping ego therapy with other dynamic therapies and micro-group psychotherapy with gestalt therapies (an association indicated by the author) improves the stability of the statistical comparisons between the effects of the two broad therapy types.

The following therapy types were distinguished at one stage in the meta-analysis.

Psychodynamic therapies were those employing concepts such as unconscious motivation, transference relationship, defense mechanisms, structural elements of personality (id, ego, superego), ego development and analysis. Therapies of this type tend to be long in duration, verbal, emotionally evocative, and historic in content. In writing, references are made frequently to Freud and his followers, as well as to Erikson and the neo-Freudian ego psychologists.

Dynamic-eclectic therapies are based on dynamic personality theories, but employ a wider range of therapeutic techniques and interactive concepts than the more orthodox Freudian theory. The influence of Sullivan and Alexander on the training of American psychiatrists is reflected in much dynamic-eclectic therapeutic practice. Therapy frequently consists of evaluative, diagnostic interviews using the medical model, as well as emotional expression and interpretation leading to greater client insight into his personal needs and dynamics.

Adlerian therapy (Adler 1929) is referenced by Dreikurs and others and is based on the never-ending strivings of the personality to escape from a sense of inferiority. Striving for superiority alienates people from love, logic, community life, and social responsibility. Therapy is verbal, evocative, conscious, historic, and interpretive, but aims toward more realistic life styles, heightened social interest and responsibility, and closer interpersonal relationships.

Hypnotherapy (Wolberg 1948) is one type of therapy that uses hypnosis as a tool for increasing relaxation and suggestibility and weakening ego defenses. As described by Lewis Wolberg, hypnotherapy is closely related to psychodynamic theory, suggesting that such neurotic states as anxiety, hysteria, and compulsions are susceptible to this treatment. Psychosomatic conditions with functional causes are also treated by hypnotherapy.

Client-centered or nondirective psychotherapy is associated with Rogers (1942), Truax, Carkhuff, Gendlin, and Axline (nondirective play therapy with children) among others. The key concepts of this therapy include the necessary conditions of therapist congruence, empathy, and unconditional positive regard for the client. By experiencing these conditions, the clients' own potentials for health lead them to self-understanding, acceptance, and reorganized perceptions of self and others.

Gestalt therapy was developed by Perls (Perls, Hefferline, and Goodman 1965) and, like Rogerian therapy, is humanistic and phenomenological in philosophy. The key concept in this therapy is awareness. The healthy person can readily bring into awareness all parts of his personality and apprehend them as an integrated whole. Therapy is a process of heightening awareness through immediate here-and-now emotional and physical experiences and exercises and integrating alienated elements in the person (e.g., healing the "splits" between body and mind, conscious and unconscious). Gestalt therapy is often associated with the human potential movement, marathon and encounter groups, which employ common constructs and processes.

Rational-emotive psychotherapy was developed by Ellis (1962) and rests on a cognitive theory of human personality and therapeutic intervention. The ABC theory holds that human reactions (C) follow from cognitions, ideas, and beliefs (B) about an event, rather than from the event itself (A). The beliefs may be either rational (logical, empirical) or irrational. These irrational beliefs are common for people in distress and pervasive in our society. They include the notion that one must be universally loved, or that failure at a task is utterly catastrophic. The therapist demonstrates the ABC theory in relation to the client's problem, convinces the client of the truth of the theory, confronts the irrational reactions, and teaches the client to confront them himself. The objective of therapy is to replace the irrational, self-defeating cognitions with logical and empirically valid cognitions.

Other cognitive therapies comprise a family of therapeutic theories related to Ellis's rational-emotive psychotherapy in that the place of cognitive processes—faulty beliefs, irrational ideas, logically inconsistent concepts—is central. Theorists in this family include George Kelley (1955), Victor Raimy (1975), and Donald Tosi (1974). They are similar in that the therapies are often active, didactic, directive, sometimes bordering on being hortatory. The therapists confront logical inconsistencies, interpret faulty generalizations and self-defeating behaviors, assign tasks to work on, and generally use suggestion and persuasion to get the client to give up his self-defeating belief system. Although some theorists have incorporated these therapies into behavioral treatments, connections with scientific behaviorism are absent from their primary expositions.

Transactional analysis is primarily associated with Eric Berne (1961) who developed a personality theory based on three ego states—the parent, adult, and child—and the interrelationship of these ego states within a person and between persons. All beliefs, cognitions, and behaviors are under the control of these ego states. Therapy consists of on-going (usually group) diagnosis and interpretation of the structural elements of communication and interaction, with the goal of improved reality testing and complementary transactions.

Reality therapy is identified with William Glasser (1965) and is based on the idea that persons who deny reality are unsuccessful and distressed. Mental illness does not exist—only misbehavior that is based on the denial of reality. Reality is achieved by the fulfillment of the basic needs—to love and be loved and to feel self-worth (success identity). The therapist establishes a personal relationship with the client; attends to present behavior rather than historical events or feelings; interprets behavior in light of the theory; encourages the formation of value judgments about correct behavior and a plan for changing behavior, rejecting excuses for a failure to change, and the development of self-discipline. More realistic ways to fulfill needs are taught to the clients, who feel better if they do better.

Systematic desensitization is a therapy based on scientific behaviorism, primarily associated with Wolpe (1974). In this therapy, anxieties are eliminated by the contiguous pairing of an aversive stimulus with a strong anxiety-competing or anxiety-antagonistic response. The usual procedure is to teach the client deep muscle relaxation (a response antagonistic to anxiety) and then introduce anxiety-provoking stimuli, arranged in hierarchies, in connection with the relaxation until the client can confront and overcome the anxiety directly. The behavioral principles involved are reciprocal inhibition, counterconditioning, or extinction.

Implosive therapy, developed by Stampfl (1970), operates on many problems similar to those addressed by systematic desensitization, and is based on classical conditioning models. The therapist directs the client's imagery so that he is forced to imagine the worst possible manifestation of his fear, and the connection between conditioned stimulus and conditioned response is extinguished.

Operant-respondent behavior therapies are a family of treatment programs in which the scientific laws of learning are invoked. The client is viewed as a passive recipient of reinforcement or conditioning. Proponents include Skinner, Staats, Bijou, and Baer.

Cognitive behavior therapies are a family of therapies in which laws of learning are applied to cognitive processes. Unlike the strictly operant or respondent theories, in cognitive-behavioral therapies, the client is more of an active agent in his own therapy, occasionally even administering the treatment himself (e.g., self-control desensitization). Modeling treatments are included in this family of therapies because the client must identify with the model and adopt the behavior for which the model (but not the client) is reinforced. Among the proponents of cognitive behaviorism are Donald Meichenbaum (1977), Albert Bandura (1968), and Mahoney (1976).

Eclectic-behavioral therapy is a collection of treatments that employ behavioral principles in training programs designed to affect a variety of emotional and behavioral variables. Assertiveness training is the principal therapy, and Lazarus (1972) and Phillips (1956) are among the proponents.

Vocational-personal development counseling involves providing skills and knowledge to clients to facilitate adaptive development. Frequently, a trait and factor approach is used with aptitude and personality testing, diagnosis, prescription, and interaction with the client to facilitate the development of personal, social, educational, and vocational skills. Among the proponents are Theo Volsky (Volsky, Magoon, Norman, and Hoyt 1965), and Williamson (1950).

"Undifferentiated counseling" refers to therapy or counseling that lacks descriptive information and references that would identify it with proponents of theory. It is usually practiced in schools (i.e., the clients were given ordinary counseling), but sometimes is used as a foil against which a more highly valued therapy can be compared. That it cannot be attributed to any single theorist or group of writers is indicative of its lack of theoretical explication.

Placebo treatments were often included in an experimental study of therapeutic effectiveness. Placebos were used to test the effects of client expectancies, therapist attention, and other nonspecific and informal therapeutic effects. The placebo treatments tested in the meta-analysis were the following: relaxation training, attention control, relaxation and suggestion, relaxation and visualization of scenes in an anxiety hierarchy, group discussion, reading and discussing a play, informational meetings, pseudo-desensitization placebo, written information about the phobic object, bibliotherapy, high expectancy placebo, visualization of reinforcing scenes, minimal contact counseling, T-scope therapy, pseudo-treatment control, and lectures.

Therapy types were formed from therapy labels, using the following procedures. In about 40 percent of the studies, there was a direct correspondence between the specific therapy and therapy type. This occurred when there were sufficient numbers of studies of a particular therapy label to produce stable statistical estimates of effects (e.g., rational-emotive psychotherapy, systematic desensitization). Otherwise, the therapy was typed on the correspondence between the experimenter's description of the therapy and key concepts associated with major therapeutic theories. The names of proponents of theory were also used to establish a connection between the label and the type of therapy. For example, a therapy labeled "intensive psychotherapy" was grouped in the psycho-dynamic therapy type, because these key concepts were mentioned in the treatment description: "transference relationship," "ego regression," "analytic insight," and "unconscious motivation." Another therapy labeled cognitive behavior modification was grouped into the cognitive behavioral therapy type, because of several associated concepts and because Donald Meichenbaum, a noted cognitive behaviorist, was referenced for the therapy.

A scale was developed to indicate the degree of confidence in classifying therapy labels into therapy types. The greater the number of concepts, descriptions, and proponents named by the experimenter and associated with a major school of thought, the higher the value assigned to this scale. The highest value (5) was given to a study when the major proponent of a theory actually participated in the study, or when the therapy sessions were recorded and rated for their fit with the theory. The low point of the scale (1) was given to studies when the experimenter provided almost no key concepts or references. On this five-point scale, 15 percent of the studies fell into the highest category, 42 percent in the next highest, 24 percent in the middle category, and 19 percent in the lowest two categories. The mean for the confidence of classification scale was 3.5 (standard deviation = 1.0).

Table 4-4 contains the therapy labels included in two therapy types: Cognitive-behavioral therapy and Behavioral therapy. The remaining lists are located in Appendix 2.

Therapy subclasses were formed from the results of a study of a multidimensional scaling of therapy types. Twenty-five clinicians and counselors enrolled in an advanced seminar in psychotherapy research were used as judges. Ten therapy types (psychoanalytic psychotherapy, psychoanalysis, Adlerian therapy, transactional analysis, rational-emotive psychotherapy, Rogerian, Gestalt therapy, behavior modification, implosive therapy, and systematic desensitization) were studied and discussed for a five-week period. Then the members of the seminar acted as judges in the multidimensional scaling study. Each judge performed a multidimensional rank ordering of the therapies (Torgerson 1958, p. 263), judging similarity among them on what-

Table 4–4.   Therapy labels within two therapy types

Therapy types	
Behavioral therapy	Cognitive behavioral therapy
Behavior modification	Verbal desensitization
Counterconditioning	Attention treatment
Operant conditioning	Contact desensitization
Aversive conditioning	Behavioral self-control
Social-skills training	Self-control desensitization
Token economy	Modeling
Conditional relaxation	Semantic desensitization
Systematic counseling	Cognitive control
Behavioral counseling	Self-modeling
Verbal reinforcement	Covert reinforcement
Self-control	Model reinforcement
Stimulus	Behavioral rehearsal
Precision teaching	Anxiety-management training
Social learning theory	Cognitive behavior modification
	Covert sensitization
	Covert assertion
	Covert modeling

ever basis he chose, articulated or unarticulated, conscious or not. The results of the Shepard (1964) multidimensional scaling appear in Figure 4–1. Three dimensions defined the space for grouping the ten therapies. One can see in the figure four classes of therapies: the cognitive or ego therapies (transactional analysis and rational-emotive psychotherapy) in the front; the dynamic therapies low in the background; the behavioral triad in the upper right; and the pair of relational or humanistic therapies (client-centered and Gestalt).

There were several departures from the therapy subclass grouping developed in the multidimensional study described above. First, there was an insufficient number of studies to carry Freudian therapy as a therapy type. Second, eclectic therapies and hypnotherapy were grouped in the dynamic subclass due to similarities between concepts and techniques described. Third, cognitive behavioral therapies were broken off into a separate subclass from behavior therapy, because of major differences in basic assumptions between the two (i.e., the acknowledgement in cognitive behavioral therapies of substantial organismic involvement). Fourth, rational-emotive psychotherapy was distinguished from other cognitive therapies, such as Kelley's fixed role therapy, cognitive restructuring, rational restructuring, rational stage-directed therapy, and cognitive rehearsal. Fifth, a subclass of developmental therapies was created to account for the addition of studies of school, vocational, and undifferentiated counseling. Following further reading and consultation,* these modifications were made on theoretical grounds.

*The authors wish to thank Dr. Victor C. Raimy, who provided valuable consultation on the therapy classification problem.

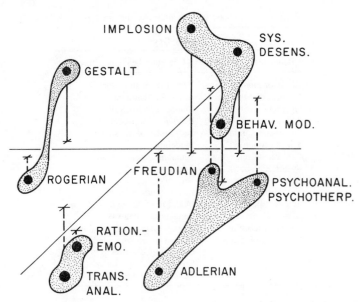

Figure 4-1. Multidimensional scaling of 10 therapies by 25 clinicians and counselors

An even coarser level of analysis necessitated the forming of therapy *classes,* following the multidimensional scaling study and conceptual analysis. The two therapy classes were named behavioral and verbal. The schema for ordering the therapy types, subclasses, and classes is presented in Figure 4-2. Although this scheme is readily defensible, it is arbitrary, since independent verification is impossible. Therefore, other groupings are possible, and the reader with a preference for other groupings will find sufficient data at a finer level of analysis to compare their effects.

Examples of Study Classification. To illustrate the process of classifying the features of the study onto the coding sheet, three examples are presented.

Willis and Edwards (1969) published a study of the effects of systematic desensitization and implosion on mouse phobia. Table 4-5 contains the classifications for this study. The study was coded as follows, for the reasons stated in parentheses.

Krumboltz and Thoresen (1964) published a study of the effect of behavioral counseling on vocational information-seeking behavior. Table 4-6 contains the results of coding this study and the reasons for the coding when judgments were made.

Reardon and Tosi (1976) studied the effects of "rational stage-directed imagery" on the self-concept and adjustment of female delinquents. Table 4-7 contains the coding variables, how the study was classified on these variables, and the basis on which judgments were made.

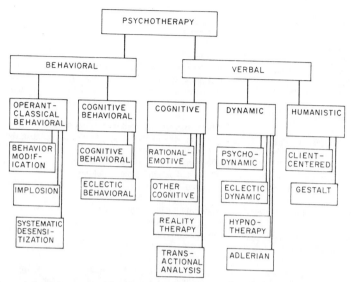

Figure 4-2. Scheme for ordering therapy types, subclasses, and classes

Data Analysis

The data from the coding forms were punched onto computer cards and transferred to permanent files. Data were analyzed, using the Statistical Package for the Social Sciences (SPSS). Analysis proceeded in three steps: (1) transforming data from control-referenced studies; (2) analysis of the full set of data; and (3) analysis of statistically controlled data.

Step One: Control-Referenced Effects

In the effort to translate all study findings into comparable terms, several problems arose. The problem of nonmetric or dichotomous outcomes that were rescued by the probit transformation has already been mentioned. A second major problem concerned experiments where two or more treatments were compared, but no untreated control group was included. If these kinds of inconsistency had not been compensated for, then the large body of literature was in danger of fracturing into several separate and seemingly incomparable portions, and much would have been lost.

When experiments compared two (or more) therapies but no control group, a method of calculating effect sizes was used that came to be called *control-referencing* of effects. The logic of this approach can be explained best, perhaps, by means of a simple example. Suppose that an experiment was performed in which therapy A was compared to an untreated control group, and an effect size of $ES_A = 1.00$ was found. Likewise, an experiment comparing therapy B and an untreated control group gave $ES_B = 0.80$. All that

Table 4-5.   Classification of a study by Willis and Edwards (1969)

Publication date	1969
Publication form	Journal
Training of experimenter	Psychology (judged from institutional affiliation)
Blinding	Experimenter did therapy (judged from tone of the report)
Diagnosis	Mouse phobic, simple phobic (no indication given of neurotic symptoms other than anxiety to rodent)
Hospitalization	None
Intelligence	Above average (inferred from client status as college student)
Client-therapist similarity	Very similar (inferred from client degree of disturbance and status as college student)
Age	20 (inferred from college student status)
Percentage male	0% (stated as all-female population)
Solicitation of client	Solicited by experimenter (stated as solicited based on extreme pre-test scores)
Assignment of clients to groups	Random (stated as matched groups on pre-test measure, then random assignment to 3 groups)
Assignment of therapist	Nonrandom (no therapist differences produced in outcomes)
Experimental mortality	0% in all groups at termination; 4% in all groups at follow-up (stated)
Internal validity	High (based on random assignment and low mortality, although the design suffered from threats to internal validity of testing and instrumentation)
Simultaneous comparison	Yes (systematic desensitization against implosion against control)
Type of treatment	(1) Systematic desensitization—behavioral subclass (2) Implosion—behavioral subclass
Confidence of classification	Rated 4 (based on inclusion of key concept and references and the commonality from experiment to experiment using these therapies)
Allegiance	Write up showed no general favor toward either treatment over the other
Modality	Individual treatment (stated)
Location	College facility (stated)
Duration	3 hours over 3 weeks (stated that the average client required 5 sessions of 25 minutes for relaxation training and hierarchy presentation; exact duration had to be estimated from these figures)
Therapist experience	5 years (no information given, coding conventions allow 5 years for Ph.D.-level psychologists)
Outcome	3 outcome measures were used: the Fear Survey Schedule (FSS, total), the Fear Thermometer, and the Behavior Avoidance Measure (BAT). The result from the Fear Thermometer paralleled those of the other two and thus were omitted. Follow-up data were reported in such a way that effect sizes were impossible to calculate. Both the BAT and the FSS were classified as measures of fear-anxiety. They were given immediately after therapy. They were rated as 5 on the reactivity scale because the scales were used as part of the treatment; the behavioral measure was taken by the nonblinded experimenter.
Effect size	Statistics were reported in the form of mean differences between groups, and F statistics from a 3-factor ANOVA. The effect sizes were as follows:

	FSS	*BAT*
Systematic desensitization	1.71	.07
Implosion	2.12	.48

Table 4-6. Classification of a study by Krumboltz and Thoresen (1964)

Publication date	1964
Publication form	Journal
Training of experimenter	Education (known by institutional affiliation)
Blinding	Experimenter (evaluators) did not do therapy, but did know group composition (no information about blinding of evaluators was given)
Diagnosis	Vocationally undecided (students who asked for counseling about future plans, grouped in "neurotic" diagnostic type)
Hospitalization	None
Intelligence	Average (estimated, in the absence of other information)
Client-therapist similarity	Moderately similar (ages differed, but socioeconomic status of community indicated similarity)
Age	16 (high school juniors)
Percentage male	50% (sample stratified by client sex)
Solicitation of clients	Clients volunteered after being given notice that counseling would be available
Assignment of client	Random (stated)
Assignment of therapist	Random
Experimental mortality	No subjects lost from any group (stated)
Internal validity	High
Simultaneous comparison	Yes (2 treatments groups and placebo group compared against control)
Type of treatment	(1) Model reinforcement—Cognitive behavioral subclass (students were shown tapes of models being reinforced for information-seeking behavior, but students were not reinforced personally)
	(2) Verbal reinforcement—Behavioral subclass (counselors verbally reinforced clients for production of information-seeking statements)
	(3) Film discussion—Placebo (clients saw and discussed a film, to control for nonspecific effects of counselor attention)
Confidence of classification	Rated 5 (highest) (because of thoroughness of description, knowledge of experimenters' theory and previous work)
Allegiance	Equal allegiance paid to each of treatments. No allegiance to placebo condition
Modality	Mixed (students were randomly assigned to individual and group treatments, but modality did not interact with outcome, so the two modes were combined for the meta-analysis)
Location	School (stated)
Duration	2 hours, 2 weeks (2 sessions, time estimated)
Experience of therapists	2 years (estimated by status in counselor-training program plus training for this experiment)
Outcome	Two outcome measures were used: frequency and variety of information-seeking behavior as estimated from responses to structured interview questions. Reactivity was rated "4" for both, because measures were self-report of clients to nonblind evaluators. These were classified as measures of vocational or personal development
Effect size	Statistics reported as treatment means and mean squares from a 4-factor analysis of variance

(continued)

Table 4-6—*Continued*

The effect sizes were as follows:

	Frequency (of information-seeking behavior)	Variety (of information-seeking behavior)
Model reinforcement	1.29	0.77
Verbal reinforcement	1.05	1.39
Placebo	0.21	0.27

one knows about the effects of therapies A and B vis-à-vis untreated controls at this point is that they are 1.00 and 0.80, respectively. An experiment is encountered in which therapies A and B are compared without a control group; suppose that the results favor therapy A by two-tenths standard deviation, i.e., $ES_{A-B} = 0.20$. It so happens in this instance that ES_{A-B} is perfectly consistent with ES_A and ES_B, and it seems eminently reasonable to decompose ES_{A-B} into $ES'_A = 1.00$ and $ES'_B = 0.80$, these being called control-referenced effects, and being consistent with the results of each of the three studies. If, however, ES_{A-B} had been equal to 0.10, the three data would not have been perfectly consistent. In this case—the expected case—it would seem reasonable to divide the inconsistency equally between therapies A and B and let $ES'_A = 0.95$ and $ES'_B = 0.85$. These control-referenced values preserve the difference between A and B that was observed in the experiment and are as close to the previously observed ES_A and ES_B as possible. The reasoning is essentially the same when ES_A and ES_B are estimates based on the average effects for all experiments in which A and B, respectively, were compared with untreated controls.*

Step Two

Meta-analysis is the analysis of analyses. The effect sizes, calculated from the statistical results of separate studies, are treated as the dependent variable in the meta-analysis. Independent variables are the characteristics of the study, the clients, the treatment, and the outcomes.

The unit of analysis is the effect size rather than the study. Four hundred seventy-five studies yielded 1,766 effect sizes, averaging 3.7 effect sizes per study. The usual format for tables of results was to list the values of the independent variable and then the average effect size ($\overline{ES}$), the standard error of the effect size ($\sigma_{\overline{ES}}$), and the number of effect sizes on which $\overline{ES}$ and $\sigma_{\overline{ES}}$ were based.

---

*A more mathematically rigorous development of the problem proceeds along the following lines: given $\overline{ES}_A$, $\overline{ES}_B$ and $\overline{ES}_{A-B}$, find ES'_A and ES'_B, the control-referenced effects corresponding to ES_{A-B}, such that ES'_A and ES'_B satisfy what might be called the conditions of preservation ($\overline{ES}_{A-B} = ES'_A - ES'_B$) and of equal division of error ($ES'_A - \overline{ES}_A = \overline{ES}_B - ES'_B$). These conditions establish two independent linear equations in two unknowns, for which the solution will be easily obtained: $ES'_A = (\overline{ES}_{A-B} + \overline{ES}_A + \overline{ES}_B)/2$ and $ES'_B = ES'_A - \overline{ES}_{A-B}$.

Table 4-7.   Classification of a study by Reardon and Tosi (1976)

Publication date	1976
Publication form	Journal (although the paper was available in unpublished form, both as a dissertation and paper read at a professional meeting, it had been accepted for journal publication)
Training of experimenter	Psychology (inferred from department affiliation)
Blinding	Experimenter was therapist (judged from report)
Diagnosis	High stress delinquents (experimenter's description), delinquent or felon
Hospitalization	None
Intelligence	Average (estimated, in the absence of other information)
Client-therapist similarity	Moderately dissimilar (because of students' identification as delinquent, age and sex differences)
Age	16 (stated)
Percentage male	0% (female population)
Solicitation	Self-presentation in response to advertised services (stated)
Assignment of clients	Random (stated)
Assignment of therapists	Random (stated)
Experimental mortality	0% from all groups
Internal validity	High
Simultaneous comparison	Treatment and placebo compared against control
Type of treatment	(1) "Rational-stage directed imagery" (subclass-cognitive) (hypnosis or intensive muscle relaxation used as aids to induce rational, cognitive restructuring)
	(2) Placebo—relaxation and suggestion to feel better
Confidence of classification	Rated 4 (many key concepts associated with Ellis, Kelley, and Raimy, plus personal communication with authors)
Allegiance	Definite allegiance toward the therapy (inferred from tone of report)
Modality	Group (stated)
Location	Residential facility (stated)
Duration	6 hours over 6 weeks (stated)
Therapist experience	3 years (inferred from status as doctoral candidates)
Outcome	Two outcomes were measured by experimenter: Tennessee Self-Concept Scale (TSCS) and the Multiple Affect Adjective Checklist (MAACL) (MAACL not included because of insufficient data reporting) TSCS rated as a 4 in reactivity (self-report on measure similar to treatment) Measure was taken immediately after therapy and 2 weeks later.
Effect size	Means from TSCS (total) were obtained from a figure. Estimates of standard deviation were made using probability values. Effect sizes are as follows:

	0 weeks post	2 weeks post
Rational-stage directed imagery	1.59	1.59
Placebo	0.74	−0.20

It is a simple matter to argue that it is unwise to collapse or coalesce all outcome measures in a study into a single measure of success or failure. A study may measure outcomes along a broad front of possible effects, some of them worked toward ardently in the therapy and others measured on the pretense of possibly picking up some remote side-effect.

But once the decision is made to permit as many measures of effect for a study as there are outcome measures taken, a host of problems—less serious than those that led to this juncture, one hopes—ensues. Studies in which wide-scale but indiscriminate testing took place may take on inordinate importance in the total body of data. Hypothetically, a study that examined a weak therapy but measured on ten outcome scales would receive ten times the weight of a study that examined a strong therapy but measured a single outcome. There are a few ways around such problems: (1) when outcomes are distinguished by type (e.g., measures of fear and anxiety, measures of self-concept), then the redundancy of studies in collections of effect sizes is far less prevalent and less severe; (2) multiple outcomes from single studies can be coalesced according to well-defined rules, provided that they have been separately calculated and recorded in the first place; thus, several outcomes would be aggregated into one outcome poststudy; (3) we have chosen to work with a body of data that preserves all of the distinctions made by the original investigator; thus, a single study might contribute one or several measures of effect size, *ES,* to the total picture. Such a body of data is "lumpy," to use the argot of statisticians; each datum is not independent of each other datum, and precisely how many "degrees of freedom" exist in the complete set of data is a question to which even the best informed judges would likely give quite different answers. In our opinion, the most reasonable recourse when reporting an aggregated finding is to begin with the most finely differentiated body of data possible (viz., each study yields as many effects as it took measurements) and report both the number of effects and the number of studies from which they arose. Those reviewers who choose to aggregate all results so that there is one outcome per study do no better when they, usually unwittingly, disregard the links and dependencies among studies that are performed by the same researcher or at the same laboratory, and the like.

Using the data from all studies, several analyses were performed. First, descriptive statistics on the characteristics of the data were obtained. It was necessary to determine, for example, the proportions of effect sizes falling into different values of the independent variables (e.g., interval validity of study, therapist experience, etc.) as a guide for further statistical analyses, as well as a check on external validity. That is, the reader must base his judgment about the generalizability of these experimental findings to the actual practice of psychotherapy by comparing the characteristics of both. Second, all continuous variables, including effect size, were intercorrelated. Third, discrete variables were cross-tabulated (e.g., therapies with outcomes, diagnoses with outcomes).

Fourth, average effect sizes ($\overline{ES}$) were obtained for different values of all the independent variables. For example, average effect sizes were obtained for each diagnostic type, each outcome type, each level of internal validity and reactivity. In this way, it is possible to determine, using the studies as a whole, the comparative effects of clients, treatments, and outcomes. Cautions in interpreting these comparisons must be noted, however. A comparison of the magnitude of effect associated with long-term (twenty or more sessions) versus short-term (ten or fewer sessions) therapy, using the meta-analysis data, is not an experimental comparison. Therapies of longer duration are likely to be used with more seriously disturbed clients. Certain types of therapy tend to be shorter and have more modest goals. These and other factors must be rival hypotheses for the interpretation of the difference in effect that is due to therapy duration. Additional controls over different rival hypotheses were exercised in Step Three of the data analysis.

Step Three

Statistical controls were instituted to estimate more accurately the comparative effectiveness of different therapies. Three types of statistical controls were used—(1) cross-classification of independent variables, (2) multiple regression analyses, and (3) the "same experiment" analysis.

Cross-classification of independent variables was used to determine, for example, the average effect of each therapy type on clients in various diagnostic categories (e.g., the effect of psychodynamic therapy on neurotics versus psychotics, the effect of client-centered therapy on measures of self-esteem versus measures of fear and anxiety). Complete cross-classification was impossible, due to the limited number of effect sizes within many interesting variables. For example, the effect of Adlerian therapy with neurotics versus psychotics on measures of adjustment versus anxiety was impossible to estimate, because of the small number of effect sizes on which such a comparison would be based. This is a general problem in reviewing research, not limited to meta-analytic procedures.

Multiple regression analysis was performed on the data as a whole, within classes and subclasses. The dependent variable was the effect size and the independent variables were determined by studying the intercorrelations generated in Step II of the analysis. Using multiple regression allowed the examination of the effect of each independent variable on effect size, with all other independent variables held constant.

The most important analysis was the "same-experiment study," which involved only the subset of studies in which an experimenter compared, *within the study,* the effects of a behavioral therapy and a verbal therapy. For example, an experimenter might have compared three groups—one which received eclectic psychotherapy (verbal therapy class), one which received systematic desensitization (behavior therapy class), and one which received no treatment (control group).

Within the "same experiment" study, all variables unrelated to the therapy would be the same for both therapy groups, i.e., the same measure would be used for both groups, they would be treated for the same length of time, with therapists of approximately the same degree of ability, and the diagnostic type would be the same for both therapies. All other preexisting client variables would be comparable in the three groups by virtue of random assignment or matching. Thus, the comparative effectiveness of therapies could be more accurately estimated in the "same experiment" study than in the data as a whole. However, one important variable could not be controlled in the "same experiment" study and that was the allegiance of the experimenter. Often one therapy in a study was obviously the favorite; the other, the also-ran.

This subset of studies was identified and average effect sizes were determined for therapy classes, broken down by diagnostic type and outcome type. Comparisons arising from the "same-experiment study" are still not experimental comparisons, since clients are not randomly assigned to *experiments*. However, several major variables that confound the interpretation of therapy effects can be ruled out with this analysis.

....

Chapter 5

Findings of the Psychotherapy Meta-analysis

In this chapter, findings of the meta-analysis of psychotherapy studies will be reported. The analysis was extensive; it lasted more than two years and resulted in literally thousands of tabulations and data summaries. Only a few of the most pertinent findings can be reported in the space available here. When a simple analysis addressed a question nearly as well as a complex analysis, the choice almost always favored the former.

The findings are organized into several broad categories. First, the general findings are reported. The questions addressed by these analyses are basic and simple: Is psychotherapy effective compared to no treatment? How large an effect does it produce? The next set of findings are addressed to questions of the relative efficacy of different specific psychotherapies and types of psychotherapy. For example, has implosive therapy been shown to be more effective than systematic desensitization; or do behavioral psychotherapies produce larger effects than verbal therapies? These questions are not only answered in general, but the comparison of specific therapies and types of therapy is also reported for different types of client (e.g., phobics, neurotics, psychotics) and outcome (e.g., anxiety, self-esteem, work and school achievement). It is important to note that such comparisons frequently lack the kind of control or internal validity that the reader may be accustomed to in treatment and control group comparisons. A particular table will invite the reader to compare the average effect of rational-emotive and implosive therapies in the treatment of fear and anxiety, but the circumstances of the two sets of studies are likely to differ. It is unnecessary and wasteful to regard the circumstances as incomparable; they are simply different in any number of relevant or irrelevant ways. The studies of rational-emotive therapy may have a greater proportion of test anxiety cases, whereas, the implosive therapy studies may be more concerned with rat phobias; or the implosive therapy clients might be slightly older, on the average, than the RET clients. These inequalities are certain to result when studies are done by different investigators under different circumstances. Extraneous influences can be controlled by randomization *within* a study comparing RET and untreated controls; but the comparison of RET's effect with the effect of implosive therapy in a separate study is confounded by a number of potential threats. Why report potentially confounded and invidious comparisons among types of therapy then? Because it is quite unclear how serious the confoundings are; to ignore all comparisons would surely result in discarding enormous amounts of important data. Moreover, experienced investigators and scholars can sense with some confidence the direction and importance of these inequalities. For example, the studies that compare implosive and systematic desensitization therapies are largely carried out in similar circumstances with similar types of client. If the difference in their effects is larger than that between systematic desensitization and hypnotherapy, say, then something credible has been learned even from a confounded comparison.

Leaving the problem of confounded comparisons at this point would be unsatisfactory. Several analyses are aimed at exercising better control over the comparison of the effects of different therapies. Three principal means exist for controlling extraneous inequalities in the comparisons of the studies. Extraneous variance is reduced by cross-classifying two variables. The effects of each therapy may be calculated for each diagnosis, for example. In this way, diagnosis is equated. Regression analysis can be employed to equate statistically two sets of studies that differ in various respects. For example, suppose ten studies of client-centered therapy and fifteen studies of reality therapy differ in that the latter used clients of average age twenty-five and the former of age eighteen. The effects of therapy can be correlated with age and an estimate obtained for the effects of each therapy for twenty-year-olds, say. This approach is the equivalent, in most respects, to the analysis of covariance. The third method of control is probably best. One can select from the entire set of data only those studies in which, for example, client-centered and reality therapy are compared under identical (or randomly equivalent) circumstances; this is accomplished by finding those experiments in which the two therapies are compared in the *same* experiment. For this body of data, called ''same experiment data,'' the two therapies are evaluated under equivalent conditions (client age, diagnosis, length of treatment, etc.). Equating the conditions of studies by ex post facto regression adjustment and by selection of the ''same experiment'' cases is the rationale behind the third set of findings to be reported.

The fourth and final group of findings reported in this chapter addresses questions of the relationship of the effects of psychotherapy to many features and conditions of the clients, their problems, and the treatment they receive. Attention is also given to methodological concerns about how the findings of studies may be related to the techniques used in the study, where the study was published, and the like.

The second general caution concerns external validity. This is the question of the extent to which the findings of research can be generalized to some population of interest. The question pertinent here is to what extent can the results of psychotherapy-outcome research be generalized and applied to the practice of psychotherapy. Will a relationship reported in this chapter, such as the correlation between duration of therapy and amount of therapeutic effect, also reveal itself in therapy conducted in "real" situations?

Determining the external validity of research is a responsibility shared by the researcher and the reader. The reader must study the context in which the research took place; the subjects involved; the description of the treatment, setting, and (in this case) therapists. These characteristics of the research must then be compared with the same characteristics in the applied setting. The reader makes an inference about the degree of similarity, the important points of difference, and then the applicability of the research finding.

The characteristics of therapy in the research literature analyzed here are tabulated in Appendix 3 and can be compared with the characteristics of therapy as it is actually practiced. Therapy conducted for the purpose of research may tend to be of shorter duration, may involve clients with less serious presenting problems, may be conducted by less experienced therapists, and may be conducted more often in academic settings. Generalizing the findings of the meta-analysis should be qualified accordingly.

The Overall Effects of Psychotherapy

Four hundred seventy-five controlled studies of psychotherapy yielded 1,766 effect-size measures. The average of effect-size measures was 0.85 (with a standard error of 0.03).* The difference in the means between groups receiving psychotherapy of any type and untreated control groups was 0.85 standard deviation units averaged across all outcome measures.

A 0.85 standard deviation effect can be understood more clearly by referring it to percents of populations of persons. Suppose that along some measure of well-being or mental health, persons are distributed according to the familiar bell-shaped normal distribution. If two separate distributions are drawn for those who receive therapy and those who do not, the distributions will be separated by 0.85 standard deviations at their means or centers. This difference is illustrated in Figure 5-1. Notice in particular that the average or median of the psychotherapy curve is located above 80 percent of the area under the control group curve. This relationship indicates that the average person who receives therapy is better off at the end of it than 80 percent of the persons who do not. Stated differently, but equivalently, the average person, who would score at the 50th percentile of the untreated control population,

*The standard error was calculated by multiplying the standard deviation of effect sizes by the square root of the number of effect sizes. It measures the unreliability of the average in an inferential statistical sense. The standard error and its interpretation are discussed in more detail below, in connection with Table 5-1, where it plays a more prominent role.

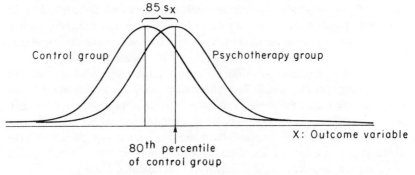

Figure 5-1. Representation of the effect of psychotherapy on any outcome (based on data from 475 controlled studies)

could expect to rise to the 80th percentile with respect to that population after receiving psychotherapy.

Little evidence was found for the alleged existence of the negative effects of psychotherapy. Only 9 percent of the effect-size measures were negative (where the mean for the control group was higher than the mean for the psychotherapy group). Nor was there convincing evidence in the dispersions of the treated groups that some members became better and some worse as a result of psychotherapy.

The estimate of the effectiveness of psychotherapy as 0.85 standard deviation units is a conservative figure, since it includes placebo treatments as well as undifferentiated counseling. Many scholars in the field would not consider these two treatments as legitimate forms of therapy. The average effect of therapy, excluding placebo treatments, is 0.89. Excluding both placebo treatments and undifferentiated counseling, the average effect rises to 0.93 standard deviation units.

Even the conservative estimate of psychotherapy is large compared to the size of effect produced by many experimental interventions in the social sciences. In elementary school, the effects of nine months of instruction on reading achievement is about 0.67 standard deviation units. The differences in achievement caused by decreasing the size of a school classroom from thirty to fifteen children is about 0.15 standard deviation units (Glass and Smith 1979). The increment in mathematics achievement caused by the introduction of computer-based instruction is 0.40 standard deviation units (Hartley 1977). The effect of television on antisocial behavior is 0.34 standard deviation units (Hearold 1979).

Compared with experimental interventions studied in the social sciences, the effect of psychotherapy is clearly substantial. Published conclusions about the absence of benefits from psychotherapy are incorrect; they are based on unrepresentative samples of the research literature or unsophisticated methods for deriving meaningful information from it.

The Effects of Different Types of Therapy

Hundreds of volumes have been devoted to the careful delineation of theories and schools of thought in psychotherapy and the features that distinguish one from the others. Advocates of each new school of psychotherapy assert that its benefits are superior to those of competing therapies. These claims are seldom supported by data demonstrating superiority.

Table 5-1 contains the average effect size for each of eighteen therapy types, with the standard deviation of the effects, the standard errors of these averages, and the number of effect sizes included in the averages. There are significant variations in the magnitude of effect produced by the therapies studied; the average effects range from a high of 2.38 standard deviation units to a low of 0.14.

The standard error of the mean is a measure of the sampling instability of an average. Different small samples from the same population would not give exactly the same average; the standard error of the mean reflects how variable the different sample averages might be. If the effect sizes that are averaged in any table here are thought of as a sample from a population, then the standard error of the mean, $\sigma_{\overline{ES}}$, can be used to determine how far the observed average might deviate from the population average. The odds favor 2-to-1 the conclusion that the sample average will be no more than $\sigma_{\overline{ES}}$ away from the population average. Other things equal, small standard errors are better than

Table 5-1. Average, standard deviation, standard error, and number of effects for each therapy type

Type of therapy (arbitrary order)	Average effect size ($\overline{ES}$)	Standard deviation	Standard error of mean σ_{ES}	Number[a] of effects (n)
1. Psychodynamic therapy	0.69	0.50	0.05	108
2. Dynamic-eclectic therapy	0.89	0.86	0.08	103
3. Adlerian therapy	0.62	0.68	0.18	15
4. Hypnotherapy	1.82	1.15	0.26	19
5. Client-centered therapy	0.62	0.87	0.07	150
6. Gestalt therapy	0.64	0.91	0.11	68
7. Rational-emotive therapy	0.68	0.54	0.08	50
8. Other cognitive therapies	2.38	2.05	0.27	57
9. Transactional analysis	0.67	0.91	0.17	28
10. Reality therapy	0.14	0.38	0.13	9
11. Systematic desensitization	1.05	1.58	0.08	373
12. Implosion	0.68	0.70	0.09	60
13. Behavior modification	0.73	0.67	0.05	201
14. Cognitive-behavioral therapy	1.13	0.83	0.07	127
15. Eclectic-behavioral therapy	0.89	0.75	0.12	37
16. Vocational-personal development	0.65	0.58	0.08	59
17. Undifferentiated counseling	0.28	0.55	0.06	97
18. Placebo treatment	0.56	0.77	0.05	200
Total	0.85	1.25	0.03	1761

[a] The number of effects, not the number of studies; 475 studies produced 1,761 effects, or about 3.7 effects per study.

large ones. In Table 5–1, for example, the sample mean for psychodynamic therapy should be nearer its true mean than should the sample mean for hypnotherapy be near its true mean, since the standard error of the latter is five times as great as the former. The standard error can be used as a means for examining the observed difference, say, between the average effects produced by types of therapy and judging whether that difference is reliable—that is, worthy of interpretation as a true difference rather than merely a random fluctuation. Throughout this chapter, a mean difference equal to two standard errors was used as a guideline for interpreting nonrandom differences between two effects.

The highest average effect size was produced by the cognitive therapies (line 8) other than, but similar to, Albert Ellis's rational-emotive psychotherapy. The therapy labels in this group included systematic rational restructuring, rational stage-directed therapy, cognitive rehearsal, and fixed-role therapy. Major proponents of theories in this group included Victor Raimy, George Kelley, and Donald Tosi. Techniques of this therapy include active persuasion and confrontation of dysfunctional ideas and beliefs. The second highest average effect size was 1.82 standard deviation units, produced by hypnotherapy (line 4). This type of therapy employed hypnosis, obviously, as a method for dealing with such problems as anxiety hysteria, compulsion neurosis (Wolberg 1948), as well as asthmatic reactions. Cognitive-behavioral therapies (line 14) such as modeling, self-reinforcement, covert sensitization, self-control desensitization and behavioral rehearsal were third highest on the ranking of therapeutic effectiveness, having an average effect size of 1.13 standard deviation units. Systematic desensitization (line 11), primarily used to alleviate phobias, was next highest, with an average effect size of 1.05. An average effect size of 0.89 standard deviation units was achieved by dynamic-eclectic (line 2) and eclectic-behavioral therapies (line 15). Several therapy types yielded average effect sizes, of similar magnitude, clustering around two-thirds of a standard deviation; none was significantly different from the others. These therapies were psychodynamic therapy ($\overline{ES} = 0.69$), Adlerian therapy ($\overline{ES} = 0.62$), client-centered therapy ($\overline{ES} = 0.62$), Gestalt therapy ($\overline{ES} = 0.64$), rational-emotive therapy ($\overline{ES} = 0.68$), transactional analysis ($\overline{ES} = 0.67$), implosion ($\overline{ES} = 0.68$), behavior modification ($\overline{ES} = 0.73$), and vocational-personal development counseling ($\overline{ES} = 0.65$).

Placebo treatments (e.g., relaxation training, pseudodesensitization therapy, minimum-contact attention control groups) yielded an average effect size of 0.56 standard deviation units. A direct comparison of this placebo effect with the therapies mentioned in the preceding paragraph would be invidious. Placebo treatments were most often used in studies of desensitization, implosion, and cognitive behavioral treatments of monosymptomatic anxieties. In such studies, the effect of the psychotherapy was about twice as great as the effect of the placebo treatment. If this two-to-one ratio of therapy to placebo effect held for the entire body of data, then line 18 in Table 5-1 would be closer to 0.4, i.e., half of 0.85, whereas, it is now closer to 0.6.

Two average effects stand out because they are small. The effect of undifferentiated counseling (i.e., therapy reported without descriptive information or references to a theory) had an average effect size of 0.28. The smallest effect size in the table is that associated with reality therapy ($\overline{ES} = 0.14$). However, only one controlled evaluation of this therapy could be located. Nine effect sizes were produced from this study. The resultant data are too sparse to support a comparison with the other therapy types and will not be interpreted further.

The foregoing comparison of the effects of different types of therapy is raw and uncontrolled. Populations of persons seeking psychological help do not randomly sort themselves into the different types of therapy. Some forms of therapy are even specifically designed for a narrow range of psychological problems. Some therapies tend to cater to less seriously disturbed clients. Professionals in hospitals prefer some therapies over others for use with seriously disturbed inpatients. Thus, it can be seen that the differences in therapeutic effect reported in Table 5-1 reflect variation in therapeutic effectiveness *plus all other* variations in client characteristics, diagnostic types, therapist experience, and choice of outcome criteria.

Three general strategies were used to control statistically the variables other than type of therapy itself, so that a more accurate view of differences among therapies could be obtained. The first of these was cross-tabulation of therapy types with diagnosis and outcome type. The second was multiple regression analysis, and the third was analysis of experiments in which one class of therapy was directly compared with another class.

Reducing Confounding by Cross-Classification

Do the average effects produced by each type of therapy vary with the type of client treated? Contained in Table 5-2 are the average effects of specific therapies cross-classified by client diagnosis. Sufficient numbers of effects were available for only part of the cross-classification. When a cell was based on fewer than ten effect-size measures, it was judged to be too unstable to be meaningful and was eliminated from the table. Thus, the effects of eleven therapies on three client diagnoses—neurotics or true phobics, simple phobics, and psychotics—are shown. Other therapy-diagnosis combinations had too few cases to permit inspection.

Several therapies produced about the same magnitude of effect for the three diagnostic types. Psychodynamic therapies, client-centered therapy, vocational-personal development counseling, cognitive-behavioral therapy, and implosive therapy produced the same magnitude of effect whether the client was neurotic, phobic, or psychotic. Both placebo treatments and systematic desensitization were more effective with simple (monosymptomatic) phobics than they were with neurotics. Behavior modification was more effective with psychotics and simple phobics than with neurotics. Rational-emotive psychotherapy was more effective with neurotics than with simple phobics. Dynamic-eclectic therapies were more effective with neurotics than with psychotics.

When effect size produced by different therapies was broken down further by the type of outcome measured in the study, interesting differences emerged. Table 5–3 shows how the size of effect of therapy varies, depending

Table 5-2.   Average, standard error, and number of effect sizes for three diagnostic types, produced by eleven therapy types

		Diagnostic type		
Therapy types		Neurotics/true phobics	Simple phobics	Psychotics
Psychodynamic	$\overline{ES}$	0.69	0.84	0.90
	$\sigma_{\overline{ES}}\ (n_{ES})$	0.05 (66)	0.06 (13)	0.16 (20)
Client-centered	$\overline{ES}$	0.63	a	0.51
	$\sigma_{\overline{ES}}\ (n_{ES})$	0.10 (97)		0.13 (12)
Systematic desensitization	$\overline{ES}$	0.92	1.12	a
	$\sigma_{\overline{ES}}\ (n_{ES})$	0.07 (87)	0.12 (246)	
Rational-emotive psychotherapy	$\overline{ES}$	1.11	0.54	a
	$\sigma_{\overline{ES}}\ (n_{ES})$	0.16 (11)	0.10 (28)	
Other cognitive	$\overline{ES}$	a	2.68	a
	$\sigma_{\overline{ES}}\ (n_{ES})$		0.36 (29)	
Behavior modification	$\overline{ES}$	0.61	0.94	0.81
	$\sigma_{\overline{ES}}\ (n_{ES})$	0.08 (84)	0.17 (21)	0.05 (24)
Dynamic-eclectic	$\overline{ES}$	0.88	a	0.54
	$\sigma_{\overline{ES}}\ (n_{ES})$	0.12 (44)		0.10 (30)
Vocational-personal development	$\overline{ES}$	0.66	0.43	0.60
	$\sigma_{\overline{ES}}\ (n_{ES})$	0.24 (14)	0.12 (12)	0.08 (20)
Cognitive-behavioral	$\overline{ES}$	0.92	1.66	a
	$\sigma_{\overline{ES}}\ (n_{ES})$	0.15 (44)	0.39 (64)	
Implosive therapy	$\overline{ES}$	0.96	0.59	a
	$\sigma_{\overline{ES}}\ (n_{ES})$	0.15 (12)	0.11 (44)	
Placebo	$\overline{ES}$	0.43	0.69	0.54
	$\sigma_{\overline{ES}}\ (n_{ES})$	0.06 (51)	0.10 (99)	0.06 (14)

a Cells with fewer than 10 effect sizes were eliminated from the table.

Table 5-3. Averages and number of effect sizes for six types of outcome produced by eight types of therapy

Therapy type		Outcome[a]					
		Fear/ anxiety	Self-esteem	Global adjustment	Emotional-somatic	Social	Work/ school
1. Psycho-dynamic	$\overline{ES}$	0.53	[b]	0.77	[b]	[b]	[b]
	n_{ES}	18		57			
2. Client-centered	$\overline{ES}$	0.63	0.85	0.64	[b]	0.43	0.54
	n_{ES}	12	30	43		18	24
3. Systematic desensitization	$\overline{ES}$	1.21	[b]	0.97	1.01	[b]	0.44
	n_{ES}	255		29	18		44
4. Cognitive	$\overline{ES}$	2.50	[b]	2.80	[b]	[b]	[b]
	n_{ES}	31		12			
5. Behavior modification	$\overline{ES}$	0.83	0.20	0.96	0.77	0.41	0.49
	n_{ES}	30	10	48	18	18	23
6. Dynamic-eclectic	$\overline{ES}$	0.97	[b]	0.67	[b]	[b]	1.78
	n_{ES}	23		42			10
7. Cognitive-behavioral	$\overline{ES}$	1.79	[b]	0.91	[b]	[b]	0.40
	n_{ES}	66		10			40
8. Placebo	$\overline{ES}$	0.66	[b]	0.60	0.67	0.24	0.50
	n_{ES}	105		27	13	12	13

[a] See Chapter 4 for a description of outcome categories.
[b] This cell had fewer than 10 effect sizes; thus it was eliminated from the table.

on what type of outcome was observed.* Regardless of what type of outcome measure was selected by the researcher, psychodynamic (line 1) and cognitive (line 4) therapies produced about the same magnitude of effect. Client-centered therapies produced relatively larger effects on measures of self-esteem and relatively smaller effects on measures of social behavior, with other effects between. Systematic desensitization produced about the same magnitude of effect for all measurement categories except measures of achievement, for which the effects of that therapy were much smaller. On measures of fear or anxiety, global measures and ratings of adjustment, and

*Examples of specific measures that fell into twelve outcome types were the following: fear-anxiety (Test Anxiety Scale, Behavioral Approach Test); self-esteem (Tennessee Self-Concept Scale, ratings of self-acceptance, real-ideal self-correlation); global adjustment (therapist ratings of improvement, symptom severity, Beck Depression Inventory); life indicators of adjustment (hospitalization, employment status, discharge from hospital); personality traits (Minnesota Multiphasic Personality Inventory, California Personality Inventory, Edwards Personal Preference Schedule); emotional-somatic (asthmatic symptoms, use of medication, migraine symptom improvement); addiction (number of cigarettes smoked, alcholic recidivism, use of drugs); social behaviors (sociometric status, social effectiveness, acceptance of others); sociopathic behaviors (probation violation, criminal contacts, correction of sexual deviance); work-school achievement (grade point average, completion of educational program, work success ratings); vocational-personal development (vocational realism, Adaptive Behavior Scale, Study Habits Inventory); and physiological measures of stress (Palmar Sweat Index, Galvanic Skin Response, pulse rate).

Table 5-4.   Averages, standard deviations, standard errors of means, and numbers of effect sizes for six therapy subclasses[a]

Therapy subclass	Average effect size $(\overline{ES})$	Standard deviation	Standard error of effect sizes $(\sigma_{\overline{ES}})$	Number of effect sizes (n)
Dynamic	0.78	0.71	0.04	255
Behavioral	0.91	1.29	0.05	646
Cognitive	1.31	1.63	0.14	145
Humanistic	0.63	0.89	0.06	218
Developmental	0.42	0.59	0.05	157
Cognitive-behavioral	1.24	2.10	0.17	157

[a] Placebo treatments were not included in therapy classes and subclasses.

emotional-somatic complaints, behavior modification produced strong effects, but smaller effects on measures of social behaviors, achievement, and self-esteem. In fact, the effect of behavior modification on self-esteem is the smallest entry in the table. The effects of dynamic-eclectic therapy were very different, depending on what was measured. Its impact on achievement was extremely high, reliably higher than its impact on global adjustment or fear and anxiety. Much smaller effects were produced by cognitive-behavioral therapies on measures of achievement than on other types of outcome.

The results from the analysis of cross-classification on therapy and diagnosis and on therapy and outcome measurement produces many empty cells and few solid answers. Even with 500 studies and 1,700 effects, the data are still too sparse to answer questions such as, "Is rational-emotive psychotherapy more effective than transactional analysis for neurotic clients?" The next necessary step was to form more general categories of therapy. Any grouping strategy blurs distinctions and is subject to dispute. Nevertheless, the potential gain in information is worth the loss of fine distinctions. The reader is referred to Chapter 4 for the discussion of the method for grouping therapies.

Effects within Therapy Subclasses

Six subclasses of therapy are distinguished in the meta-analysis of effects:*
dynamic, behavioral, cognitive, humanistic, developmental, and cognitive-

*Dynamic subclass = psychodynamic therapy, Adlerian, dynamic-eclectic and hypnotherapy. Behavioral subclass = behavior modification, systematic desensitization, and implosion. Cognitive subclass = rational-emotive therapy, transactional analysis, and other cognitive therapies (e.g., fixed-role therapy, cognitive restructuring, systematic-rational restructuring). Humanistic subclass = client-centered and gestalt therapies. Developmental subclass = vocational-personal development counseling, undifferentiated counseling. Cognitive behavioral subclass = cognitive behavioral therapies (e.g., self-management, covert conditioning, and model reinforcement), and eclectic-behavioral therapies.

behavioral. Table 5-4 contains the mean, its standard error, and the number of effect-size measures obtained for each therapy subclass. The cognitive and cognitive-behavioral subclasses produced the largest effects, reliably larger than the behavioral and dynamic subclasses, which were in turn significantly larger than the humanistic subclass. Significantly less effective than all the others was the developmental subclass.

Table 5-5 contains the average effect size obtained for each therapy subclass for eight separate client diagnoses. In this table, it can be seen that humanistic and developmental therapy subclasses produced about the same magnitude of effect, regardless of the diagnosis of the clients treated. Dynamic therapies produced about the same magnitude of effect for all diagnostic categories except delinquents and felons, for whom the effect is much greater. Behavioral therapies appear in these data to be more effective with depressives and monosymptomatic phobics than with other diagnostic types. Cognitive and cognitive-behavioral therapies were much more effective with simple phobics than with other diagnostic types.

Table 5-6 contains the average effect sizes obtained for the therapy subclasses broken down by kind of outcome. There were no therapy subclasses that produced stable effects across all types of outcome. The dynamic therapy subclass produced relatively larger effects when the outcome was a measure of work or school achievement, an emotional-somatic complaint, or an addiction than when other types of outcome were measured. The behavioral therapy subclass produced relatively larger effects for the outcomes fear-anxiety, vocational-personal development, global adjustment, or emotional-somatic complaint than for the other outcomes. Behavior therapies seemed particularly unsuccessful on measures of self-esteem, although there are only eleven such effects recorded. Cognitive therapies were much more effective on measures of fear-anxiety and global adjustment than on other measures, and rather unsuccessful on measures of work or school achievement. Humanistic therapies (e.g., client-centered and Gestalt) were much more effective on measures of self-esteem than on other types, especially life indicators of adjustment. Developmental therapies were not very effective on anything other than measures of vocational-personal development. The cognitive therapy subclass was much more successful on measures of fear-anxiety and social behavior than on other kinds of outcome.

In the cross-classification of therapy subclass and diagnosis or outcome, cells still existed where there were no effects or too few effects to yield a stable estimate of effect. An analysis of the effects of different therapies in which both diagnosis and outcome class are controlled simultaneously is impossible, even at this level of aggregation. Finding an empirical answer to the question of "what kind of therapy works best for what kind of client with what kind of therapist in what kind of setting," expressed so eloquently by Kiesler (1966) and others, seems futile from this perspective, even with an enormous data base like the one analyzed here. Not only is it unlikely that a

Table 5–5. Averages and number of effect sizes for diagnostic types produced by six therapy subclasses

Diagnostic types		Therapy subclasses					
		Dynamic	Behavioral	Cognitive	Humanistic	Developmental	Cognitive-behavioral
Neurotic	$\overline{ES}$:	0.69	0.77	0.63	0.61	0.38	0.84
	n_{ES}:	121	187	35	155	88	71
Simple phobic	$\overline{ES}$:	0.83	1.01	1.82	[a]	0.33	1.71
	n_{ES}:	14	327	49		19	64
Psychotic	$\overline{ES}$:	0.68	0.88	[a]	0.51	0.60	[a]
	n_{ES}:	50	31		12	22	
Delinquent-felon	$\overline{ES}$:	1.49	0.64	0.64	[a]	[a]	[a]
	n_{ES}:	16	19	18			
Habituee	$\overline{ES}$:	0.95	0.76	[a]	[a]	[a]	[a]
	n_{ES}:	17	27				
Emotional-somatic	$\overline{ES}$:	[a]	0.86	[a]	[a]	[a]	[a]
	n_{ES}:		30				
Handicapped	$\overline{ES}$:	[a]	[a]	[a]	0.64	0.51	[a]
	n_{ES}:				11	15	
Depressive	$\overline{ES}$:	[a]	1.18	[a]	0.50	[a]	[a]
	n_{ES}:		18		18		

[a] Data omitted because there were fewer than 10 effect sizes in the cell.

Table 5-6. Average effect size classified by therapy subclass and type of outcome

Outcome		Therapy subclass					
		Dynamic	Behavioral	Cognitive	Humanistic	Developmental	Cognitive-behavioral
Fear-anxiety	$\overline{ES}$:	0.78	1.12	1.67	0.61	0.36	1.78
	n_{ES}:	42	332	59	15	12	63
Self-esteem	$\overline{ES}$:	0.66	0.23	0.65	0.99	0.34	0.73
	n_{ES}:	15	11	10	38	11	6
Global adjustment	$\overline{ES}$:	0.73	0.96	1.86	0.57	0.44	0.97
	n_{ES}:	100	82	24	96	32	18
Life adjustment	$\overline{ES}$:	0.51	0.54	a	0.24	a	a
	n_{ES}:	17	7		7		
Emotional-somatic	$\overline{ES}$:	1.22	0.89	a	a	a	a
	n_{ES}:	7	36				
Addiction	$\overline{ES}$:	1.05	0.75	0.53	a	a	a
	n_{ES}:	11	23	6			
Sociopathic behavior	$\overline{ES}$:	a	0.48	0.59	0.34	a	a
	n_{ES}:		11	12	5		
Social behavior	$\overline{ES}$:	0.94	0.42	a	0.45	0.43	1.23
	n_{ES}:	7	20		22	8	18
Work-school achievement	$\overline{ES}$:	1.24	0.45	0.28	0.54	0.30	0.60
	n_{ES}:	17	73	10	24	59	18
Vocational-personal development	$\overline{ES}$:	a	1.04	a	a	0.85	a
	n_{ES}:		16			20	
Physiological stress	$\overline{ES}$:	a	0.60	a	a	a	0.38
	n_{ES}:		28				7

[a] Empty cell

Table 5-7.   Average, standard deviation, standard error of the mean, and number of effect sizes for three therapy classes

Therapy class	Average effect size $(\overline{ES})$	Standard deviation	Standard error of mean $(\sigma_{\overline{ES}})$	Number of effects
Verbal therapies	0.85	1.09	0.04	597
Behavioral therapies	0.98	1.50	0.05	791
Developmental therapies	0.42	0.59	0.05	157

single researcher can employ a research design incorporating all the above factors (24 cells at least), but a literature as broad as 500 studies fails to provide a collective answer.

An even more general categorization scheme was used to group therapies into verbal, behavioral, and developmental therapy classes* (see Chapter 4 for method of categorizing therapies). Table 5-7 contains the average effects for the three therapy classes, using the entire data set. The average effect size for the verbal therapy class was 0.85; for the behavioral class, the average effect was 0.98. The developmental class produced an average effect of 0.42. These figures represent the uncontrolled differences in effectiveness of the three therapy classes. Behavioral therapies are clearly superior estimated this way. But one must not overlook the fact that these estimates contain not only the true effectiveness of the therapies, but all other factors that make studies of behavior therapy different from other studies. At this point, we still cannot verify, for example, whether one therapy class might involve more seriously disturbed patients than the others; or whether one therapy class employed outcomes more susceptible to falsification than did the others. Analysis of the effects of therapy classes for different types of client and outcome measurement is the first step toward more accurate estimates of comparative effects.

Table 5-8 contains the average effects produced in the three therapy classes for each diagnostic category. The behavioral and verbal therapy classes are about equally effective when used with clients of the following types: psychotics, normals, delinquents-felons, habituees, emotional-somatic disordered, handicapped, and depressive clients. Behavior therapies were more effective than others for neurotics, true (complex) phobics, and simple (monosymptomatic) phobics. Verbal therapies were not reliably more effective for any diagnostic type. All therapy classes were equally effective in treating psychotics. For all other diagnostic types, developmental therapies produced the smallest effects.

Table 5-9 shows that verbal and behavioral therapy classes were equally effective for measures of fear-anxiety, life indicators of adjustment, personality traits, emotional-somatic complaints, addiction, sociopathic behaviors,

*Verbal class = dynamic, cognitive, and humanistic therapy subclasses. Behavioral class = behavioral and cognitive-behavioral therapy subclass. Developmental class = developmental therapy subclass.

social behaviors, and work-school achievement. Verbal therapies showed larger average effects for measures of self-esteem. Behavioral therapies revealed larger average effects for measures of global adjustment. (See page 65 above for explanation of outcomes.) Developmental therapies were least effective on all outcome types.

The above differences among therapy classes are interesting, but still contain the effects of all confounding variables. The next section contains the results of several techniques used to control and eliminate this confounding.

Equating Therapies through Regression Analysis

Virtually all methodologists, reviewers, and critics of psychotherapy research devote much attention to the factors and conditions that interact with therapy, since they may produce varying results. It is widely accepted, for example, that neurotics are easier to influence than psychotics or drug addicts and that experienced therapists are more effective than inexperienced therapists.

The findings reported so far represent the uncontrolled differences among therapies. These differences were confounded or mixed together with all other conditions and factors that theorists and methodologists claim interact with

Table 5–8. Average effect sizes and number of effects classified by therapy class and client diagnosis

		Therapy class		
Diagnosis		Verbal	Behavioral	Developmental
Neurotic-true phobic	$\overline{ES}$:	0.64	0.81	0.38
	n_{ES}:	319	246	88
Simple phobic	$\overline{ES}$:	1.61	1.13	0.33
	n_{ES}:	85	391	19
Psychotic	$\overline{ES}$:	0.65	0.85	0.59
	n_{ES}:	62	34	22
Normal	$\overline{ES}$:	0.67	[a]	[a]
	n_{ES}:	14		
Delinquents-felons	$\overline{ES}$:	1.03	0.78	[a]
	n_{ES}:	40	25	
Habituee	$\overline{ES}$:	1.07	0.82	[a]
	n_{ES}:	30	36	
Emotional-somatic disordered	$\overline{ES}$:	1.39	0.86	[a]
	n_{ES}:	10	30	
Handicapped	$\overline{ES}$:	0.59	[a]	0.52
	n_{ES}:	12		15
Depressive	$\overline{ES}$:	0.95	1.27	[a]
	n_{ES}:	26	20	

[a] Cells with less than 10 cases were eliminated from the table.

Table 5-9.   Average effect sizes and number of effects classified by therapy class
and type of outcome measure

Outcome measurement		Therapy class		
		Verbal	Behavioral	Developmental
Fear-anxiety	$\overline{ES}$:	1.21	1.22	0.36
	n_{ES}:	117	401	12
Self-esteem	$\overline{ES}$:	0.85	0.41	0.34
	n_{ES}:	65	17	11
Global adjustment	$\overline{ES}$:	0.78	0.98	0.44
	n_{ES}:	222	96	32
Life adjustment	$\overline{ES}$:	0.43	0.62	a
	n_{ES}:	24	10	
Personality traits	$\overline{ES}$:	0.04	a	a
	n_{ES}:	11		
Emotional-somatic complaint	$\overline{ES}$:	1.27	0.88	a
	n_{ES}:	11	40	
Addiction	$\overline{ES}$:	0.84	0.81	a
	n_{ES}:	20	26	
Sociopathic behavior	$\overline{ES}$:	0.54	0.53	a
	n_{ES}:	21	15	
Social behavior	$\overline{ES}$:	0.65	0.82	a
	n_{ES}:	37	37	
Work-school achievement	$\overline{ES}$:	0.70	0.49	0.30
	n_{ES}:	54	88	59
Vocational-personal development	$\overline{ES}$:	a	1.03	0.76
	n_{ES}:		23	22
Physiological measures of stress	$\overline{ES}$:	a	0.56	a
	n_{ES}:		35	

a Cells with less than 10 cases were eliminated from the table.

therapeutic effects. For example, the difference between the average effects produced by behavioral and verbal therapies on measures of global adjustment (Table 5-9) reflect not only the difference in "true" effectiveness of the two therapy groups, but also the possible influence of each of the following: differences in client diagnosis and the severity of the problem treated; differences in client motivation for therapy; differences in clients' age, sex, socioeconomic level, and similarity of the client to the therapist; differences in number of hours of therapy given to clients of the two therapy classes; differences in the average level of therapist experience, empathy, or directness; differences in the way the study was conducted and the outcome measured.

These confounding variables obscure the assessment of actual differences in effectiveness produced by the various therapies. Through multiple regression analysis, it may be possible to determine the contribution of the confounding variables and hold them constant statistically to arrive at a more accurate representation of the relative effectiveness of the therapies.

A correlation matrix of all coded variables was computed. This matrix is reproduced in Appendix 4. It was studied to determine which variables from the research reports correlated with the magnitude of effect produced by the therapies. Table 5-10 contains the correlation of effect size and all other coded variables. Contrary to prediction, few variables thought to covary with therapy effect did so. The highest correlation with effect size ($r = 0.18$) was the reactivity of measurement, i.e., the higher the rated reactivity of the instrument used in a study, the larger the measured effect size. Two other variables that merited further attention were client-therapist similarity ($r = 0.10$) and the percentage of the client group that was male ($r = -.13$). Better results were associated with studies in which the clients resembled their therapists in ethnic group, age, social and educational status, and with studies in which the clients were predominately female. However, these characteristics were highly correlated with the reactivity of measurement. This relationship indicated a cluster of studies in which groups predominately female of high social and educational levels were treated for anxiety and assessed with highly reactive instruments.

A few variables were selected for the regression analysis—client diagnosis, source of clients, client IQ, therapy mode, and internal validity. Five variables were transformed to reflect interactions and curvilinearity observed in scatterplots and plots of residuals. These were as follows: (1) age, which showed a curvilinear relationship with effect size (effect size was greater for clients in the age range nineteen to twenty-two and less with younger and older clients); (2) therapist experience in interaction with client diagnosis, with more experienced therapists assigned to the most seriously disturbed clients; and (3) follow-up time, which revealed a curvilinear relationship with effect size. A variable was created to reflect different types of outcome. Level one of this variable consisted of psychological variables of fear-anxiety, self-

Table 5-10. Correlation of effect size with seventeen variables coded from the studies

Variable	Correlation	Number of *ES* measures
Date of study publication	.07	1,764
Degree of blinding in study	−.01	1,763
Amount of hospitalization of clients	.02	1,696
Client IQ	.08	1,764
Client-therapist similarity	.10	1,764
Client age	−.00	1,753
Percent male in client group	−.13	1,425
Internal validity of study	.03	1,760
Mortality in experimental group	−.05	1,536
Mortality in control group	−.04	1,536
Duration of therapy	−.05	1,735
Number of therapists in study	−.05	1,666
Therapist experience	.00	1,637
Sample size of experimental group	−.06	1,765
Sample size of control group	−.06	1,750
Follow-up time	−.05	1,764
Reactivity of measurement	.18	1,761

esteem, measures and ratings of global adjustment, personality traits, and measures of vocational or personal development. Level two of this variable consisted of the less tractable measures of life adjustment, emotional-somatic complaints, addiction, sociopathic and social behaviors, work or school achievement, and measures of physiological stress. The regression analysis thus had sixteen independent variables and was conducted within subsets of the data corresponding to the class, subclass, and type of therapy. Table 5-11 contains the standardized regression coefficients of the independent variables within the three classes of therapy. Similar data for the subclasses of therapy are located in Table 5-12. Table 5-13 shows the pattern of correlations between the independent variables used in the regression analysis and effect size, within subclasses of therapy. The average reactivity of measures used in the evaluation of the effectivenss of each therapy subclass show how much variation there was. Evaluations of cognitive-behavioral therapies employed measures with average reactivity twice as high as measures typically used in evaluations of developmental therapies.

These results show generally that the average effect size of therapies cannot

Table 5-11. Regression analysis within therapy classes

	Unstandardized regression coefficients		
Independent variable	Verbal ($n = 596$)	Behavioral ($n = 786$)	Development ($n = 157$)
Diagnosis: neurotic, phobic, or depressive	−.14	−.22	.02
Diagnosis: delinquent, felon or habituee	.17	.04	1.01
Diagnosis: psychotic	−.25	.21	.90
Clients self-presented	−.20	.20	.35[f]
Clients solicited	.16	.10	.14
Individual therapy	−.37[a]	.14	.19
Group therapy	−.17	−.00	.09
Client IQ (1 = IQ < 95, 2 = IQ 95-115, 3 = IQ > 115)	.24[a]	.11	−.11
Client age[b]	.00	.00	−.00
Therapist experience × neurotic diagnosis[c]	.01	.05	.01
Therapist experience × delinquent diagnosis	.03	.01	−.26
Therapist experience × psychotic diagnosis	.02	−.11	.06
Internal validity (1 = low, 2 = medium, 3 = high)	.08	.13	−.00
Follow-up time[d]	.01	−.01	−.01
Outcome type[e]	−.14	−.16	−.03
Reactivity[f]	.02[a]	.02[a]	.01
Additive constant	.25	.10	.32
Multiple R	.29	.23	.36
σ_e, standard error of estimate	1.05	1.47	.58

[a] Significant ($p \leq .05$) contribution of independent variable to reliable variation in effect size
[b] Transformed age = (age − 25) $(|\text{age} - 25|)^{1/2}$
[c] Interaction terms of diagnostic variables and therapist experience
[d] Transformed months post therapy = (number of months)$^{1/2}$
[e] Outcome type: 1 = fear-anxiety, self-esteem, global adjustment, personality traits, vocational-personal development; 2 = life adjustment, emotional-somatic complaint, addiction, sociopathic and social behaviors achievement, physiological stress measures
[f] Transformed reactivity of measure = (reactivity)$^{2.25}$

Table 5-12. Regression analysis within therapy subclasses

	Unstandardized regression coefficients					
Independent variable	Dynamic (225)	Behavioral (642)	Cognitive (144)	Humanistic (218)	Cognitive-behavioral (156)	Developmental (157)
Diagnosis: neurotic, phobic, or depressive	.04	−.09	−.49	−.22	−.23	.02
Diagnosis: delinquent, felon, or habituee	.07	−.02	−1.35	1.93[a]	−.01	1.01
Diagnosis: psychotic	−.34	.16	[b]	−.18	−.85	.90
Clients self-presented	−.17	.13	1.29	−.56[c]	.56	.35[c]
Clients solicited	−.37[c]	−.02	1.24	−.80	.67	.14
Individual therapy	−.56[c]	.00	−1.77	−.42	.42	.19
Group therapy	−.55[c]	−.11	−.93	−.31	.13	.09
Client IQ	.10	.10	.67	.18	.04	−.11
Client age[d]	−.00	.00	.00	.00	−.00	−.00
Therapist experience × neurotic diagnosis[e]	−.03	.00	−.10	.08[c]	.09	.01
Therapist experience × delinquent diagnosis	.01	−.02	.32	−.34	.31	−.26
Therapist experience × psychotic diagnosis	.05	−.10	[b]	.02	.37	.06
Internal validity	.09	.06	.57[c]	−.02	.34	−.00
Follow-up time[a]	−.03[c]	.00	.11	.02	−.81	−.01
Outcome type	.19	−.20	−.56	−.20	−.24	−.03
Reactivity[f]	.01[c]	.01[c]	.01	.02^2	.02	.01
Additive constant	.67	.54	−1.70	.67	−.85	.32
Multiple R	.45	.23	.41	.46	.30	.36
σ_e, standard error of estimate	.65	1.27	1.55	.82	2.12	.58

[a] Transformed months post therapy = (number of months)$^{1/2}$

[b] The data set showed no variance on this variable; consequently, it was dropped from the regression analysis. (See Table 5-11 and page 101 for coding explanations.)

[c] Significant ($p \leq .05$) contribution to reliable variance in effect size

[d] Transformed age = $(age - 25)(|age - 25|)^{1/2}$

[e] Interaction terms of diagnostic variables and therapist experience

[f] Transformed reactivity of measure = (reactivity)$^{2.25}$

Table 5-13. Correlation of independent variables with effect size for therapy subclasses

Independent variable (used in regression analysis)	Therapy subclass					
	Dynamic	Behavioral	Cognitive	Humanistic	Cognitive-behavioral	Developmental
Diagnosis: neurotic, phobic, or depressive	-.13	.04	.18	-.09	.03	-.12
Diagnosis: delinquent, felon, or habitué	.25	-.04	-.18	.22	-.02	.10
Diagnosis: psychotic	-.08	-.01	—	-.03	-.04	.12
Client self-presented	-.07	.04	.04	-.15	-.04	.12
Clients solicited	-.12	-.00	.12	.14	.10	-.08
Individual therapy	-.17	.06	-.08	-.07	.15	.08
Group therapy	-.02	-.05	.18	.04	-.12	-.01
Client IQ	-.03	.03	.23	.05	.11	-.11
Client age	-.09	.05	.05	.01	-.03	.08
Internal validity	.12	.00	.17	-.14	.09	-.00
Follow-up time	-.11	-.04	.00	.04	-.06	-.16
Outcome type	.14	-.17	-.17	-.10	-.14	-.15
Reactivity	.04	.20	.17	.24	.22	.21
Mean effect size, $\overline{ES}$	.78	.91	1.29	.63	1.24	.42
Standard error of $\overline{ES}$	.05	.05	.14	.06	.17	.05
n_{ES}	225	642	144	218	156	157
Mean reactivity for therapy subclass	18.52	21.82	18.90	16.71	22.19	11.30

be very accurately predicted from knowledge of the characteristics of the studies. The multiple correlations never exceeded 0.50, and the median multiple correlation from these analyses is 0.33. Less than 10 percent of the variation in effect size was determined by client diagnosis, intelligence, age, mode of presentation, therapy modality, therapist experience, internal validity of the experiment, type, time, and reactivity of measurement.

The independent variable accounting for most of the variance in effect size was reactivity of measurement. Furthermore, there were reliable differences among therapy classes and subclasses with respect to average reactivity. Behavioral therapies used measures that were more highly reactive (more under the influence of therapist and client) than verbal therapies. It is conceivable that the differences in reactivity might account for some of the differences in average effect size observed among therapy types, subclasses, and classes. In other words, the question addressed with regression analysis was how the average effects produced by different therapies would change if the degree of reactivity were equated for all the therapies. The result is a statistical or ex post facto correction.

The first step was to determine the regression equations separately for the behavioral and verbal therapy classes (Table 5-11). For all independent variables *except* reactivity, the mean values for the entire set of data ($N = 1,760$) were substituted for the observed means of each therapy class. For the reactivity variable, the average of reactivity for the verbal class was entered in both sets of equations (one for verbal, one for behavioral). Then the regression weights found in the original regression analyses were applied to the values of the independent variables. The result was a statistically adjusted effect size—the estimated average effect for the two therapy classes if both classes had employed measures with the same degree of reactivity.

The results of this statistical equating of therapy classes are as follows. Whereas the uncorrected difference between verbal and behavioral therapy classes was 0.14 ($\overline{ES}_{\text{behavioral}} = 0.98$, $\overline{ES}_{\text{verbal}} = 0.84$), the difference after statistical correction for reactivity of mean differences was 0.03 ($\overline{ES}_{\text{behavioral}} = 0.91$, $\overline{ES}_{\text{verbal}} = 0.88$). Adjusting in the opposite direction—substituting the average value of reactivity observed in the behavioral class—the average corrected effect size was 0.95 for the verbal class and 0.99 for the behavioral class. These figures represent the estimated magnitude of effects if both therapy classes had used measures with the typical level of reactivity used in studies of the behavioral class. In the original uncorrected data, the behavior therapies did enjoy an advantage in magnitude of effect because of more highly reactive measures. Once this advantage was corrected, reliable differences between the two classes disappeared.

Statistical adjustment for the differences among therapy subclasses was also conducted. The average values of reactivity for the dynamic therapies (psychoanalytic, eclectic-dynamic, Adlerian, and hypnotherapy) were substituted for those of the behavioral subclass (systematic desensitization, implosive therapy, behavior modification) and average values for the full data set assigned to the other independent variables. The uncorrected difference between these two therapy subclasses was 0.13 ($\overline{ES}_{\text{behavioral}}$ = 0.91, $\overline{ES}_{\text{dynamic}}$ = 0.78). After statistical correction for differences in average reactivity of measurement, the difference was reduced to 0.03 ($\overline{ES}_{\text{behavioral}}$ = 0.90, $\overline{ES}_{\text{dynamic}}$ = 0.87). Substituting in the opposite direction, the corrected effect sizes were 0.91 for the Dynamic subclass and 0.95 for the behavioral subclass. These figures are the estimated effects that would have been observed if both therapy subclasses had used measures with reactivity values typical of the behavioral subclass. Inspection of the tables of correlations and regression analyses will indicate the magnitude and direction of corrections between other pairs of therapies.

Experimental Comparisons of Therapies—the "Same-Experiment" Data

Ex post facto statistical equating of therapies is only partly satisfactory, since many potential confounding variables remain uncontrolled. The best solution for the reduction of the influence of extraneous variables is experimental; that is, for one researcher to study the effects of two or more therapies directly, using the same kinds of client, therapy of standard duration, therapists of equivalent training, and common measurements. In this way, all extraneous variables are controlled and differences in average effects between the two therapies reflect directly on their differential effectiveness.

Some of the studies identified for this meta-analysis did compare two or more therapies directly. These studies were isolated for closer examination in the "same experiment" analyses. The relevant studies were of two types— those in which two or more therapies were simultaneously compared against a control group, and those in which the two or more therapies were tested without an untreated control group. Data from the latter group were subjected to the control-referencing procedures described in Chapter 4. Because of the small number of studies involved, the therapies were aggregated into classes; it was not possible to use specific therapies or even subclasses. Only those studies in which therapies belonged to different therapy classes were used. This procedure eliminated those studies in which, for example, systematic desensitization was compared with implosive therapy, and those in which dynamic-eclectic therapy was compared with client-centered therapy. There were 72 studies in the "same experiment analysis." Fifty-six studies were comparisons of verbal and behavioral therapies, yielding 365 effect sizes. There were 3 studies in which verbal and developmental therapies were compared, yielding 8 effect-size measures. Thirteen studies involved comparisons of behavior and developmental therapies, yielding 86 effect-size measures.

The average effect sizes were found for the three therapy classes in three sets of comparisons—studies in which a verbal therapy was compared with a developmental therapy, studies in which a behavioral therapy was compared with a developmental, and studies in which a verbal therapy was compared with a behavioral therapy. The results are contained in Table 5-14. For those studies in which verbal therapies were directly compared to developmental therapies, verbal therapies produced larger effects. In those studies in which behavioral therapies were compared directly with developmental therapies, the former were vastly superior. In the direct comparison of verbal and behavioral therapies, behavioral therapies produced reliably larger effects.

What the experimenter chose to measure greatly affected the estimates of comparative effect, as Table 5-15 shows. The superiority of behavioral over verbal therapies is shown only on measures of fear or anxiety and measures of global adjustment. When the measures are grouped, as they were in the regression analysis, into psychological and less tractable measures,* the interaction of effect size and outcome type is clearly seen. The advantage (difference in average effect) for the behavioral therapies on psychological measures is 0.25, but for less tractable measures, the advantage drops to 0.04.

Several approaches were used to answer the question of which therapy works best. The observed differences in the "same experiment" analysis are the best estimates of comparative therapy effects. The contribution of extraneous variables is best controlled experimentally. There were reliable differences observed in the magnitude of effect produced by therapies, regardless of how they were aggregated. Cognitive and cognitive-behavioral therapies produced the largest effects, and at the most general level of aggregation, behavioral therapies produced the largest effects. However, the kind of outcome measurement was related to the size of therapeutic effect observed. On measures that were less susceptible to influence, reliable differences among therapies disappeared. The developmental therapies (ordinary school counseling, unidentified and unreferenced therapies, vocational study skills, and personal skills counseling) showed very small effects.

The Effect of Therapy for Different Outcomes and Methods of Measurement

The choice of what outcome is measured, what sort of instrument is used, and when the effects are measured influences estimates of the benefits of psychotherapy. If the researcher chose to measure anxiety reduction immediately after therapy by means of a paper-and-pencil test such as the Fear Survey Schedule, he had a greater chance of demonstrating large effects than

---

*Psychological measures were fear-anxiety, self-esteem, global adjustment, personality traits, vocational-personal development. Life measures less susceptible to influence were life adjustment, emotional-somatic complaint, addiction, sociopathic and social behaviors, work or school achievement, and physiological stress.

Table 5-14. Results of "same-experiment" analysis

Comparison	Therapy class	Average effect size, $\overline{ES}$	Standard deviation	Standard error of $\overline{ES}$	Number of effect sizes	Number of studies
Verbal vs. developmental	Verbal	0.51	0.24	0.12	4	3
	Developmental	0.36	0.20	0.10	4	
Behavioral vs. developmental	Behavioral	0.95	0.64	0.09	52	13
	Developmental	0.39	0.44	0.08	34	
Verbal vs. behavioral	Verbal	0.77	0.76	0.06	187	56
	Behavioral	0.96	0.87	0.07	178	

Table 5-15.   Verbal vs. behavioral therapies in the "same experiment" studies classified by type of outcome measure

	Verbal		Behavioral	
	$\overline{ES}$	n_{ES}	$\overline{ES}$	n_{ES}
Fear-anxiety	.99	67	1.22	71
Self-esteem	.04	5	−.00	5
Global adjustment	.73	57	.98	50
Life adjustment	.41	4	.46	4
Personality traits	.30	3	.73	3
Emotional somatic complaint	.67	3	.85	1
Addiction	.85	7	.77	11
Sociopathic behavior	.55	13	.48	11
Work-school achievement	.43	13	.24	9
Vocational-personal	.69	1	1.04	1
Physiological stress	.01	2	.57	4

if he chose a physiological measure such as pulse rate three months after therapy, all other things being equal. Table 5-16 contains the effects obtained for twelve separate outcome types, averaged across therapies and all other conditions of the studies.

The largest effects, reliably larger than for any other outcome category, were associated with measures of fear or anxiety. Measures of global adjustment, emotional-somatic complaints, and vocational or personal development showed the next largest effects. Life indicators of adjustment, physiological stress, work or school achievement, and personality traits were associated with the smallest effects.

The analysis of average effect sizes produced by different therapy subclasses on the outcome classification can be recalled from Table 5-6. Fear-

Table 5-16.   Average, standard deviation, standard error of the mean, and number of effect sizes classified by type of outcome measure

Outcome measure	Average effect size $(\overline{ES})$	Standard deviation	Standard error of mean $(\sigma_{\overline{ES}})$	Number of effects
Fear-anxiety	1.12	1.72	0.07	647
Self-esteem	0.69	0.97	0.10	99
Measures and ratings of global adjustment	0.80	0.86	0.04	383
Life indicators of adjustment	0.46	0.43	0.07	35
Personality traits	0.31	0.56	0.13	18
Emotional-somatic complaint	0.84	0.56	0.07	70
Addiction	0.77	0.52	0.07	55
Sociopathic behaviors	0.55	0.40	0.06	38
Social behaviors	0.64	0.82	0.08	94
Work or school achievement	0.49	0.76	0.05	215
Vocational or personal development	0.85	1.13	0.15	59
Physiological stress	0.71	1.08	0.15	50

110 THE BENEFITS OF PSYCHOTHERAPY

anxiety was most affected by cognitive, cognitive-behavioral, and behavioral therapies. Self-esteem was affected most by humanistic therapies and least by behavioral therapies. On global measures of adjustment, cognitive, cognitive-behavioral, and behavioral therapies were most effective. On measures of addiction, social behavior, and work-school achievement, the dynamic therapies were most effective.

The longevity of therapy effects was studied by calculating the effect sizes and comparing them at various follow-up dates. Two-thirds of all 1,765 therapy effects were measured immediately after therapy, i.e., at "0 weeks" follow-up time. Other relatively popular follow-up periods were four weeks (11% of the ES's), eight weeks (4%) and fifty-two weeks (2.5%) after therapy. Four effects were measured more than ten years after therapy. A graph of the average effect sizes at each follow-up time was irregular and difficult to comprehend; even smoothing with statistical moving averages did not help reveal a basic form of the curve. The curvilinear correlation between ES and follow-up time for all 1,765 effect sizes was only 0.14. Eventually, regression analysis was chosen as the clearest representation of the relationship between measured effect size and follow-up time at which the measurement was taken. Effects were averaged in nineteen follow-up time categories extending from immediately after therapy to more than 300 weeks after. Then the average effect was regressed onto a quadratic function of time (weeks plus weeks squared). The resulting least-squares solution produced a multiple correlation of 0.78, indicating that the regression curve is an excellent fit to the graph of average effect sizes. The graph in Figure 5-2 depicts the relationship. There one sees that the estimated average effect of psychotherapy over control conditions is slightly above 0.90 standard deviation units immediately after therapy, and it falls to around one-half standard deviation at about two years (104 weeks) after therapy.

In previous sections of this chapter, it has been reported that the reactivity of outcome measurement was the best predictor of the magnitude of effect produced by psychotherapy. During the coding of the studies, reactivity was rated on a five-point scale based on the degree to which the measure could be influenced by either client or therapist, the similarity between therapy goals and the measure, or the degree of blinding in the assessment process. Measures rated low on this scale were school grade-point averages, physiological measures of stress, and ratings and assessments given by observers who were blinded, that is, unaware of the assignment of clients to therapy or control groups. Measures rated high on reactivity included therapist ratings of client improvement, measures closely associated with the treatment (such as the Irrational Beliefs Test given to clients of rational-emotive psychotherapy), behavior elicited in the presence of the therapist in high demand, high expectancy situations (such as the Behavioral Approach Test), and self-reports of the clients to therapists. Table 5-17 contains the summary of results on the reactivity measure. Its correlation with effect size was +.18. A breakdown of

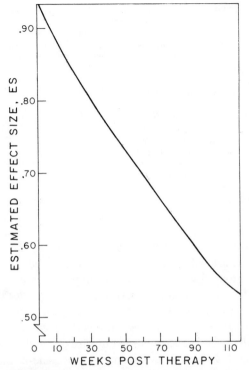

Figure 5-2. Relationship between measured effect of psychotherapy and the number of weeks after therapy at which the effect was measured (Curve is based on fitting a quadratic regression line to the mean effect sizes for each follow-up time category.)

average effect sizes for each value of the reactivity scale shows no difference in the effect sizes for the lower three values and greatly inflated average effects for the higher two values, which also constituted the majority of cases. The curvilinear correlation (Glass and Stanley 1970, pp. 150-152) of reactivity and effect size was +.28.

Two studies provide concrete examples of the relationship between reactivity and effect size. Study number 595 was an evaluation of the effects of systematic desensitization and covert positive reinforcement on the test anxiety of college students. The Suinn Test Anxiety Battery Scale (STABS) was used as the criterion and was administered immediately after therapy and twenty weeks later. This measure was rated "5" on the reactivity scale because of the close connection between the test items and the items in the anxiety hierarchy used in therapy. The other measure was an academic performance test, rated "2" on the reactivity scale, since it was constructed and administered by the experimenter. The effect size produced by systematic desensitization on the STABS at the end of therapy was 1.04 and was 1.27

Table 5-17.   Average effect size classified by each value of reactivity measurement[a]

Reactivity scale value	Examples of "instruments"	Average effect size	Standard error of mean $\sigma_{\overline{ES}}$	Number of effects
1 (low)	Galvanic skin response, grade-point average	0.55	0.06	222
2 (low average)	Blind ratings of adjustment	0.55	0.04	219
3 (average)	MMPI (Minnesota Multiphasic Personality Inventory)	0.60	0.04	213
4 (high average)	Client self-report to therapist, E-constructed questionnaire	0.92	0.03	704
5 (high)	Therapist ratings, behavior in in presence of therapist	1.19	0.06	397

[a] Average reactivity for all cases: 3.46. Correlation of reactivity and effect size: linear, $r = 0.18$; curvilinear, $\eta = 0.28$.

twenty weeks later. On the academic performance test, the effect size was -1.25, which indicated that the control group performed substantially better than the therapy group. The group in the "covert positive reinforcement" treatment had an effect of 0.50 on the STABS immediately after therapy and an effect of 1.26 twenty weeks later. On the academic performance test, the effect size was 0.36. Changes in anxiety about test performance (no doubt a valued outcome in itself) were not accompanied by changes in test performance.

Study number 1126 was an evaluation of systematic desensitization (the therapy to which the experimenter paid an obvious allegiance) and insight psychotherapy on anxiety and depressive symptoms of phobic outpatients. The therapies were compared against a placebo consisting of relaxation training. Since no untreated group was employed, the criterion statistics were subjected to control-referencing procedures described in Chapter 4. The effect size reported below reflects those transformations. Twelve measures were administered: therapist assessment of the intensity of anxiety related to the clients' primary phobia and all phobias, and depressive symptoms immediately after therapy and twelve weeks later, and the assessments of the same symptoms made by a rater who was uninformed about which clients were in the different treatment groups, also immediately after and twelve weeks after therapy. Therapist ratings were rated as highly reactive (5); and we gave blind assessments a low value (2). Table 5-18 contains the effect sizes produced by the two therapies. The three effects produced at follow-up time (main phobia, all phobias, and depression) and within reactivity categories did not differ from one another, so they were averaged for clarity of this presentation.

Two interesting findings are contained in Table 5-18. First is the difference in magnitude of effect observed by the therapist and the blind rater for both therapies and on both measurement occasions. Second is the tendency for the therapist to observe even greater effects at follow-up than at immediate post-

Table 5-18.   Effects produced by two therapies on outcome measurements at different times and different levels of reactivity (Study 1126)

Outcome measurement	Effect size for systematic desensitization	Effect size for dynamic-eclectic psychotherapy
Blind assessment at 0 weeks (average of main & total phobias, and depression)	1.21	0.61
Therapist assessment at 0 weeks	1.58	0.99
Blind assessment at 12 weeks	0.96	0.40
Therapist assessment at 12 weeks	1.93	1.06

testing, while the assessments of the blind raters show a decline in effect from post-test to follow-up. This tendency can be observed for both therapies. Physiological measures of stress (low reactivity) were also administered. Data were not reported but the authors wrote that these measures failed to yield significant treatment effects.

The influence of measurement reactivity on the magnitude of therapeutic effect cannot be denied. However, it is doubtless untrue, as some have observed, that the illusory appearance of the benefits of psychotherapy is due entirely to soft outcome measures. Even the least reactive measures, those most difficult to influence, demonstrated about a one-half standard deviation advantage of treated over untreated groups (cf. Table 5-17). The magnitude of effect from even this most conservative estimate is greater than some critics of psychotherapy have allowed.

The Effect of Therapy for Different Kinds of Clients and Presenting Problems

The clients treated in the therapy evaluation were characterized according to their diagnosis, years of previous hospitalization, age, sex, intelligence, and similarity to the therapists in social, ethnic and educational background. These characteristics were then related to the size of effect produced in the study, either by correlation analysis or cross-classifications.

Table 5-19 contains the average effect sizes produced with the twelve diagnostic types. The effects of studies that evaluated the effects of therapy on simple phobics and depressives were reliably larger than those that studied other diagnostic types. The effects associated with neurotics, true phobics, psychotics, "normals," and handicapped clients were reliably lower than those of other diagnostic types. Even the smallest effects were larger than one-half standard deviation. Therapy with psychotics was no less successful than therapy with neurotics, both showing around a two-thirds standard deviation effect. Table 5-5, which appears early in this chapter, contains the average effects produced by each subclass of therapy on three diagnostic

Table 5-19.   Average, standard error, and number of effect sizes for twelve diagnostic types

Diagnostic type	Average effect size, $\overline{ES}$	Standard deviation	Standard error $\sigma_{\overline{ES}}$	Number of effect sizes
Neurotic, true phobic	0.63	0.71	0.03	708
Simple phobic	1.12	1.82	0.07	611
Psychotic	0.68	0.48	0.04	132
Normal	0.66	0.98	0.19	26
Delinquent, felon	0.82	0.91	0.11	74
Habitué	0.88	0.85	0.10	75
Emotional-somatic disordered	0.86	0.65	0.09	57
Handicapped	0.53	0.81	0.14	36
Depressive	1.09	1.12	0.17	46

types. For neurotic clients, cognitive-behavioral therapies were the most effective, but not reliably more so than therapies in the behavioral or dynamic subclass. Developmental therapies produced the smallest magnitude of effect.

For simple phobics, the cognitive and cognitive-behavioral therapy subclasses produced extremely positive results, reliably higher than did other therapies. Behavior therapies (e.g., systematic desensitization, implosive therapy, and behavioral modification) produced results similar to those of the dynamic therapy subclass. Developmental therapies were least effective with simple phobics. For psychotics, behavior therapies produced the largest effects, but not reliably higher than the effects produced by the dynamic therapy subclass. Developmental therapies were as effective as humanistic therapies for this diagnostic type. For depressives, behavior therapies were more effective than humanistic therapies.

In a previous section of this chapter, the table of correlations of client variables with effect size was presented (Table 5-10). It showed a slightly positive correlation between magnitude of effect and client intelligence and similarity to the therapist. The more intelligent the client, the greater the effect the therapy was likely to produce. The more alike the client and therapist, the greater the effect the therapy was likely to produce. Although there was not a simple linear relationship between effect size and client age, scattergrams revealed a slight curvilinear trend. Therapy produced smaller effects among clients under eighteen and over twenty-five and larger effects in the age range between. Extent of hospitalization of the clients before therapy did not relate to the magnitude of effect produced. Client sex did relate to effect size; the greater the percentage of female clients in the study, the larger the effect produced.

Two general reservations should be pointed out about these findings. First, the correlations may be attenuated, since they are based on average values within a study, not scores on individuals. There would be more variability (hence the possibility for higher correlation with effects) in, say, a set of IQ scores from individual clients than in the average IQ's of clients in a set of studies. Second, it should be kept in mind that there was a large group of studies in which clients of above average intelligence and similarity to therapists, and often predominantly female, were treated for anxiety by behavioral or cognitive-behavioral therapies, with quite positive results. This phenomenon may account for the clustering of client variables and higher effect sizes. In this case, the correlations may be an artifact and not generalizable to studies using other types of therapy.

Group, Individual, and Other Modes of Therapy

All studies were classified according to whether the therapy was administered individually, in groups, or in a few other less common modes. In general, the mode in which therapy was delivered made no difference in its effectiveness, as Table 5–20 shows. Indeed, the average effects for group and individual therapy are remarkably similar.

Effect of Duration of Therapy

The length of therapy was recorded for each study in three ways: the number of hours of psychotherapy; the number of weeks over which the therapy lasted, and a derivative index, the rate of therapy in hours per week. The three measures were very highly intercorrelated; only one was selected for subsequent analysis: the total number of hours of therapy.

Durations of therapy ranged from one hour to over three hundred. Over two-thirds of all effects were measured in studies involving twelve or fewer hours of treatment; the average duration of therapy was fifteen and three-quarter hours. The effect of therapy bore no simple or consistent relationship to its duration. The curve that relates average effect size to number of hours of therapy twists and dips erratically. It seems to result more from what kinds of clients and problems are treated in therapies of different lengths than from some intrinsic relationship between the length of therapy and its benefits. Figure 5–3 is a graph of the curve relating effect size to therapy duration. The curve has been smoothed by a fifth-order moving average (Glass, Willson,

Table 5–20. Average, standard error, and number of effect sizes obtained for different therapy modalities

Therapy modality	Average effect size, $\overline{ES}$	Standard deviation	Standard error, $\sigma_{\overline{ES}}$	Number of effects
Individual	0.87	1.52	0.06	755
Group	0.83	1.05	0.04	862
Mixed individual & group	0.89	0.71	0.07	97
Family	0.51	0.76	0.20	15
Automated	0.52	0.69	0.16	18
Other or unknown	0.98	0.54	0.15	13

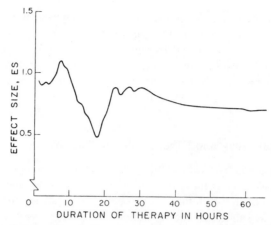

Figure 5-3. Relationship of effect size and duration of therapy (Curve is derived by a fifth-order moving average of the raw data.)

and Gottman 1975) to remove irregularities and reveal its basic shape more clearly. The curvilinear correlation between *ES* and hours of therapy is equal to 0.29; but virtually none of the relationship is linear, and the nonlinear components of the relationship make no sensible statement about the benefits of long-term and short-term therapies.

There is, however, an interesting rise in effect from one hour to seven hours and then a drop in magnitude of effect. This finding was accounted for by examining the breakdown of effect sizes by therapy duration and type of outcome measurement. The large effects in the region of one to seven hours were produced predominantly on measures of fear and anxiety by short-term behavioral therapies. In very few of these evaluations was therapy conducted for more than six or seven hours. Thus, whatever decline can be seen in Figure 5–3 is probably a consequence of that cluster of therapies. Within that cluster, there was a positive relationship between duration and effect. That is, for short-term behavioral therapies on specific anxiety, the size of effect increases somewhat with the number of hours of therapy from one to seven.

The lower effect sizes in the therapies of extremely long duration should be viewed in the light of the diagnosis and severity of the problems that clients of long-term therapies probably present. The less tractable problems are those associated with smaller effects, as well as longer time spent in therapy. Therefore, it is an oversimplification to say that longer-lasting therapies produce smaller effects (or no larger effects) than short-term therapies.

Effects of Therapist Training and Experience

The average number of years of experience of the therapists across the nearly 500 studies was three and a quarter years. To judge the external validity or generalizability of these findings to the field as a whole, one must compare this figure with the average level of experience of working psychotherapists. A plausible interpretation is that therapists participating in experimental evaluations are probably less experienced than psychotherapists in actual practice.

For the body of research, however, there was no relationship between the years of experience of the therapists in a study and the magnitude of therapeutic effect produced in that study ($r = 0.00$, Table 5-10). The interaction of therapist experience and client diagnosis was investigated in the regression analysis, but failed to explain reliable variance in effect size.

The discipline in which the therapists were trained was not recorded. However, the type of training of the experimenter was noted; it usually coincided with therapist training. In 45 percent of the cases, the experimenter was also the therapist. In many other instances, the experimenter was part of the same academic department or institution as the therapist. Table 5-21 contains the results of the classification of effect sizes by the type of training of the experimenter. Those trained in psychology obtained the largest effects. However, the confounding of this finding with the different types of problem addressed by professionals in the various fields cannot be overlooked. That is, psychiatrists were least likely to be involved with laboratory experiments of behavioral therapies on monophobic clients (that is, with those studies that produced largest effects). Experimenters trained in education produced reliably smaller therapeutic effects.

Effect of Therapy for Different Settings

All studies were classified according to the setting in which therapy was conducted. Then the size of effect associated with each setting was determined. Over half of the studies that could be coded on this variable (15 percent could not be determined) took place in some college facility, such as a psychology laboratory, therapy training center, or student mental health clinic. This setting produced the largest effects, as Table 5-22 shows. The smallest effects were produced by therapies conducted in public schools and mental health centers.

Table 5-21. Average, standard deviation, standard error, and number of effect sizes associated with different types of experimenter training

Type of training	Average effect size, $\overline{ES}$	Standard deviation	Standard error, $\sigma_{\overline{ES}}$	Number of effects
Psychology	0.94	1.25	0.04	1,141
Psychiatry	0.80	0.46	0.03	225
Education	0.61	1.44	0.04	393

Table 5-22.   Average, standard deviation, standard error, and number of effect sizes for various settings in which therapy took place

Therapy setting	Average effect size, $\overline{ES}$	Standard deviation	Standard error, $\sigma_{\overline{ES}}$	Number of effects
Public school	0.50	0.72	0.05	246
Hospital	0.73	0.51	0.04	203
Mental health center	0.47	0.68	0.13	28
Other clinic or outpatient facility	0.79	0.73	0.05	215
College facility	1.04	1.70	0.06	743
Prison	0.76	0.58	0.09	39
Residential facility	0.71	1.12	0.15	58

Effect of Therapy Produced by Studies Conducted at Different Times and Published in Different Sources

Both the year of publication and the source of publication were recorded for each study. The earliest publication date of any study located was 1910. Four controlled studies appeared before 1952 and 77 appeared before Eysenck's 1961 review. Half of the studies appeared before 1972. The year that accounted for the most studies was 1974. There was a slight relationship between the effect size produced by a study and the year in which it was published ($r = 0.07$, $n = 1,764$). There was also an interesting relationship between the year a study was published and the internal validity of its design. More recent studies were rated higher in internal validity.

The form of publication of a study also was related to reliable differences in magnitude of effect, but not in the expected direction. Of 1,765 effect sizes, 67 percent appeared in journals, 2 percent in books, 27 percent in dissertations, and 3 percent in unpublished papers (Table 5-23). The largest effects were associated with unpublished papers; however, many of these were in the process of being published. Journal articles and books were associated with about the same magnitude of effects and dissertation studies with the least, but still two-thirds of a standard deviation effect.

Effects of Psychotherapy for Different Methods of Evaluation

The desired state in experimental research or evaluation is that the independent variables account for most of the differences in measured outcomes and that differences contributed by the research methods account for only a small part. In early reviews and criticisms of psychotherapy-outcome research, it was alleged that the studies that showed positive results used inadequate methods, i.e., that poor research methods rather than efficacious treatments were responsible for the positive results observed in some studies.

In the meta-analysis, features of the research methods of each study were coded and then related to the magnitude of effect the study produced.

Experimenter Blinding. Each study was classified according to the degree of blinding in the experimental procedures. Blinding was defined as the purposeful ignorance by the person doing the outcome assessment of the placement of each client in the treated or untreated groups. In almost 45 percent of the cases, the person who ran the experiment and conducted the evaluation also acted as the therapist. This situation made experimental blinding impossible. In over half the cases, the experimenter or evaluator knew the composition of the treated and untreated groups, but did not personally conduct the therapy. In only 4 percent of the cases was the evaluator blind as to the group status of each client during outcome assessment.

The average effects produced by therapies under these three conditions are recorded in Table 5-24. The single-blind evaluations produced the largest effects, a finding opposite to the hypothesis that the greater the possibility of the experimenter to influence results in the desired direction, the larger the observed effect will be. There were, however, slightly more favorable results produced when the experimenter did the therapy than when the experimenter knew the group composition but did not personally conduct the therapy.

Experimenter Allegiance. Each study was coded according to whether there was a stated or directly inferrable preference by the evaluator for one form of therapy over another. The preference or allegiance occurred in the majority of cases and could be detected by the direction of stated research hypotheses, favorable results of previous research uncritically accepted, rationalizations after failure to find significant effects for the favored treatment, and outright praise and promotion of a point of view. Bias against comparison therapies could be detected by the opposite tone. A comparison therapy might be set up as a kind of strawman over which the favored therapy would prevail. The comparison therapy (often an ''insight therapy'') would be treated with fairly obvious disdain, and would not be given much opportunity for success.

Table 5-23.   Average, standard deviation, standard error, and number of effect sizes associated with four forms of publication

Publication form	Average effect size, $\overline{ES}$	Standard deviation	Standard error, $\sigma_{\overline{ES}}$	Number of effects
Journals	0.87	1.32	0.04	1,179
Books	0.80	0.52	0.08	42
Dissertations	0.66	0.83	0.04	483
Unpublished papers	1.96	2.13	0.27	61

Table 5-24.   Average, standard deviation, standard error, and number of effect sizes associated with different degrees of experimenter blinding

Experimenter blinding	Average effect size, $\overline{ES}$	Standard deviation	Standard error, $\sigma_{\overline{ES}}$	Number of effects
Experimenter did therapy	0.89	1.54	0.06	755
Experimenter knew composition of groups, but didn't do therapy	0.79	0.96	0.03	917
Experimenter (evaluator) blind as to group composition	1.29	1.21	0.15	66

An observation from this body of literature is that impartial evaluations are rare. Evaluations of therapy are usually conducted by admitted advocates of that therapy. There is an obvious contrast between the studies of systematic desensitization and ''an insight therapy'' on specific anxieties on the one hand, and the Sloan study (Sloan, Staples, Cristol, Yorkston, and Whipple 1975) on the other. The latter evaluators compared the effects of dynamic and behavioral therapies. Actual outpatients were used, rather than volunteers. The therapists for both kinds of therapy were highly trained, experienced, and committed to their own models. The therapy was of acceptable duration. In spite of the fact that this study was not conducted under laboratory conditions, its research methods were above reproach, having true random assignment to groups and very little mortality from samples. A variety of outcome measures (with differing levels of reactivity) were administered at several points in time. Throughout, the evaluators maintained impartiality and gave each type of therapy every chance to succeed. The results of the Sloan study were particularly interesting because they parallel the results of the meta-analysis—that both forms of therapy were effective (mean differences of therapy over control groups) and that the dynamic and behavior therapies produced virtually the same magnitude of effect. The only advantage for behavior therapy over dynamic therapy was on the highly reactive outcome measures.

In only about 12 percent of the cases in the entire literature was there balanced or undetected allegiance to the therapy tested. In the vast majority of cases, an experimenter was testing his favored method against a competitor to whom, one might reasonably suppose, the experimenter would not have wanted to lose. Table 5-25 contains the average effects associated with the three categories of experimenter allegiance. These data show a regular relationship between allegiance and magnitude of effect. Where the allegiance was in favor of the therapy, the magnitude of effect was greatest. Where there was bias against the therapy, the effect was least.

Client Solicitation.   There is a stage in the development and evaluation of a therapy in which it is desirable to test its effects in a laboratory situation,

Table 5-25. Average, standard deviation, standard error, and number of effect sizes for experimenter allegiance

Experimenter allegiance	Average effect size, $\overline{ES}$	Standard deviation	Standard error, $\sigma_{\overline{ES}}$	Number of effects
Allegiance to the therapy	0.95	1.46	0.04	1,071
Allegiance against therapy	0.66	0.77	0.04	479
Unknown or balanced allegiance	0.78	0.86	0.06	213

maintaining close control over experimental variables, and using data to modify the treatment and make it applicable for general use. For tests such as these, the use of client volunteers is often necessary. Whether results from experiments such as these can be generalized to nonexperimental subjects, that is, persons who identify psychological problems in themselves and independently seek treatment, is problematical. Effectiveness on real clients is the true test of the therapy, since the solicitation of experimental volunteers is different in many respects from the actual delivery of treatment in hospitals, mental health centers, clinics or private practice. One test of the generalizability of results observed in experimental settings is to compare the effect sizes of various methods of obtaining clients for the therapies evaluated. Similar effect sizes would indicate greater generalizability.

The studies were classified according to five methods by which the clients were obtained. Table 5-26 contains the average effect sizes associated with each method. The highest effects were produced by studies in which the

Table 5-26. Average, standard deviation, standard error of the mean, and number of effect sizes classified by the method of soliciting clients

Client solicitation	Average effect size, $\overline{ES}$	Standard deviation	Standard error, $\sigma_{\overline{ES}}$	Number of effects
Clients recognized problem and independently sought assistance	0.71	0.47	0.03	243
Clients responded to an advertisement for a special therapy program	1.00	1.03	0.06	289
Clients were identified and solicited by experimenter (e.g., in psychology class, dorm, or school) especially to participate in therapy program	0.92	1.62	0.06	810
Clients committed to hospital, prison, or residential facility and hence to therapy	0.61	0.62	0.04	277
Clients were referred by teacher M.D., etc. to participate in therapy	0.87	0.92	0.08	141

clients responded to an advertised special therapeutic program (not a continuing service such as those offered by a mental health center or clinic) and those in which the evaluators solicited the clients to participate in a therapy experiment (often as a requirement for a class). Significantly smaller effects were obtained in studies in which the clients recognized the existence of a problem, independently sought the therapy, and became part of an experiment as well. Lower still were those studies whose clients were committed to therapy by an authority as part of their hospitalization, imprisonment, or status as students. The reliable differences in effects associated with the true-to-life methods and the laboratory methods of obtaining clients is evidence against the generalizability of results of laboratory-based therapies and argues for field-based evaluation to back up research conducted under artificial arrangements.

Internal Validity. The validity of the experimental designs used in outcome evaluations has often been the nub of the argument about whether or not the literature supports the efficacy of psychotherapy. An approach typical of several reviewers (Chapter 2) has been to declare as irrelevant or inappropriate any study that does not meet certain arbitrary standards of design. Rachman (1971) impeached several studies that supported the effectiveness of psychotherapy, because of flaws in their design. In his judgment, therapeutic effects produced by a study depended on the degree of rigor of the experimental methods used in that study.

At each stage in the meta-analysis, the attempt was made to apply unbiased standards of the internal validity of experiments. Following Campbell and Stanley (1966), the criteria for judging the internal validity of a study were the method of assignment of clients to treated and untreated groups and the differential mortality of subjects from experimental groups during the treatment and assessment periods. Random assignment and low, controlled mortality eliminate nearly all threats to the internal validity of a study.

Each study was coded for the method of assignment of clients to groups and the extent of mortality from each group. There was also an overall rating of internal validity given to each study. This rating was based on method of assignment and extent of mortality, plus any other experimental method that interacted with assignment and mortality (Chapter 4). These criteria were

Table 5-27. Average, standard deviation, standard error, and number of effect sizes classified by the method of client assignment

Assignment to groups	Average effect size, $\overline{ES}$	Standard deviation	Standard error, $\sigma_{\overline{ES}}$	Number of effects
Random	0.84	1.33	0.04	1,357
Matching	0.92	0.89	0.06	234
Pre-test equation	0.74	0.78	0.08	86
Convenience sample	0.81	1.05	0.16	44
Other nonrandom assignment	0.91	1.00	0.16	40

Table 5-28.   Average, standard deviation, standard error of the mean, and number of effect sizes classified by the internal validity of the study

Rated internal validity	Average effect size, $\overline{ES}$	Standard deviation	Standard error of mean, $\sigma_{\overline{ES}}$	Number of effects
1 (low)	0.78	0.80	0.05	224
2 (medium)	0.78	0.83	0.04	378
3 (high)	0.88	1.42	0.04	1,157

clear and fair and did not go further than necessary, i.e., into textbook niceties irrelevant to control over threats to internal validity.

The majority of studies employed random assignment of clients to groups. Sixty-six percent were rated high in internal validity (i.e., used random assignment and had low, controlled mortality rates). Table 5-27 shows the average effect size produced by studies using various methods of assigning clients to treated and untreated groups. There were no reliable differences in effects that could be attributed to differences in client assignment to experimental conditions.

The correlation analysis (Table 5-10) revealed that there was no relationship between the percent of mortality in either experimental or control groups and the size of effect.

Table 5-28 contains the average effects obtained for therapies under conditions of low, medium, and high internal validity. No reliable differences in magnitude of effect can be accounted for by differences in design validity. There was a slight trend toward a positive relationship between effect and internal validity, showing that the better designed studies produced larger effects. This trend is the opposite to that implied by Rachman, viz., that only the poorly designed studies showed effects favorable to psychotherapy.

The relationship of internal validity to magnitude of effect can also be seen in Table 5-12, where the correlations with effect are broken down by therapy subclass. The dynamic, cognitive, and cognitive-behavioral therapies had effects that are positively related to internal validity. Behavioral and developmental therapies showed no relationship between internal validity and effect size. Humanistic therapies showed a negative relationship, that is, for studies of client-centered and Gestalt therapies, the more poorly designed studies produced the larger effects.

The overall relationship between design quality and magnitude of effect ($r = 0.03$, $n = 1,760$) must be explained more fully. The absence of an association means that there is no basis for discarding poor quality studies from this body of evidence. If there had been clear-cut differences in the magnitude of effect produced by good and poor studies, then reason demands that one accept as evidence those studies that have the best designs and discard the rest. Such is not the case with this body of literature. Sophisticated experimental methods are necessary to detect the effects of a weak intervention. The effects of psychotherapy are so pronounced that a sophisticated design is not required to reveal them.

Even though the methods of the experimental design are independent of effect size, the methods used in measuring effects are not. The degree of reactivity of the measurements used was highly correlated with the magnitude of effect produced by a study. Evaluation methods themselves account for large variations in effects.

Summary of Results

The aim of this study was to arrive at an estimate of the effectiveness of psychotherapy that was both comprehensive and unbiased. The estimates arrived at are based on a statistical aggregation or summary of effects representative of the research literature as a whole. They are free of the bias so often injected when the review of research is conducted by advocates of some school of therapeutic thought.

The results show unequivocally that psychotherapy is effective. Estimated for all types of therapy, client, and outcome, the average effect is 0.85 standard deviation units. This estimate is based on 475 controlled studies, 1,766 measured effects, and tens of thousands of persons. In relative terms, the effect of 0.85 standard deviations means this: an applicant for therapy who is no better off than average (i.e., is at the 50th percentile) in psychological well-being, compared to all those who have not received psychotherapy, rises to the 80th percentile as a result of psychotherapy. At the end of treatment, he is better off than 80 percent of those who need therapy but remain untreated. In absolute terms, the magnitude of therapeutic effect is greater than most interventions of social science. Not only is psychotherapy effective on the average, but there is scant evidence of negative or deterioration effects of psychotherapy.

The question of comparative effectiveness of different types of therapy does not yield a single answer. At the simplest level, therapies were merely compared for average effectiveness, disregarding any systematic differences in the kinds of client typically treated by each therapy and the types of outcome typically observed. This simple, uncontrolled comparison yielded results such as the following. Cognitive, cognitive-behavioral therapies, hypnotherapy, and systematic desensitization appeared most effective. Undifferentiated counseling was least effective. Psychodynamic, dynamic-eclectic, Adlerian, client-centered, gestalt, rational-emotive therapies, transactional analysis, implosive therapy, behavior modification, eclectic-behavioral therapy, and vocational-personal development counseling were close to the average effectiveness of all therapies. Organized into classes of therapy, the behavioral therapies were more effective than the verbal therapies, which were in turn more effective than the developmental therapies. Placebo treatments, usually consisting of relaxation training or mere attention from a therapist, showed a positive effect as large as one-half standard deviation unit, but about half as large as therapies against which placebos were compared. A more complex and sophisticated treatment of the comparative effectiveness question included making allowances for the systematically different characteristics of clients and outcomes typical of the various types of therapy. Once these varying characteristics were controlled or canceled out, a different picture emerged. The well-controlled comparisons yielded no reliable differences in effectiveness of behavioral and verbal therapies. Developmental therapies were still relatively less effective than others.

One can argue that at the most general level all outcomes can be aggregated because they represent some aspect of psychological well-being. Each evaluator chose some aspect of that global construct as a criterion in his study. The choice of outcome criteria was quite important in determining the magnitude of effects forthcoming in a study. All types of outcome measurement showed positive effects, but some types were associated with greater effects than others. Measures of fear or anxiety were associated with the largest effects. Measures of personality traits or work or school achievement showed the smallest effects. The method used to measure the outcome was also associated with the magnitude of effect measured in a study. Some measures were highly reactive—easy to influence and obvious as to the social desirability of response. The more highly reactive the measure, the greater was the magnitude of effect. The time the evaluator chose to measure the outcome also affected the estimate of therapeutic effect. If measured immediately after therapy, the magnitude of effect was around 0.90 standard deviation units. This effect drops gradually to about 0.50, if the effect is measured two years after therapy. The measurement of outcomes was critical to answering the question of comparative therapeutic effectiveness. Compared to verbal therapies, behavioral therapies were evaluated using more highly reactive measures and assessments were made closer to the end of therapy. These differences may account for what appeared to be the superiority of behavioral over verbal therapy when the two were compared without controls.

The characteristics of the clients involved in the therapy evaluation influenced the size of effects eventually produced. Depressed clients and clients with simple, monosymptomatic phobias were associated with the largest effects; psychotics, neurotics, and handicapped clients with the smallest. The more intelligent the client, the more alike the therapist and client in education and socioeconomic status, the larger the therapeutic effect was likely to be. The greater the proportion of female clients, the larger was the effect. Many methodologists demand to know the right treatment for the right client in the right setting. Yet even with a data base as large as this one, there is not sufficient information to answer the question with any confidence.

The characteristics of a therapy, other than its theoretical classification, bore surprisingly little relation to the size of effect. Individual therapy and group therapy and combinations of them were equally effective. The duration of therapy was unrelated to its measured effectiveness. The experience of the therapist was unrelated to therapeutic effectiveness, although the years of experience of therapists in the studies was quite low, on the average. Psychologist-experimenters produced larger effects than psychiatrist-experimenters, who in turn produced larger effects than education-experimenters. Any conclusion about relative effectiveness of the various professionals must be made with caution, however; or, better yet, not made at all. One might wish to know the relationship between therapeutic effectiveness and other qualities of the therapist—warmth, caring, disclosure, leading style, and the like. Yet these qualities were not studied experimentally, or, if studied, they were virtually never reported in conjunction with the outcome data; therefore, they did not enter the meta-analysis.

The allegation by critics of psychotherapy—that poor quality research methods account for the positive outcomes observed—can now be laid to rest. The degree of experimental rigor employed by the researcher was *positively* related to the size of effect produced. Greater controls were associated with slightly higher effects. Experimental mortality and the degree of blinding in the evaluation were also unrelated to outcome. Yet other features of the experiment were in fact influential in determining effect size and should be viewed critically. The method of measurement and its relationship to effect size has already been mentioned. Clients who were solicited by the experimenter especially for the study or who heard of therapy through advertisements of special therapy programs were associated with the largest effects. Smaller effects were associated with clients who recognized their problems and sought assistance on their own and those who were committed to therapy as part of a hospital or prison program. These last categories are probably the most representative of actual therapeutic practice.

Experimenter allegiance should also be viewed critically. Almost 60 percent of the treatments were tested by researchers with recognizable allegiance to the therapy. This positive allegiance was associated with larger effects.

The analyses reported in this chapter revealed many conditions that somehow elaborate, attenuate, or complicate the accurate estimation of overall psychotherapy effectiveness. Yet in spite of each qualification, and if only the most cautious and conservative estimate is made, the benefits of psychotherapy remain impressive.

Chapter 6

Reviews of Research on the
Effects of Drug Therapy
on Psychological Disorders

The early 1950s marked the beginning of a new era in the treatment of psychological disorders. Demonstration of the clinical benefits of chlorpromazine by Delay and Deniker and the effects of reserpine by Kline set in motion a wave of drug treatment for psychiatric patients. That wave is still growing, almost thirty years later. At the same time, a wave of criticism and controversy grew around the widening use of drugs in a domain that was once the sole province of psychological therapies. The criticism has ebbed and flowed over the past thirty years not only in the public sector, but in the psychiatric and psychopharmacologic disciplines, as well.

The apparent salutary effects on psychological symptoms of some early drugs like imipramine, chlorpromazine, and reserpine demanded a new or broadened theory of the causes of mental illness. The lines of argument were drawn. The somatogenic school and the psychogenic school offered competing theories of the etiology of mental illness. Still, many psychiatric researchers wrote with temperance about the good and the bad of drug therapy.

Some authors emphasized that chemotherapy was aimed at treatment rather than cure and warned that drugs could blunt patient affect, mask symptoms, reduce motivation to work at psychotherapy, increase transference hostility; that drugs could become a force for dependency due to magical thinking or reliance on the doctor for an external cure (Skobba 1960; Moriarity 1960; Sawer-Foner 1960; Arieti 1974; Group for the Advancement of Psychiatry [GAP] 1975).

Some of these same authors and others pointed to the possible benefits of drug therapy: it could make the patient more accessible to psychotherapy, help carry the patient longer so he might deal with his problems more successfully, and produce results quicker and cheaper than psychotherapy (Linn 1961; Lesse 1957; Ostow 1961; Sawer-Foner 1960). Despite the often reasoned opinion published in the psychiatric literature advocating cautious combination of drug and psychotherapy, friction still exists between the psychotherapeutic model and the psychopharmaceutic model (May 1971; Grinspoon and Greenblatt 1963; GAP 1975; Docherty 1977).

Most psychopharmacy researchers, general practitioners, and psychiatrists were long ago convinced that psychotropic drugs are effective. While these groups have moved on to questions concerning "the right drug for the right patient" (Kiesler 1971; Klett and Mosely 1965; Downing, Rickles et al. 1971), many nonmedical clinicians and the general public still question the psychotherapeutic advantages of administering drugs to mentally ill patients. In fact, psychotropic drugs have become so widely prescribed by doctors (over 200 million prescriptions in 1970, with the number rising, GAP 1975, p. 274) that reaction to its widespread drug use has generated a large constituency of critics.

Even the most widely touted evidence of benefits of drug therapy has been questioned by "social psychiatry" advocates. The well-known time series graph of U.S. mental hospital in-patient population shows its first dip from 1955 (558,900 patients) to 1956 (551,400 patients) (Davis and Kline 1969). Although this drop in resident population coincided with the widespread introduction of psychotropic drugs into hospitals, Gilligan (1965) and Klerman (1963) noted that some drug critics attribute much of this change to ". . . a number of psychological and social therapies [that] were introduced during the 1950's" (Gilligan 1965, p. 41).

A few researchers have broken with tradition to question anew the necessity for drug therapy (Carpenter 1977; Tobias 1974; Gardos and Cole 1977). As Carpenter wrote: "We believe . . . that the treatment of schizophrenia has become so extensively drug oriented that a significant impediment has arisen to the exploration of alternative therapeutic approaches. The situation has reversed from the 1950's when a commitment to psychological treatment philosophies posed a severe resistence to pharmacological innovations" (1977, p. 14).

With the field of psychiatry in a "state of siege" (Dietz 1977, p. 1356), with drugs viewed by the public as the bane not the balm of psychiatry, and with practitioners from the psychogenic school ". . . not altogether comfortable about the concurrent use of drugs and psychotherapy" (May 1971, p. 503), it is time to take a broad look at the effects of drug therapy on psychological disorders.

In a 1975 publication, the Group for the Advancement of Psychiatry (GAP) estimated that over 10,000 papers had been published about psychotropic drugs since 1960. If the rate of about 650 studies per year suggested by the 1975 publication were constant from 1954 to the present, one would estimate that over 25,000 articles have been published on all phases of psychotropic drugs. As Van Pragg put it, "The psychotropic drugs have set in motion an avalanche of research, which has moved in several different directions" (in Klein and Gittleman-Klein 1976, p. 17).

Data are constantly being generated by researchers seeking evidence of the therapeutic benefits of new drugs or new modes of drug administration. Well-known drugs are being tried on patients with symptoms previously thought to be resistant to modification. Varied therapeutic milieux are being tested to determine how they might facilitate or interfere with drug treatment. Drugs are tested in competition with psychotherapy or in conjunction with it.

There is, therefore, no dearth of evidence on the question of the benefits of drug treatment. But thousands of pieces of evidence do not guarantee understanding or intelligent policy formation. The vast literature in its fractionated state certainly has not settled professional disputes nor provided the clinician or layman with needed answers. We take the position that too many research pieces, some with conflicting results, cannot be assimilated or understood without more elaborate statistical tools.

In this study, the tools of meta-analysis were used to integrate the results of a large body of literature, thereby seeking general answers to the several pressing questions. What are the overall therapeutic benefits of drug treatments on patients with psychological disorders? What kinds of patient have benefited most from psychotropic drugs? On what kinds of outcome has drug therapy had its greatest effects? What are the general and specific effects of psychotropic drugs? Is drug therapy more or less effective than psychotherapy? Does drug therapy facilitate or inhibit the effects of psychotherapy? How do the characteristics of the studies relate to their outcomes?

The notion of investigating the marginal or average therapeutic effects of drugs as a general class may seem odd to the clinician who must decide which of many drugs is best for the specific patient at hand. Certainly, one important goal for future research is to determine the proper drug for a specific patient in the circumstances in which clinician and patient find themselves. Yet this goal has yet to be approached with a single piece of multifactorial research. No matter how important the interaction question is, we are not relieved of the responsibility of settling the still unanswered question of average, overall effectiveness of drug therapy.

Reviews of the Research Literature

There have been many attempts to impose order upon and draw generalizations from the thousands of studies on drug treatment effectiveness. Unfortunately for the reader, the conclusions of the research reviews have sometimes been contradictory. Such contradictions may be accounted for by understanding the various inclusion criteria used by authors to select studies for the review as well as the use of varying methods for assessing and summarizing the results of studies.

Compared to the vitriol that characterizes the reviews of research in psychotherapy, there is dispassion and relative consensus in the reviews of psychopharmacy. In the latter literature, there is far less partisanship, less incidence of cults of personality growing around proponents of one or another treatment, less ambiguity about treatment, and more obvious and clear-cut results. Clinicians may argue over the proper drug or the proper therapeutic dose, but this dispute pales beside the conflict between Jung's attention to the unconscious and Glasser's denial of its existence, for example. In spite of the notable differences in the tone of the two literatures, some disputes still persist in the drug therapy literature. The questions of drugs vs. psychotherapy and the efficacy of drugs in combination with psychotherapy remain open.

Drug Therapy Outcome Reviews

Like the psychotherapy-outcome reviewers, authors of many of the most comprehensive and systematic syntheses of the psychopharmacological literature reduced multifarious results to impressionistic narrative conclusions or simple box-score comparisons.

Antipsychotic Drugs. In 1969, Klein and Davis published three comprehensive reviews (on antipsychotic, mood stabilizing, and minor tranquilizing drugs), in their well-known text, *Diagnosis and Drug Treatment of Psychiatric Disorders.* Since the methodology of the three reviews was so similar, only one will be discussed in any detail here. In their review of antipsychotic drugs, 159 placebo-controlled studies with phenothiazines were tabled by outcome. Seventy-nine percent (126 studies) showed the 11 phenothiazines to be more effective than the placebo and 21 percent showed no difference. Examination of dosage relationship to outcome was made with a subsample of 61 chlorpromazine studies. It demonstrated that significant differences between phenothiazines and placebo were uniformly reported for higher drug doses, but at lower doses results were more equivocal. Data were also subdivided into a design adequacy dichotomy that revealed that studies with methodological problems "tended to find drugs ineffective" (p. 55).

Side effects were catalogued in a comprehensive table for the 10 phenothiazines that presented the percents of patients manifesting each symptom. This table on side effects is one of two systematic attempts to aggregate raw data from original studies. In fact, in justifying the use of the box-score methodology Klein and Davis note: "This type of classification-scheme is preferable to one which utilizes percent improvement figures since both the improvement criteria and the percent improvement base rates vary considerably among studies. For example, a study using an acute schizophrenic population would show a greater percentage of improvement than one using chronic schizophrenics" (p. 54).

Although it is true that criteria and base rates differ with regard to improvement from study to study, this is not found to be a compelling argument to eschew aggregation of raw data (as percentage of improvement, or some other magnitude of improvement measure). Because one study group examined drug reactions with short-term patients and another examined drug reactions with long-term patients, the likely different improvement rates (measured as the drugs vs. placebo difference) do not necessarily represent measurement artifacts. Rather, the difference may reflect genuine treatment-symptom interactions. With the proper techniques, study differences can be systematically examined to shed light on the effects these methodological mismatches have on outcomes.

In their review of the antipsychotic literature, Klein and Davis did not aggregate statistics on the magnitude of drug effects. However, despite their caveat to the contrary, in addition to box-scoring 66 placebo-controlled studies of tricylic antidepressants in their review of mood-stabilizing drugs, Klein and Davis aggregated across studies the percent of improved patients. While 40 percent of 606 placebo patients improved, 70 percent of 734 drug patients improved.

Ignored in all these reviews were data from uncontrolled studies. No breakdown by patient characteristics (sex, age, chronicity, etc.), duration of treatment,* or type of outcome measure† was reported although elaborate tables describe for each study, patient number and diagnosis, duration of study, drug dose, outcome, and design. No attempt was made to predict study results by an aggregate of study characteristics.

Davis (1965) reviewed 125 studies of phenothiazines and via box-scores showed 73 percent of the studies found drug more effective than placebo. In 1969, Davis and Klein recycled part of Davis's 1965 review of phenothiazines and showed that 77 percent of 160 double-blind placebo-controlled studies found phenothiazine to exceed placebo in effectiveness.

Campbell (1975) listed 38 drug studies of infantile autism in a summary of representative publications. Although she tabulated several study characteristics (for subjects: number, age, and diagnosis; for drug: generic name and dosage; for methodology: design, outcome variables, and analysis), she did not systematically present results by these categories. No box-score was reported, rather a narrative summary was made of the state of therapy, heavily emphasizing results from the author's own research. Uncontrolled studies were represented.

Goldstein, Clyde, and Caldwell aggregated data across studies in their 1968 review of the clinical efficacy of the butyrophenones. From ten clinical studies the number of treated chronic psychotic patients improved and unimproved was tabulated separately from the number of treated acute psychotic patients improved and unimproved. Global rating of improvement was the dependent variable. In each tabulation results from double-blinded studies were reported separately from unblinded studies. Sixty-three percent of 661 patients (chronic and acute combined) improved.

From 9 open (i.e., nonblind) studies the authors also tabulated each of four improvement categories with the median prescribed dosage for each category.

---

*Study length was reported in a table that described each study, but results were not reported by categories of study duration.

†Five selected studies reporting on schizophrenic patients examined effects of eight drugs on Blueler's psychological dimensions of schizophrenic systems.

Presumably due to the pairing of greater doses for more severe illness the relationship was negative (greater improvement with smaller doses).

Schou (1968) reviewed the efficacy of lithium in treating mania, using 43 studies, 2 of which were double-blind controlled. He reported that only one study gave equivocal results regarding lithium efficacy. In an attempt to quantify the effects of the ion, Schou summed the number of unimproved patients found in 6 studies. (The method for choosing the 6 studies was not described). About 75 percent of patients improved. There was no report of the improvement rate for untreated manic patients.

Gittleman-Klein and Klein (1968) reviewed several studies of the long-term effects of antipsychotic agents. Rather than aggregating raw data or summarizing findings via box-scores, the authors drew conclusions from separate examination of every selected study.

Hollister took this narrative, impressionistic summary method as well, when in 1969 he wrote on the current status of psychotherapeutic drugs in the treatment of human psychiatric illness. In this impressionistic review, Hollister concluded that the clinical efficacy of the antidepressant and antianxiety agents was equivocal, while the efficacy of the antipsychotic drugs was certain.

Davis (1975, 1976) investigated maintenance therapy for schizophrenia and affective disorders. He recorded the percent of patients improved in 24 double-blind studies of antipsychotic medication withdrawal. He did the same for the 8 best studies he could collect on lithium-maintenance therapy. By aggregating p values over studies in each category, Davis showed "the evidence is unequivocal that antipsychotic drugs prevent relapse" (1975, p. 1239) and that lithium is likewise certainly effective. "Size effect" or magnitude of relationship was recorded for each study by phi coefficients. Contrary to Davis, Tobias (1974) attempted to impugn research results that claimed efficacy of maintenance therapy for schizophrenia. He described several studies in great detail, highlighting threats to the internal validity of each and concluded "The foregoing review indicates that no definite statement may be made at this time concerning the effects of drug withdrawal in chronic mental patients" (p. 120).

Antidepressant Drugs. Morris and Beck (1974) reviewed the efficacy of antidepressant drugs, using 146 double-blind studies on drugs actively promoted in the United States in 1972: Of 93 studies on the tricyclic compounds, two-thirds showed the drug superior to the placebo; one-third showed no difference. This overall box-score was broken down by in- and out-patient status. The authors likewise divided box-score outcomes of the mono-amine oxidase inhibitors (MAOI's) into in- and out-patient studies, finding 8 of 13 studies to favor the drugs.

Other reviews of antidepressant drugs include Davis (1965), Cole (1964), Atkinson and Ditman (1965), Davis, Klerman, and Schildkraut (1968), and Klerman and Cole (1965). In 1965, Davis recorded the box-score outcome of 47 studies of antidepressant drugs, 68 percent showed drug superior to placebo. Almost all studies were placebo-controlled and double-blinded. In a narrative review, Cole (1964) alluded to 15 placebo-controlled studies of imipramine on depressive inpatients in which only two-thirds showed significant drug superiority, while all 3 placebo-controlled studies of imipramine on out-patients signified drug over placebo superiority.

Atkinson and Ditman (1965) surveyed 56 trials of tranylcypromine and discarded from review all but 16. The decision for exclusion was based on the authors' intent to examine only those studies in which tranylcypromine was used alone and in which the patient sample was homogeneous for a specific diagnosis. Ten of the 16 clinical trials were without control (i.e., pre-post design). Box-scores of effectiveness were broken down by design characteristics (placebo-control/double-blind, drug comparison control, and no control) and specific patient diagnosis. In a two-way classification that attempted to quantify outcomes by the patient diagnostic group, outcomes were trichotomized as follows: favorable, equivocal, unfavorable. Only 42 percent of comparisons gave results that were unequivocally favorable. No description was given of the rationale that produced the three-level outcome split.

Davis, Klerman, and Schildkraut (1968) presented box-scores for 28 and 52 double-blind placebo-controlled studies of MAOI's and tricyclics, respectively. Seventy-nine percent of the tricyclic studies showed a superiority of drug to placebo, but only 54 percent of the MAOI studies showed a superiority of drug to placebo.

Davis, Klerman, and Schildkraut's Table 2 for the MAOI box-score is reprinted here in part:

Drug		Number of studies in which	
Generic name	Trade name	Drug was more effective than placebo	Drug was equal to placebo
MAO inhibitors:			
Tranylcypromine	Parnate	2	1
Iproniazid	Marsilid	3	2
Isocarboxazid	Marplan	2	3
Nialamide	Niamid	0	3
Pheniprazin	Catron	1	1
Phenelzine	Nardil	4	3
Pargyline	Eutonyl	2	0
Etryptamine	Monase	1	0
OTHER TREATMENTS:			
Electroshock therapy		7	1
Deprol (meprobamate + benactyzine)		2	1
Chlorpromazine (in depression)		2	0

Source: J. Davis, G. Klerman, and J. Schildkraft, "Drugs Used in the Treatment of Depression," in D. H. Efron, ed., *Psychopharmacology: A Review of Progress 1957–1967*, Public Health Service Publication No. 1836, 1968. Table 2. Double-Blind Placebo Controlled Studies of the Efficacy of the Monoamine Oxidase Inhibitors and Other Treatments for Depression, Comparing the Number of Studies in Which the Drug Was More Effective Than Placebo to the Number of Studies Finding the Placebo Equal in Effectiveness.

The authors' conclusion was as follows: "As can be seen from the table, there is a definite trend for the therapeutic efficacy of tranylcypromine, iproniazid, phenelzine, and pargyline. There is considerable doubt whether isocarboxazid and nialamide are more effective than placebo" (p. 723).

One or two votes out of three should not a "trend" or "doubt" make. The reporting method used above left the question of efficacy unanswered, since results of the voting technique were equivocal.

Klerman and Cole (1965) reported box-scores by significance level, as have most of their colleagues. But, like Klein and Davis, and Goldberg et al., Klerman and Cole summed data across placebo-controlled studies. Twenty-three placebo-controlled studies on the efficacy of imipramine were located of which 18 yielded data that permitted patient dichotomization into improved or unimproved. Of the 550 patients treated with imipramine, 65 percent improved; of the 459 treated with placebo, 31 percent improved. Information is tabled for drug dose, duration of treatment, patient diagnosis, and patient setting. From this additional information, only results by patient setting are reported (71 percent of out-patients improved; 61 percent of in-patients improved). For those studies that reported results by treatment group average scores rather than the number of improved patients, the box-score decision based on significance levels of the mean differences was reported.

From 32 uncontrolled clinical trials, the authors reported "fairly general agreement that significant improvement can be expected from the use of impramine in 60 to 80 percent of various types of depression"—a finding that coincides with the 65 percent improvement reported in the controlled studies.

Rogers and Clay (1975) took a unique tack in aggregating research results on imipramine. They retrieved the original global ratings of improvement from 30 placebo-controlled studies and submitted each to Fisher's Exact Test. The results from each study were reported as p values of the chi square statistic and tabled along with information about patient setting, type, and number. No attempt was made to aggregate p values, as was done by Davis (1975, 1976). Instead, the results were analyzed by the authors' impression, the specifics of which were not credible. Interestingly, only 8 of the 30 comparisons yielded statistically significant differences between imipramine and placebo when a nondirectional hypothesis was tested at $p = 0.05$.

McNair (1974) examined 72 publications of antidepressant drug effects that appeared in the literature between 1955 and 1972. Over 400 comparisons on 13 self-report depression scales were dichotomized into statistical significance or no statistical significance categories. Only 21 percent were significant. These almost exclusively double-blind studies were separately described by patient population, research design, and drug administration information. Percent of significant outcomes from the over 400 comparisons was reported by levels of these study characteristics as well.

These comprehensive and detailed reviews of the literature described above have much in common. All dealt with specific drugs or drug groups rather than categories of drug and most reported only methodologically excellent studies whose results were offered as final assay of disputed or equivocal findings. Rather strict methodological excellence (e.g., double-blind procedure or homogeneity of patient diagnosis) was required of individual studies for inclusion in the reviews. Most reviews were narrative, using the narration to describe methods and results of studies and to point out methodological weaknesses or strengths that undermined or supported the credibility of specific findings. All reviews attempting to aggregate outcomes across studies, except McNair's, made one global judgment about the results of each study or used only one or two outcome measures (e.g., percent improved) to summarize effects. McNair did report on 400 outcomes of 72 studies and also showed correlations between study characteristics and outcome (significant vs. nonsignificant).

Nevertheless, only Davis (1975, 1976) made any attempt at estimating the magnitude of the drug effect. Some authors estimated the size of the drug effect by summing across studies the percents of improved patients in the drug vs. no drug groups. Other authors only reported box-score results that, while indicative of the frequency of positive findings, biased results in favor of large studies and did not shed light on the magnitude of drug versus control group

Table 6-1.   Number and percentage of studies reporting no difference between placebo and drug (data from reviews discussed above)

Reference	N studies (total)[a]	N studies showing no difference	Percent of total showing no difference (%)
Antipsychotics			
Klein & Davis (1969)	159	33	21
Davis (65)	125	34	27
Davis (75)	22	2	9
Davis (75)	9	1	11
Antidepressants			
Morris & Beck (74)	93 tricyclics	31	34
	13 MAOI	5	38
Davis (65)	47	15	32
Cole (64)	15 inpatients	5	33
	3 outpatients	0	0
Atkinson & Ditman (65)	18 tranylcypromine	7	39
Davis et al. (68)	28 MAOI	13	46
	52 tricyclics	11	21
Klerman & Cole (65)	25 imipramine	8	32
Rogers & Clay (75)	30 imipramine	22	73
Klein & Davis (69)	65 tricyclics	15	23
	46 MAOI	17	37
Antianxiety			
Klein & Davis (69)	97	18	19
Total	847	237	28

[a] It is certain that studies examined in one review appeared in some other review as well, making these data nonindependent.

differences. Neither box-score results nor results of combined improvement rates capture the full complexity of study outcomes, because only one overall effect is reported for studies in which many outcomes may have been measured. Finally, though the box-score results clearly favor the view that drugs are effective, over one quarter of the results point to no reliable difference between drug-treated and control patients (Table 6-1).

It should be stressed that the highly narrative nature of these reviews is crucial for the practitioner who must have detailed information about indications, contraindications, and side effects of a certain drug or drug type. But the price paid for this specificity is a more fragmented view of results, much the way a description of the history and circumstances surrounding each student's test score would give a crucial but very different and more fragmented picture of test results than would the class average. There may be a pattern to these pieces of results and this should be and has been explored by the reviewers. But it is difficult to draw hard evidence of correlations and interactions from narrative descriptions of many different studies, no matter how detailed. While such evidence is available for specific types of drug it often comes from one definitive study that identifies, for example, "the right drug for the right patient" (Klett and Mosley 1965, p. 546) or the right therapist for the right treatment (Whitehorn and Betz 1957). Applications to a less circumscribed domain (i.e., a domain of widely diverse clinical research studies) have yet to be tried.

Reviews of Drug-Plus-Psychotherapy and Drug-Versus-Psychotherapy Effects

Six reviews of empirical research studying combination therapy and drug versus psychotherapy were identified (Luborsky et al. 1975; Uhlenhuth et al. 1969; May 1968 and 1974; Gilligan 1965; GAP 1965).

All six reviews were detailed narrations of empirical studies of drugs and psychotherapy. In the main, they concluded that drug-plus-psychotherapy was more effective than psychotherapy alone, but that the combination was not more effective than drug therapy alone. They also concluded that drug therapy was better than psychotherapy so that the effects of the two treatments together produced the effect of the more effective treatment alone. This is what Uhlenhuth called a "reciprocal interaction" (p. 60).

These conclusions were based on results of between 4 and 20 studies (Table 6-2). Only Uhlenhuth and Luborsky recorded results by box-scores. Uhlenhuth recorded only drug-plus-psychotherapy versus psychotherapy and drug-plus-psychotherapy versus drug outcomes. Luborsky included those comparisons plus drug-versus-psychotherapy studies.

Author's names are listed under columns that describe study outcomes. When one study appears in more than one column it is because the review narrative described more than one study outcome.* This table was constructed by categorizing studies based on the review narrative (for this table, the Luborsky et al. review was merely reproduced). The reviews shared many studies, but not all studies were categorized into the same outcome column. For example, the GAP publication described the outcome of Klerman's research as showing that drug therapy was as effective as drug-plus-psychotherapy, but Luborsky described the same study as showing drug therapy less effective than drug-plus-psychotherapy.

Forty-six different studies gave 144 comparisons across all 6 reviews. If the same study is counted only once as a tally is taken across reviews by summing along columns of Table 6-2, the following summary of the 6 reviews can be made: Twenty-two studies showed drug-plus-psychotherapy to be superior to psychotherapy alone, but about half as many (12) showed the combination to be equal in effect to psychotherapy. Nine studies showed drug therapy to be less effective than drug-plus-psychotherapy, but 16 showed it to be equal in effect to drug plus psychotherapy. Only one study showed drug to be superior to drug-plus-psychotherapy.

While 11 studies showed drug alone to be superior to psychotherapy alone, 3 showed the opposite effect, and 5 studies found the treatments to be equally effective.

These results leave the drug-plus-psychotherapy effect ambiguous. While the preponderance of evidence suggests that the treatments offered together are better than psychotherapy alone, still 12 comparisons (of 35 addressing this question) suggest that drug-plus-psychotherapy is no better than psychotherapy alone. None suggests that drug therapy is worse. Nine comparisons suggest that drug therapy is less effective than drug-plus-psychotherapy, but 16 comparisons suggest that drug therapy is *no* less effective than drug-plus-psychotherapy. Finally, the vote is only 11 to 8 favoring the superiority of drug therapy to psychotherapy.

The ambiguity of the results across the six reviews is greater than two of the review authors suspect. Luborsky et al. suggested: "The advantage for combined treatment is striking. . . . A combination of treatments may represent more than an additive effect of two treatments—a 'getting more for one's money'—there may also be some mutually facilitative interactive benefits for the combined treatments" (p. 1004).

May (1971) found to the contrary that " there is little difference between psychotherapy plus drug and drug therapy alone for hospitalized psychotic

---

*These outcomes may even be contradictory. For example, in the May (1968) review Lorr (1962) was described as showing that drug-plus-psychotherapy was more effective than psychotherapy alone as rated by therapists, but equal to psychotherapy as rated by patients. Similarly, in May (1971), Koegler and Brill (1967) were said to have demonstrated that drug therapy was better than psychotherapy by patients' own ratings, but psychotherapy was better than drug therapy in the patients' ability to work and understand themselves.

Table 6–2. Summary of findings of six reviews on the drug-plus-psychotherapy and drug-versus-psychotherapy[a]

Reviewer	D + P > P	D + P = P	D + P > D	D + P = D	D > P	P > D	D = P	D + P Interaction	Number of studies
GAP (75)	Lorr (63) Roth (64) Rickles (66) Bellak (64) May (64) Grinspoon (68) Gorham (64)	Lorr (61) Cowden (55) Karon (65,69) Honigfeld (64)	King (58) Evangelikas (61) Klerman (74) Honigfeld (64)	May (64) Cowden (55,56)	Friedman (74) May (64)	Friedman (74)	Cowden (55)	Covi (74) (+)[b]	18
Gilligan (65)	Evangelikas (61)	Gibbs (57)	Evangelikas (61)	Cowden (56)	Evangelikas (61)	Rathod (58)			4
Uhlenhuth (69)	Evangelikas (61) Gorham (64) Grinspoon (68) Daneman (61) Lorr (63) Rickles (66) Bellak (64)	Honigfeld (64) Gibbs (57) Lorr (61)	King (58) Evangelikas (61)	Cowden (56,57) King (63) Honigfeld (64) Gorham (64) May (64)	Evangelikas (61) May (64)				15
Luborsky (75)	Gorham (64) May (65) Cowden (56) King (58) Grinspoon (67) Pascal (56) Evangelikas (61) Luborsky (54) Koegler (67) Reid (69) Daneman (61) Hesbacher (70) Rogers (54)	King (58) Gibbs (57) Lorr (63)	Gorham (64) Hogarty (73) Cowden (56) King (63) Luborsky (54) Klerman (74)	King (60) May (65) Pascal (56) Evangelikas (61) Kroeger (67)	Gorham (64) May (65) Pascal (56) Evangelikas (61) Luborsky (54) Koegler (67)		Lazaras (61)		20

Reviewer	D + P > P	D + P = P	D + P > D	D + P = D	D > P	P > D	D = P	D + P Interaction	Number of studies
May (68)	Evangelikas (61) Grinspoon (67) Hamilton (63) Greenblatt (63) May (64,65,68) Lorr (62)	Gibbs (57) Lorr (61,62) May (64,65)	Appleby (63) Gorham (64)	Fairweather (60)	King (63) Gorham (64) Cowden (56) Honigfeld (65) May (64) Rogers (67)	Cooper (61) Gorham (64) May (64,65) Lorr (62)	Cowden (56) Rathod (58)		19
May (71)	May (64,65) Grinspoon (67) Gorham (64) Evangelikas (61) Lorr (62) Rickles (66)	Cowden (55,56) Gibbs (57) Lorr (61,62)	Gorham (64)	King (58,63) Gorham (64) Cowden (56) May (64) Evangelikas (61) Lorr (62)	Gorham (64) May (68) Evangelikas (61) Lorr (62) Koegler (67)	Koegler (67)	Cowden (55,56) Koegler (67)	Lorr (62) (+)ᵇ Honigfeld (65) (−)ᵇ May (68) (−)ᵇ	17

	D + P > P	D + P = P	D + P > D	D > D + P	D + P = D	D > P	P > D	D = P	D + P Interaction
Number of studies	22	12	9	1	16	11	3	5	(+)2 (−)2

ᵃ D + P = Drug therapy-plus-psychotherapy effects
  D = Drug therapy effects
  P = Psychotherapy effects

ᵇ (+) indicates a drug-plus-psychotherapy interaction
  (−) indicates no-drug-plus-psychotherapy interaction

patients (but not for neurotic out-patients). The combination is, however, quite clearly superior to psychotherapy alone" (p. 513).

Uhlenhuth et al. represented the opinions of GAP and Gilligan when they wrote: "When all is said and done, the existing studies by no means permit firm conclusions as to the nature of the interaction between combined psychotherapy and medication" (p. 611).

Although these reviews of combination therapy are similar in style and method to the reviews of drug therapy, they are different in one important respect. They seek to answer a broader question—not what the effects of this specific drug or this class of drugs are?—but what the effects of this therapy are? And in so doing they cut across types of drug and types of psychotherapy to include a much broader range of cases than typically included in the reviews of drug effects. This sets the proper tone for inclusion of a great variety of studies, as was done in the study reported herein.

Chapter 7

Methods of the Drug Therapy Meta-analysis

This chapter contains descriptions of the methods used in the integration of studies dealing with the treatment of psychological conditions with drugs. The report of methods is divided into the following sections: selection of studies to be included, variables used to classify the study characteristics, data analysis, and restrictions on the research. The psychotherapy meta-analysis and the drug therapy meta-analysis were performed separately. Although the same philosophy of research integration underlies both, the studies were done at different times by different individuals. For this reason some definitions and coding conventions vary between the two.

Selection of Studies

The intent behind this phase of the investigation of the benefits of therapy was to draw conclusions from the whole realm of clinical drug literature. To that end, the entire population of controlled research on drug therapy was the basis for the conclusions. From the population of studies in which drug therapy was compared against controls, a random sample was selected. The population of studies in which drug therapy was compared with psychotherapy was exhausted, as was that of studies in which drug therapy in combination with psychotherapy was evaluated. In the resulting body of studies, no requirements were made to meet proper drug dose level or patient diagnosis, duration of treatment or homogeneity of patient subsample, or to include a placebo control group or test for drug ingestion. This strategy was used to eliminate the problem of selectivity so obvious in previous reviews and the resulting bias in the conclusions. Some reviewers excluded from review all those studies in which an inadequate drug dosage was administered; other authors ignored studies in which a drug was administered for too short a time to allow it to reach what they thought was its full therapeutic potency. Still others omitted studies conducted on an allegedly inappropriate patient population or on a patient population too heterogeneous to allow the symptom-specific effects of a drug to show through. Finally, most reviewers regarded a double-blind placebo-controlled methodology as an essential design feature. These tactics follow the logic set down by Downing et al. (1971), who addressed the problem of integrating research on psychotropic drug effects. "The broader or more relaxed the canons of similarity used by an investigator, the less informative will be the results emerging from the form of quantified combinations which such canons will permit him to employ" (p. 340).

These authors go on to suggest that "A search for reasons underlying atypical results in a few studies may unearth deviations in a procedure which serve to invalidate the data" (p. 344). To increase the homogeneity and validity of the sample of studies under investigation, the deviant studies should be deleted.

This advice, if adhered to conscientiously in choosing studies for inclusion in a review of drug effects, will produce evidence about a drug's effects under what are imagined to be optimal conditions; but the resulting review will not yield the proper evidence to answer the broader evaluative question: What are the effects of this drug under *typical* conditions?

The specification of basic requisites for inclusion of studies in a review has been used as an excuse to exclude articles capriciously. Some psychopharmacologists are suspicious of the motivation and product of such a strategy. Klein and Davis (1969) emphasized less the arbitrariness and more the deviousness of authors employing their own guidelines for inclusion: "With differences of opinion in psychiatry today, almost anything can be proven by a judicious selection of studies fitting one's own preconception. Similarly one might emphasize that studies which did not fit a particular preconception suffered from flaws which render their results suspect" (p. 196). Requirements that drug studies employ a certain drug dosage, patients of a certain homogeneous diagnostic group, placebo controls, or tests for drug ingestion are frequently claimed as absolutely necessary for acceptable clinical research. Reviewers claim a study lacking one or another design requirement is of such little value that it does not merit inclusion in a review of drug effects. We consider this logic too conservative, since it means ignoring research because of hunch and surmise without solid empirical evidence to substantiate that outcomes of "good" studies were different from outcomes of "poor" studies. In the present research, we treat each of these requirements as variables to be related to the measured effectiveness of the drug therapy. In this way, it can be determined whether variations in population or research design do in fact produce differences in the results of research.

The clinical drug research literature was further defined as all published clinical drug trials on mentally ill humans reported in the English language literature between 1954 and 1977. The decision to sample the population of clinical drug research was made for two reasons. First, it was felt that the sheer volume of clinical drug experiments on humans (probably about 1,500 to 2,000 in the English language literature alone) was too large to gather, read, code, and analyze. Second, because of relatively less controversy in the field, it was presumed that drug effects would be fairly consistent, more consistent, for example, than the psychotherapy literature. This greater consistency would allow rather precise estimates of drug effects from relatively fewer cases than were needed to estimate the effects of psychotherapy accurately.

The only requirement for inclusion of a study in our sample was that it employ a no-drug treatment or a placebo control group. Though previous reviewers were admonished for inclusion requirements that were too restrictive (e.g., including only double-blind placebo-controlled studies), this somewhat arbitrary line was drawn because of a conviction that without a control group, spontaneous symptom remission was too likely to be mistaken for a drug effect. Case studies, experiential reports, pre-post designs, and drug versus drug studies were omitted.

To identify more clearly the domain from which to sample, further restrictions were imposed on selection of potential studies. Studies of patients whose primary diagnosis was somatic were excluded. Thus omitted were studies of drugs used to treat patients for organic brain syndrome, epilepsy, phenylketonuria, minimal brain damage, or Down's syndrome, and studies of patients with psychophysiological disorders (asthma, backache, acne, ulcer, enuresis, angina, and the like). This criterion did not exclude studies whose primary focus was examination of neurotic or psychotic patients or patients with character disorders whose somatization of symptoms led to physiological illness. Thus, in a study of patients showing high stress or anxiety, patients may have also complained of sexual problems, sleep disturbances, or hypertension. So long as the patients were described in the aggregate as anxious, phobic, or neurotic, and they were treated with a psychotropic drug, studies of this type were eligible for inclusion. If a study dealt with patients with high blood pressure or chest pain who were treated with nitroglycerine, say, and no major emphasis was placed on underlying causal psychological dysfunction, it would be considered to fall in the domain of somatic medicine and would be excluded from the analysis. Distinctions between primarily psychological research and somatic research might not always be easily made. Nevertheless, with the conventions outlined above as guidelines and with the computerized literature search used as described below, no study identified fell into limbo between research on the mind and research on the body.

All studies of normal subjects and all studies that used *only* physiological outcomes (e.g., blood plasma levels of amines, EEG's, urinalysis) were omitted. Lastly, studies of toxic psychosis (e.g., drug-induced psychosis) or model psychosis (e.g., using hallucinogens) were not examined.

A Medical Literature and Retrieval System (MEDLARS) search from the University of Colorado Medical Center computer search facility generated all research meeting specified criteria catalogued between 1 January 1966 and 30 January 1977. (See Appendix 5 for the search specifications.) The facility catalogues all studies from approximately 2,400 journals.

Studies could not be excluded from the initial MEDLARS search because they lacked control groups or included no measures of psychological outcomes. There were some uncontrolled studies and studies designed to assess only biochemical outcomes of drug administration picked up in the initial search. Approximately 1,100 studies were located by this initial MEDLARS search.

Several studies were selected at random from the MEDLARS printouts. As the referenced articles were located and read, it became clear that many studies lacked control groups. Titles containing no allusion to the existence of a control group (via such key words as "double-blind," "crossover," "controlled," or "placebo") probably indicated studies lacking this crucial ingredient. Therefore, to reduce reference retrieval time, articles with titles containing the above-mentioned key words became the primary focus of the random sample.* Forty such studies were randomly chosen from the MEDLARS bibliography.

From the psychopharmacological literature prior to 1 January 1966, the period not covered by MEDLARS, a random sample of about fifty studies was taken from bibliographies of comprehensive review articles on the efficacy of drug treatment in psychiatric cases. In addition, studies listed in *Psychological Abstracts* between 1954 and 1966 under the heading "Therapy/drugs" were included in the population sampled. These review articles and the number of bibliographical references made in each are presented in Table 7-1. As the last reference in Table 7-1 appears the number of studies sampled from the 1954–66 *Psychological Abstracts* that became part of the pool of pre-1966 references from which studies were sampled. Once again, the emphasis on title terminology that was likely to indicate the use of a control group was applied to selection of studies from these bibliographies.

The selection of the approximately 90 articles (50 articles from the 1954 to 1966 literature; 40 articles from the 1967 to 1977 literature) was stratified so that approximately equal numbers would be represented in three major drug categories: antipsychotic, antianxiety, and antidepressant. Once these articles were assembled, a few articles were added to insure that major well-known studies and very recent articles (February and March 1977) were not overlooked. Ninety-six articles or books studying the effects of drug therapy were thus collected, read, coded, and analyzed in a manner soon to be described.

Furthermore, to answer questions about the interaction of drug therapy and psychotherapy applied in tandem, and to answer questions about the comparative efficacy of the two treatments applied independently, 55 additional arti-

---

*This tactic helps explain the large percent of placebo controlled studies that were entered into this meta-analysis.

Table 7-1.   Bibliographic references from which most pre-1966 studies were sampled

Reference	Topic	Number of studies listed in bibliography
Azcarate (1975)	Antiaggression	43
Davis (1965)	Antidepression	410
Davis et al. (1968)	Antidepression	369
Hollister (1969)	All drugs	120
Hollister (1973)	All drugs	241
Itil (1975)	Antiaggression	81
Klein & Davis (1969)	a) Mood stabilizer	472
	b) Minor tranquilizer	185
	c) Antipsychotic	420
Klerman & Cole (1965)	Antidepression	341
Morris & Beck (1974)	Antidepression	185
Sheard (1975)	Antiaggression	60
Psychological Abstracts (1954–66)	Therapy/drugs	26

cles or books were gathered. Every effort was made to locate controlled studies that pitted drug therapy against psychotherapy or a combination of drug-plus-psychotherapy against either psychotherapy alone or against a control group.

In all, 151 separate studies make up the body of studies included in this meta-analysis. Specific characteristics of each study were recorded on coding sheets, along with calculation of the magnitude of the treatment effect for the outcome variables reported.

Classification of Studies

Once the studies had been assembled, it was necessary to record two types of information from each piece of research: the conditions of the study that might relate to outcome, and the outcome itself. A coding sheet was constructed for recording as much as 56 pieces of information for each study (Appendix 6).

The information chosen for coding was thought to be descriptive of study features that might possibly relate to study outcomes. The characteristics are listed below with a brief description of the conventions used in the coding. To clarify the application of these conventions, an actual study will be coded as an example.

Conditions of the Study

Research Funding Sources. The National Institute of Mental Health, NIH, NIAAA, USPHS, or any domestic or foreign nonprofit sponsor was considered "nonprofit sponsor." The study was categorized as "drug company" if a drug company was explicitly acknowledged to have contributed *any* funding *beyond mere supply of drugs*. Even if NIMH supplied funding as well the funding source was taken to be a drug company. Merely supplying the drugs was not cause for considering the sponsor to be a drug company, since in almost all drug trials, pharmaceutical houses donated the drug tested. The study was categorized "unspecified" if no explicit acknowledgment of sponsor was made. This includes articles in which mention was made of free drugs supplied by drug companies, but no other financing information was provided.

Type of Publication. Codes of "book" (including book chapter or monograph), "major journal," or "minor journal" were given each type of publication. A "major journal" was any journal subscribed to by the University of Colorado Medical Center and bound or intended to be bound for permanent catalogue. The distinction between major and minor journals was so arbitrary that this convention seemed most defensible. Journals less widely read than *Archives of General Psychiatry* or *American Journal of Psychiatry*, but having a good reputation among a more specialized audience, were included in the major journal category (e.g., *Current Therapeutic Research, New England Journal of Medicine, Canadian Medical Association Journal, Psychiatry Quarterly*) along with those journals with larger readerships. Examples of minor journals were *Activitas Nervosa Superior, Clinical Medicine, Post Graduate Medical Journal*. Only one study was included that had not been published in some kind of journal. The results of this unpublished manuscript were included in the "minor journal" category.

Patient Diagnosis. Where at least 90 percent of the patients were reported to fall within a single major diagnosis or specific illness category, that study was coded as that illness category (e.g., psychotic). If the modal patient diagnosis or specific type accounted for fewer than 90 percent of the patients, then that study was coded "mixed," to indicate that more than one type of patient had received the treatment. Chronically ill in-patients, in-patients receiving moderate to large doses of antipsychotic medication, and delusioned patients were classified "psychotic." "Nonpsychotic" patients were those patients described as anxious, phobic, depressed, or showing drug problems. Out-patients receiving moderate to light doses of antianxiety agents or antidepressants were also included in the "nonpsychotic" category. This label was preferred over "neurotic" because neurosis has come to represent a hodge-podge of illnesses ranging from borderline psychosis to juvenile delinquency. Patients were labeled "character disorder" if they were reported to have problems with drugs, alcohol, heroin, or methadone, or were referred to as sociopaths. Studies were classified under "combination" if more than one patient group was involved.

Length of Illness. When not specifically reported, length of illness was listed as "acute" for psychotic patients who were either in a first psychotic episode or were less than 21 years old, or for nonpsychotic patients who presented themselves for therapy for the first time or were less than 25 years old. Patients were coded as "chronic" if they were in-patients for an extended period or if they were 35 or older. Patients labeled "intermediate" were between acute and chronic and between 25 and 35 years of age. If the authors of the study reported average duration of illness, then illnesses of one year or less were coded as "acute." Illness over two year's duration was labeled "chronic." Only if the authors mentioned that patients were mixed in chronicity was the study classified as "mixed."

Mean Age. The mean age was recorded for the patients in the study, either from direct report or estimate.

Percentage Male. The percentage of males in the patient group was recorded.

Socioeconomic Status. The Hollingshead taxonomy was used to classify patient socioeconomic status (SES). When SES information was not reported directly, patients in county or teaching hospitals or who receive welfare or public assistance were classified as "low." Private physician's patients or private psychologist's patients were classified as "middle." Private psychiatrist's patients were classified as "high" SES. These inferences were made because information so easily inferred and so seldom stated was deemed preferable to no information at all.

Sample Size. The number of experimental patients and control patients was summed across all treated and untreated groups to yield the total number of patients included in the study. In cross-over designs, where the same subjects served as both experimentals and controls, the total number of patients was equal to the number of patients in the experimental group (which was also the number in the control group).

Types of Treatment or Control. Treatment type was labeled "placebo" when any inactive (e.g., lactose) or active (e.g., atropine) substance was taken by a patient who was unaware that the substance was intended to have no therapeutic effect. A treatment was considered "psychotherapy" only when a concerted effort was made by researchers to create a psychologically therapeutic environment for patients. This convention reads as a tautology if one does not emphasize "concerted effort." Monthly meetings for 10 to 20 minutes with an M.D. to discuss "any problems with the medication" were not considered psychotherapy. Milieu therapy was considered psychotherapy when authors indicated that special efforts were made to create a psychologically salutary milieu. For example, a teaching hospital for psychiatric residents or a hospital that implemented new or extraordinary procedures to engage patients in group therapy, occupational or recreational therapy, or special interpatient interactions was coded as providing psychotherapy. The treatment was labeled "drug only" when drugs alone were administered as treatment. If this administration had taken place in a hospital setting or with brief meetings between the patient and the M.D. to discuss side effects or dosage requirements, and no mention was made by the author of any concerted effort to provide psychotherapy to the patient, then the treatment was coded as "drug only." The treatment was labeled "drug-plus-psychotherapy" if psychotherapy was provided the patient, as well as drugs. This psychotherapy can be as little as "brief supportive psychotherapy" or milieu therapy, but the authors of the study must have made explicit mention of the intent to provide a psychotherapeutic liaison or environment. Unintended combinations of psychotherapy with drugs were not, by these conventions, coded as "drug-plus-psychotherapy." The treatment was labeled "psychotherapy-plus-placebo" if the group receiving psychotherapy received drug placebo as well. The label "regular treatment minus drug" was given when hospitals did not provide such milieux (as above and offering no drugs to treat patients). Waiting list controls or control patients generally ignored during the study by the professional staff conducting the research were categorized as "no treatment or placebo."

Psychotherapy treatments were further categorized as: "individual behavioral" (single person, behavior modification, or systematic desensitization), "group behavioral" (group meetings to solve a specific behavioral problem, e.g., word behavior, while eschewing insights or interpretations), "individual nonbehavioral" (psychoanalysis, psychoanalytic psychotherapy, client-centered therapy, cognitive-theory-modeled therapy such as rational-emotive therapy, reality therapy, transactional analysis, Gestalt therapy), and "group nonbehavioral" (milieu therapy in which concerted effort is made to improve the physical and psychological environment of the patient).

Years of Therapist Experience. Information about the years of therapists' experience was seldom reported in the body of research comparing drugs to psychotherapy or examining the combined effects of drug and psychotherapy. Where some information was given, but the information was short of specifying the exact number of years of therapists' experience, the following conventions were developed: "extensive experience" or "several years experience" was coded as "10 years." If the senior author was one of the therapists, the study was coded as "5 years." A classification of "2 years" was given to therapists who were Ph.D.-level clinical psychology students or second-year psychiatric residents. When therapists were first-year psychiatric residents or "inexperienced therapists," the study was coded "one year." The vaguest information about therapists' experience was often missing. No attempt was made to estimate the years of experience for the psychopharmacologists or medical doctors treating the patients with drugs alone.

Duration of Treatment. The average number of months spent in therapy at the time of outcome measurement was coded. If half the patients ended therapy at 12 weeks and half ended therapy at 14 weeks, then duration would be 13 weeks or 4.2 months. If outcome measurements were made at several different points in therapy, only the measures taken at the latest point were included in the analysis. The average number of hours of psychotherapy was also recorded.

Major Drug Type. Drugs were categorized, using Hollister's (1973) taxonomy: "A more realistic nomenclature might be based on the putative clinical uses of the various drugs. Drugs used for treating anxiety in all its clinical guises would be referred to as anti-anxiety drugs; those for mental depressions, as antidepressants; and those used for treating schizophrenia and other psychoses would be termed antipsychotic drugs" (p. 7). Where the therapeutic purpose of a drug was unknown and the clinical diagnosis of patients for which the drug was prescribed was also unknown, the drug was classified as "other." Lithium and all other drugs used to treat mania were classified as antipsychotic agents. Drugs used to combat alcohol or narcotic abuse (e.g., naloxone, disulfiram, LSD, metronidazole) were classified as antidrug-dependent drugs and later, due to so few cases, were coalesced with the "other" category. Where a drug generally used to treat one genre of illness, e.g., depression, was used to treat a different type, e.g., anxiety, its drug type code remained with its more general putative clinical use. So, for example, where amitriptyline was used to treat school phobia, it was classified as an antidepressant. Where thioridazine was used to treat severe anxiety, it was classified as an antipsychotic drug. Table 8-6 contains a list of most drugs included in this study and their generic classifications.

Average Daily Dosage. Mean dosage over the duration of the experiment was recorded. If patients began on 800 milligrams (mg) per day of meprobamate for the first two weeks of therapy, were raised to 1,000 mg for the second two weeks, and received 1,500 mg the last two weeks, then the average daily dosage equaled 1,100 mgs. Where therapists could prescribe dosage within a given range, the mean dosage, unless otherwise reported, equaled one-half the range of dosages.

Severity of Side Effects. The study was coded "low" if so reported or if no side-effect information was given. A coding of "medium" was assigned if side effects were discussed but no more than two more patients were removed from the drug due to side effects than were removed from placebo due to side effects. If side effects were so severe that three or more patients were removed from treatment (or had their dosage reduced) than were lost from the placebo group, then this variable was coded "high."

Control of Drug Intake. Reports are legion of patient noncompliance with prescribed intake of drugs. To assess the effect on outcome of methods to help insure the intake of drugs, the presence or absence of such controls was recorded for each study. Studies were classified as "controlled" if there was parenteral administration, depot or implant administration, urinalysis or mouth check, or pill count. The study was classified as "no controls" if characterized by absence of control or if there was pill count showing general noncompliance with prescribed dosage, or if there was no mention of controls.

Time of Outcome Measurement. A record was made of the number of months elapsed between the time the treatment ended and the time the effects were measured. If elapsed time was under one month, but over 0 months, the code was "one month."

Types of Outcome Measurement. There were six types of outcome measurement: hospital-related outcomes, somatic symptoms, psychological symptoms, adjustment, global health, and a miscellaneous category. *Hospital-Related Outcomes* consisted of "release rate" (number or percent of patients released from an in-patient facility), "hospitalization rate" (number or percent of patients placed on in-patient status), "length of hospitalization" (number of days that patients remained on in-patient status), and "length of time in community" (number of days that patients remained in the community). Observations and ratings of patient behavior, such as ward disruption, excessive alcohol intake, and bodily functions (eating, sleeping, sexual activity) comprised *Somatic Symptoms,* which also included attitudes and behaviors relative to the use of alcohol and drugs, as well as global behavior checklists. *Psychological Symptoms* were those outcomes designed to assess patients' anxiety, depression, self-esteem, disordered cognition and ego functioning. While most behaviors were coded as somatic symptoms or adjustment problems, most pencil and paper and projective tests designed to assess intrapsychic well-being were coded as measures of psychological symptoms. A few behaviors were coded as measures of psychological symptoms because they so clearly were measures of anxiety. These were physiological measures of stress and tension—heartbeat, blood pressure, galvanic skin response, and measures of phobic behavior—ability to leave home and to go school, ability to walk among crowds, and the like. *Adjustment* consisted of "work adjustment" (attendance at work or school and ratings of work and school behavior), "hospital adjustment" (interactions with fellow patients and staff, cooperation, general demeanor), "social adjustment" (appearance, activity, speech, family life and nonhospital-related cooperation, interactions, and demeanor), "aggression," "manic behavior," "global mental health" (overall improvement or deterioration in symptoms or adjustment). The *Miscellaneous* category included outcomes which could not be classified in the others described above.

Method of Outcome Measurement. Some outcomes were measurements made by the experimenter or therapist; others were ratings made by nurses, ward attendants, the patients themselves or their relatives. How an outcome was measured might be related to the size of the drug therapy effect. Consequently, several categories were defined and outcomes coded accordingly. They were "patient self-report" (self-assessment of health, usually a global rating), "patient test" (any test of intelligence, personality or psychomotor ability), "experimenter rating" (ratings given by therapist, researcher or uninvolved third party who was not a nurse), "nurse rating" (including ward attendants or paraprofessionals), "ratings by significant others" (relative, friend, or co-patient), and "physiological assessment" (e.g., heart rate, blood pressure, galvanic skin response). When more than one method was used, it was classified as a "combination."

Susceptibility to Influence. Each outcome measure was given a rating that indicated the degree to which it was possible for the patient to influence the magnitude or direction of results. For example, if a patient wanted to appear more mentally healthy than he was, he could do so on a self-assessment merely by giving himself a higher rating. It would be more difficult to "fake good" on complex multifactor personality tests. It would be even more difficult to influence ratings given by his nurses or doctors. Points on the susceptibility to influence scale were assigned as follows. All patient self-report measures, because they were most readily influenced, were rated 5, the highest scale value. Multifactor personality tests were rated 4. Assessments by doctors, nurses, and significant others were rated 3. Cognitive tests were rated 2. Physiological measures of stress and hospitalization status (least susceptible to influence) were rated 1. It should be noted that susceptibility does not relate to the degree of blindness in the design and thus is a different construct from "reactivity of measure" (Chapter 4).

Research Design. Different research designs might produce different clinical drug trial results. Some reviewers have recommended ignoring the results of all but the best research. What is regarded as excellent research differs from reviewer to reviewer, but most agree that minimum standards of validity demand double-blind and placebo-controlled trials. Drug trials lacking a patient group that receives a drug placebo or in which effects are assessed by doctors aware of patients' assignment to the treated or control condition provide suspect evidence of drug effects. Although the validity of such research is justifiably in doubt, doubt does not constitute proof of false findings.

Rather than eliminate "poor" studies because of suspicious research design, we coded these characteristics of research design and studied their covariation with research outcomes. Major design characteristics that were coded were patient and doctor blinding, use of drug placebo as a control, method of patient assignment to groups, control of patient attrition, and global internal validity. A study was listed as "double-blind" when neither patient, experimenter, nor rater of outcome was aware of the experimental status of the patient. An outcome was listed as "single-blind" when only the therapist or rater knew what treatment the patient was given. If no information was given regarding the therapist's knowledge of treatment assignment, then such knowledge was assumed. In most cases, it was the patient who was uninformed about his treatment assignment. A study design was listed as "open" if the therapist, the patient, and the rater knew what treatment the patient was receiving. A design was listed as "placebo-controlled" if the experimental condition was tested against a drug-placebo condition. Patient assignment to experimental conditions was listed either as "random," "matched groups," or "intact groups" (existing groups such as hospital wards). The study was classified according to whether or not attrition (patients dropping out during the course of treatment) was controlled.

Each study was rated on its "global internal validity." This rating was a composite of several features of the research design: blinding, use of placebo controls, method of assigning patients to treatments, attrition, and the susceptibility to influence of the outcome measurement. A five-point scale was used. A score of 5 was assigned to studies in which (1) patients were randomly assigned to treatments, (2) placebo controls were used, (3) there was low attrition, and (4) there were blind ratings of outcomes not greatly susceptible to influence. A score of 1 was assigned to studies in which there was nonrandom assignment of patients to treatments and obvious noncomparability of treatment and control groups; or severe attrition of the samples of patients; or either of these problems plus nonblind ratings of outcomes highly susceptible to influence. Scores of 2, 3, and 4 fell between the anchor points defined above and represented some modifications or departures from the definition. A score of 3, for example, was given to studies in which there was random assignment of patients to treatments, but high or differential rates of attrition or nonblind ratings of outcomes highly susceptible to influence.

Because calculation of the internal validity of a comparison relied more on subjective judgment and general familiarity with basic threats to internal validity (e.g., Campbell and Stanley 1966) than on a prescribed formula, some examples are offered below of studies whose results are threatened the least and studies whose results are threatened the most by poor research design. The following four studies were given the lowest rating of internal validity. In Greenblatt (1965), outcomes were discharge rates, but the drug group was in one hospital and the no-drug group was in a different hospital. Since the latter was a teaching hospital with a reputation for shorter stay, the differences in discharge rates probably reflected differences in discharge policy. Although patients were assigned at random to hospitals, neither patient nor therapist was blind to treatment conditions. Cowden (1955) used nonblind ratings of ward behavior and patients were assigned to wards in some unreported (and probably nonrandom) fashion. Pretreatment data showed great differences between the treatment group and the control group. Treatment patients, reported healthier at the end of the experiment, were on the average four and one-half years younger than control patients. Analysis of variance was conducted on three treatment groups and one control group, each with a reported eight patients. The degrees of freedom were reported to be 3 and 24, with no explanation of the loss of four patients' data. In Gottlieb (1951), patients received either insulin treatments or psychotherapy. Therapists rated the patients receiving psychotherapy, but several different third parties rated patients who received insulin therapy. Attrition was great. Only 39 of 128 original psychotherapy patients were rated on improvement. Neither therapists nor raters were blind to the assignment of patients to conditions. In a study by Bassa (1965), there was complete confusion of treatments (drug or placebo). Patients were able to switch back and forth between the two treatment medications, and no records were kept of the switching. If the patient was not improved, he was switched to the comparison pill, but no record of this switch was reported. Although patients were originally randomly assigned to drug or placebo, and although the study was double blind, over half of the patients did not complete the treatment.

The following are examples of studies with the highest ratings of internal validity. Kelley (1969) tested chlordiazepoxide against a placebo for two weeks. There was random assignment, no patient attrition, and double-blind conditions. In Zwanikken (1976), the effects of penfluridol were compared to a placebo. Patients were randomly assigned to treatments, and there were no dropouts during the six months of treatment. All parties were blinded to treatment assignments. Curiously, all patients were able to obtain prescriptions for other antipsychotic drugs. While this lowered the internal validity score for all ratings of improvement, it allowed a perfect internal validity score for the outcome, showing the percent of penfluridol and placebo patients who received other antipsychotic drugs. In a study by Bennet et al. (1954), nurses made blind ratings of patients. Patients were randomly assigned to isoniazid or a placebo. All parties were blind to treatment assignment, and patients received drug or placebo for three months. No dropouts were reported. Gittleman-Klein et al. (1976) randomly assigned 61 children to receive methylphenidate or placebo; the patients were tested on the full-scale WISC. Only four children dropped out. All parties were blind to treatment assignment.

Calculation of the Effect Size. Once study characteristics were coded, the difference between the treatment and the control group results (or between the results of two treatment groups) had to be quantified. To quantify the difference in outcome measured between treated and untreated patients, the untreated patients' mean score was subtracted from the treated patients' mean, and the difference was divided by the standard deviation of the untreated patients' scores. Thus, effect sizes were measures of the superiority, if any, of treatment groups compared to control groups expressed in standard deviation units. In its simplest form, the effect size equals $(\bar{X}_D - \bar{X}_C)/s_C$ where $\bar{X}_D$ = drug group mean, $\bar{X}_C$ = control group mean, and s_C = standard deviation of the control group. The effect size metric is akin to a z-score and permits the same interpretations, assuming a normal distribution of responses to therapy. An effect size of 1.0 means that after therapy the average treated patient lies at the 84th percentile of the untreated group. Two treatments can be compared by this method as well. An effect size of +1 for drug-treated patients compared to psychotherapy patients indicates that the average drug-treated patient lies at the 84th percentile of the psychotherapy-treated group.

Simple as this effect-size measure seems to be, nonuniform reporting practices and the absence of results of the two fundamental statistics needed for its solution often complicate its calculation. Among almost 400 drug therapy effect sizes, two-thirds were calculated by methods that were more complex than the uncomplicated calculation described above.

In most of these cases, reported means, F, and t-statistics allowed for post hoc calculation of the standard deviation of an outcome measure. Where no means or standard deviations were reported, but sample sizes and p values of statistics were given, effect sizes could still be determined. The square root of within-cell mean squares from one-way analyses of variance often served as the standard deviation in the effect-size equation when only F statistics were reported. For factorial analyses of variance, the within-cell mean square had to be changed before it could be used in the effect-size calculation. Crossing the treatment with a factor that correlates with outcome reduces the within-cell mean square. This reduction must be corrected before the square root of the within-cell mean square is taken as the standard deviation in the effect-size formula. The mean square within-cells of factorial analyses of covariance had to be properly corrected both for homogenization of cell variability due to the crossing of treatment by some attribute that correlated with outcome, as well as deflation due to the correlation between dependent variable and covariate. Wherever a result was reported as "not significant," a nondirectional p value of 0.25 was arbitrarily chosen for effect-size calculation purposes. Effect sizes calculated by this method were perhaps least defensible, since the p values were based on almost no information (except that they were no smaller than 0.05). But they amounted to only four or five cases out of several hundred in the entire study. Where only sample sizes were shown and a report of "significant difference" was made, a p value of 0.05 was chosen to allow calculations of the effect size. This procedure probably yielded conservative results (i.e., consistently smaller effect sizes than may have been proper), since the 0.05 level of significance is the upper boundary of conventionally acceptable probabilities for rejecting null hypotheses. Complete explication of formulas used to reconstruct effect sizes from various statistics is located in Appendix 7. Outcomes reported as rates (e.g., rehospitalization rates or percentage improvements) were transformed into probability units or probits (Finney 1971). The control probit was subtracted from the experimental probit to yield an effect-size metric comparable to that used for continuous data.

In most studies, more than one outcome measurement was reported. Converting all reported outcomes to effect sizes proved impossible, and choice of a subset of outcomes became an important problem. Guidelines were established to keep the method of choosing outcomes consistent. Results were always chosen without prior regard to the outcome of the significance tests associated with them, so statistically significant as well as nonsignificant results were included without prejudice. When many dependent variables were measured, an attempt was made to choose the outcomes that were suggested in the text to be most likely affected by the treatment. For example, an author hypothesized that imipramine would be most effective in reducing anxiety in his phobic patients. He reported the psychiatrist's post-treatment five-point rating of patient phobia, the full-scale MMPI, the Zung depression scale, and a patient's anxiety checklist. The psychiatrist's ratings and the patients' checklist were chosen for calculation of effect sizes, since they related most directly to the major intended benefit of the therapy. Individual subscales from multidimensional tests were chosen in this fashion as well. Where more than three outcome measures fell into a category that was to be selected, one outcome was randomly chosen for inclusion.

If no outcome measure was identified by the author as most likely affected by therapy, then the measures most tractable to the treatment were chosen (e.g., anxiety measures in studies of antianxiety agents). If the most likely symptoms affected were not easily interpretable, or effects were incalculable, the most interpretable results were chosen. So, for example, if depressed neurotic patients treated with phenelzine were reported to "show healthier profiles on the Beck Depression Inventory," but no information about the mean score differences or the probability levels associated with the differences was reported, then an effect size for the Beck Depression Inventory could not be calculated. A five-point global rating of improvement reported in the study might then be substituted for this missing effect.

Generally, if overall results from multiscale tests were reported (e.g., Brief Psychiatric Rating Scale total score or Hamilton Depression Scale), these results were preferred over the test's individual scale scores (e.g., Brief Psychiatric Rating Scale anxiety score or Hamilton Retardation/Apathy Cluster). Where *all* individual scale scores for each group were reported for a multidimensional test like the MMPI, all scales were averaged and the outcome was coded as a global measure of health or illness. Where individual scale scores were reported (e.g., the D or Ma of the MMPI scales) and there were no significant differences on the other scales, then one zero was added into the effect size of reported scales for each unreported nonsignificant scale score. This conservative strategy may attenuate the overall results by adding in zeros where slightly positive effects might have been added had the details of the nonsignificant results been reported. This was done on no more than four occasions out of several hundred. If entire tests were omitted because they showed no significant differences, the results were ignored and no zeros were added into the effects of other measures that were reported. This liberal bias inflates the overall results by ignoring the unreported small or negative effects. The two counterbalancing strategies were borne of an effort to account for unreported effects, since unreported results ignored in a meta-analysis would tend to bias estimates of therapeutic efficacy.

Reliability of Coding Procedures

To test the reliability of the coding, 2 judges were enlisted to code 5 studies. One judge coded 2 studies, and one coded 3. The judges were unfamiliar with the psychopharmacological literature, but well-practiced in general coding and effect-size calculation common in meta-analysis.

The 5 studies were included in the 151 studies gathered for this meta-analysis. Each judge received a drug-only study and a study of drug-plus-psychotherapy. The studies were chosen at random from all studies under ten pages in length. This restriction of length was adopted to reduce the time necessary for the judges to devote to the task. A brief list of coding conventions was given to each judge, with a request to code only the effect size for one or two dependent variables if there were many from which to choose.

One hundred sixty-two ratings were recorded by the 2 judges over the 5 studies (not including the effect sizes themselves) and were matched with an equal number of ratings by a third judge. One hundred twenty-two (75 percent) were identical and another 13 (8 percent) were within one or two scale points for five-point rating scales or continuous variables such as patient age, duration of treatment, and the like. Seventeen percent of the ratings were placed into the wrong category or were off by more than two scale points. These incorrect codings included such inconsistencies as the rating of an outcome measure as hospital adjustment rather than work adjustment or as somatic symptoms instead of anxiety. The codings of the two judges did not differ substantially from the codings of the third.

Agreement between each judge's calculation of effect sizes and an earlier independent calculation was substantial. A sixth study was added exclusively to give another test to the replicability of effect-size calculation. This study was chosen to represent a relatively complex case for calculation. Calculated by the second judge, it is reported last in Table 7-2 below.

Table 7-2.   Effect sizes for two judges compared to those of a third judge

	Study	ES for judge	ES for judge no. 3	Size of error
Judge 1	Study 1	0.50	0.54	0.04
	Study 2	0.64	0.67	0.03
Judge 2	Study 3	−1.15	−0.95	0.20
	Study 4	0.87	0.85	0.02
	Study 5	1.58	1.58	0.00
	Study 6	1.08	0.93	0.15
		$\overline{ES} = 0.59$	$\overline{ES} = 0.60$	Average: 0.07

Example of Study Classification

To provide a concrete example of the process of classifying a study, the following description is presented. The study is by Gibbs, Wilkins, and Lauterbach (1975). The *Research Funding Source* was labeled ''unspecified,'' since there was no mention made of it. *Type of Publication* was ''major journal'' (*Journal of Clinical Experimental Psychopathology*). *Patient Diagnosis* was listed as ''combination.'' Authors reported that ''all psychoneurotic disorders were included. . . . Other clinical groups accepted for study included affective and schizophrenic psychoses'' (p. 274). *Length of Illness* was assigned a value of ''one to two years.'' No specific information on this point was provided, but the intermediate length was chosen because patients were about 26 years old and were both in- and out-patients. *Age* was given by the author as an average of ''26 years.'' Information on the *Percentage Male* of the patient group was given as ''62 percent.'' *SES* was estimated as ''middle'' based on reported information on patients' (or their dependents') status as veterans with average intelligence. *Sample Size* was listed by the authors as 25 for the experimental group and 14 for the control group. *Type of Treatment or Control* was classified as ''drug-plus-psychotherapy vs. psychotherapy-plus-placebo.'' Patients were assigned to one of three groups. Two groups received one of two different size doses of chlorpromazine (about 100 mg and about 300 mg) and psychotherapy. The results of these two groups were pooled to represent the drug-plus-psychotherapy condition. The third group received four placebo tablets daily plus psychotherapy. *Type of Psychotherapy* was classified ''individual nonbehavioral'' based on information that it was carried on at a VA hospital and conducted by two psychiatrists. *Years of Therapist Experience* was listed as ''unknown'' due to lack of direct information or clues. *Duration of Therapy* was given as ''1.5 months'' for both drug therapy and psychotherapy. The number of hours of psychotherapy was unknown. The *Major Drug Type* was listed as ''antipsychotic'' (chlorpromazine). The *Average Daily Dosage* was listed as ''200 mgs.'' This figure represents the average dosage of the two groups (one that received 100 mgs and the other that received 300 mgs) pooled to form the drug-plus-psychotherapy treatment condition. *Severity of Side Effects* was listed as "low." Four patients were reported to have side effects ranging from leukopenia to nausea to skin rash, but side effects were not so severe that any patient had to be dropped from treatment. No information was given about side effects in the placebo group. *Control of Drug Intake* was listed as "no control." Although the drug was administered orally, there was no report of pill counts or other measures to check ingestion.

Time of Outcome Measurement was listed as "zero months," because all outcomes were assessed immediately after treatment. Three outcomes were recorded under *Type of Outcome Measurement*. The Revised Malamud Psychiatric Rating Scale was recorded under measures of "global mental health" (since it was described by the authors as an "overall index of the extent of pathology"). The Minnesota Multiphasic Personality Inventory was also recorded under measures of "global mental health," since the thirteen subscales were converted to effect sizes and averaged to yield one global outcome measure. The Wechsler Bellvue intelligence test was used as a measure of disordered cognition and thus was recorded in the category "psychological symptoms." *Method of Outcome Measurement* consisted of "experimenter rating" for the Malamud Scale and "patient test" for the MMPI and Wechsler Bellvue. *Susceptibility to Influence* was rated "four" for the MMPI, "three" for the Malamud Scale and "two" for the Wechsler Bellvue, because of respectively decreasing possibilities for the patient to "fake good" and appear better off than he was.

The degree of *Blinding* in the experimental design was listed as "single-blind." Patients were unaware whether they were in the drug-plus-psychotherapy treatment group or in the placebo-plus-psychotherapy group. The psychiatrists who treated and rated patients on the Malamud Scale were, however, aware of treatment assignments. The study was listed as *Placebo-Controlled*. *Patient Assignment* to treatments was random. *Attrition Control* was quite satisfactory. All 39 patients beginning treatment were measured after the six-week trial. *Global Internal Validity* was rated separately for the Malamud Scale and the other two outcomes. The Malamud Scale yielded an outcome that was suspect, due to an "instrumentation" threat to internal validity (Campbell and Stanley 1966). Therapists who rated outcome could, without premeditation, apply different standards of improvement (i.e., different instrumentation) to the drug-plus-psychotherapy group and the placebo-plus-psychotherapy group. Consequently, the internal validity rating for the Malamud Scale was only "two." The single-blind problem was not so great a threat to the internal validity of the IQ and MMPI findings, because the therapist has less control over the results. Consequently, the internal validity rating was "four" for these two outcomes, reflecting the strength of the design due to random assignment of patients and lack of attrition. The internal validity rating was one point below perfect, because of the single rather than double-blind feature of the design.

Three *Effect Sizes* were calculated, one for each outcome: Malamud Psychiatric Rating Scale $= 0.60s_x$, Wechsler Bellvue IQ $= -.35s_x$, and MMPI $= -.14s_x$ (the average effect size for 13 subscales). The MMPI and IQ results favored the placebo-plus-psychotherapy group over the drug-plus-psychotherapy group. The Malamud Rating Scale showed the reverse result.

Data Analysis

In nearly all respects, the analysis of the data, once they were collected and coded, proceeded by the same methods discussed at the end of Chapter 4 and illustrated throughout Chapter 5. In the literature on drug therapy and in its meta-analysis, one encounters the same problems of nonindependence, scaling, "control referencing," and regression adjusting that arose in the analysis of findings on the effects of psychotherapy. The analysis of drug and psychotherapy effects and their interaction goes beyond the methods of Chapters 4 and 5 in one important respect, however. This respect must be described here and again in Chapter 8, where the results of the studies are presented.

The notion of a statistical interaction is at the heart of what is frequently claimed to be the benefits of drug and psychotherapy separately and in combination. Not enough can be written here to substitute for an extensive didactic discussion of interaction (for which the reader who needs it might see Glass and Stanley 1970, pp. 404ff., or Hopkins and Glass 1978, pp. 369ff.). But the rudiments of the notion can be conveyed. If the properties of two things cannot be predicted from their properties in isolation, they might be said to "interact," in common parlance. For example, hydrochloric acid and sodium hydroxide interact to form common salt (NaCl) and water, though neither salt nor water is present in either of the original chemicals. Oil and water remain oil and water even when mixed; they do not interact. To put the notion of interaction one step closer to its statistical meaning, one can say that if the result of combining two conditions is *not* the sum of the results of the two conditions separately, the conditions interact. A synonym for interaction in this context is nonadditivity. Imagine that an agronomist sprays acres of hay with hydrochloric acid and other acres of hay with sodium hydroxide; he is likely to harvest zero bushels per acre. But if he combines the acid and the base, which then forms salt and water, and sprays his hay with the mixture, he will probably harvest a decent yield (even though no thanks are due to the salt water spray). The sum of the HCl and NaOH effects (0 bales/acre + 0 bales/acre) does not equal the (HCl + NaOH) effect, which might be 150 bales/acre. The acid and the base have an interaction effect on the crop yield.

Consider what is often written and spoken about the relative benefits of drug and psychotherapy. Some persons believe that psychotherapy with seriously disturbed clients is not very beneficial; for example, it would score 1 on a hypothetical 10-point scale of effectiveness. Drug therapy with the seriously ill might be only slightly more beneficial, say a score of 2 on the 10-point scale. However, when drugs are used to calm the patient down or open him up and, hence, permit the psychotherapist to do his work, the benefits are exceedingly great (score 8 on the 10-point scale), so the story goes. The combined benefits of drug therapy and psychotherapy are believed to be greater than the sum of their separate effects: $8 > 1 + 2$. Thus are drug therapy and psychotherapy believed to interact in the treatment of serious psychological problems. It is unimportant at this stage that many people do not believe this is so.

The experimental literature on drug therapy and psychotherapy addresses the estimation of the separate and interactive effects of drugs and psychotherapy in a variety of ways. The variety is a nuisance. Several types of experiment can be identified that inform one about the drug effect alone, or the drug plus the interaction effect, or the psychotherapy plus the drug plus the interaction effect, and so on in various combinations. An experiment that compares clients' progress under drugs with a group of clients receiving a placebo or nothing estimates the simple drug effect. Whereas, an experiment that compares two groups of clients, one of which receives drugs-plus-psychotherapy and the other only drugs provides an estimate of the psychotherapy plus the interaction effect, since one group has the possible advantage of the separate psychotherapy effect and any benefits that result from combining drugs and psychotherapy. Denote the drug effect in isolation when compared with a placebo or no treatment by δ; denote the separate psychotherapy effect by ψ; and denote the interaction effect of the two by η. Then the comparison of drug therapy and placebo in an experiment estimates δ. The comparison of drug-plus-psychotherapy with psychotherapy estimates $\delta + \eta$ because both sides of the comparison have equal psychotherapy effects. In Table 7-3 appear the possible experimental comparisons of drug and psychotherapy and what effects these comparisons estimate.

By arranging and averaging the results from experiments of the six different types specified in Table 7-3, the separate and interactive effects of drug and psychotherapy can be estimated. The organization of data and unknown parameters in Table 7-3 can be viewed as a system of six sources of informa-

Table 7-3. The structure of experiments on the effects of drug and psychotherapy

Treatments compared in the experiment	Effects estimated by the comparison
A. Drug vs. placebo (or no treatment)	δ
B. Psychotherapy vs. placebo	ψ
C. (Drug & psychotherapy) vs. placebo	$\delta + \psi + \eta$
D. (Drug & psychotherapy) vs. drug	$\psi + \eta$
E. (Drug & psychotherapy) vs. psychotherapy	$\delta + \eta$
F. Drug vs. psychotherapy	$\delta - \psi$

tion and three unknown parameters. Least-squares estimates of the parameters can be calculated by ordinary methods.

If one wished to maintain a distinction between placebo and no-treatment control groups, there would be twelve lines in Table 7-3 instead of six, and the structure of effects would change slightly; for example, a drug vs. no-treatment experiment would estimate the drug plus the placebo effect, since the expectancy effect of administering the drug to the experimental group would not be counterbalanced by an expectancy effect for the no-treatment control group. In the analyses that follow in Chapter 8, placebo and no-treatment controls will be combined in unweighted averages, and the estimation of the placebo effect largely ignored.

....

Findings of the Drug Therapy Meta-analysis

The 112 experiments on the effects of drug therapy and drug plus psychotherapy yielded about 566 measurements of effect, which will be described and analyzed in a variety of ways in this chapter. First, the overall distribution of the drug therapy effects will be described and discussed; its gross characteristics will be compared with the findings on the effects of psychotherapy from Chapter 5. Then, the data will be analyzed to obtain estimates of the size of effects produced by drug therapy and by psychotherapy and the magnitude of their interaction when combined. Two types of data will be analyzed for this purpose; the entire data set with all its nonequivalences and confoundings, and a subset of the data in which certain comparisons of effects are controlled by merit of their having been controlled by the original investigators. Finally, the relationships of the size of the drug therapy effect with numerous characteristics of the therapy, the clients and the studies themselves will be described.

Effects of Drug Therapy

Experiments reported in the literature yielded 412 effect-size measurements for drug therapy or drug therapy combined with psychotherapy compared to a no-treatment or placebo control group. These measures represent the published literature on drug therapy or drug and psychotherapy combined.

Of the 412 values of *ES*, 49 (or 12 percent) represent effects of drug therapy and psychotherapy in combination compared to no-treatment or placebo control groups. Data from about 13,000 patients are represented in the over four hundred effect measures. Basic descriptive statistics for the 412 drug and drug-plus-psychotherapy effects are presented in Table 8-1.

There it can be seen that the average effect size is one-half standard deviation. The implications of an effect of this size for patient groups are illustrated in Figure 8-1. In the figure, two normal distributions representing hypothetical treatment and control groups of patients measured on an outcome variable are placed with 0.511 standard deviations between their means.

Table 8-1.   Descriptive statistics for 412 drug and drug-plus-psychotherapy effect sizes

Average effect size	$\overline{ES} = 0.511$		
Standard deviation of effect sizes	s_{ES}	=	0.675
Standard error of mean effect size	$s_{\overline{ES}}$	=	0.034
Number of effect sizes	N_{ES}	=	412
Number of studies	N_{studies}	=	112
Range of effect sizes	Lowest	=	-1.08
	Highest	=	5.18
Percent of negative effect sizes	$\%(-)$	=	14%

(The skewness and kurtosis of the distribution are 2.50 and 11.58, respectively.)

The average patient in the therapy group is at the 70th percentile of the untreated (or placebo) control group. Thus, the typical patient's standing on the outcome variable has been bettered by twenty percentile ranks because of treatment. Only 14 percent of the *ES*'s were negative: about 10 percent were negative for the effects of psychotherapy reported in Chapter 5. When the 363 *ES*'s for drug therapy vs. no-treatment control or placebo groups are averaged, a figure of 0.499 standard deviations results.

One is tempted to compare the average drug effect reported here with the average psychotherapy effect reported in Chapter 5. The temptation is irresistible, but the comparison must be done cautiously. More than 80 percent of the drug or drug-plus-psychotherapy experiments employed placebo control groups; the figure for psychotherapy experiments in Chapter 5 is only about 10 percent. The placebo in drug studies is usually an inert substance administered as a pill. The little data available on the question give an estimated effect of this placebo as large as one-quarter standard deviation, i.e., a placebo vs. no-treatment comparison of roughly $0.25s_x$.* So in a gross comparison of the average *ES* of Table 8-1 with the average psychotherapy effect in Table 5-1, it would be well to increase the drug effect by about 0.20 because of placebo effects. But other important inequalities remain between the two collections of studies, those of Chapter 5 and those considered here. The average drug therapy patient is older than the average client of psychotherapy (37 years vs. 22 years); he is more likely to be diagnosed as psychotic (50 percent vs. 7 percent); he is more likely to be institutionalized (47 percent vs. 17 percent); and so forth. Nearly all of the ways in which the typical drug therapy patient

---

*About 340 comparisons were made between drug therapy or drug-plus-psychotherapy and a placebo control group; their average effect size was $\overline{ES} = 0.483$. Nearly 70 effect sizes were calculated on comparison of either type of therapy with untreated control groups; their average equaled $\overline{ES} = 0.702$. A first approximation of the placebo effect would be the difference, which equals 0.22. Three studies that directly compared the placebo condition with untreated controls yield ten *ES*'s that averaged 0.28.

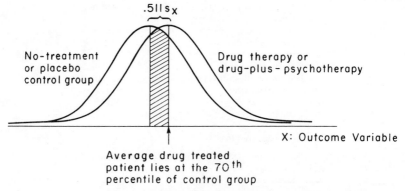

Figure 8-1. Drug therapy and drug-plus-psychotherapy effects for all outcomes, patients, drugs, and settings (based on 112 studies and 412 data points)

differs from the typical client of psychotherapy in Chapter 5 probably make the former a less likely candidate for large therapeutic gains than the latter.*

Drug and Psychotherapy Effects: Separate and Interactive

The 566 measures of effect calculated from the 112 experiments encompass varied and complicated information about the separate and interactive effects of drug and psychotherapy. In the final section of Chapter 7, the precise way in which various experimental comparisons estimate these effects was explained. In Table 8-2 appear the actual average effect sizes calculated from the findings of the 112 experiments.

As an example of how Table 8-2 can be interpreted, consider the first line of entries. A total of 55 comparisons in the 112 studies involved contrasting the scores of persons who received psychotherapy with those who received no treatment or, at most, a placebo. Such comparisons estimate the magnitude of the psychotherapy effect, ψ; the estimate equals 0.30, i.e., the psychotherapy groups averaged three-tenths standard deviation superior to the control groups on the outcome variables. Consider as a second example the 94 comparisons of drug-plus-psychotherapy with psychotherapy alone. Such comparisons estimate the separate drug effect, δ, and the interactive effect, η, which results when drug and psychotherapy are combined in the same treatment. The psychotherapy effect, ψ, is not reflected in the contrast because it is present on

---

*When the average characteristics of the drug therapy studies are substituted into the regression equations for relating study characteristics to effect size for verbal and behavioral psychotherapies in Table 5-11, estimated effects within about 0.05 of one-half standard deviation were obtained. Hence, the findings from the collection of drug therapy studies are roughly in accord with those from the psychotherapy studies conducted on comparable clients in comparable ways.

Table 8-2.   Average effect sizes from various experimental comparisons made in the experiments on drug and psychotherapy

Comparison	Parameter(s) estimated[a]	Average ES	No. of ES's
Psychotherapy vs. no-treatment or placebo	ψ	0.30	55
Drug therapy vs. no-treatment or placebo	δ	0.51	351
Drug & psychotherapy vs. drug	$\psi + \eta$	0.41	10
Drug & psychotherapy vs. psychotherapy	$\delta + \eta$	0.44	94
Drug vs. psychotherapy	$\delta - \psi$	0.10	7
Drug & psychotherapy vs. no-treatment or placebo	$\delta + \psi + \eta$	0.65	49

[a] ψ denotes the separate or "main" effect of psychotherapy;
  δ denotes the separate effect of drug therapy; and
  η denotes their interaction.

both sides of the comparison. The 94 effect sizes that estimate $\delta + \eta$ have an average of 0.44. The remainder of the table can be understood in like manner.

From simple inspection, it appears that the drug therapy effect of 0.51 is more than half again as large as the psychotherapy effect of 0.30. The interaction effect is slightly more difficult to comprehend from merely inspecting the entries in Table 8-2. That the drug-plus-psychotherapy vs. drug comparison, which estimates $\psi + \eta$, is a full one-tenth standard deviation larger than the 0.30 estimate of ψ from the first line of the table might lead one to believe that η is positive; but the comparison of the estimates of $\delta + \eta$ and δ (being 0.44 and 0.51, respectively) reverses this impression. Inspection is too arbitrary and confusing. Several comparisons in the table contain information about the same parameters; it seems reasonable that every source of information about a parameter should be used in estimating it. A complete and standard method of combining the data in Table 8-2 into estimates of the parameters is needed. Such a method is suggested when one recognizes that the two middle columns of Table 8-2 constitute a system of linear equations, three of them independent and containing three unknowns (ψ, δ, and η). The method of least-squares statistical estimation can be applied to obtain estimates of the separate and interactive effects of drug and psychotherapy.*

The estimates obtained by appropriate means to the data in Table 8-2 are as follows:

  ψ, the separate effect of psychotherapy : 0.31
  δ, the separate effect of drug therapy : 0.42
  η, the interactive effect of drug-plus-psychotherapy : 0.02

Each effect is expressed on a scale of standard deviation units. Thus, the data of Table 8-2 lead to the conclusion that with the groups of clients studied

---

*The reader wishing more detail about the estimation procedure can reproduce the solution by decomposing the second column of Table 8-2 into the product of a 6×3 matrix X (of 0's, 1's, and -1's) and the vector (ψ, δ, η), denoting the third column by y, then calculating the solution $(X^T X)^{-1} X^T y$. These methods are explained in detail in Appendix 8 for the more complicated case of the "same experiment" data that will be used in the next section of this chapter to refine the estimates of the effects.

psychotherapy produces outcomes that are about one-third standard deviation superior to the outcomes from placebo or untreated control groups. The drug effect is only about one-third greater than the psychotherapy effect. An effect of $0.31s_x$ will move an average client from the middle of the control group distribution to about the 62nd percentile; an effect of 0.42 would move the average client to only about the 66th percentile. The effects of the two therapies are not greatly different; however, we note here for the first time that the drug therapies were administered in less than half the time it took to administer the psychotherapies (2.6 months vs. 6.1 months). Any careful assessment of the relative value of drug and psychotherapy will take both effects and costs into account.

Arguments over the relative value of drug therapy and psychotherapy will be made simpler by the fact that the interactive effect of combining the two therapies is virtually zero ($\eta = 0.02$). This must not be misunderstood as implying that drug-plus-psychotherapy is ineffective; far from it. The near zero interaction effect means that when drug therapy and psychotherapy are combined, one can expect benefits to patients equal to the sum of the separate drug therapy and psychotherapy effects (0.31 + 0.42 = 0.73), no more no less. Uhlenhuth et al. (1969, p. 60) distinguished four models for the way in which drug and psychotherapy might combine to produce benefits: "1. Addition, the effect of the two interventions combined equals the sum of their individual effects. 2. Potentiation, the effect of two interventions combined is greater than the sum of their individual effects. 3. Inhibition, the effect of two interventions combined is less than the sum of their individual effects. 4. Reciprocation, the effect of two interventions combined equals the individual effect of the more potent intervention."

The first three models are what statisticians call zero, positive, and negative interaction, respectively. Of the four models, the first, "addition," best coincides with the data reported here. The "potentiation" and "inhibition" models find no support in the data of Table 8-2; the "reciprocation" model is even less in accord with the evidence.

Estimates of Effects from "Same Experiment" Data

The estimates derived from Table 8-2 are interesting, but they are based on data that may not be comparable in important respects. For example, the 55 effect sizes for the comparison of psychotherapy with untreated or placebo control groups came from studies in which 40 percent of the clients were male, 52 percent were diagnosed as psychotic, 46 percent were institutionalized, and 17 percent of the outcome measures were of psychological symptoms. The 351 effect size measures for drug therapy versus no treatment or placebo were from studies in which 50 percent of the clients were male, 44 percent were psychotic, 45 percent were institutionalized, and 32 percent of the outcome measures were of psychological symptoms. There are other differences as well between these two classes of study. These differences may confound the estimates of the relative benefits of drug therapy and psychotherapy. We hasten to add that it is conceivable that they do not confound them to any serious extent; for, in fact, the differences do not appear to be large. The average ages of the patients are nearly equal for the various types of comparison (ranging from 36.3 years to 38.0 years), the length of illness ranges only from 1.98 years to 2.20 years from one comparison to the other, and the largest difference between comparisons is in length of treatment (6.1 months for psychotherapy vs. 2.6 months for drug therapy), which is less a confounding influence than it is an intrinsic characteristic that distinguishes drug therapy from psychotherapy.

However, it is unwise to speculate about possible confounding and nonequivalence when the possibility exists of addressing their influence directly. Such a direct assessment can be achieved through use of the logic of "same experiments," which played a part in estimating the effects of verbal and behavioral psychotherapies in Chapter 5. If the estimates of the relative effects of drug therapy and psychotherapy were restricted to only those experiments in which both were applied as separate treatments, then the two types of therapy would be assessed under equivalent circumstances. On the average, those who receive drug therapy would be equivalent in age, diagnosis, gender, institutional setting, and the like, to those who received psychotherapy. Such equivalence is assured by the experimental controls (usually randomization) exercised by the original investigators. Moreover, for the studies on which the drug therapy and psychotherapy effects are based, the conditions are equivalent: the same outcome measures are administered at the same time to both groups, the same statistical treatment of data is performed, and so forth. Hence, any confounding of conditions with the experimental comparisons that may have seemed objectionable in Table 8-2 will be eliminated if those comparisons are viewed again, making certain that the treatments were compared within the same experiments.

Consider first the comparison of the drug effect and the psychotherapy effect. From the 112 studies, ten were identified in which drug therapy and psychotherapy were simultaneously compared with an untreated or placebo control group. These 10 studies yielded 35 effect size measures of the form $ES = (\bar{X}_{\text{therapy}} - \bar{X}_{\text{control}})/s_x$. The average effects are as follows:

Average effects based on comparisons
of drug and psychotherapy with
control groups within the same experiment

Drug therapy vs. control: $N = 35$ ES's	$\overline{ES} = 0.532$
Psychotherapy vs. control: $N = 35$ ES's	$\overline{ES} = 0.306$

One can be assured that the clients, therapists, outcome measures, and the like, are equivalent for this comparison of drug and psychotherapy effects. These data indicate that drug therapy is superior to psychotherapy by approximately 0.20 standard deviations, in contrast to the 0.10 standard deviation difference favoring drug therapy from the entire set of data.

However, the picture is not yet complete. Six other studies compared drug therapy and psychotherapy directly, without using an untreated or placebo control group. These studies yielded eight measures of effect size of the form $ES = (\bar{X}_{drug} - \bar{X}_{psychotherapy})/s_x$. The average effect size is as follows:

Average effect of direct comparisons
of drug and psychotherapies
from within the same experiments

Drug vs. psychotherapy: $\overline{ES} = 0.020$
$N = 8\ ES$'s

This difference, favoring drug therapy to no interesting or significant extent, is quite at odds with the 0.20 difference reported above. If the two effects are averaged, a difference in effect size favoring drug therapy over psychotherapy by about 0.10 standard deviations is obtained, $(0.20 + 0.02) \div 2 = 0.11$. If a weighted average is taken, acknowledging that the 0.20 was based on 35 ES's and the 0.02 on only 8, an average effect size is obtained that favors drug therapy over psychotherapy by 0.17 standard deviations. The superiority of drug therapy over psychotherapy is probably somewhere between one and two-tenths standard deviations. A more refined and complete analysis, which will be presented below, will clarify whether the difference is closer to 0.10 than 0.20.

A single experiment frequently encompasses more complex comparisons than merely drug therapy and psychotherapy pitted against each other or simultaneously against a control group. A common form of experiment compares drug therapy and drug-plus-psychotherapy with the same control group. As can be seen in Table 7-3, a comparison of drug therapy and control groups estimates the separate drug effect, δ; and the comparison of drug-plus-psychotherapy and controls estimates the sum of the two therapy effects and their interaction, $\delta + \psi + \eta$. Hence, the comparison of the two types of effect from the same experiment provides an excellently controlled estimate of the sum of the psychotherapy effect and the interaction effect, $\psi + \eta$. Moreover, drug and drug-plus-psychotherapy treatments are often compared directly in experiments that do not include control groups. Such a comparison likewise estimates the psychotherapy and the interaction effect. Among the 112 studies, 17 of the former type and 8 of the latter type were identified. Findings from them are summarized in the following tabulation:

Drug and drug-plus-psychotherapy compared to control groups in the same experiments	Drug and drug-plus-psychotherapy compared in the same experiments

Drug vs. control: $\overline{ES}$ = 0.457
N = 50 ES's
Drug-plus-psycho-
  therapy vs. control: $\overline{ES}$ = 0.650
N = 50 ES's
	Drug-plus-psycho-
	  therapy vs. drug: $\overline{ES}$ = 0.278
	N = 15 ES's

The 17 studies that employed control groups yield an estimate of the sum of the psychotherapy and interaction effect of $0.650 - 0.457 = 0.193$ standard deviation units. The 8 studies that compared drug and drug-plus-psychotherapy directly yield an estimate of $\psi + \eta$ of 0.278. The unweighted average of the two estimates is 0.236; the weighted average is 0.213; the two effects total something between one-fifth and one-quarter of a standard deviation. If the earlier estimates of about 0.30 of the psychotherapy effect, ψ, are sound, then there is some indication in these data that the interaction effect is slightly negative, since $\psi + \eta$ seems to be less than 0.30.

The third and last common type of experiment involves the comparison of drug-plus-psychotherapy directly with psychotherapy only, or the comparison of each with untreated or placebo control groups within the same experiment. A total of 7 such studies using control groups and 9 studies using direct comparisons were found. Each set of experiments is used to estimate the sum of the drug and the interaction effect (cf. Table 8–2). The average effect sizes are as follows:

Drug-plus-psychotherapy and psychotherapy compared to control groups within the same experiment	Drug-plus-psychotherapy and psychotherapy compared to each other within the same experiment

Drug-plus-psycho-
  therapy vs. control: $\overline{ES}$ = 0.653
N = 25 ES's
 	
Psychotherapy vs.
  Control: $\overline{ES}$ = 0.173
N = 25 ES's
	Drug-plus-psycho-
	  therapy vs. psycho-
	  therapy: $\overline{ES}$ = 0.100
	N = 27 ES's

The difference between the effects calculated with reference to the common control groups estimate the sum of the drug and interaction effect, $\delta + \eta$;

for the above data, the estimate is $0.653 - 0.173 = 0.480$, which is slightly larger than earlier estimates of the drug effect and thus indicates a slightly positive, but very small, interaction. However, the direct comparisons of drug-plus-psychotherapy and psychotherapy alone from the same experiments also estimate $\delta + \eta$ and do so with excellent control; this latter estimate equals 0.100, which is substantially less than the 0.480 estimate. Both estimates are based on about the same number of cases. Knowing nothing about why these two estimates should be different, and we are very nearly in such a position, we can average them; the resulting estimate of $\delta + \eta$ equals 0.29 standard deviations, which is well under the estimate of the separate drug effect and suggests a negative interaction.

The above estimates have taken advantage of the greater control exercised within but not necessarily across experiments. However, they are not arrived at in any systematic or unique way. To do so, one must state the estimation problem in a form more amenable to conventional statistical estimation theory. Unfortunately, the full statistical treatment of the estimation problem would tax unduly the typical reader's patience and tolerance for indigestible mathematics. Consequently, the statistics of the estimation of the drug, psychotherapy, and interaction effects from the "same experiment" data have been documented in Appendix 8, and the results alone are reported below.

Based on all 270 effect-size measures from the "same experiment" data, the estimates of effects for drug therapy, psychotherapy, and their interaction are as follows:

$$\psi = 0.32$$
$$\delta = 0.44$$
$$\eta = -0.14$$

The estimates of the separate psychotherapy and drug effects are very little different from the estimates calculated from all 566 effect sizes in the first half of this chapter. The difference between the two effects is virtually identical to the difference estimated with all of the data: $0.47 - 0.37 = 0.10$ vs. $0.44 - 0.32 = 0.12$. A one-tenth standard deviation superiority of drug therapy over psychotherapy is solidly indicated by the data, regardless of how they are viewed. The restriction of data by the "same experiment" condition made an appreciable difference only for the estimate of the interaction effect; an interaction effect of $+0.02$ became a -0.14 where greater experimental control was exercised.

The separate psychotherapy and drug therapy effects are roughly one-third to one-half standard deviation, depending on which estimates are accepted, favoring drug therapy by about one-tenth standard deviation, regardless of which estimates are taken. The interaction effect of the two therapies is negative. That is, the combined effect of administering drug and psychotherapy together is less than the sum of their separate effects.

Results Classified by Characteristics of Patients and Studies

Occasionally, interesting trends and patterns were observed when effect sizes were averaged for patients of different types (e.g., in-patient vs. out-patient, or psychotic vs. nonpsychotic), or for different features of the therapies or the studies (e.g., types of drug, types of outcome measure). Some of the more interesting findings are reported in this section. A total of about four hundred effect-size measures from the 112 studies will be analyzed here; only the effect measures from comparisons of either drug therapy or drug-plus-psychotherapy with a control group are included. Comparisons of drug therapy with psychotherapy, for example, are excluded; and about fifty effect sizes for psychotherapy vs. control are excluded, since the relationship of these effects to other characteristics was studied in the last half of Chapter 5.

Average Effect Sizes for Different Patient Diagnoses

In Table 8-3 are shown the average effects for psychotic, nonpsychotic, and other patients. (The "other" category includes effect sizes for combinations of psychotic and nonpsychotic patient samples and for the diagnosis "character disorder.") The comparison between psychotic and nonpsychotic patient outcomes shows an interesting trend in the drug-plus-psychotherapy studies. Unlike the drug-only studies, the drug-plus-psychotherapy studies show larger effects for psychotic patients than for nonpsychotic patients. This could be partly artifactual. Proportionately, half as many studies in the drug-plus-psychotherapy category for the psychotic diagnosis were placebo-controlled (9 of 29 = 31 percent) compared to the drug-plus-psychotherapy nonpsychotic diagnosis (10 of 16 = 63 percent). This problem of a disproportionate number of placebo-controlled studies in the nonpsychotic vs. psychotic categories was not present in the drug-only sample. There, approximately 90 percent of each group was composed of placebo-controlled comparisons.

When effects for comparisons with placebo control groups and untreated control groups are weighted equally, drug-plus-psychotherapy is still better for psychotic patients than nonpsychotic patients. However, there is almost no difference between psychotic and nonpsychotic patients treated by drug

Table 8-3.   Effect sizes for major diagnosis of patient

Type of patient	Drug only			Drug-plus-psychotherapy		
	$\overline{ES}$	s_{ES}	n	$\overline{ES}$	s_{ES}	n
Psychotic	.493	.434	130	.802	.645	29
Nonpsychotic	.623	.885	151	.374	.233	16
Mixed (including character disorder)	.221	.470	70			0
Totals	.498	.686	351	.650	.571	45

therapy. Effect sizes for equal weighting of placebo and untreated control comparisons are displayed below:

	Average effect sizes	
Patient diagnosis	Drug therapy	Drug-plus-psychotherapy
Psychotic	$\overline{ES} = 0.55$	$\overline{ES} = 0.69$
Nonpsychotic	$\overline{ES} = 0.60$	$\overline{ES} = 0.39$

Effect sizes for specific types of patient diagnosis are presented in Table 8-4. The superiority of drug treatment for anxious patients compared to depressed patients can be observed clearly in the table. This finding cannot be explained away by different percents of placebo-controlled studies in the two categories. Ninety-six percent of studies of depressed patients were placebo-controlled; 100 percent of studies of anxious patients were placebo-controlled.

Average Effect Sizes for In-patients and Out-patients

Nearly two hundred effect size measures were calculated from studies that assessed the effects of either drug or drug-plus-psychotherapy for patients who were institutionalized; 173 effect sizes were calculated for "out-patients." Well over one hundred effects were for mixed or indeterminate patient groups. The average of the effect sizes and their standard deviations are as follows:

	$\overline{ES}$	s_{ES}	N
In-patients	.47	.52	199
Out-patients	.60	.84	173

Approximately 81 percent of the in-patient effects and 88 percent of the out-patient effects are placebo-controlled. Hence, the superiority of the out-patient average cannot be due to the one-quarter standard deviation advantage that an untreated control study is likely to have over a placebo control study.

Table 8-4. Effect sizes for specific diagnosis

Type of patient	Drug only			Drug-plus-psychotherapy		
	$\overline{ES}$	s_{ES}	n	$\overline{ES}$	s_{ES}	n
Schizophrenic	.495	.550	108	.802	.645	29
Depressive	.367	.698	85	.460	.160	7
Anxious	.663	.950	87	.370	.232	4
Other (including character disorder and other)	.410	.650	43	.565	.064	2
Total	.495	.689	323	.693	.566	42

Table 8-5. Average effect sizes for major drug types

Type of drug	Drug therapy			Drug-plus-psychotherapy			All drug therapy		
	$\overline{ES}$	s_{ES}	n	$\overline{ES}$	s_{ES}	n	$\overline{ES}$	s_{ES}	n
Antipsychotic	.439	.512	112	.825	.644	28	.517	.580	140
Antidepressant	.403	.709	67	.440	.197	8	.407	.673	75
Antianxiety	.625	.849	130	.269	.253	7	.607	.833	137
Other (including antidrug dependent, drug type combinations, other)	.426	.473	34	.160	0	1	.418	.693	35
Totals	.501	.697	343	.651	.577	44	.518	.685	387

Twelve percent of the effects for both in-patients and out-patients were assessments of the combined effect of drug-plus-psychotherapy; hence, the comparison of the two types of patient is balanced with respect to the type of therapy given. It remains possible that in-patients were more seriously disturbed than out-patients and that their lesser improvement is to be expected.

Average Effect Sizes for Major Drug Types

Results in Table 8-5 show the average effect size for the three major types of drug and other drug types. In the three major drug types, observed trends in the drug-only research indicate that antidepressant drugs have the least effect, followed by antipsychotic drugs. Antianxiety agents did best over all. In the drug-plus-psychotherapy research, the trend was different. The antipsychotic drugs were superior to the others. This finding could be due, in part, to the fact that hospitalization-outcome measures, large in comparison to other outcome measures, comprised a much greater percent of the drug-plus-psychotherapy studies (13 percent) than they did in the drug-only studies (2.5 percent).

A further breakdown of drug types is presented in Table 8-6. Comparisons that included a combination of drugs from two different categories (e.g., the antipsychotic category and the antidepressant category) were excluded, as were drugs in the "other" category from Table 8-5. Therefore, the total number of comparisons in Table 8-6 is somewhat smaller than the number recorded in Table 8-5. No important difference in effect was revealed between the phenothiazines ($ES = 0.48$) and a conglomerate of other drugs ($ES = 0.42$) used to treat psychotic disorders. Neither did the tricyclic antidepressants evidence statistically significantly greater effects than the MAOI's or amphetamines, though the observed differences are in the expected direction favoring the tricyclics. There are no significant differences among the magnitude of effects for the benzodiazepines, the carbamates or the hypnotics, but the benzodiazepines verge on superiority. With the numbers of effects on

Table 8-6. Effect sizes for specific drugs

ANTIPSYCHOTICS

Phenothiazines

	$N_{comparisons}$ 83	$\overline{ES}$ 0.475	s_{ES} 0.55
		n	$\overline{ES}$
Chlorpromazine		40	0.55
Promethazine		2	0.41
Prochlorperazine		5	0.25
Trifluoperazine		6	0.34
Triflupromazine		3	0.81
Promazine		2	0.13
Perphenazine		11	0.31
Mepazine		2	-0.07
Fluphenazine		5	0.64
Thioridazine		5	0.17
Prochlorperazine + Trifluoperazine		4	0.85
Triflupromazine + Chlorpromazine		2	1.16

Others

	N_{comp} 30	$\overline{ES}$ 0.424	s_{ES} 0.66
		n	$\overline{ES}$
Reserpine		11	0.59
Loxapine		4	0.06
Haloperidol		1	1.45
Thiothixene		3	-0.41
Lithium		7	0.51
Pimozide		4	0.56

ANTIDEPRESSANTS

Tricyclics (TCA's)

	N_{comp} 46	$\overline{ES}$ 0.44	s_{ES} 0.40
		n	$\overline{ES}$
Imipramine		25	0.43
Amitriptyline		27	0.44
Opipramol		1	1.04
Protriptyline		3	-0.12

Monoamine oxidase inhibitors (MAOI's)

	N_{comp} 25	$\overline{ES}$ 0.29	s_{ES} 0.39
		n	$\overline{ES}$
Iproniazid		10	0.50
Isoniazid		4	0.25
Phenelzine		5	0.21
Nialamide		4	-0.09
Isocarboxazid		2	0.33

Others

	N_{comp} 8	$\overline{ES}$ 0.36	s_{ES} 0.32
Amphetamines			

ANTIANXIETY AGENTS

Benzodiazepines

	N_{comp} 64	$\overline{ES}$ 0.73	s_{ES} 1.04
		n	$\overline{ES}$
Diazepam		31	0.77
Chlordiazepoxide		22	0.14
Lorazepam		3	0.46
Prazepam		2	1.09
Oxazepam		1	3.37
Ripazepam		5	2.57

Hypnotics

	N_{comp} 12	$\overline{ES}$ 0.24	s_{ES} 0.21
		n	$\overline{ES}$
Phenobarbitol		5	0.20
Amobarbitol		7	0.27

Carbamates

	N_{comp} 44	$\overline{ES}$ 0.55	s_{ES} 0.42
		n	$\overline{ES}$
Meprobamate		39	0.54
Tybamate		5	0.66

which some average effects are based being quite small, power to detect true
differences among drugs was low.

Average Effect Sizes for Different Types of Outcomes

Among the hundreds of particular definitions and operationalizations of
therapy outcomes, five general types were distinguished: (1) hospitalization
outcomes (e.g., entry or release; length of stay); (2) somatic symptoms (e.g.,
eating, drinking alcohol, sleeping, headache, sexual dysfunction); (3)
psychological symptoms (e.g., hallucinations, delusions, depression, anxiety,
hysteria); (4) psychological adjustment (e.g., conformity to hospital routine,
general social behavior and demeanor, social withdrawal); and (5) global
improvement (gross ratings of improvement or deterioration in psychological
and physical health). These categories are described in greater detail in the
first half of Chapter 7. The average effect size in each category, along with the
number and standard deviation of effects, are reported in Table 8-7.

The classification of effects by outcome type reveals little that is interesting
or convincing. Outcomes related to release from a mental institution or length
of stay are unaccountably high, although the average is based on only fifteen
measures of effect. The impact of therapy on improvement in the area of
psychological symptoms is less than for somatic symptoms. This difference
may reflect something about the way drugs influence behavior, or it may only
reflect something about the methods by which outcomes are measured. Improvement in the area of psychological symptoms was more likely to have
been assessed with standardized personality tests or checklists than was the
disappearance of somatic symptoms. Some light may be cast on the distinction in the next section.

Average Effect Sizes for Different Methods of Outcome Measurement

In Table 8-8, the nearly four hundred effect-size measures are classified
and described in terms of how the outcomes of therapy were measured:
whether by (1) the ratings of the patient himself or his doctor, nurse, or a
person close to him, such as a spouse, parent, or other relative; (2) a
psychological test; or (3) a physiological measure of improvement. All of the
sources of ratings produced nearly the same average effect; effects measured
by psychological tests were noticeably small, particularly so when one
realizes that the tests probably tapped the same domain of outcomes toward
which the ratings were directed. Perhaps the standardized psychological inventories are too general and coarse to detect the many specific ways in
which therapeutic gains may be manifested. This same feature of the possible
insensitivity of standardized psychological tests as instruments for evaluating
the outcomes of therapy can be seen in Table 5-16. Among a dozen different

Table 8-7.   Average effect sizes for different types
of outcomes

Type of outcome	$\overline{ES}$	s_{ES}	n
Hospitalization outcomes	.95	.60	15
Somatic symptoms	.56	.66	31
Psychological symptoms	.39	.54	139
Psychological adjustment	.44	.56	58
Global improvement	.63	.81	149

types of outcome measures, "personality traits" assessed by psychological test show the lowest average effect size ($\overline{ES} = 0.31$ for 18 values of ES).

Average Effect Sizes for Different Levels of Outcome Measure Susceptibility to Falsification

Some measures of outcome permit an easy misrepresentation of the patient's well-being in circumstances where the motivation to misrepresent is strongly felt; for example, the patient's own report to the therapist of relief in symptoms such as fear or depression. Other measures (e.g., galvanic skin response) are not nearly so easily faked. Details of the categorization of outcome measure susceptibility to falsification are reported under that heading in Chapter 7. In Table 8-9, the average effect sizes are reported for the five ordered levels of susceptibility of outcome measures. As can be seen clearly, larger effects were not consistently related to higher levels of susceptibility to falsification. Indeed, no consistent relationship emerged.

The lack of a relationship between effect size and outcome measure susceptibility is somewhat surprising in view of the strong relationship between "reactivity" of outcome measure and the magnitude of the psychotherapy effect that was reported in Chapter 5. Although the susceptibility concept and the reactivity concept are related, they may be different in a few important respects. "Susceptibility," as it was employed here to distinguish conditions of outcome measurement, was separated from the blinding of either the patients or the therapists to the therapeutic conditions. Hence, a measure, which in the abstract might be readily faked, may well not have been faked in any way that could have affected the outcomes of the experiment, if both the patient and the therapist were unaware whether an active drug or a placebo had been administered. Nearly 80 percent of the effect-size measures for drug therapy were placebo-controlled. Highly fakeable measures are unlikely to yield large differences between drug therapy and placebo control groups, because the experimental demand characteristics (Rosenthal 1976) are similar in both groups. Placebo control groups were rarely used in the psychotherapy research analyzed and reported in Chapter 5; hence, the reactivity of the outcome measure was more likely to reflect the different demand characteristics of the psychotherapy and untreated control group conditions.

Table 8-8. Average effect sizes for different
methods of outcome measurement

Method of outcome measurement	$\overline{ES}$	s_{ES}	n
Ratings			
by the patient himself	.46	.76	60
by the experimenter	.56	.70	251
by his nurse	.53	.63	41
by persons close to him	.59	.39	9
Psychological tests	.26	.39	31
Physiological methods	.31	.56	4

Average Effect Sizes for Different Features of Internal Validity

The internal validity of an experimental study refers to such features of its execution as how subjects were assigned to treatments, whether assessment of outcomes was single, double, or unblinded, whether differential attrition from the treatment conditions was taken into account, and the like. The first two mentioned features of internal validity were specifically studied and are reported in Table 8-10.

Either single- or double-blinding in the assessment of results produced smaller effects on the average than in an open experiment where both the patient and the assessor of the therapeutic outcomes are aware of patients' assignments to the experimental conditions. In the bottom half of Table 8-10, it can be seen how greatly the lack of good experimental controls favors the demonstration of drug therapy effects. When patients were not matched or randomly assigned to experimental conditions, the average effect was nearly one-quarter standard deviation larger. A slight trend in this direction was noticed in the findings for the psychotherapy studies (Table 5-28), but it was not nearly so strong; there the difference between ''intact group'' assignment and more reliable methods of equating treatment groups (randomization, matching) favored the former by only about 0.06 standard deviations.

From the separate estimates of methodological influences on the findings of a drug therapy experiment, one can anticipate that the net effect of a few weaknesses in experimental design could be disconcertingly large. Suppose

Table 8-9. Average effect sizes for five levels of susceptibility
of outcome measures to falsification

Susceptibility of outcome measure to falsification	$\overline{ES}$	s_{ES}	n
1: Low (e.g., physiological measure of stress)	.78	.60	19
2: Low average	.36	.51	42
3: Average	.55	.70	255
4: High average	.33	.32	26
5: High (e.g., patient self-report of symptom change)	.46	.76	61

Table 8-10. Average effect sizes for degrees of blinding and methods of patient assignment to treatments

Degree of blinding	$\overline{ES}$	s_{ES}	n
None or "open"	.62	.51	74
Single (patient or assessor blind)	.50	.44	50
Double (patient and assessor blind)	.49	.75	271
Assignment of patients to treatments	$\overline{ES}$	s_{ES}	n
Random	.48	.65	334
Matching	.54	.51	16
Intact groups (nonrandom)	.72	.88	45

that drug A was tested in an experiment that employed untreated instead of placebo controls, in which outcomes were assessed without blinding, and patients were not randomly assigned to treatments nor matched. Drug B was tested with placebo controls, random assignment, and double-blinding. The advantage (unfairly won, of course) of not having placebo controls (0.25), not blinding measurement (0.10) and not assigning patients randomly (0.20), could amount to over one-half standard deviation for drug A over drug B.

Correlations of Selected Characteristics of Studies with Effect Size

Some characteristics of studies can be measured on a continuum, and their relationship to magnitude of the therapy effect is more conveniently expressed as a correlation coefficient than as a series of average effects for categories of the characteristic. The correlations for seven such characteristics are reported in Table 8-11. There one finds, for example, that the year in which a study was published bears little relationship to the size of the effect shown in the study. For over 350 effect-size measures taken in drug therapy studies, the correlation of *ES* with date of publication is -0.01. Although the correlation is -0.42 for 45 effects from drug-plus-psychotherapy studies, and it is statistically significantly different from zero by conventional criteria, such an odd and surprising finding should be viewed cautiously. The correlation of -0.42 is the largest (in absolute value) in the table; but there are many values and some would deviate substantially from zero if even by chance alone. Moreover, the 45 values of *ES* on which the correlation was calculated are not independent; they could have arisen from a much smaller number of studies, in which case, the degrees of freedom by which the significance test was made are too many and the reliability of the value is less than it seems. Only one characteristic of the studies showed a consistent relationship to *ES* across both drug therapy and drug-plus-psychotherapy; the percent of the patients in the study who were black correlated -0.29 with *ES* for drug therapy studies and -0.31 for a small number of drug-plus-psychotherapy studies. The negligible correlation between *ES* and follow-up time ("months after therapy that effects were measured'') may be due in part ot the very narrow range of follow-up times. Over 90 percent of outcomes were measured immediately after therapy was terminated.

The general absence of correlation of study characteristics with effect size sheds important light on the problem of confounding in comparisons of drug therapy, psychotherapy, and drug-plus-psychotherapy. In Table 8-2, data from many different studies were aggregated as though each study reflected comparable information about the effects of different types of therapy. It was acknowledged, however, that the studies assessing the effects of drug therapy alone might have somewhat different characteristics from the studies assessing drug-plus-psychotherapy. For example, the patients might have been older, on the average, or treatment might have lasted twice as long for the latter as for the former. The near zero correlations in Table 8–11 indicate, however, that nonequivalence among the classes of studies are not likely to be critical, since the respects in which studies differ are unlikely to be much related to the magnitude of the effects those studies show.

Summary

One hundred-twelve experiments were analyzed to determine the separate and combined effects of psychotherapy and drug therapy. More than 560 measures of outcome were obtained from the studies. By appropriate contrasting and combining of experimental comparisons, estimates were obtained of the magnitude of benefits of psychotherapy and drug therapy applied separately and in combination. Different approaches to data analysis yielded only slightly different estimates. The effect of drug therapy across all outcome measures was about four-tenths standard deviation units; that is, when drug

Table 8-11. Correlations of selected characteristics with effect size

Characteristic	Drug therapy		Drug-plus-psychotherapy		Total	
	Correlation, r	n	Correlation, r	n	Correlation, r	n
Year of publication	−.01	358	−.42[a]	45	−.05	403
Age	.04	324	−.24	43	.00	367
Percentage male	−.07	310	.16	43	−.04	353
Percentage white	.06	77	−.09	19	.05	96
Percentage black	−.29[b]	35	−.31	12	−.30[b]	47
Duration of treatment	.02	356	−.04	45	.03	401
Months after therapy that effects were measured	−.03	357	.19	45	.02	402

[a] $p < .01$
[b] $p < .05$

therapy was compared to a placebo control group, the effect size averaged about $\overline{ES}$ = 0.40. The comparable effect for psychotherapy treatment was about three-tenths standard deviation units ($\overline{ES}$ = 0.30). Hence, the separate effects of drug therapy and psychotherapy in the treatment of severe psychological disorders favor drug therapy by only about one-tenth standard deviation.

Three unique possibilities exist in considering the effect of combining drug therapy and psychotherapy in a single treatment regimen: (a) the magnitude of the combined treatment can equal the sum of their separate effects (an additive or noninteractive result), (b) the combined effect can exceed the sum of the separate effects (positive interaction), or (c) the combined effect may be less than the sum of the separate effects (negative interaction). The data show no support whatever for the positive interaction result. Our best estimate indicated that the combined treatments produce an effect that is slightly smaller than the sum of the effects of the two treatments applied separately (negative interaction). This finding does not imply that it is disadvantageous to combine the two treatments; indeed, in combination they yield an effect of roughly 0.60 standard deviations—larger than either separate effect. The negative interaction that was found implies that the two treatments do not combine in some synergistic or mutually facilitative way, contrary to some popular claims and misconceptions.

The analyses yielded few interesting or convincing relationships between the magnitude of drug treatment effects and characteristics of the treatment, the patients, or the properties of the experiment. Out-patients responded more favorably than in-patients. Antianxiety drugs seemed slightly more effective than antidepressant drugs. The tricyclic drugs showed slightly larger effects than the MAOI's in treatment of depression, but the differences were neither large nor consistent. Outcomes assessed by standardized psychological tests revealed particularly small effects in comparison to assessment by human raters. No relationships were obtained between magnitude of the drug treatment effect and age of patients, sex, or length of treatment.

Chapter 9

Implications for Psychotherapy
Practice, Training, and Research

The concerns of many different audiences must be addressed in this final chapter. The narrative has been carried along to this point by the telling of the story of the meta-analysis: the search for the original studies, the translation of broad concepts into numbers, the colligation of the gargantuan mass of data, the summarization of hundreds of pieces of information by a statistic or a figure. Now the reader (if he has not gagged on one or another unsavory assumption or if he has remained unconvinced that any of this really matters) rediscovers himself and his own interests. He justifiably asks what all this analysis means to him as a psychotherapist, teacher, student, or scientist. Few readers will find personal meaning in all of the implications that can be drawn out of the work reported in this book; but anyone whose professional life touches psychotherapy in any way should find something here of relevance and meaning.

Why must implications of the findings be drawn for the reader? Why is he not asked simply to draw them himself? Why are the data not permitted to speak for themselves? The data are mute—or worse, they speak with many voices in an unintelligible babel. Only the callow and obdurately scientific believe that data speak for themselves; they should be sentenced for their heresy to six months in a research laboratory or six weeks in a courtroom. Since the data do not speak for themselves, someone must speak for them, or better, with them.

We have skulked behind the figures and tables for eight chapters, unseen movers pulling strings that animate the formulas and statistics, operationalizing complex ideas and concepts, wrapped in the passive voice of positivism, invisible attendants to the engine of science grinding and bumping its way from hypotheses to facts to conclusions. We think too highly of our own work to disparage it now. It is not all whim and idiosyncrasy. Within reasonable limits of accuracy, it can be replicated by anyone who can read and calculate with intelligence (and to whom God has granted great perseverance). But when the work reaches the point where one justifiably asks what it all means to the world, whether it is anything more than a book after all, then the authors can no longer responsibly hide behind the incognito of the numbers and tables. When implications are drawn from the data, personal experience perforce intrudes; vested interests—whether they be financial, intellectual, or more personal—shape interpretations; ideological leanings incline one toward a hospitable fact and away from a hostile one.

More of one's personality may be drawn into the broad interpretation of the research than one can unabashedly admit. But let us clarify. We would be chagrined if different investigators undertaking the same task we embarked upon in Chapter 1, with the same methods and guided by the same logic, should produce substantially different numbers. However, the points we propose to make in this concluding chapter could be made in as many different ways as there are those who might make them. Some will see our findings as support for their own particular therapeutic school (e.g., "We've hardly tried our best in these silly outcome studies and look how close we are to all the other therapies" or "Look how far we've come in less than ten years, and those other therapies have been around for fifty."). Others may read the results with despair; still others with ecumenical hope.

Each interpretation, each projection of a possible future for psychotherapy will reveal something about the interpreter. To dissemble one's intellectual leanings by pretending that the broad implications of our findings follow from the numbers as unerringly as the numbers followed from the formulas would be insincere and false. So with judicious intentions, we will set down publicly those things about us that good taste allows and fairness demands.

Before all else, we are research methodologists and statisticians; for the last ten years we have worked in the field of evaluation, where value claims are illuminated by empirical inquiry. We approached the work on which this book is based primarily because of our interest in abstract problems of social science methodology, and only secondarily because of an interest in psychotherapy. When we took on the topic of psychotherapy outcomes in 1975, we were intrigued by the diversity, size, and variegated character of the research literature. We sensed that the approaches commonly adopted for making sense of large collections of research evidence were not equal to the task of summarizing psychotherapy-outcome studies. If research could be integrated more quantitatively and objectively, more might be learned. These were sentiments that swelled a statistician's heart—if the oxymoron can be ignored. We did not expect such sentiments to galvanize psychotherapy researchers into action, although we found them for the most part to be unflaggingly courteous and helpful and never less than tolerant.

To characterize our original interests in the problem solely in terms of research methodology would misrepresent them as being slightly more abstract and disinterested than they were in fact. Before we began, each of us knew psychotherapy from one chair or the other and two of us from both. We believed somewhat cautiously at the outset that psychotherapy was effective. This conviction arose from concrete, individual experience; it did not extend to the kinds of therapy most often represented in the research literature, which for all we knew at the outset could have been a fabrication and a failure. People believe much that has not been scientifically proven; and those who know science best are prepared to honor the belief, while acknowledging a lack of proof. Our belief in the efficacy of psychotherapy did not blind us to the flaws in its research foundation nor to the fact that an ultimate judgment of no scientific support for its claims would have brought us greater recognition, perhaps, than the other verdict. At the outset, our allegiance to research methodology was stronger than our allegiance to psychotherapy, and we would have quickly sacrificed the latter on the altar of the former had it been necessary. We shall watch with interest as psychotherapy grows, but we will probably not participate directly in shaping its growth beyond what we have attempted to do here. At the risk of appearing sanctimonious, we reaffirm now the allegiance we acknowledged at the outset: to science first, not to psychotherapy.

Conclusions and Implications

The forty or so tables and figures of results that stretch back across the first eight chapters are rich with particulars. But most of these are mere intimations of conclusions, suggestions for further study, provocative but thoroughly qualified statements. A conclusion that can be built upon, trusted, around which a consensus can be reached and in which enough conviction can be inspired to sustain action must be greatly overdetermined by the evidence. Redundancy and multiplicity must hammer home the same message; it must show a common view even as the data are turned from side to side. The conclusions on which recommendations are based, then, must be few but robust. In what follows, we advance only four general conclusions.

Psychotherapy is beneficial, consistently so and in many different ways. Its benefits are on a par with other expensive and ambitious interventions, such as schooling and medicine. The benefits of psychotherapy are not permanent, but then little is.

The evidence overwhelmingly supports the efficacy of psychotherapy. Journalists may continue to make copy by casting aspersions on the profession of psychotherapy, but anyone who respects and understands how empirical research is performed and what it means must acknowledge that psychotherapy has more than proven its effectiveness. Indeed, its efficacy has been demonstrated with near monotonous regularity. The post hoc rationalizations of academic critics of the psychotherapy-outcome literature (who allege that the studies, all of them, are not adequately controlled or monitored) have nearly been exhausted. They can scarcely advance new excuses without feeling embarrassed, or without raising suspicions about their motives.

Psychotherapy benefits people of all ages as reliably as schooling educates them, medicine cures them, or business turns a profit. It sometimes seeks the same goals sought by education and medicine; when it does, psychotherapy performs commendably well—so well, in fact, that it begins to threaten the artificial barriers that tradition has erected between the institutions of amelioration and cure. We are suggesting no less than that psychotherapists have a legitimate, though not exclusive, claim, substantiated by controlled research, on those roles in society, whether privately or publicly endowed, whose responsibility it is to restore to health the sick, the suffering, the alienated, and the disaffected.

It may strike many friends of psychotherapy as ironic that in the ninth decade of the twentieth century, after years of research, in spite of the backing of tens of thousands of professionals around the world, that the benefits of psychotherapy must be reaffirmed. They must be reaffirmed nonetheless, for it may be the fate of psychotherapy, perhaps more than other professions, to have its contributions gainsaid and to suffer the hostility of those who would profit from its demise.

The parity of psychotherapy with other institutions of human improvement is insured not only by its research record of consistent benefits but also by its unique contribution. Psychotherapy is *primus inter pares* for the benefits it bestows upon the inner life of its clients. For whatever contribution psychotherapy may make to its clients' social adjustment (their productivity at work or in school, their dependence on other persons and institutions), its contribution is greater to the improvement of their inner experiences of emotion, feeling, and satisfaction. Of the levers that can move society forward, psychotherapy is only one. It may not educate so well as schools; it may not produce goods and services so well as management science; it may not cure illnesses so well as medicine; but it reaches a part of life that nothing else touches so well.

The consistent demonstration of the efficacy of psychotherapy under controlled conditions commends the study of psychotherapeutic processes to scientists of many types. We were amazed at how many scientists of excellent reputation confessed to us within the past five years that they understood that psychotherapy had been disproven under controlled conditions. One does not study long what one does not believe, as we do not study ESP and UFO's. Perhaps some of the neglect of psychotherapy as an object of scientific curiosity will be corrected by the overabundant demonstration in these pages that it exists and it works.

Different types of psychotherapy (verbal or behavioral; psychodynamic, client-centered, or systematic desensitization) do not produce different types or degrees of benefit.

This conclusion could prompt one either to embrace eclectism or pluralism. We caution against the former; we favor the latter. There is little reason to suspect that eclectism, a theoretical or practical amalgam of therapeutic techniques that chance and charisma caused to be studied in the middle decades of the twentieth century, will lead to better psychotherapy or the truth about it. Good theories are not mixed from recipes: one part behaviorism, one part humanism; where truth reveals itself, it generally presents a simple, orderly countenance, not a patchwork quilt of scraps. If anything, our findings warn against an eclecticism in practice that fails to differentiate into one type or the other of psychotherapy. One of the paradoxes of psychotherapy—not unrelated to paradoxes about the scientific understanding of human behavior more fundamentally (Scriven 1966, pp. 297–99; Buck 1963)—may be that although all therapies are equally effective, one must choose only one to learn and practice.

Nor do we support the notion that a psychotherapist should be trained in many different schools of therapy, or that he should practice by applying *the* correct therapy to just the right problem (behavior modification for a case of obesity; existential therapy for a case of angst). Our results are clear on this point: in spite of clinicians' often reported sense that they tailor their methods to the individual client, and in spite of how vigorously scholars urge attention to the question of which form of psychotherapy has which effects with which types of client, our findings show no controlled empirical evidence that could serve to support the former actions, and they give every reason to think that the latter question has no answers today and may not find answers for some time to come.

Pluralism is the more intelligent alternative to eclecticism. Pluralism in psychotherapy is not the mixing of orthodoxies within a therapy hour, but rather the tolerance and nurture of alternatives at a higher level. It is not behavioral-gestaltism in the consulting room, nor necessarily one seminar in behavior technique and one in gestalt technique in every doctoral syllabus; but rather it is the recognition that no school of psychotherapy has a franchise on therapeutic efficacy. Indeed, no school of psychotherapy can claim that research proves its effects on a particular problem or type of client are superior. Pluralism means that each school of psychotherapy should be allowed to train its next generation of practitioners, conduct its research, and advance itself as a profession. The policy, or even the attitude, that excludes one school or another of psychotherapy from the academy, the mental health center, or the journals may arise from deep personal conviction, authoritarianism, or politics, but it is unwarranted by a fair comparison of demonstrated efficacy.

We did not expect that the demonstrable benefits of quite different types of psychotherapy would be so little different. It is the most startling and intriguing finding we came across. All psychotherapy researchers should be prompted to ask how it can be so. If it is truly so that major differences in technique count for little in terms of benefits, then what is to be made of the volumes devoted to the careful drawing of distinctions among styles of psychotherapy? And what is to be made of the deep divisions and animosities among different psychotherapy schools?

These are the kinds of sweeping questions that too often evoke trite and thoughtless answers. Perhaps we can avoid both. We regard it as clearly possible that all psychotherapies are equally effective, or nearly so; and that the lines drawn among psychotherapy schools are small distinctions, cherished by those who draw them, but all the same distinctions that make no important differences. Those elements that unite different types of psychotherapy may prove to be far more influential than those specific elements that distinguish them. Among certain few psychotherapy researchers this question is aptly put in terms of general or specific factors of therapeutic effectiveness. Are the benefits of psychotherapy due to a relatively small number of basic conditions shared by all types of therapy, or are they due to specific techniques present in some types of psychotherapy but not in others?

A few scholars have set aside allegiances to therapy doctrine and orthodoxy and faced this question directly. Frank (1961, 1973) found elements of persuasion common to all major forms of psychotherapy; and though advanced as an explanation of the workings of nonmedical methods of healing bodily illness, the following remarks present well his thesis as applied to psychotherapy more generally:

> The core of the techniques of healing . . . seems to lie in their ability to arouse the patient's hope, bolster his self-esteem, stir him emotionally, and strengthen his ties with a supportive group, through several features that most methods share. All involve a healer on whom the patient depends for help and who holds out hope of relief. The patient's expectations are aroused by the healer's personal attributes, by his culturally determined healing role, or, typically, by both (Frank 1973, p. 76).

Raimy (1975) revealed how quite disparate schools of psychotherapy were alike in at least one fundamental respect: whether they acknowledged it or not, they all treated clients as rational, thinking persons whose condition depends in no small way on what they believe about the world and their place in it.

Strupp (1973*a*) cast a wide net in a search for the basic ingredient of psychotherapy. In his view, all modes of psychotherapy derive their efficacy from a few fundamental factors: a helpful relationship between therapist and client, patterned after good parent-child relationships, in which the therapist is respectful, understanding, polite, and confident he can help; a power relationship from which the therapist influences the client through (1) persuasion, (2) encouragement of honesty and self-scrutiny, (3) interpretation of behaviors and ideas, (4) presentation of a personal example of maturity, or (5) manipulation of rewards; and a client who is willing and able to profit from these. (See Garfield 1973, and Strupp 1973*b*, for elaboration of these ideas.)

Each of these scholars has commended to the attention of others the importance of the general factors position. Our findings speak of communalities, not of differences: the essential equivalence of benefits from any serious attempt at psychotherapy; the surprisingly strong showing of placebo treatments, which by definition may potentiate general factors but not specific ones. The weight of the evidence that now rests in the balance so greatly favors the general factors interpretation of therapeutic efficacy that it can no longer be ignored by researchers and theoreticians. Researchers who continue merely demonstrating the superiority of their favorite therapeutic approach over untreated control groups can justifiably be accused of avoiding what several decades of research have revealed to be the significant questions about psychotherapy. Researchers who claim superior efficacy of their approach to others without having actually demonstrated it in controlled, comparative studies are guilty of chicanery or arrogance. More research is needed in which quite different types of therapy are compared; and more such research should be entrusted to neutral third parties not caught up in holy wars. The work of Sloane et al. (1975) is virtually a paradigm for the kind of research that could focus attention on the fundamental elements of psychotherapy, which make all types of it alike in its impact and different from other ways of dealing with human problems.

We must avoid the logical error of believing that we have proved a negative, namely, that specific factors do not exist. Although a few positive demonstrations would be compelling evidence for their existence, the peculiar asymmetry of logic holds that no number of failures to demonstrate them (not even 500 controlled failures) can ever prove that effective specific factors do not exist. They may still be found if one looks in the right place or in the proper way. For those inclined to continue the search for specific factors (formal logic cannot account for individuals' willingness to keep looking), we have this advice: hunt with better measuring instruments of the elements of an outcome study, the measurement of results is currently the most poorly executed. Psychotherapy-outcome research lacks nothing by way of differentiated interventions (indeed, we feel it is uselessly rich in differentiation). The literature on treatment is a veritable pharmacopoeia of prescriptions. The design of controlled experimentation has been refined to a science that is within the grasp of any researcher who owns a table of random digits and recognizes the difference between blind and sighted assessment. However, the measurement of outcomes seems to have been abandoned at a primitive stage in its development. Rating scales are thrown together with little concern expressed for their psychometric properties. Venerable paper-and-pencil tests invented for diagnosis and with roots planted vaguely in no particular theory of pathology or treatment are used to hunt for effects of short-term and highly specialized brands of psychotherapy. A superfluity of instruments exists, and too little is known about them to prefer one to another. Little is known about their structure, and less is known about their sensitivity to treatment. If specific factors do produce unique effects, they will doubtless not be discovered with instruments that are crude and poorly understood.

In a recent chapter on the evaluation of therapeutic outcomes, Bergin and Lambert (1978, pp. 171-79) posed a list of issues concerning outcome measurement that we commend to the reader for its comprehensiveness and clarity.

Differences in how psychotherapy is conducted (whether in groups or

individually, by experienced or novice therapists, for long or short periods of time, and the like) make very little difference in how beneficial it is.
When this conclusion is joined with the previous one, a generalization begins to emerge. Apparently, little that the therapist controls bears any strong relationship to the effects of psychotherapy. The method of psychotherapy counts for little; nor do such gross features of the therapy as its length, whether it is administered in groups or alone, or the training and experience of the therapist. Of course, the conclusion does not follow that the therapist, his training, and the control he exercises over therapy are irrelevant. We continue to regard the psychotherapist as indispensable—*mirabile dictu*. It may also be true that what the therapist does that affects the course of the therapy may only be observable at molecular levels seldom measured and reported in outcome studies. However, the position that the crucial process variables are often unknown, not to mention unobserved, has many advocates and hardly needs more.

An alternative implication of this and the previous conclusion is plausible. We advance it here more because it is usually neglected than because it is an unequivocal consequence of our analyses. The possibility ought to be considered more seriously that the locus of those forces that restore and ameliorate the client of psychotherapy resides more within the client himself and less within the therapist and his actions. What the client brings to psychotherapy—the will to solve a problem or be rid of it, the intelligence to apprehend contingencies and relationships, the strength to face weakness, the confidence to trust another person—may contribute more to the success of the therapy than whether it lasts twenty hours or ten, whether or not there are other clients in the room, or whether the therapist pays obeisance to Fritz Perls or Joseph Wolpe.

The habit of thought among psychotherapy researchers appears to be to disregard the client, his problem, and his resources, and focus on the therapist, what he says and does, when, how, and the like. There are more than enough intellectual traditions in American psychology to account for this particular way of construing the psychotherapeutic relationship: a behaviorism that tends to reduce the organism to a hyphen between an S and an R; a false equating of "the scientific method" with interventionist experimentation and logical positivism; an aversion to naturalistic research and *Verstehen;* a need to establish an identity for psychology that separates it from psychiatry, with its nosologies and diagnoses.

Psychotherapy is scarcely any less effective than drug therapy in the treatment of serious psychological disorders. When the two therapies are combined, the net benefits are less than the sum of their separate benefits.
The long-standing tensions between psychology and psychiatry come to the fore when one attempts to draw the implications of our findings on the separate and combined effects of drug therapy and psychotherapy. The prevailing mythology surrounding these two forms of therapy held that psychotherapy

was relatively useless with psychotics and schizophrenics, but that when drugs were administered so as to make the patient accessible to human contact, then psychotherapy could be usefully applied. This mythology reflected the power relationship that prevailed between psychiatrists and psychologists, and it was one element among many—legal sanctions by statute or by courts, illness conceptions of psychological disorders, and the like—that maintained the status difference and kept it stable.

We found no support whatever for the myth. Psychotherapy enjoys near parity with drug therapy in treating even the very serious psychological disorders. One therapy is not dependent upon the other for its effects. Together they produce greater benefits than either one could produce by itself, but their effect in combination is only slightly above their separate effects. The model to replace the myth is one of two overlapping circles in a sort of Venn diagram: drug therapy and psychotherapy each contribute about the same degree of benefits individually, with some overlap of where they work their effects.

It is grandiose to imagine the status hierarchy of psychology and psychiatry being seriously disrupted by the discarding of a single myth. However, what we have learned should cause some who think about the future of the two professions to imagine what might replace the traditional relationship. If psychotherapy comes to be regarded as a method of treatment equal in power to drug therapy, what then will happen to the relationship between psychologists and psychiatrists in the care and rehabilitation of the seriously disturbed? What will psychologists need to learn about drug therapy in their training, and, of course, what will psychiatrists need to learn of psychotherapy? How will biochemical models of mental illness be affected? What role must environment be accorded in genetic models of schizophrenia and psychotic disorders?

And so this inquiry ends where each one does: old questions are answered and, in their turn, new questions arise. Science issues only interim reports.

Coding Form Used in the Psychotherapy Meta-analysis

Benefits of psychotherapy

Card one column	Value	Information
1–5	. . . .	Study identification number
6	. . . .	Running comparison number
7–8	. . . .	Running measure number
9	. . . .	Running record number: punch 1 for card 1
		Author
10–11	. . . .	Publication date
12	. . . .	Publication form: (1) journal, (2) book, (3) thesis, (4) unpublished
13	. . . .	Training of experimenter: (1) psychology, (2) education, (3) psychiatry, (4) social work, (5) other, (6) unknown
14	. . . .	Blinding: (1) E did therapy, (2) E knew composition of groups but didn't do therapy, (3) single-blind, (4) unknown
15	. . . .	Did E call this an analogue study: (1) yes, (2) no
		Clients
16–17	. . . .	Major diagnosis: (1) neurotic or complex phobic, (2) simple phobic, (3) psychotic, (4) normal, (5) character disorder, (6) delinquent or felon, (7) habituee, (8) mixed, (9) unknown, (10) emotional/somatic complaint, (11) handicapped, (12) depressive label
18–20	. . . .	List code for label
21	. . . .	Type of phobia: (1) reptile, (2) rodent, (3) insect, (4) speech, (5) tests, (6) other performance, (7) heights, (8) other
22–23	. . . .	Average length of hospitalization in years
24	. . . .	Average intelligence: (1) below average, (2) average, 95–105, (3) above average
25	. . . .	Source of IQ: (1) stated, (2) directly inferred, (3) estimated
26	. . . .	Similarity of client to therapist: (1) very dissimilar, (2) moderately dissimilar, (3) moderately similar, (4) very similar
27–28	. . . .	Mean age to nearest year
29–30	. . . .	Percentage male
31	. . . .	SES: (1) low, (2) middle, (3) high, (blank) unknown
32	. . . .	Solicitation of clients: (1) autonomous presentation, (2) presentation in response to advertisement, (3) solicited by E, (4) committed, (5) referred

Card one Column	Value	Information
		Design
33	....	Group assignment of clients: (1) random, (2) matching, (3) pretest equation, (4) convenience sample, (5) other nonrandom
34	....	Group assignment of therapists: (1) random, (2) matching, (3) nonrandom, (4) single therapist, (5) not applicable
35	....	Internal validity: (1) low, (2) medium, (3) high
36	....	Number of threats to internal validity
37–38	....	Percentage mortality from treated groups
39–40	....	Percentage mortality from comparison group
41	....	Is more than one therapy compared simultaneously against control: (1) yes, (2) no
42	....	Number of comparisons in this study
43	....	Number of this comparison
44–45	....	Number of outcome measures within this comparison
46–47	....	Number of this outcome measure (the rest of the record deals with this outcome measure)
		Treatment
48–49	....	Type of treatment: (2) placebo, (3) psychodynamic, (4) client-centered, (5) Adlerian, (6) gestalt, (7) systematic desensitization, (8) cognitive/Ellis, (9) cognitive/other, (10) transactional analysis, (11) behavior modification, (12) eclectic/dynamic, (13) eclectic behavioral, (14) reality therapy, (15) vocational/personal development counseling, (16) cognitive behavioral, (18) implosion, (19) hypnotherapy, (20) other
		Label for therapy type
		Proponent
50–52	....	List code for label
53–55	....	List code for proponent
56	....	Confidence of classification: (1) low . . . (5) high
57	....	Class of therapy
58	....	Superclass of therapy
59	....	Type of comparison: (1) control, (2) placebo, (3) second treatment
60	....	Type of control group: (1) no treatment, (2) waiting list, (3) intact group, (4) hospital maintenance, (5) other, (blank) not control
61–62	....	Type of placebo list code
		Label of placebo type
63–65	....	Second treatment type
66	....	Allegiance of E to therapy compared: (1) yes, (2) no, (3) unknown
67	....	Modality: (1) individual, (2) group, (3) family, (4) mixed, (5) automated, (6) other, (7) unknown
68–69	....	Location of treatment: (1) school, (2) hospital, (3) mental health center, (4) other clinic, (5) other outpatient, (6) private, (7) other, (8) unknown, (9) college mental health facility, (10) prison, (11) residential facility
70–72	....	Duration of therapy in hours
73–75	....	Duration of treatment in weeks
76–77	....	Number of therapists
78–79	....	Experience of therapists in years

Card two column	Value	Information
1–5	....	Study ID
6	....	Running comparison number
7–8	....	Running measure number
9	....	Running record number: punch 2 for card 2
		Effect size
10–12	....	Sample size for treatment group
13–15	....	Sample size for comparison group
16–17	....	Outcome type: (1) fear/anxiety, (2) self-esteem, (3) test measures and ratings of global adjustment, (4) life indicators of adjustment, (5) personality traits, (6) emotional/somatic disorders, (7) addiction, (8) sociopathic behaviors, (9) social behaviors, (10) work-school achievement, (11) vocational/personal development, (12) physiological measures of stress, (13) other
		Label of outcome measure
18–20	....	List code for outcome measure
21–23	....	Number of weeks post-therapy measure was taken
24	....	Reactivity of measure: (1) low ... (5) high
25–26	....	Calculation of effect size: (1) mean difference over control S.D., (2) MS within, (3) MS total minus treatment, (4) probit, (5) chi square, (6) T table, (7) mean and P, (8) nonparametrics, (9) correlations, (10) raw data, (11) estimates, (12) other
27	....	Source of means: (1) unadjusted post-test, (2) covariance adjusted, (3) residual gains, (4) pre-post differences, (5) other
28	....	Significance of treatment effect: (0) $-.001$, (1) $-.005$, (2) $-.01$, (3) $-.05$, (4) $-.10$, (5) .10, (6) .05, (7) .01, (8) .005, (9) .001, (blank) not significant
29–34	....	Treatment group pre-mean
35–40	....	Treatment pre-standard deviation
41–46	....	Treatment post-mean
47–52	....	Treatment post-standard deviation
53–58	....	Comparison group pre-mean
59–64	....	Comparison pre-standard deviation
65–70	....	Comparison post-mean
71–76	....	Comparison post-standard deviation

Card three column	Value	Information
1–5	....	Study ID
6	....	Running comparison number
7–8	....	Running measure number
9	....	Running record number: punch 3 for card 3
10–13	....	T statistic
14–17	....	F statistic
18–22	....	Mean square within, residual, or common
23–24	....	Treatment group percentage improved
25–26	....	Comparison group percentage improved

Card three Column	Value	Information
27–30	. . . .	Effect size
31	. . . .	Class of second therapy
32	. . . .	Superclass of second therapy
33	. . . .	Allegiance of E to second therapy
34	. . . .	Modality of second therapy
35	. . . .	Location of second therapy
36–38	. . . .	Duration of second therapy in hours
39–41	. . . .	Duration of second therapy in weeks
42–43	. . . .	Number of therapists in second therapy
44–45	. . . .	Experience of therapists in second therapy
46	. . . .	Other factorial effects tested: (0) none,(1) race, (2) SES, (3)IE, (4) sex, (5) other
47	. . . .	Is this the last effect with this comparison: (1) yes, (2) no
48–51	. . . .	If yes, average effect size within this comparison
52	. . . .	Is this the last effect size in this study: (1) yes, (2) no
53–56	. . . .	If yes, average of all effect sizes in the study

....

List Codes for Diagnosis, Therapy, and Outcome Types

Specific Diagnoses Organized within Diagnostic Types

Neurotic-True (Complex) Phobic

Neurotic
Complex phobic
Poorly adjusted children
Neurotic homosexuals
Personal growth-seekers
Students in stressful training programs
Underachievers
Low achievers
Performance anxiety
Shyness
Interpersonal anxiety
Social anxiety
Anger
Sex deviants
Socially nonassertive
Externalizers
Students with behavior problems
Low sociometric status children
Inability to speak in class
Potential college dropouts
Hyperactive children

Simple (monosymptomatic) Phobics

Rat, mouse, snake, spider phobic
Speech anxiety
Test anxiety
Dental phobia
Fear of darkness
Math anxiety
Fear of blood
Acrophobia

Psychotic

Schizophrenic
Psychotic
Manic-depressive
Felons with psychiatric symptoms

Character disordered
Delinquents-Felons
Emotional-Somatic Disordered

Asthmatic
Dysmenorrhea
Sexual dysfunction
Insomnia
Enuresis
Overweight
Migraine headaches
Heart attack patients
Home dialysis patients

Handicapped

Vocational rehabilitation clients
Mentally retarded
Physically handicapped

Habitué

Smokers
Alcoholics
Drug addicts

Depressive

Specific Therapies Organized within Therapy Categories

Psychodynamic

Psychoanalysis
Psychodynamic psychotherapy
Ego therapy
Intensive psychotherapy
Leading therapy
Cathartic psychotherapy
Direct analysis
Group psychotherapy

Adlerian

Adlerian therapy
Individual analysis
DUSO

Client-centered

Rogerian therapy
Client-centered psychotherapy
Reflective therapy
Interaction psychotherapy
Nondirective play therapy

Gestalt

Gestalt therapy
Marathon group therapy
Gestalt growth group
Microgroup psychotherapy
Encounter group

Systematic Desensitization

Systematic desensitization
Reciprocal inhibition
Counterconditioning

Rational-emotive Psychotherapy
Other Cognitive Therapies

Rational stage-directed therapy
Semantic desensitization
Cognitive control
Fixed-role therapy
Rational therapy
Systematic rational restructuring
Play desensitization
Cognitive rehearsal
Verbal desensitization

Transactional Analysis
Behavior Modification

Behavior modification
Operant conditioning
Token economy
Aversive conditioning

Verbal conditioning
Conditioned relaxation
Systematic counseling
Stimulus satiation

Eclectic-dynamic

Insight therapy
Psychosomatic psychotherapy
Problem-solving group psychotherapy
Social adjustment group counseling
Traditional psychotherapy
Marital or family psychotherapy

Eclectic-Behavioral

Assertiveness training
Self-defeating behavior workshop
Desensitization plus skills counseling
Practiced imagination therapy
Behavioral rehearsal

Reality Therapy

Vocational-Personal Development Counseling

Study skills counseling
Vocational counseling
Personal achievement skills counseling
Social adjustment group counseling
Counseling and instruction about psychological processes

Cognitive-behavioral

Cognitive-behavioral therapy
Contact desensitization
Behavioral self-control
Self-control desensitization
Modeling
Modeling reinforcement
Self-reinforcement
Self-modeling
Covert reinforcement
Anxiety management training
Cognitive behavior modification
Covert sensitization
Covert assertion
Social learning theory

Implosion

Implosive therapy
Flooding

Undifferentiated Counseling

School counseling
Success sharing groups
Supportive counseling
Nondirective counseling

Specific Outcome Measures Organized within Outcome Categories

Fear-anxiety

Liebert–Morris Emotionality-Worry Scale
Behavior Avoidance Test, Approach Tests
Fear Thermometer
Fear Survey Schedule
Anxiety Achievement Scale
Suinn or Sarason Test Anxiety Scales
State-Trait Anxiety Inventory
Anxiety Card Sort
OPI Anxiety Scale
Ratings of anxiety by therapist, nurse, teacher
Performance anxiety scale
IPAT anxiety
Factorial battery of anxiety measures
Subjective units of distress
Anxiety differential
S-R Inventory of Anxiety
Spider, mouse, snake anxiety scales
Manifest Anxiety Scale
Confidence in public speaking
Ratings of speech anxiety
Fear of dental work
Math anxiety scale
Avoidance of heights
Homosexual or heterosexual anxiety
Improvement in phobic symptoms

Self-esteem

Tennessee Self-Concept Scale
Teacher, therapist, observer ratings of self-esteem
Self-ideal correlations
Piers–Harris Self-Concept Scale

Coopersmith Self-Esteem Inventory
Personal Orientation Inventory
Butler-Haigh Q-Sort
Berger's Acceptance of Self and Others

Tests and Ratings of Global Adjustment

Ratings of improvement
Ratings from Rorschach and TAT administrations
Beck Depression Inventory
Ratings of depression
Rotter I-E Locus of control
Teacher, therapist ratings of adjustment
Goal Attainment Scaling
Ability to function under stress
Neurotic symptom change
Bender-Gestalt
Adult Irrational Ideas Inventory
Irrational Beliefs Test
Mooney Problem Check List
Willoughby Scale
Omnibus Personality Inventory—personality integration
Rated absence of symptoms
Personal Orientation Inventory
Personal Beliefs Inventory
Attitude toward authority
Impulse control
Rated adjustment
Hospital Adjustment Scale
Adjective check list
Rated anger
Nurse, staff ratings of ward behavior
Psychotic Reaction Profile
Inpatient Multidimensional Psychiatric Scale
Grinker Scale
Time orientation
Ego strength
House-Tree-Person Test
Goal direction
Rogers Test of Personality Adjustment
Sentence completion test
Sematic differential
Minnesota Counseling Inventory
Dogmatism
Genuineness
Withdrawal
Prognosis
Emotional stability

Myers–Briggs Judgment Perception Scale
Morbidity

Life Indicators of Adjustment

Discharge from hospital
Hospitalizations, rehospitalizations
Time out of the hospital
Days without alcohol
Employment
Participations in pleasant events
Imprisonments, arrests, probations
Work adjustment

Personality Traits

Minnesota Multiphasic Personality Inventory
California Personality Inventory
California Test of Personality
Edwards Personal Preference Scale
IPAT
Eysenck Personality Inventory

Addiction

Days without alcohol
Legal involvements over alcohol problems
Controlled drinking
Reduced or eliminated smoking
Abstinence
Improvement in drinking behavior
Sobriety

Sociopathic Behaviors

Aggression
School misconduct
Parole violations
Recidivism
Imprisonment

Social Behaviors

Acceptance of others
FIRO-B
Sociometric status
Interpersonal distance
Interpersonal maturity

Social relations
Family adjustment
Community adjustment
Assertiveness ratings and measures
Dating behavior
Social effectiveness
Social distance
Alienation

Emotional-Somatic Complaints

Respiratory asthmatic symptoms
Number of asthmatic attacks
Lung function
Use of drugs or medication
Emergency room visits
Sleep disturbance
Enuresis
Weight loss
Pain intensity
Migraine symptoms
Dysmenorrhea
Sexual adjustment

Work and School Achievement

Intelligence tests
Academic achievement tests
Wonderlic Personnel Scale
Digit Symbols Test
Tuddenham Reputation Test
Grade point average, course grades
Mental development scales
Ratings of success in school or work
Production of verbal responses in class
Persistence in or completion of educational program
Completion of military tour of duty
School attendance

Vocational-Personal Development

Vocational maturity or adjustment
Vocational realism
Means-Ends Problem-solving Procedure
Goal-attainment Scaling
Appropriate behavior
Study habits inventory
Enjoyment of work

Task-orientation ratings
Ability to speak in class
Need for achievement
Aspiration
Attitude toward school

Physiological Measures of Stress

Palmar Sweat Print
Galvanic Skin Response
Pulse rate

Appendix 3

....

Study Characteristics for The Psychotherapy Studies

Percentage of effects for various diagnostic categories

Neurotic/true phobic	40%
Simple phobic	35%
Psychotic	8%
Normal	2%
Character disorder	0
Delinquent/felon	4%
Habituée	4%
Emotional-somatic complaint	3%
Handicapped	2%
Depressive	3%

Hospitalization

Mean	.36 years
Standard deviation	2.01

Age

Mean	22.91 years
Standard deviation	9.02

Percentage of males in study

Mean	47.95%
Standard deviation	29.63%

Percentage of effects for different solicitation categories

Autonomous presentation	14%
Presentation in response to ad	16%
Solicited by experimeter	46%
Committed	16%
Referred	8%

Percentage of therapy categories

Placebo	11%
Psychodynamic	6%
Client-centered	9%
Adlerian	1%
Gestalt	4%
Systematic desensitization	21%

(*continued*)

Cognitive (Ellis)	3%
Cognitive (other than Ellis)	3%
Transactional analysis	2%
Behavior modification	11%
Dynamic electric	6%
Eclectic behavioral	2%
Reality therapy	1%
Vocational-personal counseling	3%
Cognitive behavioral	7%
Implosion	3%
Hypnotherapy	1%
Undifferentiated counseling	6%

Percentage of different therapy modalities

Individual	43%
Group	49%
Family	1%
Mixed	6%
Automated	1%
Other	1%

Percentage of different therapy locations

School	14%
Hospital	12%
Mental health center	2%
Other clinic	5%
Other out-patient	8%
College facility	42%
Prison	2%
Residential facility	3%

Duration of therapy in hours

Mean	16.18 hours
Standard deviation	26.56

Duration of therapy in weeks

Mean	10.99 weeks
Standard deviation	13.43

Therapist experience

Mean	3.19 years
Standard deviation	2.35

Appendix 4

....

Correlation Matrix for the
Psychotherapy Meta-analysis[a]

Variables	1	2	3	4	5	6	7	8	9
1 Year of study	.00	−.10	.11	.21	−.06	−.19	.21	.12
2 Blinding		.06	−.19	−.25	.15	−.01	−.11	.32
3 Hospitalization			−.25	−.38	.37	−.02	−.03	−.02
4 IQ				.75	−.31	−.22	.02	−.01
5 Similarity					−.34	−.25	.14	−.17
6 Age						−.01	−.18	.17
7 % male							.02	.03
8 Internal validity								−.44
9 Mortality (exp.)								
10 Mortality (control)								
11 Duration								
12 N of therapists								
13 Therapist experience								
14 N of clients (exp.)								
15 N of clients (control)								
16 Time measurement								
17 Reactivity								
18 Effect size								

[a]The number of cases on which the *r*s are based range from several hundred at the least to about 1,700 at the most.

(continued)

Appendix 4 (*continued*)

10	11	12	13	14	15	16	17	18
.12	-.24	-.07	-.18	-.03	-.02	-.19	.07	.07
.41	.06	.20	-.07	.09	.07	.08	-.07	-.01
.02	.29	.11	.28	-.02	.00	.00	.05	-.02
-.08	-.33	-.17	-.05	-.26	-.28	-.09	.12	.08
-.25	-.42	-.15	-.10	-.16	-.17	-.09	.15	.10
.23	.25	.04	.10	-.07	-.09	.07	.09	.00
.01	.09	.02	.14	.24	.23	.09	-.19	-.13
-.40	-.16	.01	-.12	-.03	-.07	-.15	-.05	.03
.81	.00	.00	-.01	.04	.03	.09	-.02	-.05
	.01	-.03	.00	.04	.02	.09	-.05	-.04
		.17	.00	.04	.29	.17	-.07	-.04
			-.15	.25	.33	.09	-.07	-.05
				.01	.02	.09	-.01	.00
					.86	.26	-.14	-.06
						.22	-.14	-.06
							-.13	-.05
								.18

Appendix 5

MEDLARS Search Specifications

Search formulation—psychopharmacologic research in humans: clinical trials

1) Affective disturbances F3.126.56
   Anxiety
   Depersonalization
   Depression

2) Aggression
   Torture
   Violence

3) Neuroses
   Depression
   Depression, reactive
     Depressive neuroses
   Hypochondriacs
     Hypochondriacal neuroses
     Munchausen syndrome
   Hysteria
     Conversion reaction
       Globus hysterius
     Dissociative reaction
       Dual personality
         Multiple personalities
       Hysterical neuroses
   Neuroesthenia
   Neurocirculatory asthenia
   Neuroses anxiety
     Anxiety, castration
     Anxiety, separation
     Homesickness
   Neuroses, obsessive-compulsive
     Kleptomania
     Obsession
     Trichotillomania
   Neuroses, post-traumatic
   Neuroses, war
   Phobias
     Agraphobia
     Claustrophobia
     Phobia neuroses

4) Compulsive behavior F3.126.208
   Fire-setting behavior
   Gambling
     Risk-taking

   Obsessive behavior
   Smoking

5) Alcoholism C21.613.53.270
   Psychoses, alcoholic
     Delirium tremens
     Kersakoff's syndrome

6) Psychoses F3.709.755
   Depression, reactive, psychotic
   Folie à deux
   Paranoias
   Psychoses, involutional
     Involutional paranoid state
     Melancholic, involutional
     Paraphrenia
   Psychoses, manic-depressive
   Schizophrenia
     Schizophrenia, catatonic
     Schizophrenia, childhood
       Autism, early infant
     Schizophrenia, hebephrenia
     Schizophrenia, latent
     Schizophrenia, paranoid

7) Personality disorders
   Alcoholism
     Skid-row alcoholic
   Antisocial personality
     Sociosyntonic personality disorders
   As-if personality
   Cyclothymic personality
   Hysterical personality
   Inadequate personality
   Obsessive-compulsive personality
   Paranoia
     Paranoic personality
   Passive-aggressive personality
     Passive-dependent personality
   Schizoid personality
   Tension-discharge disorders
     Impulse-ridden personality

8) 1 or 2 or 3 or 4 or 5 or 6 or 7

9) 8 and drug therapy

10) Clinical research or research design

11) 9 and 10

12) 11 and placebos

13) 11 and (control or controlled)

14) 12 or 13

Search formulation—comparative studies between effectiveness of psychopharmacologic therapy and psychotherapy

---

1) Psychotherapy
    Analytical psychotherapy
    Brief psychotherapy
    Child psychotherapy
    Client-centered therapy
    Conjoint therapy
    Dream analysis
    Encounter-group therapy
    Existential therapy
    Experiential psychotherapy
    Expressive psychotherapy
    Family therapy
    Geriatric psychotherapy
    Gestalt therapy
    Group psychotherapy
    Hydrotherapy
    Individual psychotherapy
    Insight therapy
    Persuasion therapy
    Play therapy
    Psychoanalysis
    Psychodrama
    Psychotherapeutic counseling
    Reality therapy
    Relationship therapy
    Therapeutic community
    Transactional analysis

2) Psychopharmacology
    Drug therapy
    Pharmacotherapy
    Chemotherapy

3) 1 and 2

4) 3 and (comparison—studies on treatment-effectiveness evaluation)

Appendix 6

··

Coding Form Used
in the Drug Therapy Meta-analysis

Code sheet: drug efficacy study

Reference

Col.   Card 1

1–4   ID ... ...
5–6   Yr. of publication ... ...
7–8   Comparison for this reference ... ...
9–10   Total no. comparisons for this reference ... ...
11   Research funded by ... (1) drug co. ... (2) NIMH ... (3) other or unknown
12   Type of publication ... (1) book ... (2) major journal ... (3) minor journal ...
       (4) other
13   First author was ... (1) M.D. ... (2) Ph.D. ... (3) MSW ... (4) other or unknown

Patient information for this comparison

14   Major diagnosis ... (1) psychotic ... (2) neurotic ... (3) character dis. ... (4)
       combo ... (5) other
15   Specific type ... (1) schiz ... (2) other ... (3) dep ... (4) manic ... (5) m-d
       ... (6) aggr/hos ... (7) drug dep. ... (8) combo ... (9) anxiety
16   If mixed, modal type (major diag) ... (1) ... (2) ... (3) ... (4) ... (5)
17   Length of illness ... (1) under 1 yr. ... (2) 1 to 2 yrs. ... (3) over 2 yrs. ... (4)
       mixed

                          Acute   Intermediate   Chronic
18   If mixed, modal length ... (1) ... (2) ... (3)
19   Setting ... (1) in-patient ... (2) out-patient ... (3) mixed
20–21 Mean age to nearest yr. ... ...
22–23 Percentage male ... ...
24–25 Percentage white ... ...
26–27 Percentage black ... ...
28–29 Percentage other ... ...
30   SES ... (1) low ... (2) middle ... (3) high
31–32 Number of groups in total study ... ...
33–35 N control (this comparison) ... ...
36–38 N exp (this comparison) ... ...
39–42 N total ... ...

Notes:

(*continued*)

Col.   Card 1

Control information

43   Type ... (1) placebo ... (2) psyther ... (3) psyther + placebo ... (4) reg tmnt
        minus drug ... (5) no tmnt or plbo ... (6) no drug (marginal, P + north)
        ...(7) no psy (marginal, D + noth) ... (8) other ... (9) drug + psy
44   If psyther, type ... (1) ind beh. ... (2) grp beh. ... (3) ind non-beh. ... (4) grp
        non-beh ... (5) combo ... (6) other
        Name
45–46   Yrs. therapist exp. ... ...
47–49   Duration in months ... ...
50–52   Duration in total hours ... ...

Experimental information

53   Type ... (1) drug only ... (2) drug + psyther ... (3) psyther only ... (4) drug
        (marginal, D + P and D only) ... (5) psyther (marginal, D + P and P only) ...
        (6) placebo + psy ... (7) placebo
54/   If drug, major type ... (1) antipsychotic ... (2) antidepr ... (3) antianxiety ...
AGG   (4) antidrug dep ... (5) antimania ... (6) other ... (7) combo

Drug name(s) generic   Trade

55   If psyther, type ... (1) ind beh. ... (2) grp beh. ... (3) ind non-beh. ... (4) grp
        non-beh ... (5) combo ... (6) other
        Name
56–57   Yrs. therapist exp. ... ...
58–60   Duration in months ... ...
61–63   Duration in total hrs. ... ...

If drug is part of experimental treatment:

64–66   Duration in months ... ...
67–70   Average daily dosage in mgs. ... ...
71   Severity of side effects ... (1) low ... (2) med ... (3) high
72   Controls to insure patient took drug? ... (1) yes ... (2) no
        EG. parenteral, implant, urinalysis, mouth check

Dependent variable

73–75   Months post-trmnt measured ... ... (0 indicates during or at immediate end of
        trmnt)
76–77   Type of outcome ... (1) release rate ... (2) hospitalization rate ... (3) length stay
        ... (4) length in commun. ... (5) somatic symptoms ... (6) anxiety ... (7)
        depression ... (8) self-esteem ... (9) disorder cog.... (10) work adj.... (11)
        hosp. adj.... (12) social adj.... (13) agg/hos ... (14) manic beh ... (15) global
        severity-health ... (16) psychodynamics 170th

Col.   Card 2

1–4   ID ... ...
5–6   This comparison ... ...
7   Aggregated type outcome ... (1) hospital related 1–4 ... (2) somatic symps/eat,
        sleep, sex, alchl ... (3) psych symps 6–9, 16 ... (4) adjustment 10–14 ... (5)
        global severity-health ... (6) other
8   How rated ... (1) patient self-report ... (2) patient test ... (3) M.D. or E rating ...
        (4) nurse rtng ... (5) sig other rt ... (6) physiological ... (7) combo ... (8)
        other
9   Fakeability Low ... ...high
                          1   2   3   4   5

(*continued*)

Col.   Card 2   (*continued*)

Name of dependent variable

Design information

10   Blinding ... (1) double ... (2) single: MD knew ... (3) open; all knew—to be checked if not reported
11   Placebo-controlled ... (1) yes ... (2) no
12   Patients assigned ... (1) random ... (2) matched ... (3) existing groups ... (4) other non-ran
13   Attrition controlled or analyzed ... (1) yes ... (2) no
14   Global internal validity ... low ... ...high
1   2   3   4   5

Effect size

15–19   ... ...
20   Was comparison sig. P < .05? ... (1) yes ... (2) no
21–24   Percentage exp ... ...
25–28   Percentage control ... ...
29–35   Exp mean ... ...
36–42   Control mean ... ...
43–47   Exp S.D. ... ...
48–52   Control S.D. ... ...
53–56   Probit E.S. ... ...
57–58   Type error term (1)   (2)   (3)   (4)   (5)   (6)   (7)   (8)   (9)   ...   ...
59   Type of mean   (1) ANCOVA adj   (2) unadjusted   (3) change scores   (4) other
61–64   Common E.S. ... ... (exp mean—control mean)/S.D. control
Skip col col. 65–79
80   Punch 2 for card 2

Formulas and Conventions for Calculating Effect Sizes

I. Calculation of effect size from test statistics

A. Single classifications, no covariate

$$t = \frac{\bar{X}_T - \bar{X}_C}{\left(\frac{(n_T - 1)S_T^2 + n_C - 1)S_C^2}{n_T + n_C - 2} \left(\frac{1}{n_T} + \frac{1}{n_C} \right) \right)^{\frac{1}{2}}}$$

1. Given treatment mean ($\bar{X}_T$) and control mean ($\bar{X}_C$), t and n, calculate $\bar{S}$ where $\bar{S} = \dfrac{\bar{X}_T - \bar{X}_C}{t \left(\dfrac{1}{n_T} + \dfrac{1}{n_C} \right)^{\frac{1}{2}}}$ = square root of mean variance

$$\text{Effect size } (ES) = \frac{\bar{X}_T - \bar{X}_C}{\bar{S}}$$

2. Given $\bar{X}_T$, $\bar{X}_C$, n and probability $(p) = \alpha$ for *unreported* t, assume nondirectional probability unless otherwise stated and

find $_{\alpha/2}t_{n_1 + n_2 - 2}$
and proceed as in 1.

3. Given "mean difference is significant" and given n_T, n_C use

$$t = 1.96,$$

so

$$ES = 1.96 \left(\frac{1}{n_T} + \frac{1}{n_C} \right)^{\frac{1}{2}}$$

The following formulas are assumed for items 4–6 below:

$$F = \frac{MS_b}{MS_w} = \frac{\Sigma n_j (\bar{X}_{.j} - \bar{X}..)^2/(J - 1)}{\Sigma\Sigma(X_{ij} - \bar{X}_{.j})^2/J(n - 1)} = \frac{MS_b}{\bar{S}^2},$$

where $\bar{S}^2$ = mean within-cell variance

4. Given $\bar{X}_{T_1}, \bar{X}_{T_2}, \bar{X}_{T_3}, \ldots \bar{X}_{T_J}, \bar{X}_C$, F and $n_{T_1}, n_{T_2}, n_{T_3}, \ldots n_{T_J}, n_C$,

Calculate MS_b.

Solve for $MS_w \quad = \bar{S}^2 = \dfrac{MS_b}{F}$

$$ES = \frac{\bar{X}_{T_j} - \bar{X}_C}{\sqrt{\bar{S}^2}}$$

5. Given $\bar{X}_T, \bar{X}_C$, n and probability $(p) = \alpha$ for *unreported F*. Find $_\alpha F_{J-1, \ NJ-J}$ and proceed as in 4.

6. Given "means were significantly different," $n_1, n_2, n_3, \ldots, n_J, \bar{X}_1, \bar{X}_2, \bar{X}_3, \ldots, \bar{X}_J$, use

$_{.95}F_{J-1, \ NJ-J}$ and proceed as in 4.

B. Single classification, covariate

Proceed as in A.4, using adjusted means to arrive at adjusted MS_w. When adjusted MS_w is calculated (MS_w') convert it to MS_w by

$$MS_w(1 - r^2) = MS_w'$$

$$MS_w = \frac{MS_w'}{(1 - r^2)} \quad ,$$

where r is the correlation between variate and covariate. This value (r) is rarely reported, so it must be estimated. Below are some conventions for estimating r:

a. Measure is established psychological inventory. Two to six months elapse between measurement of variate and covariate: $r = 0.5$.

b. If six months to 1 year between reassessment: $r = 0.3$

c. Measurements are behavioral ratings made 4 months or more apart: $r = 0.25$

d. Measurements are cognitive test scores made 4 months or more (up to two years) apart: consult test manuals for test-retest reliability (coefficient of stability) or else use $r = 0.7$

e. Variate and covariate are different measures

Estimate r based on author's estimate of likely relationship between the two measures or based on your knowledge of the correlation (e.g., reading and math tests $r = 0.6$; two physiological measures $r = 0.3$).

C. Multiple classifications, no covariate

For factorial ANOVA's in which the factor or factors crossing the treatment-control factor are not of special interest (e.g., ward, hospital, private vs. public patients), the reported MS_w (for fixed models) may be an underestimate of the variance needed for the effect size. In this event, the sum of squares for the factor crossing the treatment-control dimension and the sum of squares for the interaction should be added to the sum of squares error before the effect size is calculated.

Example: $\bar{X}$ Drug = 18
$\bar{X}$ control = 10

Source of variation	Sum of squares	df	MS
Treatment (T)	768	1	768
Ward (W)	192	1	192
T × W	145	1	145
Within cells	1584	44	36

$$\text{Incorrect Effect Size} \quad \frac{18 - 10}{\sqrt{36}} = 1.33$$

$$\text{Corrected } MS_{w} = (192 + 145 + 1584)/46 = 41.76$$

$$\text{Correct Effect Size} \quad \frac{18 - 10}{\sqrt{41.76}} = 1.24$$

D. Multiple classification, covariate

In cases such as C where a covariate is involved, the MS_{w} must be corrected first for the correlation between variate and covariate, then corrected for the reduction in variance due to factorialization. Here the same consideration must be involved in estimating the correlation between variate and covariate as in the case of a single classification ANOVA with covariate, except that the correlation will be somewhat smaller than if the estimate were from a single classification study. This difference is due to the fact that the variate-covariate correlation that reduces the MS_{w} is *within cells* that have restricted range due to the factorialization. As a convention, the correlation is reduced 0.1 to 0.2 if no information is available to allow an estimate of the range restriction. Procedures in I.B. and I.C. should both be followed.

E. Dependent t test

Where t is based on correlated samples (e.g., pre-post) one must estimate the correlation between samples to solve for $\sqrt{S^2}$ below. The occasion often arises when treatment and control improvement are tested by authors, using a t test for the pre- to post-patient changes, instead of an independent t test post-treatment between treatment and control.

$$t = \frac{\bar{X}_{\text{pre}} - \bar{X}_{\text{post}}}{\left(\dfrac{S_{\text{pre}}^2}{n} + \dfrac{S_{\text{post}}^2}{n} - 2r_{pp} \dfrac{(S_{\text{pre}})(S_{\text{post}})}{n} \right)^{\frac{1}{2}}}$$

assume $S_{\text{pre}}^2 = S_{\text{post}}^2$, so

$$t = \frac{\bar{X}_{\text{pre}} - \bar{X}_{\text{post}}}{\left(\dfrac{2}{n} S^2 (1 - r) \right)^{\frac{1}{2}}}, \quad \text{then}$$

$$S^2 = \frac{(\bar{X}_{\text{pre}} - \bar{X}_{\text{post}})^2 (n)}{2t^2 (1 - r)}.$$

—Time lapse between measurements and type of measurements must be considered in estimating the correlation between time one and time two outcomes. Conventions found in I.B. apply here.

F. Repeated measures designs

Two factors (one fixed, one random): in this case, persons represent levels of a random factor and treatments are levels of the fixed factor. Here the mean square for the interaction becomes the error term for the F test of treatment effects. The mean square interaction must be corrected for the correlation between measures of patients under the two treatments to give the proper estimate of the within-cell variance. The correction formula follows:

Mean square interaction $(MSI) = S^2_{\text{within}}(1 - r)$ (Gulliksen 1950, p. 54)

$$S^2_{\text{within}} = \frac{MSI}{(1 - r)}$$

Estimate of the correlation between the patient's scores under the two treatment conditions should be made via the conventions in I.B.

Where the factors crossing the treatment-control dimension are of interest (e.g., psychotherapy–no psychotherapy crossing drug therapy–no drug therapy) the MS_{it} is left untouched.

II. Special problems
   A. Three-factor mixed model
       Two kinds of three factor mixed model in the drug therapy literature make for some confusion. The first type is the cross-over design in which treatments (drug vs. placebo, for example) are crossed by order of treatment (some patients receiving placebo first then drug and some patients receiving drug first, then placebo) with patients nested within order but crossing treatments. In this case, the F test for treatments contains the correct error term for estimating the within-cell standard deviation. That error term is the mean square for treatment by subjects within order $(MS_{TS(0)})$. If F is reported for treatment and n per treatment is known, then one can solve for MS_{within} by first solving for $MS_{TS(0)}$ using

$$\frac{MS_{\text{treatments}}}{MS_{TS(0)}} = F,$$

then correcting $MS_{TS(0)}$ to yield MS_{within} by

$$MS_{TS(0)} = MS_{\text{within}}(1 - r) \qquad \text{(as in F above)},$$

where r is the correlation (estimated as in I.B.) between subjects' scores under drug therapy and under placebo.

The second model is much like the first, but here treatments are crossed by measures (pre and post, for example) and patients cross measures, but are nested within treatments. (It should be remembered that in the first case, patients crossed treatments, but here patients are nested within treatments.) The F for treatments in this case will contain the *in*appropriate mean square for the effect-size calculation. (The mean square error of the treatment F will be subjects nested within treatments $[MS_{S(T)}]$.) Therefore, one cannot solve for the effect size standard deviation within cells, given the F and n per cell only. Instead, one must use the F test for the measures effect (pre vs. post) that contains the error term needed for the effect-size calculation (mean square for measures by subjects within treatments $[MS_{MS(T)}]$). This must be solved for $MS_{MS(T)}$ which then must be corrected by

$$MS_{MS(T)} = MS_{\text{within}}(1 - r) \qquad \text{(as above and in F)}$$

Examples of the two cases follow:

Case I.   Treatment   ANOVA table

		A	B
	1	s_1	s_1
	A then B	.	.
Order		s_{10}	s_{10}
	2	s_{11}	s_{11}
	B then A	.	.
		s_{20}	s_{20}

Source	df
Treatment (T)	1
Order (O)	1
Subject within order $S(O)$	18
$T \times O$	1
$T \times S(O)$	18

$$F_{\text{treatment}} = \frac{MS_T}{MS_{T \times S(O)}}$$

$$MS_{T \times S(O)} = MS_{\text{within}}(1 - r)$$

Estimate r, where r is the correlation between outcome measures for treatment A and B.

Case II.   Treatment   ANOVA table

		A	B
	Pre	s_1	s_{11}
		.	.
Measure		s_{10}	s_{20}
	Post	s_1	s_{11}
		.	.
		s_{10}	s_{20}

Source	df
Treatment (T)	1
Measure (M)	1
Subject within treatment $S(T)$	18
$T \times M$	1
$M \times S(T)$	18

$$F_{\text{treatment}} = \frac{MS_T}{MS_{S(T)}} \qquad \textit{Wrong MS for effect size}$$

$$F_{\text{measure}} = \frac{MS_M}{MS_{M \times S(T)}} \qquad \text{Correct MS for effect size}$$

$$MS_{\text{within}} = \frac{MS_{M \times S(T)}}{(1 - r)}$$

Estimate r, where r is the correlation between outcome scores for pre and post.

B. Wilcoxon T. Find p value for the reported T statistic and convert to appropriate parametric t statistic for the same n and p value. Solve for $\sqrt{S^2}$ as with parametric t in which you have only n and value of t.

C. Improvement rates—Given frequency distributions of global improvement ratings on scales that range from 1 to 3 or higher, calculate the means and standard deviations of the treated and control groups' raw ratings. Calculate the effect size in the standard fashion:

$$ES = \frac{\overline{X}_{\text{treatment}} - \overline{X}_{\text{control}}}{S_{\text{control}}}$$

If results are merely dichotomized (e.g., improved-unimproved), use probits to transform data to ES's.

Statistical Estimation of Effects from the "Same Experiment" Drug Therapy Data

The "same experiment" data used in Chapter 8 to refine the estimates of the drug, psychotherapy, and interaction effects have the following organization and structure:

Type of comparison	Structure of effects	$\overline{ES}$
⌈A. Drug vs. control	δ_1	.457
⌊B. Drug-plus-psychotherapy vs. control	$\delta_1 + \psi_1 + \eta_1$	.650
C. Drug-plus-psychotherapy vs. drug	$\psi_2 + \eta_2$	.278
⌈D. Drug vs. control	δ_2	.532
⌊E. Psychotherapy vs. control	ψ_3	.306
F. Drug vs. psychotherapy	$\delta_3 - \psi_4$	.020
⌈G. Drug-plus-psychotherapy vs. control	$\delta_4 + \psi_5 + \eta_3$	.653
⌊H. Psychotherapy vs. control	ψ_5	.173
I. Drug-plus-psychotherapy vs. psychotherapy	$\delta_5 + \eta_4$	.100

For example, as was reported in the text of Chapter 8, 17 studies in which drug therapy was compared to a control group yielded 50 effect-size measures averaging 0.457 (line A). The above system can be viewed as a system of linear equations. The brackets that join A with B, D with E, and G with H symbolize that these pairs of comparisons come from the same experiments. Thus, the drug effect, δ_1, in comparison A must be the same as the drug effect in comparison B. Comparisons of types B and C did not arise from only the same set of experiments; thus the ψ and η parameters could be different, as the subscripts in the above table indicate. Attempts to solve for the fourteen parameters in the table above fail for want of enough independent restrictions. Hence, certain parameters must be assumed equal before a unique solution can be found. But attempts to reduce the number of parameters by assuming certain ones equal fall short of a consistent set of equations; even when all δ's are assumed equal to a common δ and likewise for all ψ's and η's, creating only three unknown parameters, the set of nine equations is not linearly independent and no unique solution is possible. Fortunately, by assuming only three unknown parameters (δ, ψ, η) and transforming the bracketed equations into both their sums and their differences (i.e., A and B are replaced by A + B and A − B, and likewise for the other two pairs), a solvable system of linear equations is produced.

$\overline{ES}.$

A + B:	1.107 =	$\psi + 2\delta + \eta$
B − A:	.193 =	$\psi + \quad\ \eta$
C:	.278 =	$\psi + \quad\ \eta$
D + E:	.838 =	$\psi + \delta$
D − E:	.226 =	$-\psi + \delta$
F:	.020 =	$-\psi + \delta$
G − H:	.480 =	$\delta + \eta$
G + H:	.826 =	$2\psi + \delta + \eta$
I:	.100 =	$\delta + \eta$

The "same experiment" logic contributes to this formulation in one important respect. Because of the pairings of certain comparisons within the same experiments, certain of the above contrasts are known to be exact even when the assumptions of equal δ's, ψ's and η's are false. For example, that B–A estimates $\psi + \eta$ is true regardless of whether or not all experiments estimate identical δ's.

Denoting the vector of contrasts of $\overline{ES}$'s by y and factoring the system of right-hand members of the equations into X a 9×3 matrix and β a 3×1 vector, and recognizing that y can be fitted by $X\beta$ only within some degree of error, ϵ, one can apply conventional least-squared error estimation procedures to estimate the elements of β. As is well-known,

$$\hat{\beta} = (X^T X)^{-1} X^T y.$$

For the "same experiment" data,

$$(X^T X) = \begin{bmatrix} 10 & 3 & 5 \\ 3 & 10 & 5 \\ 5 & 5 & 6 \end{bmatrix}, \text{ and } y = \begin{bmatrix} 3.822 \\ 4.704 \\ 2.984 \end{bmatrix}$$

Hence, the estimates of the psychotherapy effect, the drug therapy effect, and their interaction are

$$\hat{\beta} = \begin{bmatrix} \hat{\psi} = & .32 \\ \hat{\delta} = & .44 \\ \hat{\eta} = & -.14 \end{bmatrix}$$

Bibliographies

The references used in carrying out the work reported in the text are organized into four separate bibliographies. The first is a list of all articles and books cited in the text itself. The second bibliography is a list of the outcome studies analyzed in Chapters 4 and 5. The third bibliography is a list of drug and psychotherapy combination studies analyzed in Chapters 7 and 8. The fourth bibliography is a list of drug-therapy-only outcome studies that were also analyzed in Chapters 7 and 8. Within each bibliography the references are arranged alphabetically.

General Bibliography

Adler, A. *The Practice and Theory of Individual Psychology.* New York: Humanities Press, 1929.

Ago, Y.; Ikemi, Y.; Sugita, M.; Takahashi, N.; Teshima, H.; Nagata, S.; and Inoue, S. A comparative study on somatic treatment and comprehensive treatment of bronchial asthma. *Journal of Asthma Research* 14 (1976): 37–41.

Arieti, S. An overview of schizophrenia from a predominantly psychological approach. *American Journal of Psychiatry* 131 (1974): 241.

Atkinson, R. M., and Ditman, K. S. Tranylcypromine: a review. *Clinical Pharmacology and Therapeutics* 6 (1965): 631–55.

Azcarate, C. Minor tranquilizers in the treatment of aggression. *Journal of Nervous and Mental Diseases* 160 (1975): 100–107.

Bandura, A. Modeling approaches to the modification of phobic disorders. In R. Porter (ed.), *The Role of Learning in Psychotherapy.* London: Churchill, 1968.

————. On paradigms and recycled ideologies. *Cognitive Therapy and Research* 2 (1978): 79–103.

Barendregt, J. T. A psychological investigation of the effect of group psychotherapy in patients with bronchial asthma. *Journal of Psychosomatic Research* 2 (1957): 115–19.

Barron, F., and Leary, T. F. Changes in psychoneurotic patients with and without psychotherapy. *Journal of Consulting Psychology* 19 (1955): 239–45.

Bassa, D. M., and Vora, H. D. Evaluation of efficacy of imipramine in depressive disorders: A double blind study. *American Journal of Psychiatry* 121 (1965): 1116.

Bennet, I. F.; Cohen, D.; and Starer, E. Isoniazid in treatment of the chronic schizophrenic patient. *Archives of Neurological Psychiatry* 71 (1954): 54–65.

Bergin, A. E. The evaluation of therapeutic outcomes. In Bergin, A. E. and Garfield, S. L. (eds.), *Handbook of Psychotherapy and Behavior Change.* New York: Wiley, 1971.

Bergin, A. E., and Lambert, M. J. The evaluation of therapeutic outcomes. In Garfield, S. L. and Bergin, A. E. (eds.), *Handbook of Psychotherapy and Behavior Change: An Empirical Analysis.* New York: Wiley, 1978.

Berne, E. *Transactional Analysis in Psychotherapy.* New York: Grove Press, 1961.

Bernstein, D. A. Situational factors in behavioral fear assessment: A progress report. *Behavior Therapy* 4 (1973): 41–48.

Bernstein, D. A., and Nietzel, M. T. Procedural variation in behavioral avoidance tests. *Journal of Consulting and Clinical Psychology* 41 (1973): 165–74.

Bernstein, D. A., and Paul, G. L. Some comments on therapy analogue research with small animal "phobias." *Journal of Behavior Therapy and Experimental Psychiatry* 2 (1971): 225–37.

Brill, N. Q., and Beebe, G. W. A follow-up study of war neurosis. *Veteran's Administration Medical Monographs,* 1955.

Buck, R. C. Reflexive predictions. *Philosophy of Science* 30 (1963): 359–69.

Campbell, D. T., and Stanley, J. C. *Experimental and Quasi-experimental Designs for Research.* Chicago: Rand McNally, 1966.

Campbell, M. Pharmacotherapy in early infantile autism. *Biological Psychiatry* 10 (1975): 339–423.

Carpenter, W., and McGlashan, T. The treatment of acute schizophrenia without drugs: An investigation of some current assumptions. *American Journal of Psychiatry* 134 (1977): 14–20.

Citron, K. M., et al. Hypnosis for asthma: A controlled trial. Report of the Subcommittee on Hypnotherapy for Asthma. *British Medical Journal* 10 (1968): 71–76.

Cole, J. O. Therapeutic efficacy of anti-depressant drugs. *Journal of the American Medical Association* 190 (1964): 448–55.

Cowden, R. C. Reserpine alone and as an adjunct to psychotherapy in the treatment of schizophrenia. *Archives of Neurological Psychiatry* 74 (1955): 518–22.

Davis, J. Efficacy of tranquilizing and anti-depressant drugs. *Archives of General Psychiatry* 13 (1965): 552–72.

————. Overview: Maintenance therapy in psychiatry: I. Schizophrenia. *American Journal of Psychiatry* 132 (1975): 1237–45.

————. Overview: Maintenance therapy in psychiatry: II. Schizophrenia. *American Journal of Psychiatry* 133 (1976): 1–13.

Davis, J.; Klerman, G.; and Schildkraut, J. Drugs used in the treatment of depression. In Efron, D. H. (ed.), *Psychopharmacology, a Review of Progress 1957–1967,* Public Health Service Publication No. 1836, 1968.

Davis, J., and Kline, N. Therapeutic efficacy of the phenothiazines and other anti-psychotic agents. In Black, P. (ed.), *Drugs and the Brain, Papers on Action, Use, and Abuse of Psychotropic Agents.* Baltimore: The Johns Hopkins Press, 1969.

Davis, J. D. Review of S. Rachman, *The Effects of Psychotherapy. British Journal of Psychology* 63 (1972): 642–43.

Delay, J., and Deniker, P. Les neuroplegiques en therapeutique psychiatrique. *Rapport aux Journées Therapeutiques de Paris.* Paris: Doin, 1953.

Denker, R. Results of psychoneurosis by the general practitioner. A follow-up study of 500 cases. *New York Journal of Medicine* 46 (1946): 2164–66.

Dietz, P. E. Social discrediting of psychiatry: The protasis of legal disfranchisement. *American Journal of Psychiatry* 134 (1977): 1356–60.

Docherty, J. P.; Marder, S. R.; Vankammen, D. P.; and Siris, S. G. Psychotherapy and pharmacotherapy: Conceptual issues. *American Journal of Psychiatry* 134 (1977): 529–33.

Downing, R.; Rickels, K.; Wittenborn, J. R.; and Mattsson, N. B. Interpretation of data from investigations assessing the effectiveness in psychotropic agents. In Levine, J.; Schiele, B.; and Bouthilet, L. (eds.), *Establishing the Efficacy of Psychotropic Agents*, Public Health Service Publication No. 2138, 1971.

Edwards, A. L., and Cronbach, L. J. Experimental design for research in psychotherapy. *Journal of Clinical Psychology* 8 (1952): 51–59.

Ellis, A. Outcome of employing three techniques of psychotherapy. *Journal of Clinical Psychology* 13 (1957): 344–50.

————. *Reason and Emotion in Psychotherapy*. New York: Lyle Stuart, 1962.

Eysenck, H. J. The effects of psychotherapy: An evaluation. *Journal of Consulting Psychology* 16 (1952): 319–24.

————. A reply to Luborsky's note. *British Journal of Psychology* 45 (1954): 132–33.

————. The effects of psychotherapy. In Eysenck, H. J. (ed.), *Handbook of Abnormal Psychology*. New York: Basic Books, 1961.

————. *The Effects of Psychotherapy*. New York: International Science Press, 1966.

————. The effects of psychotherapy: A reply. *Journal of Abnormal and Social Psychology* 50 (1955): 147–48.

————. The outcome problem in psychotherapy: A reply. *Psychotherapy* 1 (1964): 97–100.

————. Note on "Factors influencing the outcome of psychotherapy." *Psychological Bulletin* 78 (1972): 403–05.

————. Review of D. H. Malan's *Toward the Validation of Psychotherapy: A Replication*. *British Journal of Psychology* 68 (1977): 266.

————. An exercise in mega-silliness. *American Psychologist* 33 (1978): 517.

Finney, D. J. *Probit Analysis* (3rd ed.). Cambridge: Cambridge University Press, 1971.

Frank, J. D. *Persuasion and Healing: A Comparative Study of Psychotherapy*. Baltimore: The Johns Hopkins University Press, 1961. (Revised edition, 1973.)

Gardos, G., and Cole, J. Maintenance antipsychotic therapy: Is the cure worse than the disease? *American Journal of Psychiatry* 132 (1976): 32–36.

Garfield, S. L. Basic ingredients or common factors in psychotherapy? *Journal of Consulting and Clinical Psychology* 41 (1973): 9–12.

Gibbs, J.; Wilkens, B.; Lauterbach, C. A controlled clinical psychiatric study of chlorpromazine. *Journal of Clinical and Experimental Psychopathology* 18 (1957): 269–83.

Gilligan, J. Review of literature. In Greenblatt, M.; Solomon, M.; Evans, A.; and Brooks, G. (eds.), *Drug and Social Therapy in Chronic Schizophrenia*. Springfield, Ill.: C. C Thomas, 1965.

Gittelman-Klein, R., and Klein, D. F. Long-term effects of "anti-psychotic" agents. In Efron, D. H. (ed.), *Psychopharmacology: A Review of Progress 1957–1967*, Public Health Service Publication No. 1826 (1968): 1119–31.

Glass, G. V. The wisdom of scientific inquiry on education. *Journal of Research in Science Teaching* 9 (1972): 3–18.

————. Primary, secondary and meta-analysis of research. *Educational Researcher* 5 (1976): 3–8.

————. Integrating findings: The meta-analysis of research. In Shulman, L. (ed.), *Review of Research in Education*, Vol. 5. Itasca, Ill.: Peacock, 1977.

Glass, G. V.; Willson, V. L.; and Gottman, J. M. *Design and Analysis of Time-Series Experiments*. Boulder, Col.: Colorado Associated University Press, 1975.

Glass, G. V., and Smith, M. L. Meta-analysis of research on the relationship of class-size and achievement. *Educational Evaluation and Policy Analysis* 1 (1979): 2-16.

Glass, G. V., and Stanley, J. C. *Statistical Methods in Education and Psychology*. Englewood Cliffs, N.J.: Prentice-Hall, 1970.

Glasser, W. *Reality Therapy: A New Approach to Psychiatry*. New York: Harper and Row, 1965.

Goldstein, J.; Clyde, D.; Caldwell, J. Clinical efficacy of the butyrophenones as anti-psychotic drugs. In Efron, D. H. (ed.), *Psychopharmacology: A Review of Progress 1957-1967*, Public Health Service Publication No. 1836, 1968.

Gottlieb, J., and Hustor, P. Treatment of schizophrenics. *Journal of Nervous and Mental Diseases* 113 (1951): 237-46.

Greenblatt, M.; Soloman, M.; Evans, A.; and Brooks, G. (eds). *Drug and Social Therapy in Chronic Schizophrenia*. Springfield, Ill.: C. C Thomas, 1965.

Grinspoon, L., and Greenblatt, M. Pharmacotherapy combined with other treatment methods. *Comprehensive Psychiatry* 4 (1963): 256-62.

Groen, J. J., and Pelser, H. E. Experiences with, and results of, group psychotherapy in patients with bronchial asthma. *Journal of Psychosomatic Research* 4 (1960): 191-205.

Gross, M. L. *The Psychological Society*. New York: Random House, 1978.

Group for the Advancement of Psychiatry. *Pharmacotherapy and Psychotherapy: Paradoxes, Problems and Progress* 9 (March 1975).

Gulliksen, H. O. *Theory of Mental Tests*. New York: Wiley, 1950.

Hall, J. A. Gender effects of decoding nonverbal cues. *Psychological Bulletin* 85 (1978): 845-57.

Hartley, S. S. Meta-analysis of the effects of individually paced instruction in mathematics. Ph. D. dissertation, University of Colorado, 1977.

Hearold, S. Meta-analysis of the effects of television on social behavior. Ph. D. dissertation, University of Colorado, 1979.

Hollister, L. Clinical uses of psychotherapeutic drugs: Current status. *Clinical Pharmacology and Therapeutics* 10 (1969): 170-98.

―――. *Clinical Use of Psychotherapeutic Drugs*. Springfield, Ill.: C. C Thomas, 1973.

Hopkins, K. D., and Glass, G. V. *Basic Statistics for the Behavioral Sciences*. Englewood Cliffs, N.J.: Prentice-Hall, 1978.

Howard, K. I., and Orlinsky, D. E. Psychotherapeutic processes. *Annual Review of Psychology* (1972).

Itil, T., and Wadud, A. Treatment of human aggression with major tranquilizers, antidepressants, and newer psychotropic drugs. *Journal of Nervous and Mental Diseases* 160 (1975): 83-99.

Jackson, G. B. Methods for reviewing and integrating research in the social sciences. Final Report of Grant #DIS 76-20398, National Science Foundation. Social Science Research Group, George Washington University, 1978.

Kahn, A. V. Effectiveness of biofeedback and counterconditioning in the treatment of bronchial asthma. *Journal of Psychosomatic Research* 21 (1977): 97-104.

Kahn, A. V.; Staerk, M.; and Bonk, B. A. Role of counterconditioning in the treatment of asthma. *Journal of Asthma Research* 11 (1973): 57–61.

Kazdin, A. E. Evaluating the generality of findings in analogue therapy research. *Journal of Consulting and Clinical Psychology* 46 (1978): 673–86.

Kelley, D.; Brown, C. C.; and Shaffer, J. W. A controlled physiological, clinical and psychological evaluation of chlordiazepoxide. *British Journal of Psychiatry* 115 (1969): 1387–92.

Kelley, G. A. *Psychology of Personal Constructs.* New York: Norton, 1955.

Kiesler, D. J. Some myths of psychotherapy research and the search for a paradigm. *Psychological Bulletin* 65 (1966): 110–36.

————. Experimental designs in psychotherapy research. In Bergin, A. E., and Garfield, S. L. (eds.), *Handbook of Psychotherapy and Behavior Change.* New York: Wiley, 1971.

Klein, D. F., and Davis, J. M. *Diagnosis and Drug Treatment of Psychiatric Disorders.* Baltimore: Williams and Wilkins, 1969.

Klerman, G. Assessing the influence of the hospital milieu upon the effectiveness of psychiatric drug therapy: Problems of conceptualization and of research methodology. *Journal of Nervous and Mental Diseases* 137 (1963): 143–54.

Klerman, G., and Cole, J. Clinical pharmacology of imipramine and related antidepressant compounds. *Pharmacology Review* 17 (1965): 101–41.

Klett, C. J., and Moseley, E. C. The right drug for the right patient. *Journal of Consulting Psychology* 29 (1965): 546–51.

Kline, N. S. Use of rauwolfia serpentina benth. in neuropsychiatric conditions. *Annals of the New York Academy of Sciences* 59 (1954): 107–32.

Koegler, R. R., and Brill, N. Q. *Treatment of Psychiatric Outpatients.* New York: Appleton Century–Crofts, 1967.

Krumboltz, J. D., and Thoresen, C. E. The effect of behavioral counseling in group and individual settings on information-seeking behavior. *Journal of Counseling Psychology* 11 (1964): 324–33.

Kuhn, T. *The Structure of Scientific Revolutions.* Chicago: University of Chicago Press, 1962.

Lambert, M. J. Spontaneous remission in adult neurotic disorders: A revision and summary. *Psychological Bulletin* 83 (1976): 107–19.

Landis, C. Statistical evaluation of psychotherapeutic methods. In Hinsie, S. E. (ed.), *Concepts and Problems of Psychotherapy.* London: Heineman, 1938.

Lazarus, A. *Behavior Therapy and Beyond.* New York: McGraw–Hill, 1972.

Lesse, S. Combined use of psychotherapy with ataraxic drugs. *Diseases of the Nervous System* 18 (1957): 334–38.

Levitt, E. E. The results of psychotherapy with children: An evaluation. *Journal of Consulting Psychology* 21 (1957): 189–96.

Light, R. J., and Smith, P. V. Accumulating evidence: Procedures for resolving contradictions among different research studies. *Harvard Educational Review* 41 (1971): 429–71.

Linn, L. The use of drugs in psychotherapy. *Psychiatry Quarterly* 38 (1964): 138–48.

Lorr, M.; McNair, D. M.; and Weinstein, G. J. Early effects of chlordiazepoxide (librium) used with psychotherapy. *Journal of Psychiatric Research* 1 (1963): 257–70.

Luborsky, L. A note on Eysenck's article "The effects of psychotherapy: An evaluation." *British Journal of Psychology* 45 (1954): 129–31.

———. Another reply to Eysenck. *Psychological Bulletin* 78 (1972): 406–08.

Luborsky, L.; Singer, B.; and Luborsky, L. Comparative studies of psychotherapies.
Archives of General Psychiatry 32 (1975): 995–1008.

Mahoney, M. *Cognition and Behavior Modification*. Cambridge, Mass.: Ballinger,
1976.

Mahrer-Loughnan, G. P.; MacDonald, N.; Mason, A. A.; and Fry, L. Controlled trial
of hypnosis in the symptomatic treatment of asthma. *British Medical Journal* 4
(1962): 371–76.

Malan, D. H. The outcome problem in psychotherapy research. *Archives of General
Psychiatry* 29 (1973): 719–29.

May, P. R. A. Anti-psychotic drugs and other forms of therapy. In Efron, D. H. (ed.),
Psychopharmacology: A Review of Progress 1957–1967, Public Health Service
Publication No. 1836, 1968.

———. Psychotherapy and ataraxic drugs. In Bergin, A. E., and Garfield, S. L.
(eds.), *Handbook of Psychotherapy and Behavior Change*. New York: Wiley,
1971.

McNair, D. Self-evaluations of antidepressants. *Psychopharmacologia* 37 (1974):
281–302.

Meehl, P. E. Theoretical risks and tabular asterisks: Sir Karl, Sir Ronald, and the slow
progress of soft psychology. *Journal of Consulting and Clinical Psychology* 46
(1978): 806–34.

Meichenbaum, D. *Cognitive Behavior Modification: An Integrative Approach*. New
York: Plenum Press, 1977.

Meltzoff, J., and Kornreich, M. *Research in Psychotherapy*. Chicago: Aldine, 1970.

Miller, T. I. The effects of drug therapy on psychological disorders. Ph. D. dissertation, University of Colorado, 1977.

Moore, N. Behavior therapy in bronchial asthma: A controlled study. *Journal of
Psychosomatic Research* 9 (1965): 257–76.

Moriarity, J. D. Drug vs. psychotherapy. *Journal of Neuropsychiatry* 2 (1960):
82–85.

Morris, J., and Beck, A. The efficacy of anti-depressant drugs. *Archives of General
Psychiatry* 30 (1974): 667–74.

Ostow, M. The advantages and limitations of combined therapy. *Psychosomatics* 2
(1961): 11–15.

Paul, G. L. Strategy of outcome research in psychotherapy. *Journal of Consulting
Psychology* 31 (1967): 109–18.

Perls, F. S.; Hefferline, R. F.; and Goodman, P. *Gestalt Therapy*. New York: Dell
Publishing, 1965.

Phillips, E. L. *Psychotherapy: A Modern Theory and Practice*. London: Staples,
1957.

Rachman, S. Double standards and single standards. *Bulletin of the British Psychological Society* 30 (1977): 295.

———. *The Effects of Psychotherapy*. Oxford: Pergamon Press, 1971.

Raimy, V. *Misunderstandings of the Self*. San Francisco: Jossey–Bass Publishers,
1975.

Reardon, J. P., and Tosi, D. J. The effects of rational stage directed imagery on self-concept and reduction of psychological stress in adolescent delinquent females. *Journal of Clinical Psychology* (in press).

Rogers, C. R. *Counseling and Psychotherapy*. Boston: Houghton-Mifflin, 1942.

Rogers, C. R., and Dymond, R. *Psychotherapy and Personality Change*. Chicago: University of Chicago Press, 1954.

Rogers, S. C., and Clay, P. M. A statistical review of controlled trials of imipramine and placebo in the treatment of depressive illness. *British Journal of Psychiatry* 127 (1975): 599-603.

Rosenthal, R. *Experimenter Effects in Behavioral Research*. New York: Irvington, 1976.

———. The file drawer problem and tolerance for null results. *Psychological Bulletin* 86 (1979): 638-41.

Rosenzweig, S. A transvaluation of psychotherapy: A reply to Hans Eysenck. *Journal of Abnormal and Social Psychology* 49 (1954): 298-304.

———. Calumet. *Journal of Abnormal and Social Psychology* 50 (1955): 148.

Sawer-Foner, G. J. The role of neuroleptic medication in psychotherapeutic interaction. *Comprehensive Psychiatry* 1 (1960): 291.

Schooler, N. R. Anti-psychotic drugs and psychological treatment in schizophrenia. In Lipton, M. A.; Dimascio, A.; and Killam, K. F. (eds.), *Psychopharmacology: A Generation of Progress*. New York: Raven Press, 1978.

Schou, M. Lithium in psychiatry: A review. In Efron, D. H. (ed.), *Psychopharmacology: A Review of Progress 1957-1967*, Public Health Service Publication No. 1836, 1968.

Sclare, A. B., and Crocket, J. A. Group psychotherapy in bronchial asthma. *Journal of Psychosomatic Research* 2 (1957): 157-71.

Scriven, M. *Primary Philosophy*. New York: McGraw-Hill, 1966.

———. The methodology of evaluation. In Stake, R. E. (ed.), *AERA Monograph Series on Curriculum Evaluation*, No. 1. Chicago: Rand McNally, 1967.

———. The experimental investigation of psychoanalysis. In Hook, S. (ed.), *Philosophy, Scientific Method and Psychoanalysis*. New York: New York University Press, 1959.

Shapiro, D., and Shapiro, D. The "double standard" in evaluation of psychotherapies. *Bulletin of the British Psychological Society* 30 (1977): 209-10.

Sheard, M. Lithium in the treatment of aggression. *Journal of Nervous and Mental Diseases* 160 (1975).

Shepard, M., and Gruenberg, E. M. The age for neurosis. *Millbank Memorial Foundation Quarterly Bulletin* 35 (1957): 258-65.

Shepard, R. N. The analysis of proximities: Multidimensional scaling with an unknown distance function. I and II. *Psychometrika* 27 (1962): 125-40, 219-46.

Skobba, J. S. Drugs in psychotherapy. *Diseases of the Nervous System* 21 (1960): 586-87.

Sloane, R. B.; Staples, F. R.; Cristol, A. H.; Yorkston, N. J.; and Whipple, K. *Psychotherapy Versus Behavior Therapy*. Cambridge, Mass.: Harvard University Press, 1975.

Smith, M. L., and Glass, G. V. Meta-analysis of psychotherapy outcome studies. *American Psychologist* 32 (1977): 752-60.

Stampfl, T. G. Implosive therapy: An emphasis on covert stimulation. In Davis, D. J. (ed.), *Learning Approaches to Therapeutic Behavior Change*. Chicago: Aldine-Atherton, 1970.

Strupp, H. H. The outcome problem in psychotherapy revisited. *Psychotherapy* 1 (1963): 1-13.

———. On the basic ingredients of psychotherapy. *Journal of Consulting and Clinical Psychology* 41 (1973*a*): 1-8.

———. The interpersonal relationship as a vehicle for therapeutic learning. *Journal of Consulting and Clinical Psychology* 41 (1973*b*): 13-15.

Strupp, H. H., and Bergin, A. E. *A Bibliography of Research in Psychotherapy*. Washington, D.C.: National Institute of Mental Health, 1969.

Teuber, N. L., and Powers, E. Evaluating therapy in a delinquency prevention program. *Proceedings of the Association for Research on Nervous and Mental Disorders* 31 (1953): 138-47.

Tobias, L. L., and MacDonald, M. L. Withdrawal of maintenance drugs with long-term hospitalized mental patients: A critical review. *Psychological Review* 81 (1974): 107-25.

Torgerson, W. S. *Theory and Methods of Scaling*. New York: Wiley, 1958.

Tosi, D. J. *Youth Toward Personal Growth: A Rational-Emotive Approach*. Columbus, Ohio: Merrill, 1974.

Truax, C. B., and Carkhuff, R. R. *Toward Effective Counseling and Psychotherapy*. Chicago: Aldine, 1967.

Tukey, J. W. Conclusions vs. decisions. *Technometrics* 2 (1960): 423-33.

Uhlenhuth, E. H.; Lipman, R. S.; and Covi, L. Combined pharmacotherapy and psychotherapy. *Journal of Nervous and Mental Diseases* 148 (1969): 52-64.

Van Pragg, H. M. New developments in human psychopharmacology. In Klein, D. F., and Gittleman-Klein, R. (eds.), *Progress in Psychiatric Drug Treatment II*. New York: Brunner/Mazel, 1976.

Volsky, T.; Magoon, T.; Norman, W. T.; and Hoyt, D. P. *The Outcomes of Counseling and Psychotherapy*. Minneapolis: University of Minnesota Press, 1965.

White, K. R. The relationship between socio-economic status and academic achievement. Ph. D. dissertation, University of Colorado, 1976.

Whitehorn, J., and Betz, B. A comparison of psychotherapeutic relationships between physicians and schizophrenic patients when insulin is combined with psychotherapy and when psychotherapy is used alone. *American Journal of Psychiatry* 113 (1957): 901-10.

Williamson, E. G. *Counseling Adolescents*. New York: McGraw-Hill, 1950.

Willis, R. W., and Edwards, J. A. A study of the comparative effectiveness of systematic desensitization and implosive therapy. *Behavioral Research and Therapy* 7 (1969): 387-95.

Wolberg, L. R. *The Principles of Hypnotherapy*. New York: Grune, 1948.

Wolpe, J. *Psychotherapy by Reciprocal Inhibition*. Stanford, Calif.: Stanford University Press, 1958.

———. *The Practice of Behavior Therapy* (2nd ed.). New York: Pergamon, 1974.

Yorkston, N. J.; McHugh, R. B.; Brady, R.; Serber, M.; and Sergeant, H. G. S. Verbal desensitization in bronchial asthma. *Journal of Psychosomatic Research* 18 (1974): 371-76.

Bibliography of the Psychotherapy Meta-analysis

Ago, Y.; Ikemi, Y.; Sugita, M.; Takahashi, N.; Teshima, H.; Nagata, S.; and Inoue, S. A comparative study on somatic treatment and comprehensive treatment of bronchial asthma. *Journal of Asthma Research* 14 (1976): 37–41.

Allen, A. The use of cognitive structuring and verbal reinforcement of positive self-reference statements within a short-term group therapy session to enhance self-concept. Ph. D. dissertation, University of Arkansas, 1971.

Allen, G. J. Effectiveness of study counseling and desensitization in alleviating test anxiety in college students. *Journal of Abnormal Psychology* 77 (1971): 282–89.

Alper, T. G., and Kranzler, G. D. A comparison of the effectiveness of behavioral and client-centered approaches for the behavior problems of elementary school children. *Elementary School Guidance and Counseling* 5 (1970): 35–43.

Anderson, J. R. The effects of structured physical interactions in psychotherapy on anxiety and specific behavioral variables in children. Ph. D. dissertation, Boston University, 1974.

Andrews, W. R. Behavioral and client-centered counseling of high-school under-achievers. *Journal of Counseling Psychology* 18 (1971): 93–96.

Aponte, J. F., and Aponte, C. E. Group preprogrammed systematic desensitization without the simultaneous presentation of aversive scenes with relaxation training. *Behavior Research and Therapy* 9 (1971): 337–46.

Argue, H. A research study of the effects of behavioral group counseling upon college freshmen. Ph. D. dissertation, University of the Pacific, 1969.

Arulsigamoni, A. The relationship between self-concept and school achievement in low achieving junior high school children and the effect of counseling intervention on self-concept. Ph. D. dissertation, American University, 1972.

Ashby, J. D.; Ford, D. H.; Guerney, B. G.; and Guerney, L. F. Effects on clients of a reflective and a leading type of psychotherapy. *Psychological Monographs* 71 (1957): 1–32.

Ashen, B., and Donner, L. Covert sensitization with alcoholics: A controlled replication. *Behavioral Research and Therapy* 6 (1968): 7–12.

Baker, R. The use of operant conditioning to reinstate the speech of mute schizophrenics: A progress report. In Burns, L. E. (ed.), *Behavior Therapy in the 1970's*. Bristol: John Wright & Sons, 1970.

Bancroft, J. A comparative study of aversion and desensitization in the treatment of homosexuality. In Burns, L. E. (ed.), *Behavior Therapy in the 1970's*. Bristol: John Wright & Sons, 1970.

Bandura, A.; Blanchard, E. B.; and Ritter, B. Relative efficacy of desensitization and modeling approaches for inducing behavioral, affective, and attitudinal changes. *Journal of Personality and Social Psychology* 13 (1969): 173–99.

Barendregt, J. T. A psychological investigation of the effect of group psychotherapy in patients with bronchial asthma. *Journal of Psychosomatic Research* 2 (1957): 115–19.

Barlow, D. H.; Agras, W. S.; Leitenbert, H.; and Wincze, J. P. An experimental analysis of the effectiveness of "shaping" in reducing maladaptive avoidance behavior: An analogue study. *Behavior Research and Therapy* 8 (1970): 165–73.

Barrett, C. L. Systematic desensitization vs. implosive therapy. *Journal of Abnormal Psychology* 74 (1969): 587–92.

Barron, F., and Leary, T. F. Changes in psycho-neurotic patients with and without psychotherapy. *Journal of Consulting Psychology* 19 (1955): 239–45.

Beach, A. L. Effects of group model reinforcement counseling on achievement behavior of seventh and eighth grade students. Ph. D. dissertation, Stanford University, 1967.

Beavers, W. The comparative effect of systematic counseling and insight-relationship counseling on the task-oriented behaviors of seventh graders. Ph. D. dissertation, Michigan State University, 1970.

Becker, H. G., and Costello, C. G. Effects of graduated exposure with feedback of exposure times on snake phobias. *Journal of Consulting and Clinical Psychology* 43 (1975): 478–84.

Beckstrand, P. E. TA as a means of teaching writing in high school. *Transactional Analysis Journal* 3 (1973): 161–63.

Bekaouche, A. A study of the effectiveness of transactional analysis and transactional analysis modified on juvenile delinquents. Ph. D. dissertation, The American University, 1974.

Beletsis, J., Jr. Group psycho-therapy with chronic male schizophrenics: An evaluation of the frequency of group psychotherapy sessions as a factor affecting the results of therapy. Ph. D. dissertation, New York University, 1956.

Bell, G. E. An application of differential counseling techniques to groups of male college students experiencing vocational and educational problems. Ph. D. dissertation, The Ohio State University, 1970.

Benson, R. L., and Blocher, D. H. Evaluation of developmental counseling with groups of low achievers in a high school setting. *The School Counselor* 14 (1967) 215–20.

Bloch, J. The automated presentation of practiced imagination therapy to reduce anxiety. Ph. D. dissertation, University of Louisville, 1974.

Bookhammer, R. S.; Meyer, R. W. Schober, C. C.; and Piotrowski, A. Z. A five-year follow-up study of schizophrenics treated by Rosen's "direct analysis" compared with controls. *American Journal of Psychiatry* 123 (1966): 602–04.

Booraem, D., and Flowers, J. V. Reduction of anxiety and personal space as a function of assertion training with severely disturbed neuropsychiatric inpatients. *Psychological Reports* 30 (1972): 923–29.

Boris, T. A comparison study of the efficacy in utilizing audio-taped peer models and counselor-presented symbolic models as techniques for reducing shyness. Ph. D. dissertation, University of Maryland, 1972.

Bouffard, D. L. A comparison of response acquisition and desensitization approaches to assertion training. Ph. D. dissertation, Indiana University, 1973.

Bouillon, K. R. The comparative efficacy of nondirective group play therapy with preschool, speech or language delayed children. Ph. D. dissertation, Texas Tech University, 1973.

Boulougouris, J. C., Marks, I. M. and Marset, P. Superiority of flooding (implosion) to desensitization for reducing pathological fear. *Behavior Research and Therapy* 9 (1971): 7–16.

Boutin, G. E., and Tosi, D. J. The modification of irrational ideas and test anxiety through rational stage directed hypnotherapy. Unpublished paper. Columbus, Ohio: College of Education, The Ohio State University, 1977.

Brandsma, J. M., McCarty, D., and Wetter, R. E. Psychotherapy in alcoholism treatment: A comparison of professional and non-professional rational therapists. Paper presented to the annual meeting of the Society for Psychotherapy Research, Madison, Wisconsin, June 1977.

Breen, G. J. An interventionist group counseling approach with first year diploma school of nursing students. Ph. D. dissertation, Clark University, 1974.

Brill, N. Q., and Beebe, G. W. A follow-up study of war neuroses. Washington: V. A. Medical Monograph, 1955.

Brown, T. A. Change of self-concept with an intact group by a transactional analysis approach. Ph. D. dissertation, Southern Illinois University, 1973.

Bruce, J. The effects of group counseling on selected vocational rehabilitation clients. Ph. D. dissertation, Florida State University, 1971.

Bruyere, D. H. The effects of client-centered and behavioral group counseling on classroom behavior and self-concept of junior high school students who exhibited disruptive classroom behavior. Ph. D. dissertation, University of Oregon, 1975.

Burck, H. D. Counseling college freshmen: A three-year follow-up. *Journal of College Student Personnel* 10 (1969): 21-26.

Burck, H. D., and Cottingham, H. F. The effects of counseling low-ability, high-aspiring college freshmen. *Journal of College Student Personnel* 6 (1965): 270-83.

Cadogan, D. A. Marital group therapy in the treatment of alcoholism. *Quarterly Journal of Studies on Alcohol* 34 (1973): 1187-94.

Calhoun, S. R. The effect of counseling on a group of underachievers. *School Review* 64 (1956): 312-16.

Cameron, J. T. A preventative discipline program: Comparison of the effectiveness of two methods of group counseling with college freshmen who demonstrate a high probability for discipline involvement. Ph.D. dissertation, University of Colorado, 1969.

Campbell, D. A short-term psychotherapy for depression: A second controlled study. Ph. D. dissertation, University of Wisconsin, 1973.

Campbell, D. P. Achievements of counseled and non-counseled students twenty-five years after counseling. *Journal of Counseling Psychology* 12 (1965): 287.

_____. A counseling evaluation with a "better" control group. *Journal of Counseling Psychology* 10 (1963): 334-39.

Caplan, S. W. The effect of group counseling on junior high school boys' concepts of themselves in school. *Journal of Counseling Psychology* 4 (1957): 124-28.

Carkhuff, R. R., and Truax, C. B. Lay mental health counseling. *Journal of Consulting Psychology* 29 (1965): 426-31.

Carney, F. J. Evaluation of psychotherapy in a maximum security prison. *Seminars in Psychiatry* 3 (1971): 363-75.

Carstens, C. G. A comparison of Gestalt and behavioral treatments for social anxiety and shyness. Ph. D. dissertation, University of Connecticut, 1975.

Carter, L. G. Counseling effectiveness following treatment of counselor state anxiety. Ph. D. dissertation, East Texas State University, 1975.

Cartwright, R. D. Effects of psychotherapy on self-consistency. *Journal of Counseling Psychology* 4 (1957): 15-22.

Casas, J. M. A comparison of two medicational self-control techniques for the treatment of speech anxiety. Ph. D. dissertation, Stanford University, 1975.

Casstevens, M. Effects of modeling procedures in group counseling in the modification of disruptive school behavior with eighth grade students. Ph. D. dissertation, Arizona State University, 1969.

Cattrell, R. B.; Rickels, K.; Weise, C.; Gray, B.; and Yee, R. The effects of psychotherapy upon measured anxiety and regression. *American Journal of Psychotherapy* 20 (1966): 261.

Claiborn, W. L.; Lewis, P.; and Humble, S. Stimulus satiation and smoking: A revisit. *Journal of Clinical Psychology* 28 (1972): 416–19.

Clancy, J.; Vanderhoof, E.; and Campbell, P. Evaluation of an aversive technique as a treatment for alcoholism. *Quarterly Journal of Studies on Alcohol* 28 (1967): 1475–85.

Clements, B. E. Transitional adolescents, anxiety, and group counseling. *Personnel and Guidance Journal,* 45 (1966): 67–71.

Coche, E. A follow-up study on formerly hospitalized patients in three different treatment conditions. Paper presented at the Annual Meeting of the Society for Psychotherapy Research, Madison, Wisconsin, June 24, 1977.

Coche, E., and Douglas, A. A. Therapeutic effects of problem-solving training and play-reading groups. *Journal of Clinical Psychology* 33 (1977): 820–27.

Coche, E., and Flick, A. Problem-solving training groups for hospitalized patients. *Journal of Psychology* 91 (1975): 19–29.

Cohn, L. Effects of group counseling on freshmen nursing students. Ph. D. dissertation, Marquette University, 1972.

Coleman, M., and Glofka, P. T. Effect of group therapy on self-concept of senior nursing students. *Nursing Research* 18 (1969): 274–75.

Colman, A. D., and Baker, S. L. Utilization of an operant conditioning model for the treatment of character and behavior disorders in a military setting. *American Journal of Psychiatry* 125 (1969): 1395–1403.

Conolly, S. G. The effects of human relations training using Gestalt therapy techniques upon selected personality variables in rehabilitation clients. Ph. D. dissertation, University of Arizona, 1974.

Cooke, G. Evaluation of the efficacy of the components of reciprocal inhibition psychotherapy. *Journal of Abnormal Psychology* 73 (1968): 464–67.

Coons, W. H. Interaction and insight in group psychotherapy. *Canadian Journal of Psychology* 11 (1957): 1–8.

Coons, W. H., and Peacock, E. P. Interpersonal interaction and personality change in group psychotherapy. *Canadian Psychiatric Association Journal* 15 (1970): 347–55.

Cooper, J. E. A study of behaviour therapy in thirty psychiatric patients. *Lancet* 1 (1963): 411–15.

Cordell, G. The effect of structured group counseling on the self-concept, attendance, and achievement of absentee-prone high school students. Ph. D. dissertation, Ohio State University, 1973.

Cormik, R. D., and Dilley, T. S. Comparison of three methods of reducing test anxiety: Systematic desensitization, implosive therapy and study counseling. *Journal of Counseling Psychology* 20 (1973): 499.

Cotler, B., and Garlington, W. K. The generalization of anxiety reduction following systematic desensitization of snake anxiety. *Behavior Research and Therapy* 7 (1969): 35–40.

Coven, A. B. The effects of counseling and verbal reinforcement on the internal-external control of the disabled. Ph. D. dissertation, University of Arizona, 1970.

Crighton, J., and Jehu, D. Treatment of examination anxiety by systematic desensitization or psychotherapy in groups. *Behavior Research and Therapy* 7 (1969): 245-48.

Crouch, K. The application of group counseling and behavior modification procedures to number anxiety in a college population. Ph. D. dissertation, University of Georgia, 1970.

D'Angelo, R., and Walsh, J. An evaluation of various therapy approaches with lower socioeconomic-group children. *Journal of Psychology* 67 (1967): 59-64.

Davis, D. A. Effects of group guidance and individual counseling on citizenship and behavior. *Personnel and Guidance Journal* 38 (1959): 142-45.

Davis, H. J. The efficacy of rational-emotive imagery in the treatment of test anxiety. Ph.D. dissertation, Southern Illinois University, 1976.

Davison, G. C. The influence of systematic desensitization, relaxation, and graded exposure to imaginal aversive stimuli on the modification of phobic behavior. American Institute for Research, Creative Talent Awards Program. *Winner's Dissertation Abstracts* (1965/1966): 19-24.

————. Systematic desensitization as a counter-conditioning process. *Journal of Abnormal Psychology* 73 (1968): 91-99.

Dawley, H. H. Group implosive therapy in the treatment of test anxiety. Ph. D. dissertation, North Texas State University, 1972.

Dawley, H. H., and Wenrich, W. W. Massed group desensitization in reduction of test anxiety. *Psychological Reports* 33 (1973): 359-63.

————. Treatment of test anxiety by group implosive therapy. *Psychological Reports* 33 (1973): 383-88.

Day, R. R. Differential effects of self-administered systematic desensitization and contract management counseling sessions on test anxiety in community college students. Ph. D. dissertation, University of Virginia, 1974.

Deering, W. Behavioral and intrapsychic effects of a behavior modification (token economy) treatment program. Ph. D. dissertation, Boston University, 1974.

Deffenbacher, J. L., and Kemper, C. C. Counseling test-anxious sixth graders. *Elementary School Guidance and Counseling* 9 (1974): 22-29.

DeMoor, W. Systematic desensitization vs. prolonged high intensity stimulation (flooding). *Journal of Behavioral Therapy and Experimental Psychiatry* 1 (1970): 45-52.

Denny, D. Active, passive, and vicarious desensitization. *Journal of Counseling Psychology* 21 (1974): 369.

Denny, D. R., and Rupert, P. A. Self-control and desensitization of text anxiety. *Journal of Counseling Psychology* 24 (1977): 272-82.

Desrats, R. G. The effects of developmental and modeling group counseling on adolescents in child care institutions. Ph. D. dissertation, Lehigh University, 1975.

DeVincentis, M. D. The relative effectiveness of transactional analysis and human relations training on modifying interpersonal orientations. Ph. D. dissertation, Mississippi State University, 1974.

Dickenson, W. A., and Truax, C. B. Group counseling with college underachievers. *Personnel and Guidance Journal* 45 (1966): 243-46.

DiLoreto, A. O. *Comparative Psychology*. Chicago: Aldine-Atherton, 1971.

Doctor, R. M.; Aponte, J.; Burry, A.; and Welch, R. Group counseling versus behavior therapy in treatment of college underachievement. *Behavior Research and Therapy* 8 (1970): 87–89.

Dorfman, E. Personality outcomes of client-centered child therapy. *Psychological Monographs: General and Applied* 72 (1958): 1–21.

Duehrssen, A., and Jorswiek, E. An empirical and statistical enquiry into the therapeutic potential of psychoanalytic treatment. *Der Nervenarzt* 36 (1965): 166–69.

D'Zurilla, T. J.; Wilson, G. T.; and Nelson, R. A preliminary study of the effectiveness of graduated prolonged exposure in the treatment of irrational fear. *Behavioral Therapy* 4 (1973): 672–85.

Edinberg, M. A. Behavioral assessment and assertion training of the elderly. Ph. D. dissertation, University of Cincinnati, 1975.

Eldridge, M. S.; Witmer, J. M.; Barcikowski, R.; and Bauer, L. The effects of a group guidance program on the self-concepts of EMR children. *Measurement and Evaluation in Guidance* 9 (1977): 184–90.

Ellis, A. Outcome of employing three techniques of psychotherapy. *Journal of Clinical Psychology* 13 (1957): 344–50.

Emery, T. R., and Krumboltz, J. D. Standard vs. individualized hierarchies in desensitization to reduce test anxiety. *Journal of Counseling Psychology* 14 (1967): 204.

Endicott, N. A., and Endicott, J. Prediction of improvement in treated and untreated patients using the Rorschach prognostic rating scale. *Journal of Consulting Psychology* 28 (1964): 342–48.

Fahey, G. L., and Waller, C. H. An experimental investigation of the effectiveness of certain diagnostic and guidance procedures when applied in cases of low school achievement. *Journal of Educational Research* 34 (1941): 335–45.

Faries, M. Short-term counseling at the college level. *Journal of Counseling Psychology* 2 (1955): 182–84.

Feifel, H., and Schwartz, A. P. Group psychotherapy with acutely disturbed psychotic patients. *Journal of Consulting Psychology* 17 (1953): 113–21.

Felton, G. S., and Biggs, B. E. Teaching internalization behavior to collegiate low achievers in group psychotherapy. *Psychotherapy: Theory, Research and Practice* 9 (1972): 281–83.

Fiester, T. L. An investigation of the process and outcomes of the elimination of self-defeating behavior. Ph. D. dissertation, Michigan State University, 1973.

Finger, R., and Galassi, J. P. Effects of modifying cognitive versus emotionality responses in the treatment of test anxiety. *Journal of Consulting and Clinical Psychology* 45 (1977): 280–87.

Finney, B. C., and Val Dalsem, E. Group counseling for gifted underachieving high school students. *Journal of Counseling Psychology* 16 (1969): 87–97.

Fisher, B. Group therapy with retarded readers. *Journal of Educational Psychology* 44 (1953): 354–61.

Foreyt, J. P., and Kennedy, W. A. Treatment of overweight by aversion therapy. *Behavior Research and Therapy* 9 (1971): 29–34.

Foulds, M. L. Changes in locus of internal-external control: A growth group experience. *Comparative Group Studies* 2 (1971): 293–300.

————. Effects of a personal growth group on a measure of self-actualization. *Journal of Humanistic Psychology* 10 (1970): 33–38.

_____. Measured changes in self-actualization as a result of growth-group experience. *Psychotherapy: Theory, Research and Practice* 8 (1971): 338–41.

Foulds, M. L.; Girona, R.; and Guinan, J. F. Changes in ratings of self and others as a result of a marathon group. *Comparative Group Studies* 1 (1970): 349–55.

Foulds, M. L., and Guinan, J. F. Marathon group: Changes in ratings of self and others. *Psychotherapy: Theory, Research and Practice* 10 (1973): 30–32.

Foulds, M. L.; Guinan, J. F.; and Hannigan, P. Marathon group: Changes in scores ón the California Psychological Inventory. *Journal of College Student Personnel* 14 (1974): 474–79.

Foulds, M. L.; Guinan, J. F.; and Warehime, R. G. Marathon group: Changes in perceived locus of control. *Journal of College Student Personnel* 14 (1974): 8–11.

Foulds, M. L., and Hannigan, P. S. A gestalt marathon workshop: Effects on extraversion and neuroticism. *Journal of College Student Personnel* 17 (1976): 50–54.

_____. Effects of gestalt marathon workshops on measured self-actualization: A replication and follow-up study. *Journal of Counseling Psychology* 23 (1976): 60–65.

_____. Gestalt workshops and measured changes in self-actualization. *Journal of College Student Personnel* 18 (1977): 200–205.

_____. Gestalt marathon group: Does it increase reported self-actualization? *Psychotherapy: Theory, Research and Practice* 13 (1976): 378–82.

Friedland, B. V. Changes in problems of 9th grade students as an outcome of Adlerian group counseling. Ph. D. dissertation, West Virginia University, 1972.

Fuchs, C. Z., and Rehm, L. P. A self-control behavior therapy program for depression. *Journal of Consulting and Clinical Psychology* 45 (1977): 206–15.

Gallant, D. M. Evaluation of compulsory treatment of the alcoholic municipal court offender. In Millie, N. and Mendelson, J. (eds.) *Recent Advances in Studies of Alcoholism.* U.S. Government Printing Office, 1971.

Gallen, M., et al. A short-term follow-up of two contrasting alcoholic treatment programs: A preliminary report. *Newsletter for Research in Mental Health and Behavioral Sciences.* VA, Washington, D.C., November 1973, pp. 36–37.

Garlington, W. K., and Cotler, S. B. Systematic desensitization of test anxiety. *Behavior Research and Therapy* 6 (1968): 247–56.

Garner, W. C. The crisis intervention technique with potential college dropouts. *Personnel and Guidance Journal* 48 (1970): 552–60.

Garni, K. F. The effect of Adlerian group counseling on the academic performance of marginal commuter college students. Ph. D. dissertation, Boston University, 1972.

Gelder, M. G., and Marks, I. M. Severe agoraphobia: A controlled prospective trial of behaviour therapy. *British Journal of Psychiatry* 112 (1966): 309–19.

Gelder, M. G.; Marks, I. M.; and Wolff, H. H. Desensitization and psychotherapy in the treatment of phobic states: A controlled inquiry. *British Journal of Psychiatry* 113 (1967): 53–73.

Giantonio, C. K. Assertion training: A social skill development technique with chronic schizophrenic inpatients. Ph. D. dissertation, University of Notre Dame, 1976.

Gibbons, D.; Kelborne, L.; Saunders, A.; and Castles, C. The cognitive control of behavior: A comparison of systematic desensitization and hypnotically-induced "directed experience" techniques. *American Journal of Clinical Hypnosis* 12 (1970): 141–45.

Gilbreath, S. H. Group counseling with male underachieving college volunteers. *Personnel and Guidance Journal* 45 (1967): 469–76.

Gillian, P., and Rachman, S. An experimental investigation of desensitization in phobic patients. *British Journal of Psychiatry* 124 (1974): 392–401.

Gilliland, B. E. Small group counseling with Negro adolescents in a public high school. *Journal of Counseling Psychology* 15 (1968): 147–52.

Golburgh, S. J., and Glanz, E. C. Group counseling with students unable to speak in class. *Journal of College Student Personnel* 2 (1962): 102–03, 128.

Gold, R. D. Alteration of the self concept and attitude toward others using group behavior modification. Ph. D. dissertation, Arizona State University, 1971.

Goldfried, M. R.; Linehan, M. M.; and Smith, J. L. Reduction of test anxiety through cognitive restructuring. *Journal of Consulting and Clinical Psychology* 46 (1978): 32–39.

Gonyea, G. C. Appropriateness of vocational choice of counseled and uncounseled college students. *Journal of Counseling Psychology* 10 (1963): 269–75.

Goodstein, L. D. Five-year follow-up of counseling effectiveness with probationary college students. *Journal of Counseling Psychology* 14 (1967): 436.

Gourley, M. H. The effects of individual counseling, group guidance, and verbal reinforcement on the academic progress of underachievers. Ph. D. dissertation, University of North Carolina, 1970.

Grande, L. M. A comparison of rational-emotive therapy, attention placebo and no-treatment groups in the reduction of interpersonal anxiety. Ph. D. dissertation, Arizona State University, 1975.

Gripp, R. F., and Magaro, P. A. A token economy program evaluation with untreated control ward comparisons. *Behavior Research and Therapy* 9 (1971): 137–49.

Groen, J. J., and Pelser, H. E. Experiences with, and results of, group psychotherapy in patients with bronchial asthma. *Journal of Psychosomatic Research* 4 (1960): 191–205.

Groenheim, H. An analysis of self ideal discrepancy scores of a counseled and uncounseled group of high school students. Ph. D. dissertation, Florida State University, 1968.

Groveman, A. M. Effects of study skills counseling and behavioral self-control methods on the academic performance of college students. Ph. D. dissertation, University of Missouri–Columbia, 1975.

Gruen, W. Effects of brief psychotherapy during the hospitalization period on the recovery process in heart attacks. *Journal of Consulting and Clinical Psychology* 43 (1975): 223–32.

Guidry, L., and Randolph, D. Covert reinforcement in the treatment of test anxiety. *Journal of Counseling Psychology* 21 (1974): 260.

Guinan, J. F., and Foulds, M. L. Marathon group: Facilitator of personal growth? *Journal of Counseling Psychology* 17 (1970): 145–49.

Guthrie, G. M., and O'Neill, H. W. The effects of dormitory counseling on academic achievement. *Personnel and Guidance Journal* 31 (1953): 307–09.

Haddle, H. W. The efficacy of automated group systematic desensitization as a strategy to modify attitudes toward disabled persons. Ph. D. dissertation, Georgia State University, 1973.

Halama, J. J. The effects of assertion training and simulation instructions on laboratory and "real life" refusal behavior. Ph. D. dissertation, University of California–Los Angeles, 1976.

Hanson, J. T., and Sander, D. L. Differential effects of individual and group counseling in realism of vocational choice. *Journal of Counseling Psychology* 20 (1973): 541.

Hardage, N. C. A comparison of the efficacy of treatments of classroom behavior management and group counseling for use with potential dropouts. Ph. D. dissertation, University of Southern Mississippi, 1972.

Harding, M. A comparison of the effectiveness of three approaches to altering behavior of seventh grade boys. Ph.D. dissertation, University of Nebraska, 1969.

Harrington, S. A. The effects of basic encounter group experience with prospective counselors. Ph. D. dissertation, University of Colorado, 1971.

Harris, M. B., and Trujillo, A. E. Improving study habits of junior high students through self-management vs. group discussion. *Journal of Counseling Psychology* 22 (1975): 513–17.

Hartlage, L. C. Subprofessional therapists' use of reinforcement versus traditional psychotherapeutic techniques with schizophrenics. *Journal of Consulting and Clinical Psychology* 34 (1970): 181–83.

Haskins, D. L. B. Desensitization of test anxiety in junior high school students. Ph. D. dissertation, Colorado State University, 1972.

Hawk, R. Four approaches to drug abuse education: An investigation of high school counselors' ability to withhold reinforcement in behavioral counseling. Ph. D. dissertation, Pennsylvania State University, 1972.

Hazlehurst, C. D., Jr. Test of an exhaustion theory of implosive therapy. Ph. D. dissertation, University of Texas–Austin, 1972.

Heap, R. F.; Bablitt, W. E.; Moore, C. H.; and Hord, J. E. Behavior-milieu therapy with chronic neuropsychiatric patients. *Journal of Abnormal Psychology* 76 (1970): 349–54.

Hedquist, F. J., and Weinhold, B. K. Behavioral group counseling with socially anxious and unassertive college students. *Journal of Counseling Psychology* 17 (1970): 237–42.

Hein, V. A study of group counseling with selected high school freshmen. Ph. D. dissertation, Northwestern University, 1969.

Hekamat, H. Systematic versus semantic desensitization and implosive therapy: A comparative study. *Journal of Consulting and Clinical Psychology* 40 (1973): 202–09.

Henderson, J. D., and Scoles, P. E., Jr. Conditioning techniques in a community based operant environment for psychotic men. *Behavior Therapy* 1 (1970): 245–57.

Herman, B. An investigation to determine the relationship of anxiety and reading disability and to study the effects of group and individual counseling on reading improvement. Ph. D. dissertation, University of New Mexico, 1972.

Hervey, E. P. Comparison of three and six weeks of group model-reinforcement counseling for improving study habits and attitudes of junior high school students. Ph. D. dissertation, University of Wisconsin, 1970.

Hogan, R. A., and Kirchner, J. H. Preliminary report of the extinction of learned fears via short-term implosive therapy. *Journal of Abnormal Psychology* 72 (1967): 106-09.

————. Implosive, eclectic, verbal and bibliotherapies in the treatment of fears of snakes. *Behavior Research and Therapy* 6 (1968): 167-71.

Holroyd, K. A. Cognition and desensitization in the group treatment of test anxiety. Ph. D. dissertation, University of Miami, 1975.

Horne, A. M., and Matson, J. L. A comparison of modeling, desensitization, flooding, study skills, and control groups for reducing test anxiety. *Behavior Therapy* 8 (1977): 1-8.

House, R. M. The effects of nondirective group play therapy upon the sociometric status and self-concept of selected second grade children. Ph. D. dissertation, Oregon State University, 1970.

Howard, J. R. The effect of group-counseling techniques on feelings of alienation of black college freshmen. Ph. D. dissertation, Fordham University, 1974.

Hoyser, E. E. Therapeutic nondirective play with low achievers in reading. Ph. D. dissertation, Oregon State University, 1971.

Huddleston, R. J. The effects of a reinforcement-counseling procedure on the social behavior and sociometric status of elementary school students. Ph. D. dissertation, University of Oregon, 1972.

Hunt, G. M., and Azrin, N. A community-reinforcement approach to alcoholism. *Behavior Research and Therapy* 11 (1973): 91-104.

Hussain, M. Z. Desensitization and flooding (implosion) in treatment of phobias. *American Journal of Psychiatry* 127 (1971): 1509-14.

Husted, J. R. The effect of method of systematic desensitization and presence of sexual communication in the treatment of female sexual anxiety by counterconditioning. Ph. D. dissertation, University of California–Los Angeles, 1972.

Hyman, J. R. Systematic desensitization of mathematics anxiety in high school students: The role of mediating responses, imagery, emotionality, and expectancy. Ph. D. dissertation, Wayne State University, 1973.

Intarakumnerd, T. The effects of transactional analysis on the self-concept of Thai students who are enrolled in Mississippi universities. Ph. D. dissertation, Mississippi State University, 1976.

Ivey, A. E. The academic performance of students counseled at a university counseling service. *Journal of Counseling Psychology* 9 (1962): 347-52.

Jacobs, E., and Croake, J. W. Rational emotive theory applied to groups. *Journal of College Student Personnel* 17 (1976): 127-29.

Jacobson, H. A. Reciprocal inhibition and implosive therapy: A comparative study of fear of snakes. Ph. D. dissertation, Memphis State University, 1970.

Jarmon, D. G. Differential effectiveness of rational-emotive therapy, bibliotherapy and attentive-placebo in the treatment of speech anxiety. Ph. D. dissertation, Southern Illinois University, 1972.

Jersild, A. T. *The Meaning of Psychotherapy in the Teacher's Life and Work.* New York: Teachers College Bureau of Publications, 1963.

Jesness, C. F. Comparative effectiveness of behavioral modification and transactional analysis programs for delinquents. *Journal of Consulting and Clinical Psychology* 43 (1975): 758-79.

Joanning, H. Behavioral rehearsal in group treatment of socially nonassertive individuals. *Journal of College Student Personnel* 17 (1976): 313-18.

Johnson, T.; Tyler, V., Jr.; Thompson, R.; and Jones, E. Systematic desensitization and assertive training in the treatment of speech anxiety in middle-school students. *Psychology in the Schools* 8 (1971): 263-67.

Jones, F. D., and Peters, H. N. An experimental evaluation of group psychotherapy. *Journal of Abnormal and Social Psychology* 47 (1952): 345-53.

Jones, R. M. *An Application of Psychoanalysis to Education*. Springfield, Ill.: C. C Thomas, 1960.

Kanter, N. J. A comparison of self-control desensitization and systematic rational restructuring for the reduction of interpersonal anxiety. Ph. D. dissertation, SUNY-Stony Brook, 1975.

Karst, T. O., and Trexler, L. D. Initial study using fixed role and rational-emotive therapy in treating public speaking anxiety. *Journal of Consulting and Clinical Psychology* 34 (1970): 360-66.

Kass, E. The effect of short-term group desensitization on text anxiety. Ph. D. dissertation, Arizona State University, 1969.

Kass, W. A. Incentive and drive in systematic desensitization. Ph. D. dissertation, St. Louis University, 1973.

Katahn, M.; Strenger, S.; and Chessy, N. Group counseling and behavior therapy with test-anxious college students. *Journal of Consulting Psychology* 30 (1966): 544-49.

Kazdin, A. E. Covert modeling and the reduction of avoidance behavior. *Journal of Abnormal Psychology* 81 (1973): 87-95.

Kelley, C. A. Play desensitization of fear of darkness in preschool children. Ph. D. dissertation, University of Iowa, 1973.

Keutzer, C. S. Behavior modification of smoking: The experimental investigation of diverse techniques. *Behavior Research and Therapy* 6 (1968): 137-57.

Khan, A. U. Effectiveness of biofeedback and counterconditioning in the treatment of bronchial asthma. *Journal of Psychosomatic Research* 21 (1977): 97-104.

Khan, A. V.; Staerk, M.; and Bonk, B. A. Role of counterconditioning in the treatment of asthma. *Journal of Asthma Research* 11 (1973): 57-61.

Kinnick, B. C., and Shannon, J. T. The effect of counseling on peer group acceptance of socially rejected students. *The School Counselor* 12 (1965): 162-66.

Kissin, B.; Platz, A.; and Su, W. H. Social and psychological factors in the treatment of chronic alcoholism. *Journal of Psychiatric Research* 8 (1970): 13-27.

Knox, T. The effect of transactional analysis groups on the internal-external locus of control. Ph. D. dissertation, University of Arkansas, 1973.

Koenig, K. P., and Masters, J. Experimental treatment of habitual smoking. *Behavior Research and Therapy* 3 (1965): 235-43.

Kondas, O. Reduction of examination anxiety and "stage-fright" by group desensitization and relaxation. *Behavior Research and Therapy* 5 (1967): 275-81.

Kostka, M. P., and Galassi, J. P. Group desensitization versus covert positive reinforcement in the reduction of test anxiety. *Journal of Counseling Psychology* 21 (1974): 464-68.

Kradel, P. F., Jr. Adlerian role playing for the reorientation and reeducation of high school students with behavior problems. Ph. D. dissertation, West Virginia University, 1972.

Kranzler, G. D.; Mayer, G. R.; Dyer, C. O.; and Munger, P. F. Counseling with elementary school children: An experimental study. *Personnel and Guidance Journal* 44 (1966): 944–49.

Krop, N.; Calhoon, B.; and Verrier, R. Modification of the "self-concept" of emotionally disturbed children by covert reinforcement. *Behavior Therapy* 2 (1971): 201–04.

Krumboltz, J. D., and Schroeder, W. W. Promoting career planning through reinforcement. *Personnel and Guidance Journal* 44 (1965): 19–26.

Krumboltz, J. D., and Thoresen, C. E. The effect of behavioral counseling in group and individual settings on information-seeking behavior. *Journal of Counseling Psychology* 11 (1964): 324–33.

Lang, P. J.; Melamed, B. G.; and Hart, J. A psychophysiological analysis of fear modification using an automated desensitization procedure. *Journal of Abnormal Psychology* 76 (1970): 220–34.

Laxer, R. M.; Quarter, J.; Kooman, A.; and Walker, K. Systematic desensitization and relaxation of high test-anxious secondary school students. *Journal of Counseling Psychology* 16 (1969): 446.

Laxer, R. M., and Walker, K. Counterconditioning versus relaxation in the desensitization of test anxiety. *Journal of Counseling Psychology* 17 (1970): 431.

Lazarus, A. A. Behavior rehearsal vs. non-directive therapy vs. advice in effecting behavior change. *Behavior Research and Therapy* 4 (1966): 209–12.

———. Behavior therapy and graded structure. In Ciba Foundation, *The Role of Learning in Psychotherapy*. London: Churchill, 1968.

———. Group therapy of phobic disorders by systematic desensitization. *Journal of Abnormal and Social Psychology* 63 (1961): 504–10.

Lee, D. Y. Evaluation of a group counseling program designed to enhance social adjustment of mentally retarded adults. *Journal of Counseling Psychology* 24 (1977): 319–23.

Leitenberg, H.; Agras, W. S.; and Barlow, D. H. Contribution of selective positive reinforcement and therapeutic instructions to systematic desensitization therapy. *Journal of Abnormal Psychology* 74 (1969): 113–18.

Lester, B. G. A comparison of relationship counseling and relationship counseling combined with modified systematic desensitization in reducing test anxiety in middle school pupils. Ph. D. dissertation, University of Virginia, 1973.

Levinson, T., and Sereny, G. An experimental evaluation of "insight" therapy for the chronic alcoholic. *Canadian Psychiatric Association Journal* 14 (1969): 143–46.

Levis, D. J., and Carera, R. Effects of 10 hours of implosive therapy in the treatment of outpatients: A preliminary report. *Journal of Abnormal Psychology* 72 (1967): 504–08.

Levity, I. N. The effects of reciprocal inhibition on children's manifest anxiety. Ph. D. dissertation, Yeshiva University, 1974.

Liberman, R. A behavioral approach to group dynamics. *Behavior Therapy* 1 (1970): 141–75.

Lieberman, R. Behavioral group therapy: A controlled study. *British Journal of Psychiatry* 119 (1971): 535–44.

Lightner, M. L. Gestalt therapy: An investigation on its effects with anxiety and time orientation. Ph. D. dissertation, United States International University, 1976.

Link, W. E. Psychotherapy outcome in the treatment of hyperaggressive boys: A comparison of behavioristic and traditional techniques. Ph. D. dissertation, University of Utah, 1968.

Lomont, J. F., and Brock, L. Cognitive factors in systematic desensitization. *Behavior Research and Therapy* 9 (1971): 187–95.

————. Stimulus hierarchy generalization in systematic desensitization. *Behavior Research and Therapy* 9 (1971): 197–208.

Lutker, E. R. The effect of two treatments on interpersonal anxiety. Ph. D. dissertation, Colorado State University, 1975.

Mahrer-Loughnan, G. P.; MacDonald, N.; Mason, A. A.; and Fry, L. Controlled trial of hypnosis in the symptomatic treatment of asthma. *British Medical Journal* 4 (1962): 371–76.

Maley, R. F.; Feldman, C. L.; and Ruskin, R. S. Evaluation of patient improvement in a token economy treatment program. *Journal of Abnormal Psychology* 82 (1973): 141–44.

Marcia, J. E.; Rubin, B. M.; and Efran, J. S. Systematic desensitization: Expectancy change or counterconditioning. *Journal of Abnormal Psychology* 74 (1969): 382–85.

Marks, I.; Gelder, M.; Bancroft, J.; and O'Neill, M. Sexual deviants two years after electric aversion. *British Journal of Psychiatry* 117 (1970): 173–85.

Marks, I. M., and Gelder, M. G. A controlled retrospective study of behavior therapy in phobic patients. *British Journal of Psychiatry* 111 (1965): 561–73.

Marks, I. Phobic disorders four years after treatment: A prospective follow-up. *British Journal of Psychiatry* 118 (1971): 683–88.

Marks, J.; Sonoda, B.; and Schalock, R. Reinforcement versus relationship therapy for schizophrenics. *Journal of Abnormal Psychology* 73 (1968): 397–402.

Marshall, W. L.; Presse, L.; and Andrews, W. R. A self-administered program for public speaking anxiety. *Behavior Research and Therapy* 14 (1976): 33–39.

Martin, P. J. Anxiety extinction and therapeutic suggestion in implosive therapy. Ph.D. dissertation, University of Kentucky, 1971.

Martinson, W. D., and Lerface, J. P. Comparison of individual counseling and a social program with non-daters. *Journal of Counseling Psychology* 17 (1970): 36.

Massimo, J., and Shore, M. The effectiveness of a comprehensive, vocationally oriented psychotherapeutic program for adolescent delinquent boys. *American Journal of Psychiatry* 33 (1963): 57–68.

Matthews, D. B. The effects of reality therapy on reported self-concept, social adjustment, reading achievement, and discipline of fourth and fifth grades in two elementary schools. Ph. D. dissertation, University of South Carolina, 1972.

Matulef, N. J.; Warman, R. E.; and Brock, T. C. Effects of brief vocational counseling on temporal orientation. *Journal of Counseling Psychology* 11 (1964): 352–56.

Maxwell, W. A. The relative efficacy and generality of systematic desensitization and induced anxiety as psychotherapeutic techniques. Ph. D. dissertation, University of South Dakota, 1972.

Mayer, G. R.; Kranzler, G. D.; and Matthes, W. A. Elementary school counseling and peer relations. *The Personnel and Guidance Journal* 46 (1967): 360–65.

McCance, C., and McCance, P. F. Alcoholism in north-east Scotland: Its treatment and outcome. *British Journal of Psychiatry* 115 (1969): 189–98.

McClenaghan, J. C. The effects of transactional analysis workshops on interpersonal relationship and communication behaviors. Ph. D. dissertation, University of Colorado, 1976.

McCollum, P. S., and Anderson, R. P. Group counseling with reading disabled children. *Journal of Counseling Psychology* 21 (1974): 150–55.

McCormack, E. J. The effectiveness of group systematic desensitization for the reduction of anxiety in counselor trainees in the individual counseling practicum setting. Ph. D. dissertation, The Florida State University, 1975.

McDaniel, W. V. Changes that occur with mild mental defectives following two approaches to group counseling: Directive and group centered. Ph. D. dissertation, North Texas State University, 1971.

McFall, R. M., and Lillesand, D. B. Behavior rehearsal with modeling and coaching in assertion training. In Matazarro, J. D. (ed.), *Psychotherapy 1971*, pp. 450–57. Chicago: Aldine–Atherton, 1972.

McFall, R. M., and Marston, A. R. An experimental investigation of behavior rehearsal in assertive training. *Journal of Abnormal Psychology* 76 (1970): 295–303.

McGlynn, F. D. Graded imagination and relaxation as components of experimental desensitization. *Journal of Nervous and Mental Disease* 156 (1973): 377–85.

———. Individual vs. standardized hierarchies in the systematic desensitization of snake-avoidance. *Behavior Research and Therapy* 9 (1971): 1–5.

McGlynn, F. D.; Mealiea, W. L., Jr.; and Nawas, M. M. Systematic desensitization of snake-avoidance under two conditions of suggestion. *Psychological Reports* 25 (1969): 220–22.

McGlynn, F. D.; Reynolds, E. J.; and Linder, L. H. Systematic desensitization with pre-treatment and intro-treatment therapeutic instructions. *Behavior Research and Therapy* 9 (1971): 57–63.

McGuiness, T. P. Cognitive modification vs. assertive training in the treatment of nonassertive college students. Ph. D. dissertation, University of Pennsylvania, 1976.

McReynolds, W. T., and Tori, C. A further assessment of attention-placebo effects and demand characteristics in studies of systematic desensitization. *Journal of Consulting and Clinical Psychology* 38 (1972): 261–64.

Mealiea, W. L., and Nawas, M. M. Comparative effectiveness of systematic desensitization and implosive therapy in the treatment of snake phobia. *Journal of Behavior Therapy and Experimental Psychiatry* 2 (1971): 85–94.

Meichenbaum, D. H., and Gilmore, J. B. Group insight versus group desensitization in treating speech anxiety. In Matazarro, J. D. (ed.), *Psychotherapy 1971*, pp. 513–23. Chicago: Aldine–Atherton, 1972.

Merenda, P. F., and Rothney, J. W. Evaluating the effects of counseling—eight years after. *Journal of Counseling Psychology* 5 (1958): 163–68.

Messina, J. A comparative study of parent consultation and conjoint family counseling. Ph. D. dissertation, State University of New York–Buffalo, 1974.

Meyer, J. B. Behavioral-reinforcement counseling with rural Wisconsin high school youth. Ph. D. dissertation, University of Wisconsin, 1968.

Meyer, J. B.; Strowig, W.; and Hasford, R. E. Behavioral-reinforcement counseling with rural high school youth. *Journal of Counseling Psychology* 17 (1970): 127.

Miller, J. K. An investigation of group desensitization with test anxious seventh and eighth grade students. Ph. D. dissertation, Washington State University, 1971.

Miller, L. C.; Barrett, C. L.; Hampe, E.; and Noble, H. Comparison of reciprocal inhibition psychotherapy and waiting list control for phobic children. *Journal of Abnormal Psychology* 79 (1972): 269-79.

Mitchell, K. R. A psychotherapy approach to the treatment of migraine. *British Journal of Psychiatry* 119 (1971): 533-34.

_____. Note on treatment of migraine using behavior therapy techniques. *Psychological Reports* 28 (1971): 171-72.

Mitchell, K. R., and Ingham, R. The effects of general anxiety on group desensitization of test anxiety. *Behavior Research and Therapy* 8 (1970): 69-78.

Mitchell, K. R.; Hall, R. F.; and Piatkowski, O. E. A group program for bright failing underachievers. *Journal of College Student Personnel* 16 (1975): 306-12.

Mitchell, K. R., and Ng, K. T. Effects of group counseling and behavior therapy on the academic achievement of test-anxious students. *Journal of Counseling Psychology* 19 (1972): 491-97.

Moore, N. Behavior therapy in bronchial asthma: A controlled study. *Journal of Psychosomatic Research* 9 (1965): 257-76.

Morey, E. Locus of control as a variable in the effectiveness of two RET styles. Ph. D. dissertation, University of South Dakota, 1973.

Morton, R. B. An experiment in brief psychotherapy. *Psychological Monographs* 69 (1955): 1-386.

Moss, M. K., and Arend, R. A. Self-directed contact desensitization. *Journal of Consulting and Clinical Psychology* 45 (1977): 730-38.

Moulin, E. K. Effects of client-centered group counseling using play media on the intelligence, achievement and psycholinguistic abilities of underachieving primary school children. Ph. D. dissertation, University of Toledo, 1968.

Nally, M. J. AMT: A treatment for delinquents. Ph. D. dissertation, Colorado State University, 1975.

Nash, P. C. Treatment of math anxiety through systematic desensitization and insight-oriented therapy groups. Ph. D. dissertation, Arizona State University, 1970.

Nation, K.; Kohne, J.; and Harrington, S. The effects of group counseling on the self concepts of typical junior high school students. *Research Paper No. 34*. Boulder, Col.: Laboratory of Educational Research, University of Colorado, 1970.

Naun, R. Comparison of group counseling approaches with Puerto Rican boys in an inner city high school. Ph. D. dissertation, Fordham University, 1971.

Nawas, M. M.; Fishman, S. T.; and Pucel, J. C. A standardized desensitization program applicable to group and individual treatments. *Behavior Research and Therapy* 8 (1970): 49-56.

Nawas, M. M.; Welsch, W. V.; and Fishman, S. T. The comparative effectiveness of pairing aversive imagery with relaxation, neutral tasks and muscular tension in reducing snake phobias. *Behavior Research and Therapy* 6 (1970): 63-68.

Naylar, J. L., and Clement, P. W. Prediction and comparison of outcome in systematic desensitization and implosion. *Behavior Research and Therapy* 10 (1972): 235-46.

Newton, J. R., and Stein, L. I. Implosive therapy, duration of hospitalization, and degree of coordination of aftercare services with alcoholics. Proceedings of the First Annual Meeting of the National Institute for APA, 1972.

Ney, P. G.; Palvesky, A. E.; and Markeley, J. Relative effectiveness of operant conditioning and play therapy in childhood schizophrenia. *Journal of Autism and Childhood Schizophrenia* 1 (1971): 337–49.

Nichols, M. P. Outcome of brief cathartic psychotherapy. *Journal of Consulting and Clinical Psychology* 42 (1974): 403–10.

Nichols, R. C. Gestalt therapy: Some aspects of self support, independence, and responsibility. Ph. D. dissertation, University of Tennessee, 1973.

Noe, H. S., Jr. The effect of modeling on chronic schizophrenic behavior. Ph. D. dissertation, The University of Tennessee, 1974.

Obler, M. Multivariate approaches to psychotherapy with sexual dysfunction. *The Counseling Psychologist* 5 (1975): 55–60.

Obler, M., and Terwilliger, R. F. Pilot study on the effectiveness of systematic desensitization with neurologically impaired children with phobic disorders. *Journal of Consulting and Clinical Psychology* 34 (1970): 314–18.

————. Pilot study on the effectiveness of systematic desensitization among children with phobic disorders. Proceedings of the 77th Annual Convention of American Psychological Association, 1969.

O'Connor, R. D. Modification of social withdrawal through symbolic modeling. *Journal of Applied Behavior Analysis* 2 (1969): 15–22.

O'Donnel, J. N. Marathon group therapy and marathon in vivo group desensitization: A comparison of treatments for interpersonal performance anxiety. Ph. D. dissertation, Northwestern University, 1972.

O'Leary, W. C., Jr. An investigation to determine the effects of two methods of group counseling on the self-concept and work adjustment of psychiatric patients. Ph.D. dissertation, University of South Carolina, 1974.

Oliveau, D. C. Systematic desensitization in an experimental setting: A follow-up study. *Behavior Research and Therapy* 7 (1969): 1377–80.

Oliveau, D. C.; Agras, W. S.; Lettenbe, H.; Moore, R. C.; and Wright, D. E. Systematic desensitization, therapeutically oriented instructions and selective positive reinforcement. *Behavior Research and Therapy* 7 (1969): 27–33.

Olkowski, T. A practical and theroetical investigation into the treatment of phobic behavior. Ph. D. dissertation, University of Louisville, 1973.

Olsen, J. E. An analysis of short-term training effects upon female high school students' measured assertiveness. Ph.D. dissertation, Purdue University, 1975.

O'Neil, M. The effect of Glasser peer group counseling upon academic performance, self-satisfaction, personal worth, social interaction, and self esteem of low achieving female college freshmen. Ph. D. dissertation, University of Akron, 1973.

O'Neill, R. H. The treatment of anxiety in the physically disabled by three different variations of systematic desensitization. Ph. D. dissertation, University of North Dakota, 1974.

Orlow, L. An experimental study of the effects of group counseling with behavior problem children at the elementary school level. Ph. D. dissertation, The Catholic University of America, 1972.

Ostrom, T. M.; Steele, C. M.; Rosenblood, L. K.; and Mirels, H. L. Modification of delinquent behavior. *Journal of Applied Social Psychology* 1 (1971): 118–36.

Padfield, M. The comparative effects of two counseling approaches on the intensity of depression among rural women of low socio-economic status. *Journal of Counseling Psychology* 23 (1976): 209–14.

Parson, B. V., Jr., and Alexander, J. F. Short-term family intervention: A therapy outcome study. *Journal of Consulting and Clinical Psychology* 41 (1973): 195–201.

Pascale, J. R. Increasing classroom participation of college students: A comparison of group systematic desensitization with group discussion, counseling and group reading. Ph. D. dissertation, State University of New York-Albany, 1969.

Patterson, V.; Levene, H.; and Berger, L. Treatment and training outcomes with two time-limited therapies. *Archives of General Psychiatry* 25 (1971): 161–67.

Paul, G. L. *Effects of insight, desensitization and attention placebo treatment of anxiety*. Stanford, Calif.: Stanford University Press, 1966.

Paul, G. L., and Shannon, D. T. Treatment of anxiety through systematic desensitization in therapy groups. *Journal of Abnormal Psychology* 71 (1966): 124–35.

Peck, C. Desensitization for the treatment of fear in the high level adult retardate. Ph.D. dissertation, University of Wisconsin, 1974.

Penick, S. B.; Filion, R.; Fox, S.; and Stunkard, A. J. Behavior modification in the treatment of obesity. *Psychosomatic Medicine* 33 (1971): 49–55.

Persons, R. W. Relationship between psychotherapy with institutionalized delinquent boys and subsequent community adjustment. Proceedings of the 74th Annual Convention of the American Psychological Association, 1966, pp. 187–88.

Persons, R. W., and Pepinsky, H. B. Convergence in psychotherapy with delinquent boys. *Journal of Counseling Psychology* 13 (1966): 329–34.

Peyman, D. A. R. An investigation of the effects of group psychotherapy on chronic schizophrenic patients. *Group Psychotherapy* 9 (1956): 35–39.

Pinto, L., and Fugenbaum, L. Effects of clinical counseling on college achievement. *Journal of Counseling Psychology* 21 (1974): 409.

Platt, J. M. Efficacy of the Adlerian model in elementary school counseling. Ph. D. dissertation, University of Arizona, 1970.

Poser, E. G. The effect of therapists' training on group therapeutic outcome. *Journal of Consulting Psychology* 30 (1966): 283–89.

Posmer, K. M. The effect of two modalities of group counseling for secondary school seniors upon their locus-of-control expectancies. Ph. D. dissertation, Northern Illinois University, 1975.

Prochaska, J. O. Symptom and dynamic cues in the implosive treatment of test anxiety. *Journal of Abnormal Psychology* 77 (1971): 133–42.

Proctor, S. Duration of exposure to items and pretreatment training as factors in systematic desensitization therapy. In Rubin, R. D. and Frank, C. M. (eds.), *Advances in Behavior Therapy*. New York: Academic Press, 1968.

Pucel, J. C. Systematic desensitization and the reduction of social anxiety: The efficacy of using such a treatment technique as part of an alcoholic treatment program. Ph. D. dissertation, University of Missouri, 1972.

Pucel, J. C., and Nawas, M. M. Effects of sex pairings of experimenter and subject on the outcome of systematic desensitization. *Journal of Behavior Therapy and Experimental Psychiatry* 1 (1970): 103–07.

Quarter, J. J., and Laxer, R. M. A structured program of teaching and counseling for conduct problem students in a junior high school. *Journal of Educational Research* 63 (1970): 229–31.

Quattlebaum, R. A study of the effectiveness of nondirective counseling and play therapy with maladjusted fifth grade pupils. Ph.D. dissertation, University of Alabama, 1970.

Rathus, S. A. An experimental investigation of assertive training in a group setting. *Journal of Behavior Therapy and Experimental Psychiatry* 3 (1972): 81–86.

Reardon, J. P., and Tosi, D. J. The effects of rational stage directed imagery on self concept and reduction of psychological stress in adolescent delinquent females. *Journal of Clinical Psychology* (in press).

Rehm, L. P., and Marston, A. R. Reduction of social anxiety through modification of self-reinforcement: An instigation therapy technique. *Journal of Consulting and Clinical Psychology* 32 (1968): 5.

Reich, S. K. The effects of group systematic desensitization on the symptoms of primary dysmenorrhea. Ph. D. dissertation, University of New Mexico, 1972.

Reister, B. W. A treatment outcome study: Two group treatments and their outcomes in relation to state and trait anxiety. Ph. D. dissertation, Indiana University, 1975.

Rhinard, L. D. A comparison of the effectiveness of non-directive play therapy and behavior modification approaches. Ph. D. dissertation, Florida State University, 1969.

Richardson, F. C. Short-term desensitization therapy on test anxiety: Three types of control. Ph. D. dissertation, Colorado State University, 1971.

Richardson, F. C., and Suinn, R. M. A comparison of traditional systematic desensitization, accelerated massed desensitization, and anxiety management training in the treatment of mathematics anxiety. *Behavior Therapy* 4 (1973): 212–18.

Richter, M. O. Systematic desensitization of social anxiety in junior college students. Ph. D. dissertation, University of Pennsylvania, 1974.

Rihani, S. The comparative effects of implosive therapy and systematic desensitization upon counselor trainees' anxiety and ability to communicate emotions. Ph. D. dissertation, Michigan State University, 1972.

Rimm, D. C.; DeGroot, J. C.; Boord, P.; Heiman, J.; and Dillow, P. V. Systematic desensitization of an anger response. *Behavior Research and Therapy* 9 (1971): 273–80.

Rimm, D. C., and Mahoney, M. J. The application of reinforcement and participant modeling procedures in the treatment of snake-phobic behavior. *Behavior Research and Therapy* 7 (1969): 369–76.

Rimm, D. C., and Medeiros, D. C. The role of muscle relaxation in participant modeling. *Behavior Research and Therapy* 8 (1970): 127–32.

Rimm, D. C.; Saunders, W. D.; and Westel, W. Thought stopping and covert assertion in the treatment of snake phobics. *Journal of Consulting and Clinical Psychology* 43 (1975): 92–93.

Ritter, B. Treatment of acrophobia with contact desensitization. *Behavior Research and Therapy* 1 (1969): 41–45.

Roessler, R.; Cook, D.; and Lillard, D. Effects of systematic group counseling on work adjustment clients. *Journal of Counseling Psychology* 24 (1977): 313–17.

Rogers, C. R.; Gendlin, E. T.; Kiesler, D.; and Truax, C. B. *The Therapeutic Relationship and Its Impact: A Study of Psychotherapy with Schizophrenics.* Madison: University of Wisconsin Press, 1967.

Rosen, G. M.; Glasgow, R. E.: and Barrera, M. A controlled study to assess the clinical efficacy of totally self-administered systematic desensitization. *Journal of Consulting and Clinical Psychology* 44 (1976): 208–17.

Rosentover, I. Group counseling of the underachieving high school student as related to self-image and academic success. Ph. D. dissertation, Rutgers University, 1974.

Roth, R. M.; Mauksch, H. O.; and Peiser, K. The non-achievement syndrome, group therapy and achievement change. *Personnel and Guidance Journal* 46 (1967): 393–98.

Ruff, R. Human dimensions of in-service teacher consultation. Ph. D. dissertation, Illinois Institute of Technology, 1974.

Russell, R. K. The use of systematic desensitization and conditioned relaxation in the treatment of public speaking anxiety. Ph. D. dissertation, University of Illinois-Champaign, 1972.

Russell, R. K., and Miller, D. E. A comparison between group systematic desensitization and cue-controlled relaxation in the treatment of test anxiety. *Behavior Therapy* 6 (1975): 172–77.

Rutledge, P. B. Effects of short-term multiple treatment group counseling on social interaction perceptions of isolate-rejectees in fifth and sixth grades. Ph. D. dissertation, University of Kentucky, 1974.

Ryan, T. A. Long-term effects of behavioral counseling. Proceedings of the 75th Annual Convention of the American Psychological Association, 1967, pp. 357–58.

———. Effect of an integrated counseling program to improve vocational decision-making of community college youth. ERIC Document ED 021132, February 1968.

Ryan, V. L.; Krall, C. A.; and Hodges, W. F. Self-concept change in behavior modification. *Journal of Consulting and Clinical Psychology* 44 (1976): 638–45.

Sachs, L. B., and Bean, H. Comparison of smoking treatments. *Behavior Therapy* 1 (1970): 465–72.

Sacks, J. M., and Berger, S. Group therapy techniques with hospitalized chronic schizophrenic patients. *Journal of Consulting Psychology* 18 (1954): 297–302.

Salmon, S. The relationship between a counselor training program in Gestalt self-awareness exercises and two measures of counseling effectiveness. Ph. D. dissertation, Indiana State University, 1972.

Sanchez, M. The effects of client-centered group counseling on self-concept and certain attitudes of seventh and eighth grade students. Ph. D. dissertation, United States International University, 1969.

Sarason, I. G., and Ganzer, V. J. Modeling and group discussion in the rehabilitation of juvenile delinquents. *Journal of Counseling Psychology* 20 (1973): 442–49.

Sarkisian, R. A. The use of ideal models in covert rehearsal to influence self-concept. Ph. D. dissertation, University of California–Berkeley, 1974.

Scarborough, B. B., and Wright, J. C. The assessment of an educational guidance clinic. *Journal of Counseling Psychology* 4 (1957): 283–86.

Schaefer, H. H. Twelve month follow-up of behaviorally trained ex-alcoholic social drinkers. *Behavior Therapy* 3 (1972): 286–89.

Schaffer, H. H., and Martin, P. L. Behavioral therapy for "apathy" of hospitalized schizophrenics. *Psychological Reports* 19 (1966): 1147–58.

Schlien, J. M.; Mosak, H. H.; and Dreikurs, R. Effect of time limits: A comparison of two psychotherapies. *Journal of Counseling Psychology* 9 (1962): 31–34.

Schott, J. F.; Burtness, K. H.; and Wilson, K. W. Breaking down barriers with alcoholics: Marathons. Proceedings, 81st Annual Convention of the American Psychological Association, 1973, pp. 389–90.

Schwartz, J. L., and Dubitzky, M. Clinical reduction of smoking. *Addictions* 14 (1967): 35–44.

Scissons, E. H., and Njaa, L. J. Massed automated systematic desensitization of test anxiety: A comparison of group and individual treatment. *Journal of Consulting and Clinical Psychology* 41 (1953): 470.

Sclare, A. B., and Crocket, J. A. Group psychotherapy in bronchial asthma. *Journal of Psychosomatic Research* 2 (1957): 157–71.

Seeman, J.; Barry, E.; and Ellinwood, C. Interpersonal assessment of play therapy outcome. *Psychotherapy: Theory, Research and Practice* 1 (1964): 64–66.

Semon, R. G., and Goldstein, N. The effectiveness of group psychotherapy with chronic schizophrenic patients and an evaluation of different therapeutic methods. *Journal of Consulting Psychology* 21 (1957): 317–22.

Shannon, D. A study of the effectiveness of two procedures of counseling with small groups of underachievers with average intelligence in the eighth and ninth grades. Ph. D. dissertation, St. Louis University, 1971.

Shapiro, S. B., and Knapp, D. M. The effect of ego therapy on personality integration. *Psychotherapy: Theory, Research and Practice* 8 (1971): 208–12.

Shattan, S. P.; Dcamp, L.; Fujii, E.; Fross, G. G.; and Wolff, R. J. Group treatment of conditionally discharged patients in a mental health clinic. *American Journal of Psychiatry* 122 (1966): 798–805.

Shaw, B. F. Comparison of cognitive therapy and behavior therapy in the treatment of depression. *Journal of Consulting and Clinical Psychology* 45 (1977): 543–51.

Shaw, D., and Thoresen, C. Effects of modeling and desensitizations in reducing dentist phobia. *Journal of Counseling Psychology* 21 (1974): 415.

Shaw, M. W. The effects of automated group desensitization. Ph. D. dissertation, Washington State University, 1975.

Shean, G. D., and Zeidberg, Z. Token reinforcement therapy: A comparison of matched groups. *Journal of Behavior Therapy and Experimental Psychiatry* 2 (1971): 95–105.

Sheldon, A. An evaluation of psychiatric after-care. *British Journal of Psychiatry* 110 (1964): 662–67.

Sheldon, W. D., and Landsman, T. An investigation of non-directive group therapy with students in academic difficulty. *Journal of Consulting Psychology* 14 (1950): 210–15.

Shelley, E. L. V., and Johnson, W. F., Jr. Evaluating an "organized counseling service for youthful offenders." *Journal of Counseling Psychology* 8 (1961): 351–54.

Shipley, C. R. A behavioral treatment for depression. Ph. D. dissertation, University of Iowa, 1972.

Shoberg, J. D. Systematic desensitization versus implosive therapy in the treatment of phobic college females. Ph. D. dissertation, Southern Illinois University, 1971.

Shore, M., and Massimo, J. Comprehensive, vocationally-oriented psychotherapy for adolescent boys: A follow-up study. *American Journal of Orthopsychiatry* 36 (1966): 609–15.

Shur, M. S. A group counseling program for low self-esteem preadolescent females in the fifth grade. Ph. D. dissertation, University of Pittsburgh, 1975.

Sloan, R. B.; Staples, F. R.; Cristol, A. H.; Yorkston, N. J.; and Whipple, K. *Psychotherapy versus Behavior Therapy.* Cambridge, Mass.: Harvard University Press, 1975.

Smith, M. G. Cognitive rehearsal: A systematic investigation of a psychotherapeutic innovation. Ph. D. dissertation, University of Colorado, 1974.

Smith, R., and Evans, T. R. Comparison of experimental group guidance and individual counseling as facilitators of vocational development. *Journal of Counseling Psychology* 20 (1973): 202.

Smith, R. E., and Nye, S. L. A comparison of implosive therapy and systematic desensitization in the treatment of test anxiety. *Journal of Consulting and Clinical Psychology* 41 (1973): 37–42.

Sobell, M. B., and Sobell, L. C. Alcoholics treated by individualized behavior therapy: One year treatment outcome. *Behavior Research and Therapy* 11 (1973): 599–618.

Solberg, S. J. A comparison of alternative desensitization procedures for treatment of flight phobia. Ph. D. dissertation, University of Minnesota, 1974.

Spiegler, M. D.; Cooley, E. J.; Marshall, G. J.; Prince II, H. T.; Puckett, S. P.; and Skenazy, J. A. A self-control versus a counterconditioning paradigm for systematic desensitization: An experimental comparison. *Journal of Counseling Psychology* 23 (1976): 83–86.

Spielberger, C. D.; Weitz, H.; and Denny, J. P. Group counseling and the academic performance of anxious college freshmen. *Journal of Counseling Psychology* 9 (1962): 195–204.

Steinmark, S. W., and Borkovec, T. D. Active and placebo treatment effects on moderate insomnia under countermand and positive demand instruction. *Journal of Abnormal Psychology* 83 (1974): 157–63.

Stone, A. R.; Frank, J. D.; Nash, E. H.; and Imber, S. D. An intensive five-year follow-up study of treated psychiatric outpatients. *Journal of Nervous and Mental Disease* 133 (1961): 410–22.

Storm, T., and Cutler, R. E. Systematic desensitization in the treatment of alcoholics. Unpublished manuscript, Dept. of Psychology, University of British Columbia, 1970.

Stotsky, B. A.; Daston, P. G.; and Vardack, C. N. An evaluation of the counseling of chronic schizophrenics. *Journal of Counseling Psychology* 2 (1955): 248–55.

Straatmeyer, A. The effectiveness of rational-emotive therapy in the reduction of speech anxiety. Ph. D. dissertation, University of South Dakota, 1974.

Straight, E. M. Evaluation of group therapy by follow-up study of formerly hospitalized patients. *Group Psychotherapy* 13 (1960): 110–18.

Subcommittee on Hypnotherapy in Asthma, British Tuberculosis Association, K. M. Citron, Chairman. Hypnosis for asthma—a controlled trial. *British Medical Journal* 4 (1968): 71–76.

Suenger, G. Patterns of change among "treated" and "untreated" patients seen in psychiatric community mental health clinics. *Journal of Nervous and Mental Disease* 150 (1970): 37–50.

Suinn, R. M. The desensitization of test anxiety by group and individual treatment. *Behavior Research and Therapy* 6 (1968): 385–87.

Suinn, R. M., and Richardson, F. Anxiety management training: A nonspecific behavior therapy program for anxiety control. *Behavior Therapy* 2 (1971): 498–510.

Suinn, R. M.; Jorgensen, G. T.; Steward, S. T.; and McGuirk, F. D. Fears as attitudes: Experimental reduction of fear through reinforcement. *Journal of Abnormal Psychology* 78 (1971): 272–79.

Sullivan, D. S.; Johnson, A.; and Bratkovitch, J. Reduction of behavioral deficit in organic brain damage by use of hypnosis. *Journal of Clinical Psychology* 30 (1974): 96–98.

Taylor, D. W., Jr. A comparison of group desensitization with two control procedures in the treatment of test anxiety. *Behavior Research and Therapy* 9 (1971): 281–84.

Taylor, F. R. Systematic desensitization of dating anxiety. Ph. D. dissertation, Arizona State University, 1972.

Taylor, W. F. Direct versus indirect intervention in elementary group counseling. Ph.D. dissertation, University of Akron, 1971.

Teuber, N. L., and Powers, E. Evaluating therapy in a delinquency prevention program. *Proceedings of the Association for Research on Nervous and Mental Disease* 31 (1953): 138–47. Baltimore: Williams & Wilkins.

Thelen, M. H., and Harris, C. S. Personality of college underachievers who improve with group psychotherapy. *Personnel and Guidance Journal* 46 (1968): 561–66.

Thompson, J. W. A comparison of four behavior therapies in the treatment of test anxiety in college students. Ph. D. dissertation, University of Arkansas, 1976.

Thoresen, C. E., and Krumboltz, T. D. Relationship of counselor reinforcement of selected responses to external behavior. *Journal of Counseling Psychology* 14 (1967): 140.

Thoresen, C. E.; Krumboltz, T. D.; and Varenhorst, B. Sex of counselors and models: Effect on client career exploration. *Journal of Counseling Psychology* 14 (1967): 503.

Tiegerman, S. Effects of assertive training and cognitive components of rational therapy on assertive behaviors and interpersonal anxiety. Ph. D. dissertation, Hofstra University, 1975.

Tori, C., and Worell, L. Reduction of human avoidant behavior: A comparison of counterconditioning, expectancy, and cognitive information approaches. *Journal of Consulting and Clinical Psychology* 41 (1973): 269–78.

Tosi, D. J.; Upshaw, K.; Lande, A.; and Waldron, M. A. Group counseling with non-verbalizing elementary students. *Journal of Counseling Psychology* 18 (1971): 437–40.

Trexler, L. D., and Karst, T. O. Rational-emotive therapy, placebo, and no-treatment effects on public-speaking anxiety. *Journal of Abnormal Psychology* 79 (1972): 60–67.

Trier, C. Effectiveness of two versions of rational restructuring in reducing speech anxiety: An experimental analogue. Ph. D. dissertation, State University of New York at Stoney Brook, 1974.

Truax, C. B. Effects of client-centered psychotherapy with schizophrenic patients: Nine years pretherapy and nine years posttherapy hospitalization. *Journal of Consulting and Clinical Psychology* 45 (1970): 417–22.

Truax, C. B., and Wittmer, J. Patient non-personal reference during psychotherapy and therapeutic outcome. *Journal of Clinical Psychology* 27 (1971): 300–02.

Truax, C. B.; Wargo, D. G.; and Silber, L. D. Effects of group psychotherapy with high accurate empathy and nonpossessive warmth upon female institutionalized delinquents. *Journal of Abnormal Psychology* 71 (1966): 267–74.

Truax, R. A., and Tourney, G. Male homosexuals in group psychotherapy. *Disorders of Nervous System* 32 (1971): 707-11.

Tucker, J. E. Group psychotherapy with chronic psychotic soiling patients. *Journal of Consulting Psychology* 20 (1956): 430.

Twentyman, C. T., and McFall, R. M. Behavioral training of social skills in shy males. *Journal of Consulting and Clinical Psychology* 43 (1975): 384-95.

Tyler, F. B., and Gatz, M. Development of individual psychosocial competence in a high school setting. *Journal of Consulting and Clinical Psychology* 45 (1977): 441-49.

Varble, D. L., and Landfield, A. W. Validity of the self-ideal discrepancy as a criterion measure for success in psychotherapy—A replication. *Journal of Counseling Psychology* 16 (1969): 150-56.

Vernallis, F. F., and Reinart, R. E. An evaluation of goal directed group psychotherapy with hospitalized patients. *Group Psychotherapy* 14 (1961): 5-12.

Vernallis, F. F.; Straight, E. M.; Cook, A. D.; and Stimpert, W. E. The group therapist in the treatment of chronic schizophrenics. *Group Psychotherapy* 18 (1965): 241-46.

Vogler, R. E.; Lunde, S. E.; Johnson, G. R.; and Martin, P. L. Electrical aversion conditioning with chronic alcoholics. *Journal of Consulting and Clinical Psychology* 34 (1970): 302-07.

Vosbeck, P. D. An exploratory study of the effects of counseling. Masters thesis, University of Minnesota, 1959.

Wachowiak, D. G. Model reinforcement counseling with college males. *Journal of Counseling Psychology* 19 (1972): 387.

Waldkoetter, R. O. A comparative guidance study: Group counseling with selected African student-teachers. *Personnel and Guidance Journal* 40 (1962): 638-42.

Walker, R. G., and Kelley, F. E. Short-term psychotherapy with schizophrenic patients evaluated over a three-year follow-up period. *Acta Psychiatrica Scandinarica* 35 (1960): 34-56.

Ward, H. C. Effects of non-directive group counseling upon selective cognitive functioning and interpersonal relationships of junior high students. Ph. D. dissertation, East Texas State University, 1966.

Warne, M. M.; Canter, A. H.; and Wiznia, B. Analysis and follow-up of patients with psychiatric disorders. *American Journal of Psychotherapy* 7 (1953): 278-88.

Warner, R. An investigation of the effectiveness of verbal reinforcement and model reinforcement counseling on alienated high school students. Ph. D. dissertation, State University of New York–Buffalo, 1969.

Weingarten, C. Systematic desensitization vs. accelerated mass desensitization with speech-anxious subjects. Ph. D. dissertation, Purdue University, 1973.

Wenger, R. T. An examination of the effects of treatment in a therapeutic community versus the custodial approach in a penal system. Ph. D. dissertation, Long Island University, 1974.

West, W. B. An investigation of the significance of client-centered play therapy as a counseling technique. Ph. D. dissertation, North Texas State University, 1969.

Whitman, T. L. Modification of chronic smoking behavior: A comparison of three approaches. *Behavior Research and Therapy* 7 (1969): 257-63.

Williams, J. E. Changes in self and other perceptions following brief educational-vocational counseling. *Journal of Counseling Psychology* 9 (1962): 18-30.

Willis, R. W. Study of the comparative effectiveness of systematic desensitization and implosive therapy. Ph. D. dissertation, University of Tennessee, 1968.

Willis, R. W., and Edwards, J. A. A study of the comparative effectiveness of systematic desensitization and implosive therapy. *Behavior Research and Therapy* 7 (1969): 387-95.

Wilson, C. J.; Muzekari, L. H.; Schneps, S. A.; and Wilson, D. M. Time-limited group counseling for chronic home hemodialysis patients. *Journal of Counseling Psychology* 21 (1974): 376-79.

Winborn, B., and Schmidt, L. G. The effectiveness of short-term group counseling. *Journal of Educational Research* 55 (1962): 169-73.

Wincze, J. P., and Caird, W. K. The effects of systematic desensitization and video desensitization in the treatment of essential sexual dysfunction in women. *Behavior Therapy* 7 (1976): 335-42.

Winkler, R. C.; Teigland, J. J.; Munger, P. F.; and Kranzler, G. D. The effects of selected counseling and remedial techniques on underachieving elementary school students. *Journal of Counseling Psychology* 12 (1965): 384.

Wirt, M.; Betz, R.; and Engle, K. The effects of group counseling on the self-concepts of counselor candidates. *Counselor Education and Supervision* 58 (1969): 189-94.

Wolk, R. L., and Goldfarb, A. I. The response to group psychotherapy of aged recent admissions compared with long-term mental hospital patients. *American Journal of Psychiatry* 123 (1967): 1251-57.

Wollersheim, J. P. Effectiveness of group therapy based upon learning principles in the treatment of overweight women. *Journal of Abnormal Psychology* 76 (1970): 462-74.

Woodward, R. B. The effects of transactional analysis on the self-concepts, social adjustment and grade point averages of intellectually advantaged, intellectually normal and intellectually disadvantaged sixth grade students. Ph. D. dissertation, Mississippi State University, 1974.

Woody, R. H., and Schauble, P. G. Desensitization of fear by video tapes. *Journal of Clinical Psychotherapy* 25 (1969): 102-03.

Wright, J. C. The relative efficacy of systematic desensitization and behavior training in the modification of university quiz section participation difficulties. Ph. D. dissertation, University of Wisconsin, 1972.

————. A comparison of systematic desensitization and social skill acquisition in the modification of a social fear. *Behavior Therapy* 7 (1976): 205-10.

Yates, L. E. A comparison of the effects of individual non-directive play therapy and structured teacher guidance upon second grade students of low sociometric status: An experimental study. Ph. D. dissertation, University of Florida, 1974.

Yorkston, N. J.; McHugh, R. B.; Brady, R.; Serber, M.; and Sergeant, H. G. S. Verbal desensitization in bronchial asthma. *Journal of Psychosomatic Research* 18 (1974): 371-76.

Zeisset, R. M. Desensitization and relaxation in the modification of psychiatric patients' interview behavior. *Journal of Abnormal Psychology* 73 (1968): 18-24.

Zemore, R. Systematic desensitization as a method of teaching a general anxiety-reducing skill. *Journal of Consulting and Clinical Psychology* 43 (1975): 157-61.

Zirkle, G. A. Five minute psychotherapy. *American Journal of Psychiatry* 118 (1961): 544–46.

Bibliography of Drug Therapy and Psychotherapy Combination Studies

The following studies involve the comparison of drug therapy and psychotherapy in various combinations.

Bellack, L., and Chassan, J. An approach to the evaluation of drug effect during psychotherapy: A double blind study of a single case. *Journal of Nervous and Mental Diseases* 139 (1964).

Bellack, L.; Chassan, J.; Gediman, H.; and Hurvich, M. Ego functioning of analytic psychotherapy combined with drug therapy. *Journal of Nervous and Mental Diseases* 157 (1973): 465–69.

Blair, D., and Brady, D. Recent advances in the treatment of schizophrenia: group training and the tranquilizers. *Journal of Mental Science* 104 (1958): 625.

Brill, N. Q.; Koegler, R. R. and others. Controlled study of psychiatric outpatient treatment. *Archives of General Psychiatry* 10 (1964): 581–95.

Bullard, D.; Hoffman, B.; and Havens, L. The relative value of tranquilizing drugs and social and psychological therapies in chronic schizophrenia. *Psychiatric Quarterly* 34 (1960): 293–306.

Carpenter, W., and McGlashan, T. The treatment of acute schizophrenia without drugs: An investigation of some current assumptions. *American Journal of Psychiatry* 134 (1977): 14–20.

Claghorn, J. L.; Johnstone, E. E.; Cook, T. H.; and Itschner, L. Group therapy and maintenance treatment of schizophrenia. *Archives of General Psychiatry* 31 (1974): 361–65.

Cooper, B. Grouping and tranquilizers in the chronic ward. *British Journal of Medical Psychology* 34 (1961): 157–62.

Covi, L.; Lipman, R.; Derogatis, L.; Smith, J.; and Pattison, J. Drugs and group psychotherapy in neurotic depression. *American Journal of Psychiatry* 131 (1974): 191–99.

Cowden, R. C.; Zax, M.; and Sproks, J. A. Reserpine alone and as an adjunct to psychotherapy in the treatment of schizophrenia. *Archives of Neurological Psychiatry* 74 (1955): 518–22.

Cowden, R.; Zax, M.; Hague, J.; and Finney, R. C. Chlorpromazine alone and as an adjunct to group psychotherapy in the treatment of psychiatric patients. *American Journal of Psychiatry* 112 (1956): 898–902.

Cytryn, L.; Gilbert, A.; and Eisenberg, L. The effectiveness of tranquilizing drugs plus supportive psychotherapy in treating behavior disorders of children: A double blind study of eighty outpatients. *American Journal of Orthopsychiatry* 30 (1960): 113–29.

Daneman, E. A. Imipramine in office management of depressive reactions. *Diseases of the Nervous System* (April 1961): 213–17.

Evangelakis, M. G. De-institutionalization of patients (the triad of trifluoperazine—group therapy—adjunctive therapy). *Diseases of the Nervous System* 22 (1961): 26–32.

Friedman, Alfred S. Interaction of drug therapy with marital therapy in depressive patients. *Archives of General Psychiatry* 32 (1975): 619–37.

Gittelman-Klein, R., and Klein, D. F. Controlled imipramine treatment of school phobia. *Archives of General Psychiatry* 25 (1971): 204–07.

Goldstein, M.; Rodnick, E.; Evans, J.; May, P.; and Steinberg, M. Drug and family therapy in the aftercare treatment of acute schizophrenia. Unpublished manuscript, UCLA Psychiatric Department, 1978.

Gorham, D. R.; Pokorny, A.; and Moseley, E. C. Effects of phenothiazine and/or group psychotherapy with schizophrenics. *Diseases of the Nervous System* 25 (1964): 77–86.

Gottlieb, J., and Hustor, P. Treatment of schizophrenics. *Journal of Nervous and Mental Diseases* 113 (1951): 237–46.

Greenblatt, M.; Solomon, M.; Evans, A.; and Brooks, G. (eds.). *Drug and Social Therapy in Chronic Schizophrenia*. Springfield, Ill.: Charles C Thomas, 1965.

Grinspoon, L.; Ewalt, J.; and Shader, R. Psychotherapy and pharmacotherapy in chronic schizophrenia. *American Journal of Psychiatry* 124 (June 1968): 1645–52.

―――. Long-term treatment of chronic schizophrenia: A preliminary report. *International Journal of Psychiatry* 4 (1967): 116–28.

Groen, J. J., and Pelser, H. E. Experiences with and results of group psychotherapy in patients with bronchial asthma. *Journal of Psychosomatic Research* 4 (1960): 191–205.

Hamill, W., and Fontana, A. F. The immediate effects of chloropromazine in newly admitted schizophrenic patients. *American Journal of Psychiatry* 132 (1975): 1022–26.

Hamilton, M.; Smith, A.; Lapidus, H.; and Cadogan, E. A controlled triad of thiopropazate dihydrochloride (Dartalan), chlorpromazine and occupational therapy in chronic schizophrenics. *Journal of Mental Science* 106 (1960): 40–55.

Hamilton, M.; Hordern, A.; Waldrop, F. N.; and Lofft, J. A controlled trial on the value of prochlorperazine, trifluoperazine and intensive group therapy. *British Journal of Psychiatry* 109 (1963): 510–22.

Hesbacher, P. T.; Rickels, K.; Gordon, P.; Gray, B.; Meckelnberg, R.; Weise, C.; and Vandervort, W. Setting, patient and doctor effects on drug response in neurotic patients: I. Differential attrition, dosage deviation and side reaction responses to treatment. *Psychopharmacologia* 18 (1970): 180–208.

Hesbacher, P.; Rickels, K.; Hutchinson, J.; Raab, E.; Sablosky, L.; Whalen, E.; and Phillips, F. J. Setting, patient, and doctor effects on drug response in neurotic patients: II. Differential improvement. *Psychopharmacologia* 18 (1970): 209–26.

Hogarty, G. E.; Goldberg, S. C.; Schooler, N. R.; and Ulrich, R. F. Drug and sociotherapy in the after-care of schizophrenic patients: II and III. *Archives of General Psychiatry* 31 (1974): 603–18.

Honigfeld, G.; Rosenblum, M.; Blumenthal, I.; Lambert, H.; and Roberts, A. Behavioral improvement in the older schizophrenic patients: Drug and social therapies. *American Geriatrics Society Journal* 13 (1965): 57–72.

Jacobs, M. A.; Globus, G.; and Heim, E. Reduction in symptomatology in ambulatory patients. *Archives of General Psychiatry* 15 (1966-): 45–53.

Jenner, F. A.; Kerry, R. J.; and Parkin, D. A controlled trial of methaminodiazepoxide (chlordiazepoxide, 'Librium') in the treatment of anxiety in neurotic patients. *Journal of Mental Science* 107 (1961): 575–82.

Karon, B. P., and Grady, W. Intellectual test changes in schizophrenic patients in the first six months of treatment. *Psychotherapy: Theory, Research and Practice* 6 (1969): 88-96.

Karon, B. P., and Vandenbos, G. R. Experience, medication and the effectiveness of psychotherapy with schizophrenics. *British Journal of Psychiatry* 116 (1970): 427-28.

King, P. D. Controlled study of group psychotherapy in schizophrenics receiving chlorpromazine. *Psychiatry Digest* (March 1963): 21-26.

_____. Regressive EST, chlorpromazine, and group therapy in treatment of hospitalized chronic schizophrenics. *American Journal of Psychiatry* 115 (1958): 354-61.

Kissin, B., and Platz, A. The use of drugs in the long-term rehabilitation of chronic alcoholics. In Efron, D. H. (ed.), *Psychopharmacology: A Review of Progress 1957-1967*, Public Health Service Publication No. 1836, 1968.

Klerman, G. L.; Dimascio, A.; Weissman, M.; Prusoff, B.; and Paykel, E. Treatment of depression by drugs and psychotherapy. *American Journal of Psychiatry* 131 (1974): 186-91.

Kurland, A. A.; McCabe, L.; and Hamilton, T. E. Contingent naloxone (N-allynoroxymorphone) treatment of the paroled narcotic addict. *International Pharmacopsychiatry* 10 (1975): 151-68.

Lipman, R. S., and Covi, L. Outpatient treatment of neurotic depression: Medication and group psychotherapy. In Spitzer, R. L., and Klein, D. F. (eds.), *Evaluation of Psychological Therapies*. Baltimore: The Johns Hopkins Press, 1976.

Lipsedge, M. S.; Hajioff, J.; Huggins, P.; Napier, L.; Pearce, J.; Pike, D.; and Rich, M. The management of severe agorophobia: A comparison of iproniazid and systematic desensitization. *Psychopharmacologia* 32 (1973): 67-80.

Lorr, M.; McNair, D. M.; et al. Early effects of chlordiazepoxide (Librium) used with psychotherapy. *Journal of Psychiatric Research* 1 (1963): 257-70.

_____. Meprobamate and chlorpromazine in psychotherapy: Some effects on anxiety and hostility of outpatients. *Archives of General Psychiatry* 4 (1961): 381-89.

McLaughlin, B. E.; Harris, J.; and Ryan, F. A double blind study involving Listica, Librium, and placebo as an adjunct to supportive psychotherapy in a psychiatric clinic. *Diseases of the Nervous System* 22 (1961): 41-43.

May, P. R. A. *Treatment of Schizophrenia*. New York: Science House, 1968.

May, P. R. A., and Tuma, H. Treatment of schizophrenia. *British Journal of Psychiatry* 111 (1965): 503-10.

_____. The effect of psychotherapy and Stelazine on length of hospital stay, release rate and supplemental treatment of schizophrenic patients. *Journal of Nervous and Mental Diseases* 139 (1964): 362-69.

Meneksha, S., and Harry, T. V. A. Lorazepam in sexual disorders. *British Journal of Clinical Practice* 29 (1976): 175-76.

Paykel, E.; DiMascio, A.; Haskell, D.; and Prusoff, B. Effects of maintenance amitriptyline and psychotherapy on symptoms of depression. *Psychological Medicine* 5 (1975): 151-68.

Podobnikar, I. G. Implementation of psychotherapy by Librium in a pioneering rural-industrial psychiatric practice. *Psychosomatics* 12 (1971): 205-09.

Rickels, K.; Cattell, R.; Weise, C.; Gray, B.; Yee, R.; Mallin, A.; and Aaronson, H. Controlled psychopharmacological research in private psychiatric practice. *Psychopharmacologia* 9 (1966): 288-306.

Roth, I.; Rhudick, P.; Shaskan, D.; Slobin, M.; Wilkinson, A.; and Young, H. Long-term effects on psychotherapy of initial treatment conditions. *Journal of Psychiatric Research* 2 (1964): 283-97.

Rush, A. M.; Beck, A. T.; Kovacs, M.; and Hollon, S. Comparative efficacy of cognitive therapy and pharmacotherapy in the treatment of depressed outpatients. *Cognitive Therapy and Research* 1 (1977): 17-37.

Shader, R.; Grinspoon, L.; Ewalt, J.; and Zahn, D. Drug responses in schizophrenia. In Sankar, D. U. (ed.), *Schizophrenia, Current Concepts and Research*. Hicksville, New York: P. J. D. Publications, 1969, pp. 161-73.

Solyom, L.; Heseltine, G. F. D.; McClure, D. J.; Solyom, C.; Ledwidge, B.; and Steinberg, G. Behavior therapy versus drug therapy in the treatment of phobic neurosis. *Canadian Psychiatric Association Journal* 18 (1973): 25-31.

Soskin, R. Personality and attitude change after two alcohol treatment programs. *Quarterly Journal of Studies on Alcohol* 31 (1970): 920-31.

Titchener, J. L.; Sheldon, M. B.: and Ross, W. D. Changes in blood pressure of hypertensive patients with and without group psychotherapy. *Journal of Psychomatic Research* 4 (1959): 10-12.

Weissman, M.; Klerman, G. L.; Paykel, E. S.; Prusoff, B.; and Hanson, B. Treatment effects on the social adjustment of depressed patients. *Archives of General Psychiatry* 30 (1974): 771-78.

Whitehorn, J. C., and Betz, B. J. A comparison of psychotherapeutic relationships between physicians and schizophrenic patients when insulin is combined with psychotherapy and when psychotherapy is used alone. *American Journal of Psychiatry* 113 (1957): 901-10.

Wirt, R. D., and Simon, W. *Differential Treatment and Prognosis in Schizophrenia*. Springfield: Charles C Thomas, 1959.

Woody, G. E.. O'Brien, C. P.: and Rickels, K. Depression and anxiety in heroin addicts: A placebo controlled study of doxepin in combination with methadone. *American Journal of Psychiatry* 132 (1975): 447-49.

Zitrin, C.; Klein, D.; Lindemann, C.; Tobak, P.; Rock, M.; Kaplan, J. H.; and Ganz, V. H. Comparison of short-term treatment regimens in phobic patients: A preliminary report. In Spitzer, R. L., and Klein, D. F. (eds.), *Evaluation of Psychological Therapies*. Baltimore: The Johns Hopkins Press, 1976.

Zitrin, C.; and Klein, D. Imipramine, behavior therapy and phobia. Paper presented at the 13th Annual Meeting of the ACNP, December 1974.

Bibliography of Studies Involving Only Drug Therapy

Abse, D. W.; Curtis, T. E.; Dahlstrom, W. G.; Hawkins, D. R.; and Toops, T. C. The use of reserpine in the management of acute mental disturbance on an in-patient service: A preliminary report. *Journal of Nervous and Mental Diseases* 124 (1956): 239-45.

Ashby, W. R. A clinical trial of imipramine (Tofranil) on depressed patients. *Journal of Mental Science* 107 (1961): 547-51.

Baeckland, F.; Lundwall, L.; Kissin, B.; and Shanahan, T. Correlates in disulfiram treatment of alcoholism. *Journal of Nervous and Mental Diseases* 153 (1971): 1-9.

Baldini, J., and Meary, E. R. Controlled trials of an amitriptyline-fluphenazine combination in depressive neuroses and psychoses: A collaborative study. *Current Therapeutic Research* 12 (1970): 84-93.

Bassa, D. M., and Vora, H. D. Evaluation of efficacy of imipramine in depressive disorders: A double blind study. *American Journal of Psychiatry* 121 (1965): 1116.

Bennet, I. F.; Cohen, D.; and Starer, E. Isoniazid in treatment of the chronic schizophrenic patient. *Archives of Neurological Psychiatry* 71 (1954): 54-65.

Bodnar, S., and Catterill, T. B. Amitriptyline in emotional states associated with the climacteric. *Psychosomatics* 8 (1972): 117-19.

Brick, H. Effects of tybamate on depressive and anxiety states in penitentiary inmates: A preliminary report. *International Journal of Neuropsychiatry* 2 (1966): 637-44.

Brooker, D. K.; Rapeschi, R.; and Murray, L. Negative results of a trial of penicillamine in chronic schizophrenia. *Post Graduate Medical Journal* 44 (October 1968 Supplement): 48-55.

Butterworth, A. T. Depression associated with alcohol withdrawal. *Quarterly Journal of Studies on Alcohol* 32 (1971): 343-48.

Champlin, F. B.; Cotter, C. F.; Moskowitz, M. D.; Rossman, M.; Sheppard, C.; and Merlis, S. A comparison of chlormezanone, meprobamate and placebo. *Clinical Pharmacology and Therapeutics* 9 (1968): 11-15.

Charalampous, K. D.; Freemesser, G. F.; Malev, J.; and Ford, K. Loxapine succinate: A controlled double blind study in schizophrenia. *Current Therapeutic Research* 16 (1974): 829-37.

Chieffi, M. A two-part double blind study of the anti-neurotic action of tybamate. *Diseases of the Nervous System* 126 (1965): 369-74.

Claghorn, J. L. A comparative study of loxapine succinate, librium and placebo in neurotic outpatients. *Current Therapeutic Research* 15 (1973): 8-12.

Clinical Psychiatry Committee. Clinical trial of the treatment of depressive illness. *British Medical Journal* 1 (1965): 881-86.

Cole, C.; Patterson, R. M.; Craig, J. B.; Thomas, W. E.; Ristine, L. P.; Stahly, M.; and Pasamanik, B. A controlled study of efficacy of iproniazid in treatment of depression. *Archives of General Psychiatry* 1 (1959): 513-18.

Collins, A. D., and Dundas, J. A double blind trial of amitriptyline-perphenazine, perphenazine and placebo in chronic withdrawn inert schizophrenia. *British Journal of Psychiatry* 113 (1967): 1425-29.

Collins, P.; Sakalis, G.; and Minn, P. L. Clinical response to a potential non-sedative anxiolytic. *Current Therapeutic Research* 19 (1976): 512-15.

Conners, C. K.; Tisenberg, L.; and Barcoi, A. Effect of dextroamphetamine on children. *Archives of General Psychiatry* 17 (1967): 478-85.

Cromwell, H. A. Controlled evaluation of psychotherapeutic drug in internal medicine. *Clinical Medicine* 70 (1963): 2239-44.

Diamond, L. S., and Marks, J. B. Discontinuance of tranquilizers among chronic schizophrenic patients receiving maintenance dosage. *Journal of Nervous and Mental Diseases* 131 (1960): 247-54.

Diamond, S. Double blind controlled study of amitriptyline/perphenazine combination in medical office patients with depression and anxiety. *Psychosomatics* 7 (1966): 371-75.

Downing, R. W., and Rickels, K. Self-report of hostility and the incidence of side reactions in neurotic outpatients treated with tranquilizing drugs and placebo. *Journal of Consulting Psychology* 31 (1967): 71–76.

Dunlop, E., and Weisberg, J. Double-blind study of prazepam in the treatment of anxiety. *Psychomatics* 9 (1968): 235–38.

Dunner, D.; Stallone, D.; and Fieve, R. R. Lithium carbonate and affective disorders. *Archives of General Psychiatry* 33 (1976): 117–20.

Egan, W. P., and Goetz, R. Effect of metronidazole on drinking by alcoholics. *Quarterly Journal of Studies on Alcohol* 29 (1968).

Feuret, S. I. Chlorazepate dipotassium, diazepam and placebo in chronic anxiety. *Current Therapeutic Research* 15 (1973): 449–59.

Fink, M.; Klein, D. F.; and Kramer, J. C. Clinical efficacy of chlorpromazine-procyclidine combination, imipramine and placebo in depressive disorders. *Psychopharmacologia* 7 (1965): 27–36.

Foote, E. S. Combined chlorpromazine and reserpine in the treatment of chronic psychotics. *Journal of Mental Science* 104 (1958): 201–05.

Friedman, C.; DeMonbray, M. S.; Hamilton, V. Imipramine (Tofranil) in depressive states: A controlled trial with inpatients. *Journal of Mental Science* 107 (1961): 948–53.

Gallant, D. M.; Bishop, M. P.; Nesselhof, W.; and Fulmer, T. E. JB-8181 anti-depressant activity in outpatients. *Current Therapeutic Research* 6 (1964): 69–70.

Gilgash, C. A. Thorazine therapy with catatonic schizophrenics in relation to Wechsler verbal and performance subtest companions. *Journal of Clinical Psychology* 17 (1961): 95.

Gittelman-Klein, R., and Klein, D. F. Methylphenidate effects in learning disabilities. *Archives of General Psychiatry* 33 (1976): 655–68.

Glatt, M. M.; George, H. R.; and Frisch, E. P. Evaluation of chlormethiazole in treatment for alcohol withdrawal syndrome. *Acta Psychiatrica Scandinavia* 42 (1966, Supplement 192): 121–37.

Goller, E. S. A controlled trial of reserpine in chronic schizophrenia. *Journal of Mental Science* 106 (1960): 1408–12.

Gordon, P. E. Meprobamate and benactyzine (Deprol) in the treatment of depression in general practice. *Diseases of the Nervous System* 28 (1967): 234–40.

Greenberg, L. A.; Lester D.; Dora, A.; Greenhouse, R.; and Rosenfeld, J. An evaluation of meprobamate in the treatment of alcoholism. *Annals of the New York Academy of Sciences* 67 (1957).

Gross, H. S. A double blind comparison of once-a-day pimozide, trifluoperazine and placebo in the maintenance care of chronic schizophrenic outpatients. *Current Therapeutic Research* 16 (1974): 696–705.

Gwynne, P. H., Hundziak, M.; Kautschitsch, J.; Lefton, M.; and Pasamanick, B. Efficacy of trifluoperazine on withdrawal in chronic schizophrenics. *Journal of Nervous and Mental Diseases* 134 (1962): 451–55.

Hanyzova, Z.; Chloupkova, K.; Bojanorsky, J.; Bouchal, M.; and Synkova, J. A clinical comparison of placebo, diazepam and diazepoxide at short time application in neuroses. *Acta Nervosa Superior* (Praha), 8: 4 (1966): 438–39.

Hare, H. P. Comparison of diazepam, chlorpromazine and a placebo in psychiatric practice. *Journal of New Drugs* 3 (1963): 233–40.

Heilizer, F. The effects of chlorpromazine upon psychomotor and psychiatric behavior of chronic schizophrenic patients. *Journal of Nervous and Mental Diseases* 128 (1959): 358–64.

Heller, G. C., and Black, D. A. Meprobamate in the treatment of tension states. *Journal of Mental Science* 103 (1957): 581–88.

Inglis, J.; Caird, W. K.; and Sloane, R. B. An objective assessment of the effects of nialamide on depressed patients. *Canadian Psychiatric Association Journal* 84 (1961): 1059–63.

Inglis, J.; Jones, R. P.; and Sloane, R. B. A psychiatric and psychological study of amitriptyline as an antidepressant. *Canadian Medical Association Journal* 88 (1963): 797–98.

Joshi, V. G. Controlled clinical trial of isocarboxazid ("Marplan") in hospital psychiatry. *Journal of Mental Science* 107 (1961): 567, 571.

Kasich, A. M.; Richards, D. J.; and Vanov, S. K. Lorazepam in the management of anxiety associated with chronic gastrointestinal disease: A double blind study. *Current Therapeutic Research* 19 (1976): 292–306.

Kelley, D.; Brown, C. C.; and Shaffer, J. W. A controlled physiological, clinical, and psychological evaluation of chlordiazepoxide. *British Journal of Psychiatry* 115 (1969): 1387–92.

Kurland, A. A.; Hanlon, T. E.; Tatom, M. H.; Ota, K. Y.; and Simpoulos, A. M. The comparative effectiveness of six phenothiazine compounds, phenobarbital and inert placebo in the treatment of acutely ill patients: Global measures of severity. *Journal of Nervous and Mental Diseases* 133 (1961): 1–17.

Lee, H. Use of haloperidol in a hard core chronic schizophrenic population. *Psychosomatics* 9 (1968): 267–71.

Levin, M. L. A comparison of the effects of phenobarbital, promethazine, chlorpromazine and placebo upon mental health hospital patients. *Journal of Consulting Psychology* 23 (1959): 167–70.

Lipman, R. S.; Covi, L.; Derogatis, L. R.; Rickels, K.; and Uhlenhuth, E. H. Medication, anxiety reduction and patient report of significant life situation events. *Diseases of the Nervous System* 32 (1971): 240–44.

McLaughlin, B.; Rickels, K.; Abidi, M.; and Toro, R. Meprobamate-benactyzine (Deprol) and placebo in two depressed outpatient populations. *Psychosomatics* 10 (1969): 73–81.

Maggs, R. Treatment of manic illness with lithium carbonate. *British Journal of Psychiatry* 109 (1963): 826–29.

Master, R. S. Amitriptyline in depressive states. *British Journal of Psychiatry* 109 (1963): 826–29.

Mendelson, J. H.; Rossi, M.; Bernstein, J.; and Kuehne, J. Propanolol and behavior of alcohol addicts after acute alcohol ingestion. *Clinical Pharmacology and Therapeutics* 15 (1974): 571–78.

Miller, A., and Baker, E. F. W. Imipramine, a clinical evaluation in a variety of settings: A controlled study of chronic depressed states treated with antidepressant drugs. *Canadian Psychiatric Association Journal* 5 (1960): 150–54.

Morgenstern, F. V.; Funck, E. C.; and Holt, W. Comparative short-term evaluation of triflupromazine HCl, chlorpromazine HCl, and placebo in acutely disturbed patients. *New York State Medical Journal* 60 (1960): 254–58.

Nesselhof, W., and Gallant, D. M. A double blind comparison of WY-3498, diazepam, and placebo in psychiatric outpatients. *American Journal of Psychiatry* 121 (1965): 809, 811.

Orvin, G. H. Treatment of the phobic obsessive compulsive patient with oxazepam, and improved benzodiazepine compound. *Psychosomatics* 8 (1968): 278-80.

Overall, J. E.; Hollister, L. E.; Pokorny, A. D.; Casey, J. F.; and Katz, G. Drug therapy in depression: Controlled evaluation of imipramine, isocarboxazide, dextroamphetamine and placebo. *Clinical Pharmacology and Therapeutics* 3 (1962): 16-22.

Pahnke, W.; Kurland, A.; Unger, S.; Savage, C.; and Grof, S. The experimental use of psychedelic (LSD) psychotherapy. *Journal of the American Medical Association* 212 (1970): 1856-63.

Pasamanick, B.; Scarpitti, F. R.; Lefton, M.; Dinitz, S.; Wernert, J. J.; and McPheeters, H. Home vs. hospital care for schizophrenics. *Journal of the American Medical Association* 187 (1964): 177-81.

Pishkin, V.; Shurley, J. T.; and Wolfgang, A. Stress, psychophysiological and cognitive indices in an acute double blind study with hydroxyzine in psychiatric patients. *Archives of General Psychiatry* 16 (1967): 471-78.

Prien, R. F.; Caffey, E. M.; and Klett, C. J. Prophylactic efficacy of lithium carbonate in manic depressive illness. *Archives of General Psychiatry* 28 (1973): 337-41.

Ramsay, I.; Greer, S.; and Bagley, C. Propanolol in neurotic and thyrotoxic anxiety. *British Journal of Psychiatry* 122 (1973): 555-60.

Raskin, A., and Crook, T. H. Antidepressants in black and white patients. *Archives of General Psychiatry* 32 (1975): 643-49.

Raskin, A.; Schulterbrandt, J. G.; Reatig, N.; Crook, T.; and Odle, D. Depression subtypes and response to phenelzine, diazepam, and placebo. *Archives of General Psychiatry* 30 (1974): 66-75.

Raymond, M. J.; Lucas, C. J.; Beesley, M. C.; and O'Connell, B. A. A trial of five tranquilizing drugs in psychoneurosis. *British Medical Journal* 2 (1957): 63-66.

Rees, L., and Davies, B. A controlled trial of phenelzine (Nardil) in the treatment of severe depressive illness. *Journal of Mental Science* 107 (1961): 560-66.

Rickles, K.; Clark, T.; Ewing, J. H. Evaluation of tranquilizing drugs in medical outpatients. *Journal of the American Medical Association* 171 (1959): 1649-56.

Rickles, K.; Gordon, P. E.; Meckelnburg, R.; Sablosky, L.; Whalen, E.; and Pion, H. Iprindole in neurotic depressed general practice patients: A controlled study. *Psychomatics* 9 (1968): 208-14.

Rifkin, A.; Quitkin, F.; Rabiner, C.; and Klein, D. Fluphenazine decanoate, fluphenazine HCl given orally and placebo in remitted schizophrenics. *Archives of General Psychiatry* 34 (1977): 633-44.

Schneyer, J. J., Goodman, L. I.; and Borgen, L. A. Ripazepam (Cl-683): Double blind comparison with placebo in anxious patients. *Journal of Clinical Pharmacology* 16 (1976): 377-83.

Segal, M. M., and Shapiro, K. L. A clinical comparison study of the effects of reserpine and placebo on anxiety. *Archives of General Psychiatry* 81 (1959): 392-98.

Shaffer, J. W.; Freinik, W. R.; Wolf, S.; Foxwell, N.; and Kurland, A. A controlled evaluation of chlordiazepoxide (Librium) in the treatment of convalescing alcoholics. *Journal of Nervous and Mental Diseases* 137 (1963): 494-507.

Shepard, F. S. A study of opipramol in general practice. *The Practitioner* 195 (1965): 92-95.

Small, J.; Kellams, J.; Milstein, V.; and Moore, J. A placebo controlled study of lithium combined with neuroleptics in chronic schizophrenic patients. *American Journal of Psychiatry* 132 1315-17.

Spohn, H. E.; Lacoursie, R. B.; Thompson, K.; and Coyne, L. Phenothiazine effects on psychological and physiological dysfunctions in schizophrenics. *Archives of General Psychiatry* 34 (1977): 633-44.

Teja, J. S.; Grey, W. H.; Clum, J.; and Warren, K. Tranquilizers or anti-depressants for chronic schizophrenics: A long-term study. *Australian and New Zealand Journal of Psychiatry* 9 (1975): 241-47.

Tucker, K., and Wilensky, H. A clinical evaluation of meprobamate therapy in a chronic schizophrenic population. *American Journal of Psychiatry* 113 (1957): 678-703.

Turek, S.; Ota, K.; Brown, C.; Massari, F.; and Kurland, A. Tiotixene and thioridazine in alcoholism treatment. *Quarterly Journal of Studies on Alcohol* 34 (1973): 853-59.

Tyndel, M.; Fraser, J. G.; and Hartleib, C. J. Metronidazole as an adjuvant in the treatment of alcoholism. *British Journal of Addiction* 64 (1969): 57-61.

Weinstock, R.; Fisher, S.; Spillane, J.; Ise, C.; Shaw, D.; and Torop, P. Effects of protriptyline and perphenazaine in neurotic depressed outpatients. *Journal of Clinical Pharmacology* 15 (1975): 627-30.

Wyatt, R. J.; Vaughn, T.; Galanter, M.; Kaplan, J.; and Green, R. Behavioral change of chronic schizophrenic patients given L-5 hydoxytryptophan. *Science* 177 (1972): 1142-26.

Zwanikken, G. J. Penfluridol (R-16341) a long lasting oral neuroleptic, as maintenance therapy for schizophrenia and mentally retarded patients. *Psychiatrica Neurologia Neurochirugia* 76 (1973): 83-92.

Name Index

Subject Index

....

Acceptance of others, 66, 93, 201
Adaptive Behavior Scale, 93
Addiction: diagnosis of, 61, 96, 98, 99, 102-4, 114, 146, 191, 196, 204; drug treatment of, 149; measures of, 66, 95, 97, 98, 100, 102, 109, 110, 193, 201
Adjective check list, 200
Adjustment: global measures of, 66, 93-95, 97, 99, 100, 102, 107, 109, 110, 150, 175, 176, 193; life measures of, 66, 93, 95, 97, 98, 100, 102, 109, 150, 175, 176, 193
Adlerian therapy, 71, 74, 76, 77, 89, 90, 94, 105, 192, 197, 204
Affective disorders, 132, 149, 157, 196
Affiliation of experimenter, 59, 60, 117, 191
Age of client. See Client characteristics
Alcoholism, 61, 93, 196, 201. See also Addiction
Allegiance of experimenter, 64, 78, 79, 81, 112, 119, 121, 192
American Psychoanalytic Association, 29
Amitriptyline, 149, 174
Analogue study, 20-22, 56, 57, 191
Antiaggression drugs, 145
Antianxiety drugs, 131, 132, 144-46, 149, 173, 174, 180
Antidepressant drugs, 131-34, 144-46, 149, 173, 174, 180
Antipsychotic drugs, 130, 132, 144, 146, 149, 153, 157, 173, 174
Anxiety, 66, 115, 146, 149, 172; measures of, 78, 93-95, 97, 98, 100-103, 107, 109, 116, 193, 199
Anxiety Achievement Scale, 199
Anxiety management training, 75, 198
"Apples and Oranges," 47, 48
Assertiveness training (assertion-structured therapy), 15, 198; measures of, 66, 202
Assessment (measurement) of outcomes, 8, 21, 22, 49, 51, 56, 59, 63, 65, 66, 69, 107, 112, 119, 124, 151, 158, 175, 177, 187
Assignment of clients to groups, 10, 13, 18, 21, 49, 62-64, 78, 79, 81, 122, 123, 152, 153, 158, 167, 177, 178, 192
Asthma, 39-46, 61, 93, 202
Attendance, school, 202
Attrition, 11, 18, 59, 63, 64, 78, 79, 81, 101, 122, 123, 152, 153, 158, 177, 192, 205
"Average therapeutic effects," 1, 16, 32, 33, 42, 129, 163, 180
Aversive conditioning, 75, 197

Beck Depression Inventory, 93, 200
Behavioral Approach Test, 67, 68, 78, 93, 199
Behavioral counseling, 75, 198
Behavioral rehearsal, 198

Behavioral self-control, 75, 198
Behavioral subclass of therapy, 72, 75, 77-79, 94-97, 103-6, 110, 114, 115, 123
Behavioral therapy class, 75-77, 98-100, 102, 105-9
Behavior disorders, 61
Behavior modification, 73-77, 89, 90, 92-94, 106, 114, 148, 192, 197, 198, 205
Behavior therapy, 2, 3, 14, 17, 18, 20-23, 26, 44-46, 56, 116, 148
Bender-Gestalt, 200
Benzodiazepines. See Antianxiety drugs
Bibliotherapy, 57, 73
Blind assessment and experimentation, 18, 59, 60, 64, 67, 78, 79, 81, 101, 112, 113, 119, 120, 131-35, 142-44, 151-53, 158, 176-78, 191, 206
"Box score" method, 20, 21, 37, 38, 130-37
Brain damage, 61

California Personality Inventory, 93, 101
Carbamates. See Antianxiety drugs
"Cathartic psychotherapy," 196
Character disorder, 61, 143, 146, 171, 191, 196, 204
Children, therapy with, 14, 15, 22, 23, 41
Chlordiazepoxide, 153, 174
Chlorpromazine, 127, 130, 157, 174
Classification of studies, 55, 59-63, 76, 78-81, 145-53, 191-94, 210-12
"Class" of therapy, 75-77, 98-100, 102, 105-7, 192
Client-centered therapy, 17, 32, 56, 57, 69, 71, 74-77, 89-95, 123, 148, 192, 197, 204
Client characteristics, 30, 32, 33, 82, 114, 115, 180; age, 44-46, 55, 59, 78, 79, 81, 101-5, 113, 147, 157, 163, 167, 179, 191, 204, 206; intelligence, 59, 62, 78, 79, 81, 101-5, 113-15, 191, 206; race, 179; sex, 55, 59, 78, 79, 81, 101, 114, 115, 147, 157, 166, 179, 191, 204, 206; similarity to therapist, 59, 62, 78-81, 101, 113-15, 191, 206; socioeconomic status, 62, 101, 113, 147, 157, 191
Coding of studies. See Classification of studies
Cognitive-behavioral subclass of therapy, 77, 81, 94-97, 102-4, 110, 114, 115, 123
Cognitive-behavioral therapy, 75, 77, 89, 90, 92-94, 107, 192, 198, 205
Cognitive behavior modification, 74, 75, 198
Cognitive rehearsal, 75, 197
Cognitive restructuring, 75, 94
Cognitive subclass of therapy, 77, 81, 94-97, 103, 104, 110, 114, 123